METATHEORY in
SOCIAL SCIENCE

METATHEORY in SOCIAL SCIENCE

Pluralisms and Subjectivities

Edited by
Donald W. Fiske and Richard A. Shweder

The University of Chicago Press
Chicago and London

DONALD W. FISKE is professor of behavioral sciences at the
University of Chicago. His most recent books are *Strategies
for Personality Research* and, with S. Duncan, *Face-to-Face
Interaction*. RICHARD A. SHWEDER is professor in the
Committee on Human Development at the University of
Chicago and has written widely on cross-cultural cognitive
and affective development.

The University of Chicago Press, Chicago 60637
The University of Chicago Press, Ltd., London
© 1986 by The University of Chicago
All rights reserved. Published 1986
Printed in the United States of America

95 94 93 92 91 90 89   543

LIBRARY OF CONGRESS CATALOGING-IN-PUBLICATION DATA

Main entry under title:
Metatheory in social science.

     Proceedings of a conference on "Potentialities
for Knowledge in Social Sciences," held at the
University of Chicago, Sept. 11–14, 1983.
     Bibliography: p.
     Includes index.
     1. Social sciences—Philosophy—Congresses.
2. Social sciences—Methodology—Congresses.
3. Social sciences—Research—Congresses. 4. Knowledge,
Theory of—Congresses.   I. Fiske, Donald Winslow,
1916–   II. Shweder, Richard A.
H22.M47   1986   300'.1   85–16383
ISBN 0-226-25191-8
ISBN 0-226-25192-6 (pbk.)

Contents

Preface   vii

Conference Participants   ix

Introduction: Uneasy Social Science
  Richard A. Shweder and Donald W. Fiske   1

1 Three Scientific World Views and the Covering
  Law Model
    Roy D'Andrade   19

2 Generalization and the Social Psychology of
  "Other Worlds"
    Philip E. Converse   42

3 Specificity of Method and Knowledge in Social Science
    Donald W. Fiske   61

4 Social Inquiry by and for Earthlings
    Lee J. Cronbach   83

5 Science's Social System of Validity-Enhancing Collective
  Belief Change and the Problems of the Social Sciences
    Donald T. Campbell   108

6 Correspondence versus Autonomy in the Language
  of Understanding Human Action
    Kenneth J. Gergen   136

7 Divergent Rationalities
    Richard A. Shweder   163

8 Explanation in the Social Sciences and in Life Situations
    Paul F. Secord   197

v

9 Some Uses and Misuses of the Social Sciences
  in Medicine
    Arthur Kleinman   222

10 Social Measurement as the Creation of Expert Systems
    Aaron V. Cicourel   246

11 The Forms and Functions of Social Knowledge
    Donald N. Levine   271

12 Non-Linear Behavior
    Frank M. Richter   284

13 Heuristics and the Study of Human Behavior
    William C. Wimsatt   293

14 What Social Scientists Don't Understand
    Paul E. Meehl   315

15 Philosophy of Science and the Potentials for Knowledge
   in the Social Sciences
    Alexander Rosenberg   339

16 Similarity and Collaboration within the Sciences
    Philip S. Holzman   347

17 Two Extremes on the Social Science Commitment
   Continuum
    Barbara Frankel   353

18 Pluralisms and Subjectivities
    Donald W. Fiske and Richard A. Shweder   362

   Bibliography   371

   Author Index   379

   Subject Index   385

Preface

This book presents the products of the conference "Potentialities for Knowledge in Social Science" held at the University of Chicago 11–14 September 1983. The prospectus for the conference proposed an examination of the kinds of knowledge that now exist and those that are possible in the social sciences. While the prospectus provided a general orientation for the preliminary conference papers, each author advanced his own evaluation of the state of knowledge in the social sciences and his own thesis about where the social sciences can or cannot, should or should not, go. The assessments and proposals that emerged are quite diverse and offer a wide range of views about the aims of social science research and the forms of social science knowledge. Pluralisms abound and various subjectivities are examined.

The score of participants at the conference represented several social science disciplines, including psychology, anthropology, sociology, and psychiatry (see pp. ix–x). To ensure breadth of perspective, two philosophers of science and a physical scientist (a geophysicist) were also invited. A decision to limit the size of the group forced the omission of representatives from several disciplines—most notably political science, economics, history, and biopsychology. The contents of the book are nevertheless of broad scope and have some relevance for all parts of the social and behavioral sciences.

This book is one of the few in which theoretical issues in the philosophy of the social sciences are addressed primarily by practicing social researchers. What is presented here may not fully cover all views about where the social sciences are, and where they can go, but it is a provocative set of assessments and proposals, each expressive of a somewhat different conception of science in general, and social science in particular. Each author believes progress of some kind is possible, but only if . . .

The point on which there is most consensus among the authors is perhaps implicit. The very fact that the authors accepted our invitation to the conference and prepared themselves for it indicates that there are issues and problems about the social sciences that need further thought and closer examination. While we believe that most readers will agree, we hope that all readers will find that the contents of this book help them gain a clearer perspective on the possibilities for the social sciences and, perhaps, contribute to their perceptions of their own research work. This volume is intended for conceptualizers in social science and for investigators working on basic or applied problems who are not completely satisfied with the state of social science. It offers something to apprentice graduate students and to master craftsmen, as well as to colleagues in other disciplines and the curious laity. The text does not assume much background, although some chapters discuss one or another moderately technical issue. We have attempted to eliminate technical terms wherever possible. In most of the places where such terms are necessary to the author's meaning, they have been briefly explained. In no case, we believe, will the reader's unfamiliarity with a technical word made it impossible to gather the import of the author's thesis.

We gratefully acknowledge the support for the conference and the preparation of this book provided by a grant from the National Institute of Mental Health (1 R13MH 37238). We are especially indebted to Louis Wienckowski and David Pearl for their interest in the project and their contributions at the conference; and to Laurence Chalip, who made the physical arrangements for the conference and handled the extensive advance distributions of materials with great care and efficiency.

Conference Participants

DONALD T. CAMPBELL, Departments of Psychology and Social Relations, Lehigh University

AARON V. CICOUREL, Department of Sociology, University of California, San Diego

JOHN CLAUSEN, Institute of Human Development, University of California, Berkeley

PHILIP E. CONVERSE, Institute for Social Research, University of Michigan

LEE J. CRONBACH, Stanford Center for Youth Development, Stanford University

ROY D'ANDRADE, Department of Anthropology, University of California, San Diego

DONALD W. FISKE, Department of Behavioral Sciences, University of Chicago

BARBARA FRANKEL, Department of Social Relations, Lehigh University

KENNETH J. GERGEN, Department of Psychology, Swarthmore College

PHILIP S. HOLZMAN, Department of Psychology and Social Relations, Harvard University

ARTHUR KLEINMAN, Department of Anthropology, Harvard University

DONALD N. LEVINE, Department of Sociology, University of Chicago

PAUL E. MEEHL, Psychiatric Research Unit, University of Minnesota

DAVID PEARL, Behavioral and Social Science Research Branch, National Institute of Mental Health

FRANK M. RICHTER, Department of Geophysical Sciences, University of Chicago

ALEXANDER ROSENBERG, Department of Philosophy, Syracuse University

PAUL F. SECORD, College of Education, University of Houston

RICHARD A. SHWEDER, Committee on Human Development, University of Chicago

LOUIS A. WIENCKOWSKI, Division of Extramural Research Programs, National Institute of Mental Health

WILLIAM WIMSATT, Department of Philosophy, University of Chicago

HANS ZEISEL, Law School, University of Chicago

Introduction: Uneasy Social Science

Richard A. Shweder and Donald W. Fiske

Social science research institutions are hotbeds of pluralistic activity, each scientist holding that "progress is being made on the problem on which I am working." At the same time, and perhaps paradoxically, there has been in the social sciences, at least in recent years, a vague sense of unease about the overall rate of progress of the disciplines. A small, but visible, iconoclastic literature has emerged (see Bibliography) either challenging the scientific status of social research or expressing concern about the accomplishments of the social sciences. Some have even talked of a "crisis" in social inquiry. The essays in this volume accept that challenge and examine the concerns of that crisis literature; they appraise the current state of our knowledge or set forth proposals for acquiring valid and useful social and behavioral knowledge.

It is noteworthy that the prevailing positive mood among practicing social scientists is accompanied by an understandable desire not to be disturbed by worries about the foundations of the science or generalized concerns about a purported lack of progress. There is probably a great deal of wisdom implicit in that desire not to be disturbed, for it can be rather hazardous to believe that there are standard criteria for judging the overall progress of a discipline or field of knowledge or to impose those criteria on one's thinking. Of course, the practitioners of a science are always trying to accomplish something or other, and each practitioner knows what progress means for him or her—it means doing even better what he or she is now doing. But beyond that, there may well be no common currency for measuring progress, no way to make summary evaluations across the range of activities; and we are, perhaps, well advised to resist, even by means of indifference, any attempt to mint such a currency. Indeed, such indifference may be justified even when the attempted assessment of overall progress assumes the

1

rather bland form of a list of all the diverse things going on, for a list, almost by definition, does not add up to something unified or coherent, nor should it. To demand or announce an assessment of the progress of a field of inquiry is to risk forcing each focused but individualistic program of intense activity into a Procrustean bed. No one wants that. When such an act is permitted, it is typically for ideological or political reasons—or in the name of some "higher purpose" like funding.

Moreover, as students of the history of the sciences, we probably have good reason to beware of standardized, explicit, and precise criteria for judging and regulating the development of a science. Clarity of aim is an uncertain virtue in a healthy science: some activities that turn out to be important seemed aimless originally, and scientists who do have clear aims in mind are often aimed in different directions or at each other. Typically, in a healthy, developing science, the work at the growing edge is highly contested. Typically there are prominent scientists who find it impossible to understand each other. Typically there is relatively little consensus about what the next step should be and what the yardstick is for measuring final success. Indeed, one thing we can learn from the history of the sciences is that the criteria of progress in science are task-specific, diverse, ambiguous, and shifting. No one criterion has served as a general standard or a universal ideal. Nor, taken together, do the diverse criteria add up to a unified index of progress. At times in the development of a science, there is a premium on controlled laboratory experimentation or mathematical forumlation, but just as often there is not. Knowledge in a science can occasionally be reduced to a small set of universal causal laws, but typically it cannot. At times, it makes sense to try to predict the future, but not always. One cannot even say that it is always advisable to stick to the presumed facts or to insist upon agreement about the meaning of new concepts. There are times in the history of science when ignoring the apparent facts has paid off. And there are times, perhaps now, when pressing for consensus on the meaning of progress can be rigidifying and positively destructive. So it is quite understandable, perhaps even a form of wisdom, that most practicing social scientists do not want to be bothered by the crisis literature in the social sciences or worry about abstract formulations about the possibility of a social science.

Scientists must confront their individual research problems with some optimism. The positive mood that prevails among most social scientists is not merely the blind optimism of narrowly focused technicians who would rather not be disturbed by esoteric questions about science and progress. If pressed, most social scientists can, without too much difficulty, point proudly to knowledge that has accumulated about many particular topics, to technical advances in research methods, to success at actuarial prediction and assessment of skills, and to various counterintuitive research findings, documenting that certain prominent folk beliefs are contrary to empirical evidence. For a comprehensive and generally upbeat assessment of things, social scientists can turn to the report of the Committee on Basic Research in the Behavioral and Social Sciences, formed by the National Academy of Sciences–National Research Council. Part of the charge of that committee was to identify "illustrative areas of basic research in the social sciences that have developed analytic frameworks of high social utility" and areas "that are likely to be of high value, significance and/or social utility in the near future" (Adams et al. 1982, 1). An upbeat tone can also be found in more restricted contexts, where, for example, the Behavioral Sciences Research Review Panel identified for the National Institute of Mental Health research topics in the social sciences that, on the basis of significant recent developments, "appear to be especially promising for their potential contributions to the understanding of mental illness and health" (Clausen et al. 1983, 1). The gloom-and-doom message that sometimes emerges in the crisis literature is not that difficult to oppose.

There is, however, an alternative approach to the crisis literature in the social sciences, namely, to take seriously the issues it raises. If that literature were merely the imposition of misconceived criteria for assessing progress, it would deserve to be ignored. If that literature were merely a one-sided pessimistic enumeration of failures, it would deserve to be dismissed. But despite its shortcomings, it is more than that. The crisis literature raises to consciousness many of the assumptions that we as practicing social scientists take for granted about the nature of our science and our subject matter and the relationship between them. Those assumptions have a decisive influence on what problems we select for study and how we go about conceptualizing and investigating them. It is the view of the editors of this book that those assumptions are too important to be taken for granted and too much a part of our ongoing research enterprises to be left only to philosophers to think about (but compare the views of Meehl and Rosenberg, chaps. 14 and 15). Thus, instead of ignoring or dismissing the crisis literature, we have decided to address it and offer a variety of responses to it. The Bibliography which sampled the social science crisis literature, was shared by all conference participants a year prior to our meeting (see p. 371).

Several sources of uneasiness disturb those who are troubled about the social sciences. Whether or not one is troubled by those things, they are the kinds of things with which one must come to terms, especially if one is concerned with the potentialities for the growth of knowledge in the social sciences. For one thing, the typical or modal social science generalization is rather restricted in scope, bound to a particular population studied at a particular historical time in a particular culture, often even bounded by the particular methodology (so-called method effect) used in the investigation. The discovery that social science generalizations are typically narrow in scope is not new. Nagel makes the point in 1961 in his book *The Structure of Science* and he cites a reference from 1934, which makes the same point. Although in 1984 it is not impossible to generate at least a short list of valid universal generalizations in the social sciences, what Nagel had to say in 1961 still seems apt: "[The] conclusions reached by controlled study of sample data drawn from one society are not likely to be valid for a sample obtained from another society. Unlike the laws of physics and chemistry, generalizations in the social sciences therefore have at best only a severely restricted scope, limited to social phenomena occurring during a relatively brief historical epoch within special institutional settings" (p. 459). Acknowledging that human action is mediated by existing "technologies and traditions," Nagel suggests that "the possibility must certainly be admitted that nontrivial but reliably established laws about social phenomena will always have only a narrowly restricted generality" (p. 460). A law can be "universal" only for a homogenous set of objects or events.

The scene today is not unlike that described by Nagel. While several universals have been discovered—Berlin and Kay's generalizations (1969) about the evolution of basic color terms, Barker's generalizations (1971) about the influence of group size on responsible social behavior, Ekman's work (1973) on universal facial expressions for emotion, the discovery of a universal schema underlying the perception of personality (White 1980), several noteworthy findings concerning language universals (Greenberg 1966; Dixon 1977)—they are the occasional exceptions to the rule that social science generalizations are not very general. Indeed, over the past twenty years, the restrictions that bound social science generalizations seem to have increased, as the results of laboratory experiments did not generalize well outside the lab, as experimental research was shown to be vulnerable to expectancy effects, setting effects, even paid subject effects, and as method effects proved to be so substantial that slight changes in research method produced major alterations in the patterning of one's findings.

There are several ways one might react to this state of affairs. For example, assuming that any science worthy of its name must uncover universal generalizations about its subject matter, Nagel (1961) rose to the defense of the idea of a social science by attacking the view that universal laws of social phenomena are in principle impossible and by convincing his readers that, despite the record of narrowly restricted generalizations, the possibility could never be totally ruled out that there exist social laws valid for all societies and for all time. The assumption that any science worthy of its name must uncover generalizations of broad scope is compatible, as well, with other diverse reactions: deep concern over the fact that "generalizations decay" (Cronbach 1975); a renunciation of the very idea of a social science, or at least a renunciation of the idea that human subjectivity, identified with free will and the human spirit, can be studied scientifically (Gergen 1973; Rosenberg 1983); hope for the future growth of a young science accompanied by special feelings of pride in those universal generalizations that have been discovered (Converse 1982). Another option is to deny the assumption, to argue instead that universal generalizations are not the sine qua non of science, that "not all hypotheses of interest to a scientist are universal generalizations" (Edelson 1984, 28). One particular variant of this view is that social scientists should pride themselves in "thick description," knowing a lot about each case, documenting local events accurately, and generalizing within cases, not across cases (Geertz 1973). Each of these options receives expression in this book.

A second cause for uneasiness among those who are troubled about the social sciences is the persistence, even entrenchment, of multiple paradigms or schools of thought and the lack of convergence over time in the theories and concepts that guide research and are used to interpret evidence. There is a healthy empirical tradition in the social sciences and a richness of rigorously produced research findings; nevertheless, no reduction seems to be occurring in the diversity of conceptualizations and higher-order theories, and many basic issues never seem to get resolved. Perhaps that is why some critics see the social sciences as a game in which the players generate interpretations within the grammar of some unassailable paradigm (Freudian, Darwinian, Marxist, behaviorist, etc.) for events that have already happened, a practice reminiscent of Geertz's proverbial Mexican peasant, the one who first shoots the hole in the fence and then paints the bullseye around it (1973, 26). One reaction to the endemic diversity of theories, claims, and approaches is to view social science as myth, religion, or ideology. Another possible reaction is to argue that the social organization of the mature sciences favors a winnowing out of theories and that it is time for the social sciences to attend to the social system of science and to follow that example accordingly. One might also react by eschewing an interest in theory and attending instead to the accumulation of "facts," although in this book and elsewhere, some argue that social science has difficulty reaching agreement on just what the "facts" are. Yet another reaction is to question the assumption that convergence of belief is a criterion for maturity in science and to examine the alternative assumption that diversity of viewpoint is compatible with rationality and objectivity. Each of these options is explored in this book.

A third thing that bothers those who are troubled about the social sciences concerns the relationship between social science research and the practical demands of society. Confronted with policy questions about such topics as the effects of forced busing, the effects of educational or therapeutic interventions, the direction of social revolutions and religious movements in foreign lands, the impact of tax cuts on savings behavior, and so on, there seem to be, in the eye of the critics, only two types of social scientists: those who are frequently wrong but never in doubt, and those who say "Well, it's all very complex" and then hang up the phone. The truth, of course, probably lies somewhere in between, and perhaps a bit off to the side, for there are many areas in which social science research has yielded socially useful knowledge. Think, for example, of IQ and educational testing, opinion polling, economic indicators, the Bureau of the Census, psychosomatic medicine, the strategic use of game theory, and behavior therapy. If we broaden our notion of useful knowledge to include ideas and theories that alter our consciousness, self-consciousness, values, and goals, then the impact of social science conceptualizations—for example, Freudian, Marxist, neoutilitarian, sociobiological, and relativistic—must be judged to be enormous.

A fourth and final source of uneasiness for those who are troubled about the social sciences is its distinctive subject matter—human subjectivity. Unlike the physical sciences, social science knowledge is designed to help us understand and explain subjective experience and such "things" as meanings, intentions, ideas, values, and emotions—non-things that Descartes long ago placed beyond the reach of the mechanistic sciences. The questions are still with us whether a science of subjectivity is possible, what that science of subjectivity might look like, and how it is similar to and different from, on the one hand, the physical sciences, and on the other hand, the humanities. Lurking behind such questions is an even broader issue: What are the criteria, if any, that distinguish (good) science from (bad) protoscience from nonscience from nonsense?

Each chapter in this volume addresses one or more of these four problem areas for the social sciences: the problem of general versus not-so-general generalizations, the problem of pluralism or multiple paradigms, the problem of useful versus not so useful knowledge, and the problem of science versus nonscience.

D'Andrade's essay (chap. 1) presents an ethnographic account of the diversity of models and ideals of science among practicing scientists. The essay advances several arguments which, quoting D'Andrade, can be summarized as follows:

> First, that the sciences contain at least three very different world views, that of the physical sciences, that of the natural sciences, and that of the semiotic sciences; second, that the pursuit of "general laws" is characteristic primarily of the physical sciences; third, that some of the natural sciences, such as biology, have done well despite that fact that they have not found general laws; fourth, that in the social sciences there is considerable division between the natural science approach and the semiotic approach without a reasonable synthesis in view; and fifth, that the emphasis on predicting or explaining individual events as a scientific activity is misguided because of the difficulties of establishing the appropriate boundary conditions.

D'Andrade argues that Hempel's famous "covering law" model is not the ideal form for all scientific thinking, and he examines the foundations of those semiotic or semantic sciences that eschew an interest in lawlike generalizations and seek, instead, to understand "imposed order."

In chapter 2, Converse argues that "a model of science that suggests that either we can, in T. S. Eliot's word, 'roll the universe into a ball' with one grand summary expression like $E = mc^2$, or we are not engaging in science is a false model." Arguing that what you think about, your subject matter, is decisive for how you think,

Converse introduces the notion that each science has its own "texture." He asks, What model of science should a social psychologist choose? He notes that the texture of the biological sciences has become distinct from the texture of the physical sciences and looks forward to the development of a mature social science with a texture of its own. What is distinctive of the subject matter of the social sciences, Converse argues, is its complexity. What makes it a science is that it is aimed at the "systematic decoding of observed regularities and the reduction of the regularities to more parsimonious and general principles that account for wide ranges of phenotypic detail." What should not rule it out as a science, any more than it rules out geology, is that it is "firmly wedded to historical circumstance."

In chapter 3, Fiske examines the problem of method variance in the psychological sciences and the incommensurability and lack of convergence of findings across methods. He likens the production of knowledge in the social sciences to a daily newspaper: "Just as in one day's newspaper, the sports page, the neighborhood news section, and the music reviews report quite unrelated events, so do the various methods in social science. . . . Even when the same event is the object to which several methods are applied, the resultng sets of data can be expected to have little or no covariation." His assessment of the current scene is that knowledge in the social sciences is highly fragmentary, composed of "multiple discrete parcels," and that the specificity of knowledge is related to variations in the types of protocols used to generate data, the size scale of the objects investigated, the time scale over which objects have been studied, and the extent to which data production relies on words and the inferential judgments of observers. Fiske argues that progress will come in the social sciences by discovering new types of protocols, by identifying basic behavioral processes, by more exactly defining the objects of inquiry, and by introducing more controls over the process of data production.

Cronbach (chap. 4) identifies several false ideals of science that he believes have had a repressive effect on the psychological sciences. Among the false ideals is the quest for timeless knowledge and the desire to view the world from a position of transcendent objectivity. "When we ask our theories to 'cut nature closer to the joint,' we ask too much. . . . Many a realist wants concepts to name entities that exist in nature quite apart from man's construing. Social inquiry, I think, would be better off without that aspiration." Cronbach argues that the development of a social physics is highly unlikely and that in the near future we will not witness explanatory theories of broad scope. He suggests that "social science is cumulative, not in possessing ever-more-refined answers about fixed questions, but in possessing an ever-richer repertoire of questions." He believes that, in the short run at least, development will come from adopting a more pluralistic approach in which there is greater respect for the accurate and reliable description of local events and for historical documentation and in which it is recognized that progress in science can come even from poorly formed, vague, and untestable ideas. As a model of effective, generative research, Cronbach analyzes the Hawthorne research on the social psychology of the workplace at Western Electric Company and identifies several research strategies that he recommends to future researchers.

Taken together, the chapters by Converse, Fiske, and Cronbach provide alternative assessments of the social and psychological sciences, more or less within the broad framework of the physical science and natural science models as described by D'Andrade. By "physical sciences," D'Andrade means those concerned with stating laws of behavior. By "natural sciences," he means those concerned with what things are made of and how they work, that is to say, mechanisms. In chapter 5, Campbell holds to the unity of scientific method but also offers a bridge to the chapters by Gergen and Shweder, which examine some of the implications and possibilities of D'Andrade's third model of science, the semiotic model.

Under the basic proposition that there are requirements for being scientific that hold for both physical and social sciences, Campbell argues that many of the problems of the social sciences are due to the lack of effective "disputatious" communities of scholars, who challenge each other's specific truth claims with cross-validation and critical argument. Too many schools of thought are engaged in producing "illustrations" rather than "evidence" for assertions of descriptive facts and theoretical interpretations. For many reasons, including shortage of scholars, these assertions go unchallenged. The difficulty of producing convincing "demonstrations" is a part of the problem. While arguing for a unity of scientific method, to date best exemplified in the physical and biological sciences, Campbell's paper provides transitions to later chapters denying that unity. His acceptance of epistemological relativism (as distinguished from ontological nihilism) offers a dialectic with Gergen's more radical relativism. Campbell's parenthetical comments on validity-seeking hermeneutics (atypical of the hermeneutics most frequently invoked by postpositivist social scientists) and the overlap it might have with postpositivist theory of physical science methods of validity-enhancing belief change provide a bridge to the "interpretive" (or semiotic) models of D'Andrade, Gergen, Shweder, and Cicourel. The chapter can be taken as a rigorous program for a scientific hermeneutics.

In chapter 6, Gergen advances the provocative claim that no psychological theory has ever been abandoned "for reasons of clear observational failure." His essay is a lucid articulation of a radical relativist sociology of science, but it is far more than just that. The essay examines and makes use of key principles of contextualism, constructivism, deconstructionist hermeneutics, and principles from the analysis of the language of action. The central concern of the essay is the relationship, or lack of relationship, between descriptive language and the world of action that language is designed to represent. Gergen rejects the correspondence theory of the relationship between language and reality and, along with that rejection, raises serious doubts about the objectivity and rationality of social science. Identifying a series of principled reasons for believing that there is an inherent indeterminacy to scientific interpretations, Gergen argues that the descriptive and explanatory constructions of social science are "fundamentally free to vary across context of usage." The implication is that virtually any theory—Freudian, Skinnerian, social-learning, role-rule—can be used to describe and explain any action, and "should be capable of absorbing all empirical outcomes." The constraints on interpretation are not empirical or logical but reside primarily in a social process whereby communities of scholars "negotiate" the way in which language will be applied across diverse contexts. Gergen argues that the particular modes of discourse of science that result from the process of negotiation are never value free or ideologically neutral, and he views science as a force for or against social transformation.

Shweder (chap. 7) examines what he believes to be the false contrasts between objectivity and subjectivity, postivism and hermeneutics, science and religion, rationality and superstition, with special reference to the role of those contrasts in discussions about the nature of the social sciences. Drawing on historical and cross-cultural materials, Shweder tries to show that ideas about witchcraft, reincarnation, and the reality of dreams are of a genus not unlike that of our own scientific theories, and adopting the "native point of view," he examines the rationality and explanatory power of those theories. Promoting the concept of "divergent rationalities" and the idea that not everything that is rational must be universal, he introduces an alternative position into current debates in anthropology about whether so-called religious doctrines are "symbolic" or "irrational." Shweder argues that the contrast between subjectivity and objectivity, science and religion, and so forth, has been overdrawn, one unfortunate result of which is to rule out the possibility of a genuine "science of subjectivity" while forcing upon the social scientist the false choice of treating the social sciences as either a physical science or a humanity. As a plausible alternative, Shweder describes a world of subject-dependent objects (nothing in particular exists apart from our theoretical attempt to understand it) and objectlike subjectivity. Such a world requires a broadened concept of "rationality" and "meaning" in which convergence of belief is not the sine qua non of objectivity. Divergent rationalities are possible, for example, cults, cultures, and the diverse social science schools of thought.

In chapter 8, Secord proposes a "realist" view of science, which he contrasts with the now standard view of science as influenced by positivism. He argues that "scientific laws are to be conceived as causal principles or tendencies rooted in the nature of the relevant entities and not as reflecting regular concomitance between events." He calls for a science focused on "generative mechanisms," and he rejects both the view that "the main task of the behavioral sciences is to discover the regularities in behavior" and the view that explanation of an event is accomplished "through deduction from universal laws that are applicable to the phenomenon." Secord believes that much of social and psychological theory is vacuous because, unlike physical theory, it is unable to specify the conditions under which relationships hold. This leads him to a discussion of the difference between material objects and living organisms, closed and open systems, and to a critical evaluation of laboratory research in the human sciences. The essay concludes with an examination of the role of ordinary language in scientific social understanding and the potential applicability of social science knowledge to real-world problems.

The two chapters by Kleinman and Cicourel (chaps. 9 and 10) take a look at social science knowledge in the context of real-world institutions and problems. While mental health is brought into some of the other chapters, Kleinman focuses on medicine in general and mental health in particular, and Cicourel considers diagnostic and research procedures for gathering information from patients and other subjects. Kleinman advances the proposition that the social sciences are more relevant to day-to-day problems of health care than are the biological sciences, but the main goal of his essay is to explore a paradox: "Why do the social sciences remain marginal in medicine in spite of their obvious relevance?" Kleinman identifies numerous domains of relevant social science research in medicine—research on psychosomatic illness and stress, epidemiology, health service delivery, social support networks, social class and illness, affective functioning, psychotherapeutic outcomes, cross-cultural studies on somatization, work in medical anthropology on the distinction between illness and disease, and much more. He attributes the marginality of social science research in medical settings to several factors, including a dominant biomedical paradigm expressive of a cultural epistemology favoring empiricism and materialism, the demands of a preprofessional education, the isolation of social science research papers from the medical science journals, and many other systemic and institutional forces that affect the practice of science. Kleinman identifies potentially important areas of contribution for the social sciences in medicine, not the least of which is the questioning of core assumptions and values and the development of a scientific language for talking about subjective experience, relationships, and meaning. Acknowledging that the cognate fields of social medicine, psychiatry, public health, and bioethics are "passing through conceptual doldrums," he sounds a clarion call for supradisciplinary efforts to develop "bridging ideas" between social science and medicine.

Cicourel examines the process by which the products of mental test instruments, survey questionnaires, and structured or open-ended diagnostic interviews are produced. He notes that the popular use of formal and standardized measuring instruments "has not been accompanied by an explicit effort to study the subjects' or respondents' language, reasoning, and comprehension while being tested, completing a questionnaire, or responding to interview questions that are open-ended." In other words, the nature of individuals' mental processes in producing test responses has been presupposed or taken for granted. Reviewing recent developments in cognitive science and artificial intelligence, with special reference to the distinction between declarative and procedural knowledge and the differences between formal and natural languages, Cicourel discusses some of the tensions between the algorithmic, formalistic, context-free assumptions of the information-processing model implicit in, for example, expert systems for medical diagnosis, psychometric tests, and survey research questionnaires and the nonalgorithmic, context-dependent characteristics of the practical discourse and reasoning processes of interviewees, sub-

jects, and respondents. He calls for a reconsideration of the way we
design assessment devices as we learn more about the interaction of
informal and formal knowledge processes, and he raises questions
about the ecological validity of current measuring instruments.

In chapter 11, Levine advances a position of "methodological
pluralism." He argues that the effort to discover a unitary privileged type of knowledge or essential criteria of "real science" must
fail "because of the irreducible variety of values, norms, and
motives that organize all kinds of action, contemplative as well as
conative or practical." Examining what he refers to as the "Babel of
contending intellectual positions in our time," Levine holds that it
is possible for each of two or more conflicting approaches of knowledge to attain a status of cognitive privilege. Presenting a classification of cognitive features that are the constitutive components of
any approach to social knowledge, Levine breaks down intellectual
approaches into seven elements, including, for example, "empirical procedures," "explanatory logics," "epistemic products." In
the light of his analysis of the elementary components of any approach to social knowledge, Levine argues that endless confusion
results from labeling someone a positivist or a Marxist or an empiricist or a Freudian or a Durkheimian. According to Levine, his
analytic scheme "provides a more coherent way for critics to assess
the value of different kinds of social knowledge—to indicate what
kinds of social knowledge may legitimately claim privileged status,
and why."

While chapters 1–11 of the book are revised or expanded versions of materials presented at the conference, the next six chapters
present the reactions, commentaries, criticisms, or observations
stimulated by the conference papers and discussions. They vary
considerably in their tone and in their conception of social science
research.

In chapter 12, Richter, a geophysicist, presents his reactions to
the conference in a discussion of nonlinear behavior. Richter,
whose own research is on problems in plate tectonics and fluid dynamics, argues that complexity is the natural outgrowth of the dynamics governing nonlinear systems and that, to the extent the
social sciences are studying nonlinear systems, "complexity need
not be a reflection of some deficiency in the modes of discourse or
analysis, but may well be an inherent property of the systems being
studied." Richter constructs a model of a nonlinear system interre-
lating fear, guilt, and aggressiveness. He tries to show that in nonlinear systems, generalizations about behavior are quite context

dependent and "may even be contradictory when derived from different sets of observations taken at different times." Nevertheless,
the equations describing the underlying dynamics of the system
can be relatively simple; Richter argues that social science research
might be aimed "at understanding particular elements of this dynamic, instead of seeking universally valid statements about behavior itself." His overall view is that there is no single standard for
scientific achievement in the physical sciences, that there are notable similarities between areas of the social sciences and the physical
sciences, and that one of the "external" political problems for the
social sciences is "not so much that it studies man, but that all men
judge its success."

In chapter 13, Wimsatt argues that the phenomenon of unpredictability is quite common throughout all the sciences and is not
distinctive of the social sciences. When the covering law model of
explanation does hold, suggests Wimsatt, it is because we have been
able to isolate systems, treat their properties as context independent, and manipulate them as simple idealizations. The major aim
of Wimsatt's chapter, however, is to examine the role of
"heuristics" in scientific and everyday problem solving: the cost-
effective advantages of heuristic (vs. algorithmic) procedures as
well as the systematic biases engendered by reliance on problem-
solving heuristics. Wimsatt, a philosopher of biology and the social
sciences, poses the question, Why have most major evolutionary
theorists favored explanations in terms of "individual selection"
over "group selection"? He argues that extant mathematical models attempting "to assess the relative efficacy of individual and
group selection processes" have been systematically biased in favor
of individual selection because of the reductionist model-building
heuristics that are built into the models. Wimsatt identifies several
features that characterize a "heuristic" problem-solving procedure
and distinguish it from an algorithmic procedure.

Meehl (chap. 14) takes us on a spirited tour of the conceptual
foundations of science. Reacting to themes and issues that came up
in conference discussions, he presents his own tripartite division of
science into functional-dynamic theories, structural-functional theories, and evolutionary theories; and he addresses issues having to
do with quantification, open concepts, realism, the covering law
model of explanation, and the imputation of motives or intentions.
Critical of idealism, relativism, abstract discussions about the
nature of science, and social scientists' spending too much time on
problems best dealt with by philosophers, Meehl says we all know

that logical positivism is dead and that too much time was spent at the conference saying so. He speculates that the function of such discussions is to "relieve scientific guilt feelings or inferiority feelings about our disciplines," and he believes that an "intellectual gloominess" associated with a relative lack of credentialed knowledge characterizes various parts of the social sciences. "It is as if somebody said 'Well, maybe clinical psychology isn't up to the standards of historical geology or medical genetics, let alone theoretical physics, but we needn't be so fussy about our concepts and the empirical support for them because logical positivism, which was so stringent on that score, is a nefarious doctrine, and we are no longer bound by it.'" Meehl then advances the "controversial thesis" that "owing to the abusive reliance in the sciences upon significance testing—rather than point or interval estimation, curve shape, or ordination—the usual article summarizing the state of the evidence on a theory (such as appears in the *Psychological Bulletin*) is nearly useless."

In chapter 15, Rosenberg, a philosopher of science, argues that philosophy of science has little to contribute to the social sciences, which from his point of view is merely another way of saying that all theoretical discussions should be put aside until a relatively late date in the development of a science. He argues that there is no principled line to be drawn between science and philosophy, no formal way to distinguish, for example, the empirical from the metaphysical. There is, however, a continuum that extends from factual reports and lower-level findings and generalizations to high-level theory; and, Rosenberg argues, progress is more likely to come in the social sciences by piling up findings rather than engaging in theoretical dispute. Presenting the idea that "data never point to a unique theory and are always compatible with mutually inconsistent theories" (compare Gergen's chapter), Rosenberg is doubtful that theoretical consensus can ever be achieved. Nevertheless, he suggests that agreement can be secured about what we need to know or find out, without recourse to theory or, which amounts to the same thing, philosophy.

In chapter 16, Holzman presents an argument for the unity of the sciences and against the view that "the social sciences are in a domain separate from the natural sciences." On the one hand, he advances the view that all phenomena are context dependent and that "reasons" can be "causes." On the other hand, he opposes any attempt to restrict social science inquiry to the study of meaning, since that "would rule out a whole set of regularities that call for

social science investigation with respect to lawful regularities."
Holzman goes on to present a gloomy assessment of social science
contributions to the field of mental health and mental illness, a
failure he attributes in part to an overconcern with methodology
and a retreat from nomothetic science (compare Kleinman's chapter). He calls for the development of the institution of supradisciplinary committees to identify "important issues that need study."

In chapter 17, Frankel uses Fiske's essay as a taking off point for
a critique of the unity of science position (or "methodological unitarianism") and "neopositivism" characteristic of several chapters
in the book. She argues that among the conference participants,
"the outlook appeared most dim to those strongly committed to
traditional norms of unified science, and least so to those willing to
consider that science may not be unifiable." Frankel outlines a position of scientific pluralism or "methodological polytheism." She
recommends that we not lament the "noise introduced into social
science by the humanness of human beings" and addresses the
problem of reductionism and emergentism in science.

A final summary chapter by Fiske and Shweder (chap. 18) identifies several topics concerning pluralism versus monism and subjectivity versus objectivity that recurred in the conference discussion
and in various chapters of the book.

Reading these chapters back to back, one is struck by the richness
and variety of the formulations, the diversity of the ways in which
any two chapters might be said to be alike or different, the shifting
quality of the alliances that might be formed among authors, and the
numerous points of tension. Some chapters emphasize the similarities among the sciences, others emphasize the differences, and
the similarities and differences that are emphasized are not necessarily the same ones from chapter to chapter. Some authors rededi-
cate themselves to a search for lawlike regularities in behavior;
others renounce that quest. Hermeneutics has its advocates and its
detractors. The achievements of the social sciences and their contributions (for example, to medicine) are variously assessed.

The volume in which these essays have been placed side by side
has been entitled *Metatheory in Social Science*. Taken together, the
essays are representative of the postpositivist intellectual climate of
our times. There was once a time, not so long ago, when the very
idea of rationality was equated with the results and findings of
positive (i.e., objective) science. The results of positive science were
considered worthy of respect because scientists had possession of a
unitary method for discovering truths, and they knew how to em-

ploy that method to discover useful knowledge. Over the last several decades, that picture of science and the equation of science and rationality have taken their lumps. The drift in contemporary thinking has been to raise serious doubts about whether there are any standards, canons, or methods definitive of scientific or rational thinking. The idea of objectivity associated with positive science has been under attack from many quarters, and it has been variously defended, clarified, revised, and abandoned. The essays in this volume represent the wide range of alternative positions concerning science and subjectivity-objectivity that one might credibly adopt in a postpositivist world.

References

Adams, R. McC.; Smelser, N. J.; and Treiman, D. J. 1982. *Behavioral and social science research: A national resource.* Part 1. Washington, D.C.: National Academy Press.

Barker, R. 1971. Individual motivation and the behavior-setting claim. In *Comparative perspectives on social psychology,* ed. W. W. Lambert and R. Weisbrod. Boston: Little Brown.

Berlin, B., and Kay, P. 1969. *Basic color terms.* Berkeley: University of California Press.

Clausen, J., et al. 1989. *Behavioral science research in mental health: An assessment of the state of the science and recommendations for research directions.* Rockville, Md.: Department of Health and Human Services.

Converse, P. E. 1982. Response to lecture by Professor Cronbach. In *The social sciences: Their nature and uses,* ed. W. H. Kruskal. Chicago: University of Chicago Press.

Cronbach, L. J. 1975. Beyond the two disciplines of scientific psychology. *American Psychologist* 30:116–27.

Dixon, R. M. W. 1977. Where have all the adjectives gone? *Studies in Language* 1:19–80.

Edelson, M. 1984. *Hypothesis and evidence in psychoanalysis.* Chicago: University of Chicago Press.

Ekman, P. 1973. Cross-cultural studies of facial expression. In *Darwin and facial expression,* ed. P. Ekman. New York: Academic Press.

Geertz, C. 1973. Thick description. In *Interpretation of cultures,* ed. C. Geertz. New York: Basic Books.

Gergen, K. J. 1973. Social psychology as history. *Journal of Personality and Social Psychology* 26: 309–20.

Greenberg, J. 1966. *Language universals.* The Hague: Mouton.

Nagel, E. 1961. *The structure of science.* New York: Harcourt, Brace and World.

Rosenberg, A. 1983. Human science and biological science: Defects and opportunities. In *Scientific explanation and understanding*, ed. N. Rescher. Lanham, Md.: University Press of America.

White, G. 1980. Conceptual universals in interpersonal language. *American Anthropologist* 82:759–81.

1 Three Scientific World Views and the Covering Law Model

Roy D'Andrade

The Covering Law Model

This paper questions the descriptive adequacy of the covering law model of science and, in doing so, attempts to clarify the nature of some of the problems confronted by the social sciences and by psychology. The covering law model is a well-known description by C. G. Hempel of the nature of scientific explanation, first presented in "The Function of General Laws in History" (1965), and amplified in later papers. The covering law model of science seems close to the way people think about science: on the surface, the model seems unexceptional. Its main outline goes as follows:

1. Science consists of a search for "general laws" to explain events.

2. The statement of a general law can have different logical forms, but it typically makes a universal generalization across some domain of events, for example, "All gases expand when heated under constant pressure."

3. The main function of general laws is to connect events in patterns, which are usually referred to as "explanation" and "prediction." The pattern for an explanation is

    a. statement of antecedent conditions $C1, \ldots, Cn$.

    b. a set of general laws $L1, \ldots, Ln$.

    c. the derivation of a proposition from $C1, \ldots, Cn$ and $L1, \ldots, Ln$ that asserts E should occur.

The event E is the thing to be explained; the antecedent conditions and general laws constitute the explanation. For example:

> To an observer in a rowboat, that part of an oar which is under water appears to be bent upwards. The phenomenon is explained by means of general laws—mainly the law of refraction and the law that water is an optically denser medium than air—and by reference to certain antecedent conditions—especially the facts that part

19

of the oar is in the water, part in the air, and that the oar is practically a straight piece of wood. (Hempel 1965, 246)

Hempel notes that the same formal analysis applies to prediction, and the only difference between the two is of a "pragmatic
character" (ibid., 249). If we already know that the event E has
happened, the application of a suitable set of statements afterward,
$C1, \ldots, Cn, L1, \ldots, Ln$, constitutes an explanation. If the statements $C1, \ldots, Cn, L1, \ldots, Ln$ are known, and E is derived prior to
the occurrence of the phenomenon it describes, then we speak of a
prediction.

Major debates about the covering law model have involved
whether it corresponds to what historians do, or could do, and
whether it can be used more generally in explanation of human
behavior (see, for example, von Wright 1971). There has also been
an extended and inconclusive discussion of the necessary and sufficient characteristics a statement must have to be a general law
(Nagel 1961).

Another very different kind of objection to the covering law
model is that it does not give a reasonable description of science in
general. Is all science characterized by a search for general laws? As
an anthropologist interested in culturally learned cognitive models,
I have noticed that my friends and acquaintances in the different
sciences talk differently about their research worlds. It is not just
that the names of things are different; there seem to be quite different world views that characterize the various disciplines.

I group these scientific world views in three classes. The first
class corresponds roughly to the so-called physical sciences: physics, chemistry, astronomy, and related engineering fields. The second group of world views consists primarily of biology, geology,
some aspects of meteorology and oceanography, much of economics and psychology, and some fields of anthropology and sociology.
With a small change in the normal meaning, these might be called
the "natural" sciences. The third group has no culturally given
name but will be called here the "semiotic" sciences because of their
central interest in the study of systems of meaning. This group
consists of linguistics and some fields of psychology, anthropology,
and sociology.

The world view of the physical sciences seems to picture an almost completely homogenous universe where all generalizations
apply equally through all time. There are only a few basic objects
and a few forces, and their interrelations can be stated in quan-

titative mathematical form. Quantitative statements, using only a few terms, and with minimal restrictions on boundary conditions, serve as the prototype for the concept "law." Within the physical sciences there is a constant attempt to simplify and reduce in number the set of basic objects and relations. There is also the sense that everything is the way it is because of some deep necessity, which is what one tries to capture in the statement of a law (see, for example, Feynman 1965 for a fine exposition of this world view).

In contrast to the physical science world, the world of the natural scientist is very lumpy or patchy. For example, on the planet Earth, DNA is made of certain large molecules grouped together in a certain way. Perhaps it could have been made out of different molecules and still accomplished the same functions. On other planets with other environments, one might expect something like DNA to arise but to be made of different components and perhaps to accomplish the same functions through very different processes. The description of DNA is thus, not the description of a law, but rather the description of a complex contingent mechanism.

One of the basic analogies used in the natural sciences is that the things being studied—DNA, the cell, the spleen, the body, the ecological community—are "machines." The basic questions are, What is it made of? How does it work? Generalizations about how things work are often complex, true only of one particular kind of thing, and are usually best stated in a simplified natural language. While one can speak of things like "Mendelian laws" or "Weber's law" in the natural sciences, it is understood these kinds of quantitative statements are actually the derived outcomes of other more basic processes, rather than basic laws in themselves.

There are those who think the natural sciences fail as science in precisely the ways they are different from the physical sciences. That is, one could say that to the degree the generalizations of biology or meteorology or psychology are limited to only certain objects existing for only a certain period of time and describable only with long, complex natural-language statements, to that degree, the natural sciences are poor science. However, this gives the physical sciences too privileged a position; most scientists agree modern biology is "doing well" as a science despite that fact that its generalizations do not look like the laws of physics.

To what extent do the natural sciences fail to conform to the covering law model? If any generalization is considered to be a general law, there is no problem on this issue. But to consider a statement like "The copying of mammalian RNA transcripts into

DNA and the subsequent integration of the complementary DNA (cDNA) back into the genome does occur, and may account for as much as 20 percent of some mammalian genomes" to be a law would be an odd and deviant use of English. In standard English, a law means something much more specific than a "generalization"—it means a very general proposition about the quantitative relations between a small number of elements. In this sense, the covering law model is inaccurate when it states that all science consists of a search for real "general laws." One can read an entire article in *Science* on research findings in biology and not encounter anything a scientist would call a general law. In a similar vein, Converse has contrasted physics, chemistry, and biology:

> The fact of the matter is that even within what are conventionally called the "hard sciences," there are enormous differences in intellectual texture from one discipline to the next. . . . Groping to find an illustration of differences in texture, let us consider the question of the mathematical equation . . . $E = mc^2$. If you take one small step, say, over into chemistry, reliance on this kind of simple deterministic equation is much less. . . . Or go on another step to biology: there the pinnacle of achievement of recent history is the cracking of the genetic code. So what is the equation like $E = mc^2$ that summarizes all this? Well, there isn't one, because the discovery is of a totally different texture, one that is crucial, powerful, but that does not lend itself to this form of expression. (p. 45 below)

The implication of the covering law model that scientific explanation requires the discovery of general laws becomes even more inadequate as a description for the semiotic sciences. This type of science world view consists of those fields that study "imposed" order based on "meaning" rather than on natural or physical order. Linguists, for example, study a complex kind of ordering that humans impose upon the world. This kind of order creates meaning and is created by the attempt to convey meaning. It is an arbitrary order, which can change rapidly and which varies from place to place and time to time. A page of a book, for instance, exhibits a high degree of imposed order, with neatly separated lines of text and almost identical characters. Somehow, this physical order creates meaning.

It is not just language that is an imposed order that creates things that have meaning. The normative uniformities of dress and behavior are also an imposed order. Material culture—tables and chairs, buildings and cities—is the reification of human ideas in solid medium. A dance or ritual is another kind of reification, an order created in process and movement. These are perceptible cultural objects. Equally impressive are the imperceptible cultural objects, things like nation-states, statuses, laws, and other intersubjectivity shared notions (D'Andrade 1984).

How can we understand imposed order? As scientists, what questions should we ask about such things, other than simply to list them? What the semiotic sciences seek to answer is questions about how order is generated, or what kind of more abstract order lies behind the order we see. For example, each word in a dictionary is a small piece of order. In fact, we could say that for each word in a good dictionary, we have a "lawlike generalization"—whenever, for example, the word "cat" is used by a normal speaker of English, the word will refer to "a small carnivorous animal (*felis catus*) kept by humans as a domestic pet and for catching various pests, like mice and rats" or "a person who is like a cat in some manner." This is a generalization of considerable scope (imagine how many times the word "cat" is used in the English-speaking world in a year) and reasonable accuracy. However, the presentation of a large dictionary as a demonstration that the human sciences have lots of laws seems wrong—but exactly how is it wrong?

The task for someone studying the lexicon of a language is to try to find an upper level, a more abstract kind of order in the multiplicity of lower-level orderings. The field of semantics has advanced considerably in the past twenty years, beginning with the early work on componential analysis, through the analysis of polysemy (multiplicity of meanings) and the grammatical constituents of ordinary words, to the current interest in prototypes and the "frame," or idealized cognitive model, presupposed in the meaning of a term (for a general statement, see Lakoff 1982). Related to work in semantics is the investigation of "folk models," that is, the beliefs of a social group about the nature and operation of cultural objects such as gender, illness, morality, marriage, and mind. Folk models range from relatively implicit, tacit cognitive constructions, such as the standard English-language model for speech acts (Cicourel 1980; Wish, D'Andrade & Goodnow 1980), to relatively explicit models, such as the American model for illness (D'Andrade 1976). The work, both in semantics and in folk models, attempts to show how meanings are organized into higher order systems that guide the individual in constructing experience and making inferences (Quinn, in press).

It is not the case, however, that all social scientists are interested in finding meaningful order within a multiplicity of ordered mean-

ings. Most economists and many anthropologists and sociologists
are interested in discovering the way various institutions are related. Their world view is essentially that of the natural scientist, in
that they see the economy or society or culture as a machine. It is an
odd machine, to be sure, since it is always changing its structure
and how it functions and since it is partly under the conscious direction of human agents. But in its more routine and ordinary operation, it can be described as a machinelike collection of
interacting parts, the overall system showing a certain degree of
self-maintenance.

The issue of how the undoubted capacity of humans to create
meaning and order is related to the operation of the social or cui
tural or economic machinery has been a long-standing debate. Max
Weber saw the socioeconomic machinery as running along in "rou-
tinized" fashion much of the time. However, on occasion, the machinery could be strongly affected by cultural meaning systems, as
in the case of the Protestant ethic in the sixteenth century in Europe. At such times, the machine could be restructured by order-
imposing meaning systems, but after a time, the new system would
become institutionalized and run again almost as if it were independent of whatever meanings it might have for its human actors.
Talcott Parsons stressed the way cultural meaning systems work
continuously to "legitimatize," through the establishment of "values," the current operation of the socioeconomic machinery and to
"structure" the personalities of the human agents. For the Marxist,
meaning and reordering enter into the operation of the machinery
when accurate (rather than false) class consciousness is achieved,
which brings revolution or other kinds of restructuring of the
machine.

The point here is that from the perspective that sees the socioeconomic world as a natural object, a thing with interrelated
parts, the human order-imposing and meaning-creating capacity
can be treated as part of the machinery. But it is a tricky part, since
it can radically alter the machine itself. From the perspective that
sees the socioeconomic world as an imposed order, generated out
of symbolic structures, the natural science vision of society as a machine is much more problematic. The ethnomethodological critique, for example, points to the fact that the parts and edges of the
machinery do not have hard boundaries, but are always being
"construed" and "negotiated" by the actors. For the eth-
nomethodologist, even what constitutes a scientific fact—including
the scientific facts of the hard sciences—is itself an interpretive,

negotiated achievement, not the simple identification of a "brute fact" (for examples, see Cicourel 1983; Garfinkel, Lynch & Livingston 1981; Knorr-Cetina 1981; Latour & Woolgar 1979).

Within anthropology, there has been a shift in orientation from the natural science view of classical social anthropology to the semiotic view of symbolic anthropology. Malinowski and Radcliffe-Brown both saw the sociocultural world as an organism (a self-reproducing machine) with internal structures functionally related to each other. They seemed to have differed on the range of functions that could be profitably studied and on who was to be the central figure in British anthropology, but these, after all, were minor disagreements. That vision has been abandoned by most of modern cultural anthropology. The viewpoint that has replaced classical social anthropology, whether structuralist or psychologically oriented, stresses the symbolic aspects of culture. The reasons for this shift appear to be complex, involving such factors as the general movement away from behaviorism and toward the study of the mind, the impact of European phenomenology, the rejection of positivism, and the not inconsequential fact that much of classical social anthropology had become dull and almost irrelevant, a production of standard monographs on the social structure of similar tribal groups.

The intellectual division between the natural science approach and the semiotic approach appears to be very deep (Agar 1982; Kirk & Miller 1983). On one hand, the natural–social science world view sees a complex system of causes as the web of interdependence and functional relations among the structural parts. The role of the scientist is to isolate these structures and measure these causes. The semiotic–social science world view, on the other hand, sees a complex generation of meanings and symbols that serve to structure social action. The causes operate primarily, not across institutions, but within the human mind.

Both the natural–social science approach and the semiotic–social science approach make generalizations, but the generalizations are quite different in character. The generalizations of natural–social science sometimes sound like laws, except for the long list of often unstated qualifications. Thus, while a generalization like "As population density increases, the degree of societal complexity increases" is stated in completely general form, it is not to be taken as having the exactitude of Newtonian mechanics, and it is understood as contingent on a variety of unstated factors. Furthermore, as in the case of the Mendelian laws, such social science "laws" are not really considered to be the basic phenomena. In the case of the generalization about population density and social complexity, for example, it is understood that this probabilistic relation occurs because of the operation of various unstated basic processes involving the way an increase in group size creates opportunities and problems, the way humans adapt to opportunities and problems, the way these adaptive solutions feed back into increases in resources that make further increases in group size possible, and so on.

Semiotic–social science generalizations, in contrast, typically sound like interpretations, totally contingent on time, place, and person. Thus a generalization like "For the Balinese, the court and capital were an exemplary center, a microcosm of the supernatural order, and the material embodiment of political order" is clearly specific to a time and a place and gives an interpretation of a kind of understanding held by the Balinese that guided choice and action (see Geertz 1980).

Sometimes the charge is made that semiotic–social science generalizations are not really science because they are too local, too subjective, and too hard to falsify. This has been accepted by many anthropologists, for example, who have come to think of themselves as humanists rather than scientists. It is also argued that natural–social science generalizations are not really scientific because they too are usually time, place, and person specific and often so vague in formulation as to be almost impossible to falsify. However, unlike the semiotically oriented social scientists, the natural–social scientists have been unwilling to accept the attribution that they are not doing science, however much the failure to find "good general laws" pains them. The general point is that the covering law model fits the semiotic approach even less than it does the natural science approach. From the perspective presented here, the basic problem with the covering law model is in its use of the term "law." A more adequate model would stress that the way the generalizations develop in any domain should be appropriate to the kinds of order and regularity found in that domain.

It may seem that the stress placed here on the inadequacy of the term "general laws" is unnecessary, that everyone recognizes that the different fields of science, however partitioned, will have different canons of generalization. Nevertheless, it is doubtful whether such recognition is even common. What seems to have happened is that Hempel and others took an ideal form, general law, as the prototype of a "generalization." The social sciences and psychology then measured themselves, and were measured by oth-

ers, according to how closely they fit this ideal. Once the ideal was
in place, the useful and slowly improving generalizations of psychology and the social sciences looked so far from it as to raise the
question whether they were science at all. Gergen, for example,
states:

> A fundamental difference exists between the bulk of the phe-
> nomena of concern to the natural as opposed to the sociobehavior-
> al scientist. There is ample reason to believe that the phenomena of
> focal concern to the latter are far less stable (enduring, reliable, or
> replicable) then those of interest to the former. . . . To place the
> matter squarely, it may be ventured that with all its attempts to
> emulate natural science inquiry, the past century of sociobehavioral
> research and theory has failed to yield a principle as reliable as
> Archimedes' principle of hydrostatics or Galileo's law of uniformly
> accelerated motion. (1982, 12)

> There appears to be little justification for the immense effort de-
> voted to the empirical substantiation of fundamental laws of
> human conduct. There would seem to be few patterns of human
> action, regardless of the durability to date, that are not subject to
> significant alteration. (ibid., 34)

> With the status of fundamental laws thus impugned, traditional
> research pursuits are also thrown into jeopardy. What function is
> to be served, it may be asked, in the attempt to verify or discredit
> basic theories of human conduct? . . . Without answers to these
> questions, we confront the collapse of the common assumption that
> with continued research on a given problem, scientific knowledge
> may accumulate over time. (ibid., 35)

The basic assumption here seems to be that limited generalizations are not science since science consists of finding fundamental
laws, not limited generalizations. But why is it that limited generalizations are not science? Is not a good science one in which the
scope of the generalizations fits the extent of regularity found in
the phenomena? A small but growing number of psychologists and
social scientists have noted the gap between current achievement
and the physical science ideal of general laws without concluding
that the entire enterprise is a failure. Cronbach, for example,
states:

> All this begins to suggest that general, lasting, definite "laws" are in
> principle beyond the reach of social science, that sheer empirical
> generalization is doomed as a research strategy. Extrapolation to

> new circumstances apparently has to rest on a rhetorical argument,
> one that relies on *qualitative* beliefs about the processes at work in
> the old and new situation. . . . Skepticism regarding generalizations
> that reach beyond time, place, population expresses a constructive
> attitude, not nihilism. The sooner all social scientists are aware that
> data never speak for themselves, that without a carefully framed
> statement of boundary conditions generalizations are misleading
> or trivially vague, and that forecasts depend on substantive conjec-
> tures, the sooner will social science be consistently a source of en-
> lightenment. (1982, 70–71)

Another difficulty with the covering law model concerns the notion of what it is that science explains. As stated by Hempel (1965),
science explains "events." The examples of events given by Hempel
are things like the bursting of a car radiator on a cold night and the
expansion of a soap bubble on a warm glass. While it is true that
science can explain such events, it is usually the case that what scientists spend effort trying to understand are not isolated events but
certain regular phenomena. The description of any regular phenomenon is itself a generalization. Thus if one rubs a glass rod with
a silk cloth, the rod will attract bits of brass leaf. This is a good solid
generalization. What scientists usually do is to try to explain generalizations with other generalizations and to develop systems of interrelated generalizations.

Thus whole systems of generalizations are involved in explanation and prediction—what Cronbach and Meehl (1955) and others
have termed the "nomological network." All scientists work on constructing such systems, not on trying to explain particular events.
Only if the boundary conditions are known do such systems of generalizations have the power to predict certain events. The qualifica-
tion is important, in that many psychologists and social scientists
believe they should be able to predict behavior, which they take to
mean that they should be able to predict the particular actions of
particular persons. Many psychologists and social scientists further
believe that to the extent that they cannot do this, they do not have
a good science. But being able to predict or explain particular
events is not a good test of whether a science has found out something, since particular events have idiosyncratic boundary conditions, which make either prediction or explanation very difficult
(Meehl 1978). For example, it would be silly to say that the physical
sciences are a failure because they cannot predict when some
bridge is going to fall down or explain why the earth only has one
moon. What sciences generally explain is a regular phenomenon of

some sort—like the acceleration of falling bodies or the elliptical orbits of the moon and the planets—where the boundary conditions tend to be much fewer in number and much more ascertainable than in the case of particular events. It is easier to develop and apply an explanatory account when one knows what it is that one is explaining.

Thus a more appropriate task for psychology and the social sciences is to account for the kinds of regular phenomena we can observe naturally or produce in the laboratory. It would be a better test of progress if psychologists and social scientists held themselves accountable for being able to explain or predict such phenomena as the relation between number of items presented to subjects and the accuracy of recall or the relation between prestige and wealth, not such idiosyncratic events as whether Mrs. Puffaway will quit smoking or whether Mr. Seemsodd will have a psychotic break or whether Someland will declare war on Someotherland.

The importance placed on the development of systems of generalizations and the relative unimportance of particular explanations in science is nicely illustrated by the history of the study of electricity. In the eighteenth century, the electrification of glass by silk and other kinds of frictional electricity became phenomena of interest. Scientists began to develop a series of ideas about what might account for these phenomena. There was a controversy about whether electricity was a fluid, and if so, whether there was just one type of fluid, or two. Finally, through a whole system of generalizations, the glass rod phenomena were connected to a wide range of other phenomena, such as lightning, cathode rays, and eventually magnetism and the structure of the atom. What is of special interest is that the explanation for why electrons go from one surface to another is still not worked out for things like glass and silk; these phenomena turn out to involve the physics of complex solids, which is not well developed (Weinberg 1983, 19). Once the system of generalizations began to develop, the thing of interest, was the system itself, not the "explanation" for the electrification of glass rods.

PSYCHOLOGY, SCIENCE, AND MEANING

To this point, the discussion has focused on the social sciences and the inadequacies of the covering law model. A number of arguments have been presented: first, that the sciences contain at least three very different world views, that of the physical sciences, that of the natural sciences, and that of the semiotic sciences; second, that the pursuit of "general laws" is characteristic primarily of the physical sciences; third, that some of the natural sciences, such as biology, have done well despite the fact they have not found general laws; fourth, that in the social sciences there is considerable division between the natural science approach and the semiotic approach without a reasonable synthesis in view; and fifth, that the emphasis on predicting or explaining individual events as a scientific activity is misguided because of the difficulties of establishing the appropriate boundary conditions.

A number of the issues listed above apply to the field of psychology. In general, psychology has a natural science approach, in that it thinks of the mind, or the brain, or the psyche, or personality, as a machinelike thing with structural parts that have complex functional relations. While the computer analogy is recent, past theorists have used as their metaphors items from the technology of their day. John Marshall (1977) has pointed out that such metaphors as the hydraulic model of movement and motivation, the storehouse/library model of memory, the calculating machine model of thought, the multiple photocopy model of memory, and the mechanical governor model of human executive capacity all extend back in time, in some cases to early Greek civilization. However, there is a problem with the pure machine approach to the study of the psyche related to the fact that the mind learns things, incorporates into itself information from the external world. Learning by itself would not constitute a problem if one could always draw a line between the machinery and what has been learned, rather like the way we distinguish between the "architecture" of a computer and the "programs" it runs. But often it is hard to distinguish between hardware and software. To the extent that what is learned becomes itself a part of the machinery, the distinction between learned content and built-in processor dissolves.

This problem is not salient at present in the study of perception or animal learning, and it only intrudes on occasion into fields like memory (but see Cole et al., 1971). It is very salient, however, where a great deal of learning is needed before one can even observe the effects of the machinery of interest, as in the fields of social psychology and personality. Gergen and others have argued with force that many of the findings in these fields are at least in part the result of cultural uniformities rather than of the operation of purely psychological "laws" (Gergen 1982). Thomas Laundauer, a psychologist friend of mine, once described social psychology as a "subtle way of doing ethnography." Perhaps he should have included a number of other fields in psychology as well. However, just because much of human behavior is a blend of innate psychological mechanisms and learned cultural and idiosyncratic meanings, this does not make it impossible to study "scientifically."

Since much of human learning is verbal learning, the same semiotic issues about meaning that divide the social sciences also divide various fields of psychology. Skinner and others have pointed out that a large part of the vocabulary we normally use to describe human actions depends on identifying various inner states such as "intentions" and "motives." Inner states typically involve meanings, that is, symbolic constructions about the world (Schneider 1976). Human intentions often involve highly propositional states of affairs, such as doing what is right, being truthful, cutting costs, and so on. These intentional or propositional states are learned constructs that depend on language for their comprehension and transmission to other people. One can try to purify the descriptive language to be used in psychology, as Skinner did, but at the cost of removing from the language—and hence denying the application to people—of every kind of internal cybernetic system. For most psychologists this is too high a cost to pay.

However, while leaving meaning out of the vocabulary of human action has a high cost, keeping it in also has its cost. One of the problems with meaning is that in being something imposed on the world—on acoustic sounds to make words, on shapes to make letters, on movements to make gestures—it is arbitrary, not natural. Meanings are construed, not given, from arbitrary signs. But how can one know how any other person in the world actually construes things? It is not given in the nature of the thing. This can lead to a kind of despair about the possibility of doing science on semiotic material (Gergen 1982; Fiske 1979; Rosenberg 1983a). The issue here is that to the degree the same physical event can mean different things, the establishment of an empirical science based solely on the observation of human action becomes problematic. This is sometimes referred to as the problem of intersubjectivity, where the term "intersubjectivity" refers to a state of affairs in which two or more people understand that they are experiencing events the same way.

One simple approach to the issue of intersubjectivity is to assume things have their conventional meanings. For example, the designer of a questionnaire assumes that respondents will construe questions according to the usual linguistic and social conventions and will answer following the same conventions. While it is recognized that some respondents will bring idiosyncratic constructions to the process, this kind of "error" is expected to be random and is thereby not expected to affect measures of central tendency. However, there are problems in relying on convention to determine meanings, even in the case of questionnaires (Cicourel 1982). In much of human interaction, the meaning of what is said is underdetermined, not completely fixed, so that multiple interpretations are common. Relevant here is the ethnomethodological point that whatever intersubjective agreement is reached on most matters is accomplished only after some negotiation between the participants. Moreover, in many cases, the conventional approach to the interpretation of meanings cannot be applied because the event to be understood does not have a conventional interpretation. For example, one cannot understand dreams the way one can understand questions from a questionnaire. To the extent the person is not aware of how he or she is construing events, one cannot ask directly. It does not seem to be possible to get at the meaning of neurotic symptoms or various cultural rites and rituals by simply asking.

The same difficulty that occurs in trying to understand the meanings involved in a dream or a ritual also surface in trying to understand everyday actions. For example, in taking to task the assumption that behavior patterns are stable over the life cycle, Gergen describes the case of Charles Wilson.

> Wilson was a big, handsome boy who grew up in a small Texas town. He starred in football, basketball, and track, and managed at the same time to achieve high academic marks. He attended a Methodist church near his father's small grocery store and gas station. In his junior year of high school, Wilson was voted outstanding member of his class. How was Wilson to develop during the college years? In this case, we find that within two years of his leaving his hometown, Wilson was an active participant in the notorious Manson gang. Together, the group slaughtered almost a dozen persons without any significant motive; Wilson's specialty was carving initials in the corpses. (1982, 150).

From this description, it sounds as if Wilson changed drastically. But we do not know what any of this meant to Wilson. He may have always acted in ways to get certain kinds of group reactions, and what changed was, not how he saw the world and what he was trying to do, but rather what kinds of actions got him the things he wanted. Or he may have outwardly conformed while in his hometown but been full of fantasies that he finally found he could enact with the Manson gang. Or he may indeed have drastically changed—because of drugs, because of a shift in identity, or whatever. The point is, once one takes in the interior view of action, one cannot say that someone has changed, or not changed, on the basis of an exterior description of behavior of the kind given above.

This raises our original question, How can one determine meanings? If conventional assignments of meaning fit only a restricted class of events (typically events that are close to ordinary talk), how can the events to which conventional assignments of meaning do not apply be understood? If we cannot determine nonconventional meanings with some degree of reliability and validity, then it will be impossible to develop any scientific understanding of human action that is oriented by nonconventional meanings. This is an area of considerable controversy. The problem is not that we lack the ability to interpret human actions. The extensive works of classical Freudians, Kohutians, Marxists, Lévi-Straussian structuralists, and a variety of other interpreters of the human scene indicate that the problem is not a lack of hypotheses about the meaning of actions. The problem is to determine which hypotheses are valid.

One method of narrowing the range of possible interpretations is to gather more data. Thus, given just a dream, many interpretations are possible. But given the dream plus a series of free associations to the dream, constraints are added, in that the interpretation must fit more facts. The use of a whole corpus of myths, rather than a single myth, exemplified in the work of Lévi-Strauss, is another means of adding constraints. Victor Turner's use of native exegesis (explanation by local informants), plus various contextual and performance factors in interpreting symbolic systems, is another approach to limiting possible hypotheses through increasing the body of material to be accounted for.

The development of these hermeneutic traditions within the social sciences and psychology has happened through a series of partially independent inventions and reinventions. Although these methods are criticized because different interpreters with different theoretical backgrounds still do not come to the same conclusions, it should be stressed that there is the potential of an enormous increase in fidelity of interpretation through taking account of wider rather than narrower ranges of relevant material. Further, the fact that different interpretations of the same material remain plausible even when expanded textual materials are considered indicates that it may well be the case that there is more than one meaning for most important symbolic systems. It does not make science impossible if symbols have more than one meaning, but it would make science, or any sensible commentary, impossible if every symbol meant everything.

While the development of hermeneutic or interpretative methods in psychology and the social sciences has been much commented on, another method of studying systems of meaning has developed almost unnoticed. This is the experimental method, and it has received less attention because it did not use the usual paraphernalia of the laboratory and also because its practitioners were concerned with very different issues of control than is standard in laboratory experimentation (D'Andrade, 1984). That is, the standard laboratory experiment in psychology has been concerned with making stimulus material uniform across subjects, with controlling as many conditions as possible, and with ensuring that responses are constrained into countable equivalence classes. This has made it possible to do the same experiment on a relatively large number of subjects and to isolate the effective stimulus conditions that produce the results of interest. However, the problem that confronts someone who is trying to study cultural or individual meaning systems is, not the determination of the external conditions that produce some effect, but rather the determination of certain internal conditions thought to guide the subject's actions.

In trying to discover what a set of things means to someone—whether one wants to know what the categories of plants are in a language, what the propositions are that some group of people use to diagnose, treat, and understand the course of illnesses, or the propositions that people hold about their marriages—one needs to get the subjects to communicate. The communications between the investigator and the subject, or informant, or client, becomes a major focus of experimental concern, in the same way that the control over the effective stimulus conditions becomes a major focus of concern in the laboratory experiment. If the subjects do not communicate fully and truthfully, because of distrust or dislike or some other reaction to the investigator, the information obtained from the probe or intervention will be distorted. Thus in studying meaning systems, there has come to be a great emphasis on methods for maintaining rapport and ways of establishing and monitoring transference.

It might be objected that this so-called nonlaboratory experimental method is nothing more than simple interviewing. It should be made clear that not all interviewing involves doing an experiment. If the investigator asks an informant how many people in a village own their own farming land simply to get an estimate of how many people own their own farming land, no experiment has been done. An experiment requires three things: first, that the investigator have an idea about how things might be; second, that he has a way to relate this idea about how things might be to observations that could be made on something; and third, that the investigator has the ability or power to produce the phenomena to be observed. For example, consider the situation of an investigator who has reason to believe that a group of people attribute most deaths to witchcraft. The investigator's approach could be entirely naturalistic and observational, and he could wait and watch and listen for confirming or disconfirming events. But the right events happen infrequently, and often people don't state what is to them obvious or talk about things that are considered unmentionable. In this situation, most ethnographers would ask questions, probe, argue with informants, and use a variety of interviewing techniques to find out what they believe. In doing this, the investigator slowly builds a model of what the informants believe and continually tests this model by direct and indirect queries.

There are a number of other ways in which the anthropological experimental approach to the study of meaning differs from standard laboratory procedures. Since communication is always risky and since understanding on the part of either the informant or the investigator of what is being said is usually incomplete, the study of meaning usually involves a long series of questions and answers on the same topic, where the questions are asked at different times and in different ways. Rarely is there anything like a crucial experiment. Instead, the investigator's understanding grows with repeated questions, probes, interventions, as well as with whatever naturalistic observation is possible. The great advantages of the experimental method are that one can produce phenomena at will, rather than having to wait for the right kind of event to occur naturally, and that one can disconnect otherwise correlated conditions. As Campbell has argued, many kinds of experimental intervention can be used in the social sciences that have the potential of greatly reducing the kind of causal equivocality that arises from naturalistic observation (Campbell 1982; Campbell & Stanley 1966; Cook & Campbell 1979). If the people one is studying pretend that they know nothing about witchcraft because they are afraid that they will be suspected of being witches themselves if they reveal too much knowledge, the task is to disconnect the fears of accusation from the informant's presentation of information about witchcraft. Without the correct information about witchcraft, many of the things that happen in daily life—patterns of interpersonal avoidance, fear reactions to various events, even group antagonisms— remain equivocal. Such and such a reaction may be due to witchcraft fears, but maybe not. To get the needed information in this sort of situation is not a simple matter, but a combination of interest, acceptance, and care can usually build the kind of trust needed.

The fact that one has to operate with meanings to do experiments to discover meanings leads some commentors to negative conclusions. For example, Rosenberg says:

> If the identity of an intentional state is determined by the proposition it contains and if beliefs can be false and desires unattained, then we cannot decide what beliefs or desires an agent has by finding out whether any proposition about the world independent of his intentions is true or false. Of course we can and do discover peoples' intentional states: by asking them; but this method is itself intentional; their responses to our questions will only be counted as replies, as the utterance of meaningful speech, as actions, if we assume that they are sincere, and understand the meaning of the language in which we put our questions; that is, if we assume they desire to answer truthfully, and believe that the utterances they emit will attain this desire. . . . Now, there is nothing improper about this intentional circle so far as our every day non-scientific purposes are concerned. But social science seeks to sharpen its explanations and predictions of human behavior beyond the common-sense level. Therefore, it must break out of this intentional circle: we must find a way of identifying movements as actions without assuming the movements were caused by intentional states. (1983b, 70–71)

What is not clear to me is why it is necessary to break out of the intentional circle in order to sharpen explanations and predictions. There is no principle that says one cannot use meaning to study meaning, and Rosenberg agrees that ordinary people do so with some degree of success. Why can't social scientists do better by refining the methods of ordinary interaction? Rosenberg concludes that even behaviorism fails to completely break out of the "intentional circle," and that for this reason among others, the social sciences should be replaced by natural science approaches, such as sociobiology. That is, he simply rejects the possibility of any kind of science that deals with meaning, and he turns to pure natural science as the only route to general laws that might apply to people. This kind of Draconian solution would simply leave most human phenomena unstudied.

What, then, about social psychology and the study of personality? There seems to be agreement that these two areas have real problems, and that they are the two fields in which there is the greatest degree of involvement with meanings, or intentional states, or with learned symbolic material. Doesn't this show that meanings are hard to bring into science? My answer is that meanings are indeed hard to bring into science, but it doesn't follow that meanings should be kept out.

In fact, the problems of social psychology and the study of personality seem quite different in character. As seen by an outsider, the problem of social psychology is not that nothing is being found out—there is considerable new activity each year, and novel findings and new theoretical formulations. The major problems that seem to bedevil the field are those like the degree to which the findings of the laboratory have any relation to the things that people do in ordinary life, the degree to which findings represent historically conditioned cultural attitudes rather than deep psychological process, and the way in which the exploration of a particular phenomenon seems to lead to a dead end, with no general findings outside of the understanding of how to produce a certain limited class of effects.

All of these strike me as real concerns. It may well be very difficult to get laboratory findings to relate to ordinary life events because of the complex way in which multiple systems influence common actions. That does not indicate that the laboratory findings are unimportant or even irrelevant. It means that understanding the web of organized complexity in which ordinary life actions are embedded will prove to be a difficult venture, a kind of Mount Everest for those who want the challenge:

> The point here is precisely that specific behaviors—like most events in the world—cannot be explained as the simple manifestation of some single law or principle. What we have is interacting levels of stratification. Indeed, the acts of persons are open-systemic events in which a wide variety of systems and structures are involved, systems that are physical, biological, psychological and . . . sociological as well. This posture leads to the conclusion that laboratory psychology should not be aimed at explaining behavior—action in the world; its purpose is far more circumscribed. The explanation of behavior, as we shall see, is properly a multi-

disciplinary effort and, though based on the behavioral sciences,
necessarily transcends them to involve both biology and the social
sciences. (Manicas & Secord 1983, 405)

Another perceived failing, the fact that some or even many of
the findings of social psychology reflect at least in part cultural
ideas and attitudes, will, I believe, turn out to be a strength in the
field, since an important and distinctive thing about humans is that
psychological processes do interact with cultural and idiosyncratic
learning. Social psychologists are as well equipped to study this
kind of interdisciplinary problem as anyone else. Finally, the sense
that social psychologists keep finding interesting phenomena that
turn out not to lead to any strong or deep underlying psychological
regularities seems to me a disappointment based on a very incorrect estimate of the complexity of the human psychic apparatus.
Even viewed as machines, humans are not simple, and deep, simple
regularities will probably only be found at a relatively high level of
abstraction, connecting various kinds of what appear at first to be
distinct phenomena.

The problems of the field of personality seem much more difficult than the problems of social psychology. The current issues
about person consistency versus situational variation in behavior
strike me as indicative of the need for a reconceptualization of the
field (Fiske 1979). A great investment was made in the search for
different kinds of persons, which led to an emphasis on trait typologies and character assessment. Many of the early factor-analyt-
ic findings of ratings and questionnaires concerning character
types were based, I believe, on the artifacts that emerge when humans are asked to make ratings on others or themselves on the
basis of information held in long-term memory—a systematic distortion caused the effects of semantic similarity on memory-based
judgment (D'Andrade 1974; Shweder 1977; Shweder & D'Andrade 1980). Recent work has not found support for cross-situational consistency in behavior, although the issue remains controversial (Mischel & Peake 1982). It would appear that the search for
different kinds of persons has not proved fruitful, and a search for
something else is now in order.

Perhaps if personality were seen as the operation of certain processes—affective, conceptual, judgmental, intentional, or whatever—then the task for the field would be to determine what these
processes are, how they interact, and what creates them and trig-
gers them. But to study process, one must observe process (or the
effects of process). This is hard to do in natural settings and is not

effectively done by standard psychometric techniques. The place where these processes are most directly observable is in psychotherapy. As suggested above, the study of meaning can be made much more effective when experimental intervention can be used. The therapist is a kind of experimentor trying various interventions and observing the outcome. The natural alliance between clinicians and academic psychologists interested in personality was disrupted in the 1960s when new clinical training procedures were mandated and many departments of psychology dropped their clinical programs. The rise of psychotherapy as a profession, and the concomitant effects of professionalization seems to have worked against the use of psychotherapy as the academic laboratory for the study of personality. It is my view that not until academic psychology develops some way to observe the processes of interest in the study of personality will the field begin to make any strong advance. One cannot expect to improve upon Freud by observing less about human beings than he did.

CONCLUSION

This paper has presented two general arguments. First, the stress on general laws, exemplified in Hempel's covering law model, has set up an ideal against which no science but physics can come out well. This has led to misdirected criticism, because the problems of psychology, or sociology, or anthropology, are not that it has failed to find general laws, since it is unlikely the kind of phenomena being studied—systems of organized complexity—exhibit simple, widespread noninteractive regularities. What does seem to be possible, and what has been accomplished so far, is the development of a sense of how some of these systems of organized complexity work.

Second, the study of meanings is a part of both the social sciences and psychology. The study of systems of meaning involves a somewhat different world view than that of the natural sciences, and for a variety of reasons, the study of meanings has been controversial in both the social sciences and in psychology. More than half a century after Max Weber and Sigmund Freud, it is time to become aware of the necessity of incorporating the study of meaning into the social sciences and psychology.

References

Agar, M. 1982. Toward an ethnographic language. 1982. *American Anthropologist* 84:779–95.

Campbell, D. T. 1982. Experiments as arguments. *Knowledge, Creation, Diffusion, Utilization* 3:327–37.

Campbell, D. T., and Stanley J. 1966. *Experiments and quasi-experimental designs for research*. Boston: Houghton Mifflin.

Cicourel, A. V. 1980. Three models of discourse analysis: The role of social structure. *Discourse Processes* 3:101–32.

———. 1982. Interviews, surveys, and ecological validity. *American Sociologist* 17:11–20.

———. 1983. Language and the structure of belief in medical communication. *Proceedings of the sixth world congress of the International Association of Applied Linguistics*.

Cole, M.; Gay, J.; Glick, J. A.; and Sharp, D. W. 1971. *The cultural context of learning and thinking*. New York: Basic Books.

Cook, T. D., and Campbell, D. T. 1979. *Quasi-experimentation: Design and analysis for field settings*. Chicago: Rand McNally.

Cronbach, L. J. 1982. Prudent aspirations for social inquiry. In *The social sciences: Their nature and uses*, ed. W. H. Kruskal. Chicago: University of Chicago Press.

Cronbach, L. J., and Meehl, P. E. 1955. Construct validity in psychological tests. *Psychological Bulletin* 52:281–302.

D'Andrade, R. G. 1974. Memory and the assessment of behavior. In *Measurement in the social sciences*, ed. H. Blalock, Jr. Chicago: Aldine.

———. 1976. A propositional analysis of U.S. American beliefs about illness. In *Meanings in anthropology*, ed. K. Basso and H. Selby. Albuquerque: University of New Mexico Press.

———. 1984. Cultural meaning systems. In *Culture Theory: Essays on mind, self, and emotion*, ed. R. A. Shweder and R. A. LeVine. New York: Cambridge University Press.

———. In Press. A folk model of the mind. In *Culture models*, ed.. N. Quinn and D. Holland. New York: Cambridge University Press.

Feynman, R. 1965. *The character of physical law*. Cambridge, Mass.: MIT Press.

Fiske, D. W. 1979. Two worlds of psychological phenomena. *American Psychologist* 34:733–39.

Garfinkel, H.; Lynch, M.; and Livingston, E. 1981. The work of discovering science construed with materials from the optically discovered pulsar. *Philosophy of Social Science* 11:131–58.

Geertz, C. 1980. *Negara: The theatre state in nineteenth-century Bali*. Princeton: Princeton University Press.

Gergen, K. J. 1982. *Toward transformation in social knowledge*. New York: Springer-Verlag.

Hempel, C. G. 1965. The function of general laws in history. (*Journal of Philosophy* 39 [1942]:35–48). In *Aspects of scientific explanation and other essays in the philosophy of science*. New York: Free Press.

Kirk, J., and Miller, M. L. 1983. Ethnography, hermeneutics, and science: A response to Agar. Manuscript.

Knorr-Cetina, K. G. 1981. *The manufacture of knowledge.* New York: Pergamon Press.

Lakoff, G. 1982. Categories and cognitive models. *Berkeley Cognitive Science Report,* no. 2. Berkeley: University of California Cognitive Science Program.

Latour, B., and Woolgar, S. 1979. *Laboratory life: The social construction of scientific facts.* Beverley Hills: Sage.

Manicas, P. T., and Secord, P. F. 1983. Implications for psychology of the new philosophy of science. *American Psychologist* 38:399–413.

Marshall, J. 1977. Minds, machines and metaphors. *Social Studies of Science* 7:475–88.

Meehl, P. E. 1978. Theoretical risks and tabular asterisks: Sir Karl, Sir Ronald, and the slow progress of soft psychology. *Journal of Consulting and Clinical Psychology* 46:806–34.

Mischel, W., and Peake, P. K. 1982. Beyond deja vu in the search for cross-situational consistency. *Psychological Review* 89:730–55.

Nagel, E. 1961. *The structure of science.* New York: Harcourt, Brace and World.

Quinn, N. In press. American marriage and the model of need fulfillment: An application of folk social psychology. In *Cultural models,* ed. N. Quinn and D. Holland. New York: Cambridge University Press.

Rosenberg, A. 1983a. Human science and biological science: Defects and opportunities. In *Scientific explanation and understanding,* ed. N. Rescher. Lanham, Md.: University Press of America.

Rosenberg, A. 1983b. The human sciences: Obstacles and opportunities. *Syracuse Scholar* 4, 63–68.

Schneider, D. 1976. Notes toward a theory of culture. In *Meaning in Anthropology,* ed. K. Basso and H. Selby. Albuquerque: University of New Mexico Press.

Shweder, R. A. 1977. Illusory correlation and the MMPI controversy. *Journal of Consulting and Clinical Psychology* 45:917–24.

Shweder, R. A., and D'Andrade, R. G. 1980. The systematic distortion hypothesis. In *Fallible judgment in behavioral research,* ed. R. A. Shweder. New Directions for Methodology of Social and Behavioral Science, no. 4. San Francisco: Jossey-Bass.

von Wright, G. H. 1971. *Explanation and understanding.* Ithaca: Cornell University Press.

Weinberg, S. 1983. *The discovery of subatomic particles.* New York: W. H. Freeman and Co.

Wish, M.; D'Andrade, R. G.; and Goodnow, J. E. 1980. Dimensions of interpersonal communication: Correspondences between structures for speech acts and bipolar scales. *Journal of Personality and Social Psychology* 39:848–60.

2 Generalization and the Social Psychology of "Other Worlds"

Philip E. Converse

The topic I have chosen for my remarks is the problem of generalization, the formation of general statements from observed variability in special cases.[1] Now this is one of the oldest chestnuts in the philosophy of science, and I am nearly embarrassed to bring it up. The chief reason why I decided to address it here is because of a series of events that struck me rather forcefully a year or so ago. At that time, I attended the fiftieth anniversary of the erection of the Social Science Building at the University of Chicago. Part of the program involved a series of papers generally designed to comment on the state of the social sciences—implicity, their state fifty years later.

What stunned me was the deeply discouraged tone of the occasion: it had the flavor more of a wake than of a celebration. Across the symposium, there were many symptoms of this pervasive pessimism. I shall merely choose one of the most foreceful and articulate examples, provided by Lee Cronbach. He commented on the near impossibility of arriving at any satisfactory generalizations in social science, in part because of points of methodological recalcitrance that he felt were insuperable (a subject upon which he is an acknowledged master), but in part as well because of the growing awareness that various findings that, by experiment or field observation, appear to be very robust and general where they were developed turn out to travel poorly when you go to other worlds. That is, what you may think you have learned of a general nature here in this country often turns out not to replicate in, say, Africa.[2] This was, to be sure, but one example of the downbeat tone that so perplexed me, although obviously it is the specific instance of the pessimism that I have singled out to work with here.

My perplexity at the sea of discouragement in which I found myself was briskly relieved by the dinner speech presented by the

42

university's president, Hanna Gray. Being a good historian, she
had taken pains to string together a lengthy series of quotations
gleaned from the corresponding symposium on social science held
in 1954 at the time of the twenty-fifth anniversary of the Social
Science Building; and as I listened to the quotes, suddenly there it
all was. In 1954, social scientists saw themselves as being on the
brink of two major coups; one scientific, one political. The scientific coup, of course, was the imminent arrival at the apex of an
exact science of human affairs, reduced to a few crucial mathematical equations. The political coup was that of unerring policy
problem solution by a new breed of philosopher-kings. Against
such a backdrop, the pessimism suddenly made sense to me. After
all, it was a full quarter century later, and we still were not there.
To my mind, it quickly shaped up as a problem of remarkable expectations, ca. 1954, coupled with remarkable understandings as to
what a scientific enterprise is all about—a curious choice of scientific models, as I shall develop the matter momentarily.

As Hanna Gray talked, I was put in mind of a lengthy evening's
conversation I once had during a chance encounter in a small town
in France with a well-known American social scientist in 1959. To
my surprise, he was in considerable depression at the state of social
science. Being but a year beyond finishing my own doctorate and
still feeling high, I spent much of the conversation trying to weed
out where such a dismal depression could be coming from. I finally
boiled it down in my mind to these propositions, which he made
more or less explicit: Here it was 1959; social science had been
seriously underway for thirty years, or fifty years, or one-hundred
years, depending upon how you wanted to count, and we still had
not had Sir Isaac Newton yet.

I was privately appalled, because I was confronted with the fact
that his understandings of either science or of social science were
vastly different from my own. I morbidly commissioned a card file
in my mind that I entitled "Waiting for Newton," and I have been
filing bits and pieces away there for many years. Sure enough, Lee
Cronbach in his paper stole a line I had been saving: "Waiting for
Newton is like waiting for Godot." Sure enough, as Hanna Gray
recreated 1954 in living color that evening, I realized that my 1959
conversation partner had been on the faculty at the University of
Chicago in 1954.

Obviously, there is a problem of exaggerated expectations here,
expectations that somehow I never shared. I think my long-run
aspirations for social science are as towering as anyone else's, or

likely I would not be here. On the other hand, it was vivid to me in the 1959 conversation that my own sense of the time for various forms of progress where social science was concerned was vastly different—I would say "orders of magnitude different"—than those I was encountering. In the 1979 symposium, or in the reconstruction of 1954, the problem was identical.

I should not leave you with the impression that all social scientists in the early 1950s were swept along with these expectations. Newcomb, for one, was alarmed by them. As early as 1951, commenting on the rapid takeoff of social psychology as a specialty, he expressed in public print his fear that this takeoff "might be based upon expectations which are greater than anything which we can deliver in the near future" (Newcomb 1951, 31). But overblown original expectations were the obvious culprit in the downbeat tone of the 1979 Chicago symposium. However, I do not want to leave the matter purely to expectations. That merely raises the next question: "Where did those exaggerated expectations come from?" And one source that I should like to develop for you is something I have found to be a curious view in that generation as to what real science is, or can expect to be under varying conditions.

Of course there are models and models of science. The going model that most gripped social scientists of the period was largely exhausted by such pinnacle events as the glorious triple play from Brahe to Kepler to Newton, or perhaps the Maxwell equations, certainly $E = mc^2$. That was science. Could social psychology be a science, arriving at such beautiful, incredibly parsimonious and apparently timeless generalizations, true "universal laws," as the saying goes? And if it can, why do our generalizations falter merely in passing from one culture to another? It is hard to form an answer without deciding first what model of science one wants. The $E = mc^2$ model is fantastically inspiring, but it is not the only one.

At this point, it should have become clear that my topic involves what has been called in recent years "the crisis of confidence in social psychology." Hence I have reviewed that recent subliterature as it stands in social psychology, including Gergen's judgment that social psychology cannot be a science like the others (i.e., a "real science") because it cannot truly generalize: "The observed regularities, and thus the major theoretical principles, are firmly wedded to historical circumstances" (Gergen 1973, 315). We are left to conclude that social psychology should lower its sights by about forty leagues and concentrate as Gergen says on providing merely "a systematic account of contemporary affairs."

I agree profoundly with some of this, as you shall see, including the play of historical forces in rearranging key parameters of social process under some circumstances. But I disagree equally profoundly with some of the more pathetic implications that tend to be drawn from such an argument. Obviously, a crucial question remains "When is a science a science?" Or "What model of science, IF ANY, does the social psychologist choose?" For example, if being "firmly wedded to historical circumstance" is sufficient to disqualify the investigation as "science," then we must hastily, if perhaps apologetically, inform geology it is not, and has never been, a science, for it is hard to imagine a body of inquiry more firmly, and in the nature of things, exclusively, "wedded to historical circumstance." We might be embarrassed about the demotion, for after all, one of the major exciting developments in what is customarily seen as "hard science" in the past twenty years has been provided by geology in the theory of plate tectonics.

The fact of the matter is that even within what are conventionally called the "hard sciences," there are enormous differences in intellectual texture from one discipline to the next. "Texture" is a vague word, but I shall stick to it. If you wish me to be more formal, I mean by any given "texture" a unique location in a space of very high order, so high in fact that it would boggle the mind to count all the dimensions, much less label them. Groping to find an illustration of differences in texture, let us consider the question of the mathematical equation, which is certainly the centerpiece of the model of science as $E = mc^2$. If you take one small step, say, over into chemistry, reliance on this kind of simple deterministic equation is much less. Do you remember, for example, what the bread-and-butter equations in chemistry look like—the ones with those funny hollow arrows describing what to expect as chemical reactions? They have a distinctly different texture, as I am using the word. Or go on another step to biology: there the pinnacle achievement of recent history is the cracking of the genetic code. So what is the equation like $E = mc^2$ that summarizes all this? Well, there isn't one, because the discovery is of a totally different texture, one that is crucial, powerful, but that does not lend itself to this form of expression.

Social psychologists have a central equation, too: it reads $B = f(P, S)$, or translating into English, "Behavior is a function of person and situation." Now that is a proposition nobly striving toward the epitome of $E = mc^2$. There is something of a shortfall, however. Among other things, we may feel it is a bit underspecified. I shall return to it later. The broad point here is that even the hard sciences differ markedly in general texture, and if one asks where these differences come from, it would seem that they arise in the most straightforward way from differences in texture of the subject matter itself from science to science. What could be more appropriate?

Actually, if we would like to be a step less simplistic, it is worth registering the fact that the $E = mc^2$ model covers only a small if lofty part of the bodies of inquiry normally lumped together as "physics." Many segments of the leading edge of physics have pushed progressively toward increasing complexity without the relief provided by this kind of major simplification, and it is less than obvious in many such areas—the study of turbulence is a case in point—that there is any reason to expect such a simplification. Thus even physics displays multiple "textures" within its own domain, and while $E = mc^2$ is certainly an inspiring success story, it stops very well short of sweeping out the accumulation of useful knowledge, even where purely physical phenomena are concerned.

All of this leaves us with the fundamental question as to why the social sciences have felt that in working down this potential shopping list of models of science, the $E = mc^2$ texture is exactly the right one for its own distinctive subject matter. If I were asked offhand whether physics or biology were more likely to be the right "texture" to serve as a template for the social sciences, it would seem on the face of it that biology would be a better choice, for the simple reason that it, like social science, deals with the nature of living things. The fact that this matters, even at the level of basic thought patterns as inquiry is pursued, is best illustrated by some of the scolding given physicists by biologists like Ernst Mayr (see Lewin 1982), who feel that physicists suffer a trained incapacity to think in fruitful ways about animate objects, however adept they may be in the realms of the inanimate. The texture of the target of inquiry does matter vitally, it appears, even in how we begin to think about it, and the gap between physics and biology is already a major chasm in these regards.

But if the gap between physics and biology is large, and the social sciences seem better matched to biology, there is perhaps no reason to insist that, decades down the road, a more mature social science be patterned even after biology. Its own subject matter is quite distinct in texture from that of biology. Is it not quite possible that in due time a more mature social science will look as different from biology as biology already does from physics? This surmise does not, of course, tell us just what its texture might be, although now and again suggestions of this kind are made (see, for example, Brickman 1980 on the future of social psychology). But it does invite us not to foreclose our thinking prematurely, and certainly not to surrender quite so quickly to the counsel of despair that says if we encounter major obstacles trying to do science as $E = mc^2$, we may as well retire to write poetry, for the enterprise is doomed to failure.

Here a footnote and a caution. I am most emphatically not suggesting that social scientists may as well stop using mathematical summaries and equations of the same general form—even the deterministic form—of $E = mc^2$. There are a number of these expressions about, even in the social sciences, and many are highly useful, just as many of their counterparts are in chemistry, biology, and even geology. My point is this: a model of science that suggests that either we can, in T. S. Eliot's words, "roll the universe into a ball" with one grand summary expression like $E = mc^2$ or we are not engaging in science is a false model, as other admittedly hard sciences of high achievement eloquently demonstrate.

There are many other points at which social science understanding of what a scientific enterprise is about, modeled after two or three of the most famous mountain peaks in physics, seems to me naive, pedestrian, and on toward self-defeating. Working science is not, in the main, the thrilling last, mad twelve-hour dash from the final camp to the summit of Mount Everest. As someone has recently said, actual working science is ninety-nine percent dogged footsoldiery—the infinite preparations for the expedition and long periods of slogging around in the foothills, simply full of trial and error, painstakingly measuring, assembling, and ruminating about relatively low-grade information. Newton knew this and even enshrined the fact in one of his more famous comments on his own work: "If I have seen farther than most men, it is because I have stood on the shoulders of giants." Newton, brilliant man, not only did science consummately, but also understood its social organization more keenly than some of the earlier generations of social scientists have.

I have said that the textures of subject matters differ. One major difference between the stuff of social science and the stuff of a science like physics I shall mention only briefly, not because it is unimportant—quite to the contrary, I see it as absolutely crucial—but I shall pass it by briefly because it is boringly familiar to all of us: the subject matter is more complex, and by some orders of magnitude. Every social scientist is prepared to bring that bromide out in self-defense, and it is true.

But I do want to note that while social scientists are aware of the complexity problem, they are still capable of making statements about it that astonish me and land in my Waiting for Newton file. Thus many seem capable of the following hypothetical train of thought: "Physics, in its first serious two-hundred years, scaled and planted a flag on top of such-and-such number of peaks, of such-and-such high altitude. Social science can't be expected to move as fast in its first serious two-hundred years. Instead, to cover parallel ground, it will probably take us two-hundred-thirty or maybe even two-hundred-fifty years." When I read this between the lines, I despair, because while lip service is rendered to complexity, the speaker seems to lack all understanding of what I think it has to mean. I would think of the complexity differences in terms of orders of magnitude, and if parallel accomplishments could be calibrated, it would not surprise me if social science took five-hundred years to match the accomplishment of the first fifty years of physics.

Complexity has many faces, but one of its more obvious manifestations is plain in the data with which we work from day to day. Many years ago, a next-door neighbor who was an animal experimentalist in our psychology department said the following to me one day. "Phil," he said, "I don't see how you social psychology people put up with data from human beings. I've worked all my life with rats, but last year I got involved in a human learning experiment. It's the very last time I ever will, too—I've never seen such messy data. I couldn't wait to get back to my good clean rat data." So you see, where social psychology first went wrong was in its choice of subject matter. The differential messiness of data is itself a crucial diagnostic datum, and one that I have been known to exploit in some of my own work.

Another set of clips from my Waiting for Newton file is related to the issue of complexity, but casts it in a different light. It is also a shining example of pluralistic ignorance from one science to the next. An essay by an eminent biologist, addressed to his fellow biologists three or four years ago, commented that as every biologist was well aware, the research biologist labored under a very distinctive curse. What was this peculiarly biological curse? It was the knowledge that every question answered simply served to raise ten new questions. Now we can pity the biologist. After all, suppose you answer five questions and find yourself fifty questions deeper in debt—anybody can see that's a losing game, and they ought to get out of it while they've still got their shirts.

Well to me, this endless branching and fractionation is the very hallmark of what inquiry is about. I suspect that the amount of branching is itself a function of the underlying complexity of the subject matter, and I suspect we shall see a great deal more of it in the next two to three hundred years of social science. But one of the explicit laments at the Chicago symposium, predictably, was that we clearly were making no progress since it was obvious that anything we thought we learned simply raised a large number of new questions.

There are more items in my Waiting for Newton file than we can hope to review here. Some bring us to issues of the strategy of inquiry. One of these, for example, which is unwelcome in an audience of psychologists, has to do with the appropriate level of aggregation at which we might best proceed in the early stages of inquiry. It is my distinct impression that highly aggregated data on human populations show much clearer and more historically durable regularities than do more microscopic studies of individual decision making and performance, where data often get messy in the extreme. If we mentally thumb through the history of science, there is nothing at all surprising about this feature of aggregation. Inquiry moved quite rapidly to Boyle's law relating pressure and volume as macrocosmic characteristics of gases (later adding temperature) and only much more slowly—and with the help of the earlier insights—proceeded to devise the kinetic theory of gases and finally atomic theory. It is not always guaranteed that one should describe the forest before the trees. However, it is often a useful procedure, since one can waste a great deal of effort trying to decode Brownian motion on a molecule-for-molecule basis; and it seems to me that some of the deeper discouragement expressed about the future of social science comes from those who have flirted most closely with that risk.

I hope I have said enough by now to suggest why my view of plausible time horizons for the progress of social inquiry is so different from those I sensed in my colleagues at Chicago, and why high dismay and discouragement is only to be expected, if your expectations are geared to vastly shorter time frames. So let me now begin to redeem my title a bit more incisively.

We are troubled, it seems, as to the ultimate possibility of generalization about human beings interacting with their social surround, in part because stray research findings that seem robust enough for the United States fail to replicate or yield bizarre results when moved to Africa or some other world. I have two broad sets of comments about this dismal state of affairs. The first set, which I do for fun, is to observe with malice aforethought that even the hard sciences have their "other-world" problems as well. Here are two examples.

It should not have escaped your attention at the time of the Saturn flyby a few years ago, that data coming back threw the presiding scientists into great consternation. It was not one oddity or two: almost everything new being learned about Saturn's rings risked being something that, relative to the extant state of learning, seemed physically impossible. "The absurd has become commonplace!" was the summary report from the space center.

Now you will say, "That is quite different." They will soon find that no basic physical laws are being broken in the vicinity of Saturn. They will rapidly rejuggle and recombine the many concepts and basic rules about matter in motion that they have long stored away and show us that all of these absurdities are no more than apparent, mere fallout from the fact that we know so little about the details of local conditions that influence these phenomena. Of course this remonstrance is true enough. In fact, almost immediately it turned out that certain of the absurdities, not only could be accounted for, but even had been predicted in advance by a specialist in ring dynamics in a fugitive paper not known to space center personnel. This left, however, a further batch of absurdities yet to be tidied up and squared with existing theory.

Such a tidying up will surely happen, and rapidly. This is the joy of a mature science, long underway, with a lot of lore in its back pockets, and dealing with a relatively simple subject matter. But the metastructure of the problem, as distinct from its likely speed of solution, does not differ whatever in my mind from the discovery that a new batch of data from Africa fails to look like those to which we have been accustomed from the United States. As social scientists, we should be among the last to forget that local governing conditions in Africa may differ from those in the United States and may be as imperfectly understood at the moment as those that physicists have encountered in the vicinity of Saturn. Instead, I gather that because of such episodes, along with their counterparts in time (the historical problem), it is recommended that we conclude, in dismay, that powerful generalizations about human beings and their social surround are out of reach.

The physical scientist in contrast seems to lick his chops at the new round of detective work, and hence the contributions to systematic knowledge, that the absurd findings will enable. This is very much as he licks his chops at the theoretical possibility that out through the black holes of this universe lie other universes where at least some of what we see today as universal laws will not in fact hold. What fun it would be to decode a structure of totally new regularities!

A step closer to home, biology has its other-world problems as well. This should not surprise us; after all, the study of biology is every bit as "firmly wedded to historical circumstance" as is geology or planetary science, and in fact its time frame is considerably less majestic. My biology example is not the most incisive I might choose, but I take it because it is intriguing in itself and because it has had some amusing policy implications in the recent past. It turns out that a general rule across mammalian species is that while infants not only thrive on maternal milk but are crucially dependent on it, the adults do not drink milk at all. In fact, it can be shown that they can't digest it, and in the past few years it has been learned why. There is a highly specific enzyme in the gut of infant mammals that permits milk to be digested, and this enzyme tends to disappear as the animal matures. Now this is the general picture for mammals. However, two-and-one-sixth species are exceptions to this rule. One exception is a species of seal. The odd sixth of a species is—you guessed it—human beings. Those messy human data again.

What is the odd sixth of the adult human species whose internal biology includes the enzyme, as opposed to the other five sixths whose internal biology does not? Well, it isn't racial, as commonly construed. It cross-cuts racial lines in significant degree. The answer to this biological riddle is one that is "firmly wedded to historical and geographical circumstance." In particular, the sixth of the human race housing the enzyme necessary for milk digestion is either located at, or is stock from, two primary geographic centers on the earth's surface that, while racially distinct, happen to have been for millennia centers of cattle raising. One of these areas is in central Africa; the other is, of course, northern Europe, which, by migration, means many of us here.

The amusing policy implication refers to the point in the 1950s when a French premier, horrified at the level of alcoholism in the French population, launched a major governmental campaign to get the French to switch from wine and brandy to milk. All that this left out was the fact that, in general, the French lack the enzyme to be able to digest milk as adults.

Within the purposes of much medical and biological research, the human anatomy is largely homogenous over the universe of specimens. What this means, among other things, is that sampling strategies for the selection of subjects is of limited necessity. However, the degree of homogeneity must ever be seen as relative to the purposes of inquiry and in some areas, such as paleobiology, is a source of hot dispute even at the moment. Where other medical and biological purposes are concerned, such as idiosyncratic biochemistries reacting in unpredictible ways to the introduction of various drugs, heterogeneity is nearly the rule. And as recourse to epidemiological procedures suggests, the study of variation in human biology in time and space can often be serendipitously rewarding.

In short, then, the "harder" sciences are not without their otherworld problems. What is different, perhaps, is that they respond to these problems more as challenges or opportunities than as defeats. Social scientists, it seems to me, should pay heed.

Woven through all of my remarks, but not yet made explicit, is the radical possibility that our received stereotypes about what get called "the universal laws of true science," as opposed to all other classes of empirical assertions, may be a distinction that is artificial and simplistic. By "universal laws" I mean what is usually meant: precise assertions that, within ridiculously few specified conditions, none of which is a sheer limitation in time or space (such as the next universe over), we are convinced will hold. A different view might accept the time and space relativity of all such assertions and accept the fact that there is an exceedingly long gradient of time and space frames that are conditions on generalizations of all types. Naturally, along such a gradient, the longer and broader the better. But there is a gradient; it is not an absolute dichotomy.[3]

If we lack such a handy dichotomy, how do we know what to certify as a true science? Well, I am not much interested in those either-or definitions. My own view is that a science devotes itself to the systematic decoding of observed regularities and the reduction of the regularities to more parsimonious and general principles that account for wide ranges of phenotypic detail. As long as one is engaged in such activity, one is doing science, although there is an implicit pact that if one is doing science, then one is relentlessly attempting to move knowledge up that inclined gradient toward greater generality in time and space.

In this light, then, let us return for another look at an equation like "Behavior is a function of person and situation." I have never known whether to laugh or cry at that. I understand that Mark

Twain, asked to comment on the music of Richard Wagner, observed that "Wagner's music is really better than it sounds." If we drop the snide edge, that is roughly how I feel about the equation. It is almost vacuous, but it is really better than it sounds. I find myself turning to it in my mind far more often than I would have expected on first hearing.

I shall not linger for very long on the person term in that equation, save to raise a question or two about the likely scope in time and space of generalizations hinged in persons. On the one hand, one can imagine very high-order generalizations about behavioral dispositions brought by persons to situations that might be expected to hold over very large spans of time and space and that would not be so vacuous as to be unsatisfying. On the other hand, it is obvious that the configuration we think of as the person—the hard wiring, the biochemistry, the physical, mental, and emotional capacities and their limits—is a configuration "firmly wedded to historical circumstance." The configuration is a product of evolution, and to speak of "persons" at all—"persons as we know them," we imply—suggests its own intrinsic restrictions in time and space with regard to any relevant attempts at generalization.

I do not say this to be discouraging, nor am I discouraged about it. The time frame for generalization even within these limits remains awesome, and a great deal can be learned about the person term that is systematic, reasonably parsimonious, and tremendously useful in understanding the social world about us, without our needing to apologize for the fact that the information may be less than universal or eternal truth, or without our feeling reduced to mere description of contemporary affairs. At the same time, it is worth keeping a reasonable eye on the likely boundaries of generalization, writ small as well as large. We may well be wary, for example, of generalization by investigator fiat, which is one of the difficulties when our results do not travel well. Perhaps we are becoming more appropriately humble, but time was when sampling strategies in dealing with persons could be dispensed with on grounds that the investigator was, after all, dealing with generic properties of human beings, such that if you have studied one person, by preconception and fiat, you must have studied them all. Granted, there are manifest differences in the generality of assertions and processes. We can often see where the path tilts upward—we know a priori that some phenomena are likely to be more general than others. But ultimately the proof of the pudding is empirical, and it does not pay to be glib about the uniformity of the species with respect to one or another property or process without subjecting the guess to reasonable test.

It is when we turn to the other term in the equation, to situations, that history and historicity in the shorter-term senses of the word threaten to come pouring in on us, undermining generalization. Social psychologists have not, in general, done very well by the situation term, although it is obvious that behavior is inevitably imbedded in a situation; and there has been a respectable amount of ferment in recent years over the possibility that our conclusions are less robust than they might be because we fail to take situations sufficiently into account, and in particular, the interaction terms associated with persons and situations. It is easy to suspect that when results of some vintage and pedigree in one culture fail to travel well, to replicate routinely in other worlds, the difficulty most often lies in an inadequate understanding of the situation term.

It is of course not easy to deal with situations in a systematic way, and the reasons are legion. Situations are vastly too complex, involving dimensions without end. They display great varieties of "texture," as I have been using the word. Obviously you do not get far trying to describe them in toto, holistically, in special cases that confront you. You must abstract a limited set of properties from them—and the more limited, such as one, two, or three, the better. But how do you know you are singling out the right one? This is of course crucial in experimental settings, where there is designed to be controlled variation in a particular dimension—or perhaps two or three—abstracted from a complex situation otherwise supposedly held constant. Although randomization is a line of defense against being misled by further hidden situational variation, difficulties of this sort appear to harass our work mightily, even when we have not yet stepped across cultures.

Over the years, various strategies have been suggested and occasionally used for handling the situation term in the equation. What all have in common, and necessarily so, is a major degree of abstraction from the complexity of actual situations. However, they proceed in different ways, and some of these ways seem to me to be less fruitful than others. I cannot, for example, get excited by the erection of long lists of hierarchial structures of highly abstract situation "properties" said by the author to be generically crucial for social psychologists. To my mind what needs to be abstracted from any given situation is often highly specific to the intellectual problem at hand, and such general-purpose lists are of little use. Or again, sometimes situations are precoded less in terms of objective situation characteristics than in terms of what the situations are supposed to mean to the observer, ranging from "highly stressful" over to "not stressful at all." The problems here are obvious. Some subjects will not experience the situation as expected, especially if they are human beings and not rats. We often can leave this as unexplained variation in the normal way, although it occurs to me once again that this general strategy may be particularly vulnerable to concealed deformations of meaning in traveling from one cultural world to the next.

A rather different strategy is close to bread-and-butter in the more macroscopic areas in which I work, where experiment is for the most part out of reach. This is to work backward inductively from observed differences on some dependent variable of interest to a sense of the underlying generating processes, which often come to direct attention specifically to some differential features of situations as repetitively encountered by the persons involved. A prototypic example familiar to social psychologists might be the work of Robert Zajonc with birth order, where initial differences in measured intelligence by sibling situation seemed robust enough across cultures to be worth explaining. The apparent underlying generating mechanisms go right to situations repetitively experienced, although it is a summation or integration over what for each actor must be many thousands of "situations" over the course of childhood, interacting with parents or other adults, or with siblings younger or older, in ways that produced systematic variation in the richness of the intellectual environment.

But it is not necessary to leave the surmises presumptive. We can, as in classic epidemiological procedure, work our way through increasingly fine-grained investigation until closure can be reached by demonstration, not presumption. The main point is that there are systematic ways to proceed on such riddles involving situations that are the heart of what inquiry is about. It is my contention that when findings that appear robust in one world fail to replicate in some other world, it should be the beginning of a new round of inquiry, not a point of abandonment, much less taken as proof that social science can't generalize. My own conviction has grown over the years that, with some frequency, the key that unlocks the riddle lies very close to the surface, if one is willing to pay even brief attention to peculiarities of the "situation" more broadly construed. Much of my own cross-cultural work has been off in domains of political behavior, and I have seen these keys near the surface quite often.

Here is an example. One phenomenon in the operation of electoral systems is partisanship or party identification. We thought we knew a good deal about the dynamics of party identifications as individual processes over time, including their growth, reinforcement, intergenerational transmission, and the like, although almost all of this lore was based on data from the United States. These dynamic patterns would usually be plausibly reproduced abroad, although as data came in from more countries, a number of non-replications began to appear.

Thus in larger work that Roy Pierce and I have been doing in France (Converse & Pierce 1985), several of these crucial dynamic patterns seemed almost undiscernible. Now where political parties are concerned, there are patent differences in the electoral situation confronting the French voter and that confronting the American voter that are pretty obvious. One is the multiplicity of political parties there and, if one pays a stitch of attention to history, their noteworthy instability over time. It is easily shown that the dynamics of these identifications map much more nicely to the American ones where sympathizers of the most enduring parties are concerned. Furthermore, it turns out that there are some microregions in France that do operate effectively as two-party systems. These are areas long staked out as battlegrounds between two major national parties, where other parties do not bother to present themselves, and where the two parties involved have existed as objects of orientation over a long period of time.

When we set the other voters aside to concentrate on those voters operating American style, lo and behold, there were clear signs of the American dynamics. So the first-glance obscurity of the French case was not some inexplicable product of oddities in French political temperament or political culture, proving again that cross-national generalization is impossible, but instead something simply traceable to manifest differences in the structure of the situation in which the modal Frenchman and the modal American operate. The formation of this assessment acts in turn to enrich our understanding of the way in which situations impinge upon our psychological terms, shaping their parameters.

As another example, sticking to the same circle of ideas about processes underlying partisanship, one of the strongest and most familiar demographic correlates of such identifications is age, where the relationship is normally positive and is fairly substantial as these matters go. This has to be seen, however, as nothing but a superficial relationship, because age in itself is rarely the variable of theoretical interest, but only a crude indicator or tracer for general underlying time-dependent processes. We thought that we had a grasp on the terms of that underlying process as a simple learning pattern. But if you pursue its internal logic at all far, you arrive at the realization that under certain specifiable historic conditions, namely, voting systems of a certain early intermediate vintage, you should find the superficial relationship of partisanship with age actively reversed in its sign. Up until recently, I had never seen such a reversed relationship in real life, and as far as I know, nobody else ever had either.

However, two years or so ago, I was asked to Venezuela to do some consulting in a setting where I knew my hosts had replicated our measurements in a national election. I knew what continent Venezuela was on, but not much else. In order not to embarrass myself locally, I took on a plane with me one of those small eighth-grade primers covering the rudiments of Venezuelan geography, history, and politics. A half hour into my reading, I said to myself, "Aha—at last I am going to see one of these reversed relationships I have been expecting." My hosts could not have been less interested in that particular cross-tabulation, although they inundated me with every other conceivable piece of computer output. But I kept asking for that one table, and finally they went out and ran it for me. When they brought it back, there was the reversed relationship—not arguably reversed, so that you had to pucker and squint to imagine it was there, but unquestionably and admirably reversed, just as it should have been, although nobody had ever seen a table like that before.[4]

This was an instance, of course, where in advance we had the underlying handle, the more general principle that would help us not only to confirm the superficial rule, but to predict the exceptions as well. Nonetheless, I have often reflected that had we not had the handle in advance, how unfortunate it would have been to have taken the reversed relationship as yet another proof that generalization in social science is impossible.

I have no desire to leave you with the sense that I am claiming any special talent in decoding cross-national oddities in social science results. There are many "non-fits" that I have seen in cross-national data that have left me sorely puzzled, including even an occasional batch of data on partisanship that I continue to find perplexing. Indeed, my record is no better than the kind of trial and error that all of us slog through most of the time that goes by the name "inquiry." But I see enough glints cross-nationally of superficial oddity undergirded by higher-order regularity that I am troubled by any tendency to fluster when such oddities appear. Nor do I wish to give you, with these simple examples, a sense that such regularities always lie near the surface. Obviously, they often will not. Many lie deeply matted in cultural peculiarities that, at the moment, we know not of.

In other words, the way will be long—remember my time frames for social science progress. I didn't promise you a rose garden. We do not yet have in our backyard anything like the neat and growing lore that physicists can work from in decoding the absurd behavior of Saturn's rings. Our counterpart for that lore is itself emerging, but its progress is slow and halting. We don't even have much data of a systematic, theoretically informed sort across wide expanses of time and space. What we have is a little patch about this here, and a little patch about that there. And since such information is costly to elicit, it will be very slow a-building.

As all this begins to fill in, not only will we become more adept at solving exotic oddities rapidly, but levels of generalization will inch upward as well. I suspect that we shall discover surprising limits and conditional restrictions that must be placed on phenomena we were convinced a priori were utterly generic, but also, and most intriguingly I should say, we shall discover patterns of strong regularity for which we are theoretically quite unprepared, yet which reproduce themselves in surprising degree from world to world and hence urgently demand explanation. Nobody looks much in this direction these days, but ultimately looking there may be as fruitful in reorienting our understanding of human behaviors as the current testing of some of our primitive preconceptions.

It is true that social psychology does reach out in all social science directions, particularly as we are willing to come to serious grips with the "situation" term. It must cope with social structure, with political and economic institutions, with cultural values, and with historical sequencing. Its very scope makes progress seem slow. But if we resist turning impatience to despair, it can be a broadly rewarding effort.

Notes

1. This paper was originally presented in very similar form as the ninth annual Katz-Newcomb Lecture, April 1981, at the University of Michigan. I am indebted to Professor Donald Levine, coparticipant in this conference, for the observation that much of my perspective here on the rela-

tionship between the social and natural sciences does little but recapitulate the theses of Auguste Comte, who first tried to discuss these relationships in a systematic way more than a century ago. Since my spiritual introduction to the possibility of a true social science thirty-five years ago was largely through a reading of Comte, I am sure that the similarities are not accidental, despite a massive intervening amnesia about the details of Comte's work

2. Papers of this symposium have now been published, including Cronbach's paper entitled "Prudent Aspirations for Social Inquiry" (Kruskal 1982, 61–81). There is some natural overlap between a letter of comment I wrote at the time and the beginning of this lecture.

3. Gergen (1973) is commendably sensitive, where social psychology is concerned, to this issue and calls for more systematic exploration of variations in such historical "durability." I applaud and am merely pointing out that durability is obviously limited in some of natural science and, some would say, is never infinite.

4. The data were proprietary, and I did not try to publish the table involved. However, more recently and independent of my own interest in the matter, I have learned that Torres (1983), working with Venezuelan electoral data, has found it necessary to import the same body of theory I was using (cf. Converse 1969, for the main statement) in order to understand the patterns shown by partisanship recently in that country, especially across age cohorts. His primary data come from a Caracas sample, whereas the data I saw were from a national sample. There are minor differences in the details of the data, probably attributable to the absence of rural votes at the periphery, but the same theory seems required to understand the main lines of the findings.

References

Brickman, P. 1980. A social psychology of human concerns. In *The development of social psychology,* ed. R. Gilmour and S. Duck. London: Academic Press.

Converse, P. E. 1969. Of time and partisan stability. *Comparative Political Studies,* 2:139–71.

Converse, P. E., and Pierce, R. 1985. *Political representation in France.* Cambridge: Harvard University Press.

Gergen, K. J. 1973. Social psychology as history. *Journal of Personality and Social Psychology* 26:309–20.

Kruskal, W. H., ed. 1982. *The social sciences: Their nature and uses.* Chicago: University of Chicago Press.

Lewin, R. 1982. Biology is not postage stamp collecting. *Science* 216:718.

Newcomb, T. M. 1951. Social psychological theory: Integrating individual and social approaches. In *Social psychology at the crossroads*, ed. H. Rohrer and M. Sherif. New York: Harper.

Torres, A. 1983. Partisanship and floating electoral behavior in Venezuela. Ph.D. diss., Massachusetts Institute of Technology.

3 Specificity of Method and Knowledge in Social Science

Donald W. Fiske

Social science has accumulated many diverse bodies of knowledge.[1] Each specific parcel is separate, almost insulated from the others. Among the dozens of discrete discoveries in experimental psychology alone, Newell (1973) lists perceptual illusions and serial position effects in free recall. Social psychology has the Prisoner's Dilemma and the risky shift effect. At an intermediate level, psychology has problem solving and the classical maze learning in rats. Of still larger scope is the comprehensive array of human experience as interpreted by psychoanalysis. The scale varies with the questions being asked.

This diversity has two main bases: the selection of the behavior to be studied and the choice of a way or ways to observe and measure it. These are the two parts of method as the term will be used in this paper. The first part is the protocol, the sequence of behavior of one or more organisms on which the investigator focuses. People's experience can be subsumed under behavior because we can know about that experience only from some behavior, usually verbal behavior. Part of the protocol is the specification of the other physical or psychological events or conditions occurring at the same time as the behavior studied, such as the constancies in the setting for the behavior: What objects are present? What persons? What are the orientations of the various persons?

The measuring procedures are applied to some aspect of the protocol as a whole or to some designated units within it. Obviously the same protocol, such as a conversation, can be observed and measured in a large number of ways, depending upon the investigator's interests. Independent measuring procedures applied to the same set of protocols or even to the same units within a protocol typically generate more or less independent arrays of measurements. Although some convergence may appear, it is notorious that each array contains much variance specific to it. From the examples of Campbell and Fiske (1959) through the intercorrelation matrices published during the last quarter century, the prevailing specificity of methods is more striking than the modest degrees of convergence.

The argument of this paper is that knowledge in social science is fragmented, is composed of multiple discrete parcels, and that the separateness or specificity of those bodies of knowledge is a consequence, not only of different objects of inquiry, but also of method specificity. Each method is one basis for knowledge, one discriminable way of knowing—perhaps not in the technical epistemological sense that the phrase is used by philosophers, but in a pragmatic sense. Each method, each way of knowing, gives us a kind of knowledge. Each measuring procedure is applied to a protocol obtained under a particular set of conditions and provides information about some aspects or properties of that protocol. Each method sets for the observer a cognitive task that involves the processing of input from a protocol to produce data.

In most of social-behavioral science today, the knowledge in one parcel cannot be firmly related to that in other parcels for several reasons. First, the data and the findings obtained by one measuring procedure typically fail to be duplicated by those from another procedure, even when applied to the same protocol. Second, a single kind of protocol commonly yields data and findings that cannot be coordinated with those from another kind of protocol. Third, the conditions under which the protocol is obtained ordinarily affect the data and the findings.

The challenge to social-behavioral science is to minimize the degree of specificity in bodies of knowledge by reducing the contribution of method specificity. At best, the current bodies of knowledge can be linked to each other only tenuously. Gains are made by identifying significant new protocols involving basic behavioral processes, by recording the protocols, and by controlling the process of producing data so as to minimize the known sources of specificity in measurements.

Another factor associated with the disparateness of our bodies of knowledge is the absence of testable theories that encompass even a few of these parcels. For each parcel that has a considerable accumulation of established findings, some conceptual interpretations and perhaps even a minitheory or two are typically present. But no clear and firm linkages exist between the conceptual work in one body and that for other bodies. The lack of well-developed inclusive theories can be attributed in part to the specificity of our knowledge. Yet that specificity itself is in part due to the absence of adequate general theory. Theory can guide observation and the interpretation of empirical relationships at the same time that empirical work provides grist for the mill of the theorist. Each can contribute to or hold back the other.

Related to this condition is our poor conceptual understanding of our methods of observing and measuring. In a mature science, each measuring procedure has a rationale based on general substantive theory. Each application of such a procedure is an instance of the phenomena explained by a part of that substantive theory. For example, each of the many ways of measuring temperature is based on a known physical principle. In the absence of consensually accepted theory in social-behavioral science, we choose measuring procedures that seem to work. Our selection is pragmatic, if not intuitive. Since our measuring procedures themselves involve social-behavioral processes, a better understanding of those processes could be a step toward a more adequate substantive theory. Similarly, any progress toward better theory should contribute to improved theoretical understanding of our measuring procedures (see Fiske, in press).

In distinct protocols, different things are examined, so separate bodies of knowledge are obtained. But when are two protocols distinct and when are they of the same kind? A major difficulty in social science research lies in the categorization of protocols into homogeneous sets. (If only social science could identify large aggregates of homogeneous events or objects, like the particles in a gas, for which precise laws hold!) The investigator decides which protocols are appropriate for the problem being studied. Other scientists must find that selection satisfactory, and they must be able to identify other protocols that can be considered interchangeable so that they can conduct research on the same problem and perhaps even attempt to replicate the investigator's study. For this categorization of protocols, the investigator must provide criteria that are independent of the variables being measured. Such criteria describing the conditions are themselves measurements on at least qualitative (present or absent) scales. Even in experimental psychology, apparently similar protocols may yield different findings when the breed of rat (see Jones & Fennell 1965 on Tolman's rats compared to those of the Hull-Spence group) or the kind of wood used for animal bedding (Vesell 1967) differs.

What protocols can be labeled as the products of a person with a mental illness? Will dream reports do? Are interview transcripts sufficient? What are the protocols by which one identifies an expert system (as discussed by Cicourel in this volume, chap. 10) or a potentiality shared by persons in varying degrees (see Secord's essay, chap. 8)? Perhaps the clearest examples of the problem of categorization appear in the identification of relevant segments or units within a protocol. For instance, insofar as the content of each instance of thought disorder is unique, how are such events to be identified in a person's verbal behavior?

Consider research in the area of psychotherapy. It includes several bodies of knowledge, with one cluster derived from the protocols of treatment sessions and another from experiences outside those sessions. The several protocols from treatment include videotapes or other recordings and also the mental records, the memories of the sessions retained by the therapist and those retained by the patient. From each separate protocol, a distinct set of data is produced by each of the various procedures used. For example, the videotapes of single sessions have been judged as a whole, coded for one kind of content or another, and analyzed in terms of the periods of silence.

LEVEL AND SCALE

On the way to selecting protocols, the investigator chooses for study some events or objects possessing the properties or attributes that are to be examined. Over a range of research programs, such properties vary in level of abstraction. Consider alienation. It can be applied to a momentary feeling or the expression of such a feeling, to the state of a person lasting hours or days, to a person as a more or less enduring characteristic, to a group of persons, or to a culture or nation. As Levine (1968) warns, the latter applications are problematic because the persons within the group or culture do not have equal degrees of alienation and do not manifest it in exactly the same way. In fact, all levels above the bottom one are abstractions, and the attribute does not apply homogeneously throughout any available or potential protocol. For instance, a person's experience of alienation is not continuous and unremitting, and such experiences at different times do not involve a constant degree of alienation.

Alongside this dimension of abstraction is a range of sizes of objects measured. In the example above, the size varies from the person to the group to the culture. Within psychology, still smaller objects are studied: neural pathways, organs, and even cells. But more basic is the size or duration of the temporal event or events providing the material for the measuring process. Behavior is behaving; it changes over time. Although the fundamental unit of measurement is the assigning of a property to an action or change, most measurement in social-behavioral science assigns a property to a set of actions viewed as having something in common: talking rapidly refers to the rate at which one element in speaking succeeds another; being seen as friendly may involve the rates or intensities of several qualitatively different acts, including smiling, looking at other people, and speaking certain words. In the alienation example, the property "alienated" could be applied to a single adjective in a person's speech, but more commonly, it is applied to several manifestations over a shorter or longer period of time. Applications to groups of cultures are even more complex; they may in some way aggregate the attributions made to individual members or the inferences made to several behaviors carried out by different persons, as in suicides.

Associated with level of abstraction and with size of that which is measured is the breadth of the conceptual property assigned in measuring. Suicide is more concrete than being alienated. Rate of talking or moving is more specific than being tense or aroused. A Skinnerian bar-press is narrower than "seeks food." When the property or attribute does not describe a particular action but subsumes many diverse patterns of behavior, there is an apparent gain in conceptual simplicity at the cost of precision. Most common trait and attitude labels refer to heterogeneous manifestations.

The various groups of social-behavioral scientists work with properties at varying levels of abstraction and breadth, applying the properties to units of diverse sizes and extents. Cross-classifications on these scales yield multiple cells, within each of which a body of research can develop. At this time, the conceptual linkages between the resulting parcels of knowledge, even those for adjacent cells, are limited and tenuous.

THE DATA-PRODUCING PROCESS

Each set of protocols is typically the basis for a single body of knowledge. In the research producing that knowledge, a single procedure is often used to measure a basic dependent variable, and a standard procedure is used to assess each major independent variable. As noted earlier, each datum generated by a given procedure is the product of a behavioral process about which we have little firm knowledge. In contrast to the extended duration of behavioral protocols or even segments of protocols to which properties are attributed, the process of assigning a measurement is fairly rapid. Recognizing an instance of a designated act may take less than a second. Choosing an answer to a questionnaire item can take only a couple of seconds. Judging the degree to which a trait label applies to a person takes only a little longer. Minutes, hours, or years of experience with the person judged are reduced to a few images or impressions in the cognitive activity resulting in the datum. Although our knowledge of data-producing processes is very limited, we know enough to realize that they are quite complex. For evidence on the process of manifesting mental ability, as in producing responses to items in an intelligence test, see the work of Sternberg (e.g., 1983).

In social-behavioral measurement, the person producing the data is a crucial source of method specificity. The longer and more complex the process by which a datum is produced, the greater the likelihood that characteristics of the particular data producer will affect the process and the resulting datum. The larger the contribution from the individual observer, the lower the agreement between observers and the greater the specificity of each observer's data. In a sense, each observer can be seen as a specific measuring procedure.

The longer, more complex observer processes involve interpretive or inferential judgments, judgments about the extent of variables with verbal labels and definitions. In addition, the measuring task is presented to the observer in verbal terms. This reliance on words is a major factor in observer disagreement. In addition, the protocols are often in words; for example, they may be verbal reports or conversations. Investigators tend to assume that the meanings of verbal materials are sufficiently shared so that the investigator's meanings can be taken as those of the observer and even those of the subject to a large extent. Unfortunately, studies of words and their meanings show that not only connotations but also denotations vary among persons using words or perceiving them (see Fiske 1978, chap. 2; and Fiske 1981 for additional discussions of words and language imprecision).

Considerable research has been done on the meanings of words when used as stimuli—as in the questions asked in survey research or in written questionnaires. Frequently, the words used in phrasing a question affect the distribution of responses (Sudman & Bradburn 1982; Turner & Krauss 1978). The problem of course involves, not only the specific word (how often is "often"?), but also the interpretation of the word in a given context (Pepper 1981; Pepper & Prytulak 1974).

Words make a major contribution to procedure specificity, and that specificity severely handicaps research in many areas of social science. The multiple bodies of knowledge in the social and behavioral sciences can be roughly ordered in terms of dependence upon words. The less the data on a topic depend upon words, the more systematic and cumulative have been the findings. Within psychology, there is the range from physiological psychology through psychophysics, cognition, and social psychology to personality. Across traditional disciplines, there is the polar contrast between econometrics and ethnography. Within the field of mental health, the differentiation is not as marked. While the verbal pole is epitomized by psychoanalysis, the other extreme—as represented for example by biological psychiatry—is still handicapped by interpretations of words used in diagnostic classifications.

The dependence on words has another consequence. It provides an opportunity for the individuality, if not idiosyncrasy, of investigators' personal orientations or world views to affect their research activities—their interpretations and construals of data, their formulations of findings and conclusions. With considerable individuality in these facets of each investigator's work, any consensus among investigators on generalizations must be somewhat loose. To be acceptable to most of the investigators associated with a particular body of knowledge, a generalization has to be stated in fairly broad terms.

Each investigator can be viewed as a measuring procedure, as an instrument for obtaining knowledge. From this viewpoint, we can consider how the individuality of the investigator can contribute specificity. On the basis of accumulated experience, each investigator has acquired personal connotations for both everyday and technical words. In addition, each has a subjective phenomenal domain that he or she is trying to understand and a distinguishable way of conceptualizing it. Finally, investigators in social science also vary widely in their norms and their styles of work. Some are willing to use and trust data derived from complex cognitive interpretations and inferences of observers; others want behavioral records on which observers agree closely. Some will settle for weak and unstable relationships between variables; others accept only strong effects. Investigators working on a given substantive problem typically converge on a preferred method and agree fairly well on their norms for acceptable data and findings. Thus bodies of knowledge are differentiated by the style of those who have contributed to them.

Another factor contributing to procedure specificity is the use of delayed reports as raw data. When a lengthy protocol is the basis of an interpretive judgment, the final part of the data-producing process occurs after the experiencing of the protocol and must depend upon images and impressions retained in the observer's memory. Clear instances are self-reports and ratings by peers who have known the subject over months or years. But even the retrieval of very recent experiences must be used with great care, as Ericsson and Simon (1980) point out. Much more complex is the ethnographer's use of informants, a practice that adds the informant's retrieving and distilling of impressions about standard practices and beliefs to the ethnographer's selective recording of the informant's words.

So we have specificity in measurement procedures insofar as they vary with the type of protocol and with separate aspects of each type, as in judging traits from an interview in contrast to counting smiles during a conversation. For coping with specificity between procedures, our best strategy is to try to understand how the several types of protocols and the aspects of protocols assessed by discrete procedures contribute to the relative independence of the arrays of data. In addition, we have specificity within the products of a procedure, specificity associated with each application of it. This can stem from the observer's individualistic cognitive processing of the protocol, including the interpretations given the words in the protocol and the words in the measuring task. For the tasks involved in measuring procedures commonly used today, we have done about as much as we can to reduce observer specificity.

Can Bodies of Knowledge Be Tied Together?

Incontrovertible is the empirical fact that findings are largely specific to the method or methods used. The discreteness of the data from each procedure has led to the production of separate bodies of knowledge. These bodies will remain separate. Just as in one day's newspaper, the sports pages, the neighborhood news section, and the movie reviews report quite unrelated events, so do the various methods in social science. But even when the same event is the object to which several methods are applied, the resulting sets of data can be expected to have little or no covariation. When a sunset is observed by an artist, a sailor, and an air pollution specialist, the three observations are incommensurate. The artist perceives the whole picture, the sailor looks for diagnostic meteorological signs, and the pollution specialist looks for evidence of particulate matter.

The optimist can sustain faith by noting Kuhn's view of the history of science: "The early developmental stages of most sciences have been characterized by continual competition between a number of distinct views of nature. . . . What differentiated these various schools was . . . what we . . . call their incommensurable ways of seeing the world and of practicing science in it. . . . In the early stages of the development of any science different men confronting the same range of phenomena, but not usually the same particular phenomena, describe and interpret them in different ways" (1970, 4, 17). The pessimist doubts that the history of natural science will be repeated by social science, believing it more likely that diverse bodies of knowledge will always exist in social science because they involve different things known differently.

Findings from data aimed at concepts at one level of abstracting will ordinarily be difficult to link firmly with results pertaining to a different level. When two bodies of knowledge apply to separate objects of inquiry, such as individuals and groups, it is very difficult to integrate their substantive contents. Even when the same protocols are being studied, the units to which properties are ascribed strongly affect the nature of the findings. Compare judgments of thirty-minute videotapes of interactions with codings of occurrences of specific behaviors within each record, as in the work of Shweder and D'Andrade (1979, 1980). As another example, speech examined as sound patterns yields knowledge distinct from speech studied as content with meaning. Note that the protocol for speech as sound patterns is analyzed as a record of moment-to-moment changes while content is interpreted in terms of units with longer durations. Similarly, interaction research can be classified by the types of methods used. Observers can be employed to judge an interaction as a whole, making interpretations leading to inferences about attributes of participants (as in research on the leaderless group discussion). Alternatively, they can code each remark into categories such as those in the Interaction Process Analysis of Bales (1950). Within the growing body of research on the nonverbal side of interactions, some researchers focus on understanding particular kinds of actions, such as greeting behavior (Kendon & Ferber 1973). Others code a set of actions related to the structure of the conversation, as in examining the exchange of speaking turns (Duncan & Fiske 1977, chap. 11). Still another set of investigators work with purely physical methods (e.g., Jaffe & Feldstein

1970; Feldstein & Welkowitz 1978). Thus we have multiple bodies of knowledge about face-to-face interactions, bodies that can be distinguished by the aspect studied and, within aspect, by the particular procedure or type of procedure employed.

In some research areas, bodies of knowledge can be compared and contrasted fairly objectively, rather than by judgmental summaries and evaluations. The techniques of meta-analysis permit the averaging of sets of investigations using the same or similar methods. For example, in *The Benefits of Psychotherapy* (1980), Smith, Glass, and Miller provide summary statistics not only for kinds of treatments but also for types of methods for measuring the effects: more reactive procedures show larger mean effects, presumably as a result of positive biases in therapists and patients.

Thus meta-analysis enables us to pull together the knowledge that has been obtained by each particular method of obtaining data and then to make comparisons among them as a way to decide on next steps in research in the area. By portraying the variation around each average, it enables the investigator to identify subsets of research studies and to look for previously unrecognized sources of effects. At best, meta-analysis is a fairly objective way of assessing the state of knowledge on a given topic. At worst, people note only the summarizing mean-effect size and jump to broad inferential conclusions that ignore the extensive variation among effects and the diverse conditions generating them.

How Will Knowledge in Social Science Advance?

The best prediction of a person's behavior has been found to be that the person will do what he or she did last time in the same situation. Similarly, the best prediction of what will happen in social science is one based on what has happened. Hence it is most probable that social science will continue to develop the many discrete bodies of knowledge now extant and will initiate additional parcels, each identified with a kind of protocol and with a method or set of methods for producing data.

Some bodies of knowledge go out of fashion and are set aside, residing on library shelves, with no further additions to them. Among these are ones where the findings have proved specific to the method or to a special experimental setting and no fruitful extensions have been established (e.g., maze learning in rats). Other bodies of knowledge persist, with slow accretions. Persistence characterizes many bodies of knowledge that are deemed pertinent to societal problems, to issues with which society contends, issues that social scientists want to settle. Examples of societal problems are delinquency, alcoholism, and personal maladjustment (see also Fiske 1978, especially chaps. 9, 10). Bodies of knowledge also persist because they involve verbal abstractions, for example, "aggression" and "culture," that are derived from the way people have construed their everyday experience. Like everyone else, social scientists want to understand their everyday experience and their conceptualizations of it. Most of the topics studied by social scientists come from such experience. The topics are labeled by terms from the lay language or by terms one small step removed from common speech, for example, "socioeconomic class," "stages of development."

Such bodies of knowledge persist and continue to expand in spite of only minimal signs of progress, without showing any major quantal steps or critical transformations. What changes in social science can be taken as scientific revolutions? One reason why social science hangs on to its findings, concepts, and loose generalizations is that it has not developed a consensus on bases for rejecting any of them. To be sure, some findings are viewed skeptically because the studies generating them have apparent artifacts and because potential threats to the validity of the findings have not been eliminated in the plan for the research (Cook & Campbell 1979). But many findings are accepted because they are consistent with the approximate knowledge that social scientists and lay people have acquired from everyday experience.

Similarly, concepts persist, especially those that we find we can apply to our everyday experience. Rarely are concepts rejected, and rarely are generalizations, propositions, and theoretical statements overturned in social science. Most conceptual statements in social science persist because they are formulated in such a way that they cannot be disproved (cf. Popper 1959). Contrary empirical evidence can be ignored as not relevant or as indicating merely that the proposition does not apply under some contrived set of circumstances. Part of the problem stems from the failure of social theorists to specify the boundary conditions, the limits within which their proposition is asserted to be held.

One major strength of the multitrait-multimethod model of analysis (Campbell & Fiske 1959) is that it provides bases for rejecting a concept. If several measures of one concept do not covary highly, the utility of the concept is thrown into question. That model also throws light on method specificity. Although the problem of isolating method factors by quantitative means is still not well resolved, the model does provide evidence for intrusive effects of methods. If measurements from two methods do not agree well, then one or both methods are introducing excessive specific effects or they are not measuring the same concept. Some assumption must be rejected.

SIGNIFICANT PROGRESS

More crucial for the advance of social science knowledge than the persistence of current bodies of knowledge and the occasional shelving of others is the creation of new bodies of knowledge. The most significant of these are parcels where the researchers have managed to avoid or overcome the obstacle of method specificity, and as a consequence, investigators can begin to develop linkages between the parcels. These new bodies have some of the interrelated characteristics examined below.

Discovering New Major Protocols

Some bodies of knowledge are simply more important than others because they have major implications for human functioning. For example, Kleitman and his colleagues opened up the study of sleep, and later the study of dreaming, by discovering that dreaming occurred during periods of rapid eye movements (Aserinsky & Kleitman 1953). Another major development was initiated by Sperry's Nobel Prize-winning demonstration of the separate functioning of the two hemispheres in the brain. Although highly atypical clinical cases provided the first clues that the two hemispheres could function independently, this finding led to demonstrations that they do so function in normal cases. The basic variable, the identification of the hemisphere processing the input, can be determined in several ways that seem free of effects from procedure specificity. It is notable that these two advances involved locating the object of study in space and time, thus enabling the protocols to be circumscribed and specified.

These two examples are neurophysiological; it is not as easy to find a clear instance of a major new protocol in the purely behavioral area. The clearest is the identification of instrumental conditioning, focusing on the consequents of an action rather than on the antecedents. The result has been an enormous body of research and knowledge, perhaps best viewed as several related bodies of knowledge. The work on variable-interval reinforcement has broad ramifications, and the research on behavior modifications has had major impact on the field of mental health. The discovery of such major protocols exemplifies the statement of Bhaskar that "perhaps the most significant type of event in the history of any science is that in which it refines—redefines—its object of inquiry" (1982, 276).

Identifying Basic Behavioral Processes

The analysis of sleep and the differentiation of hemispheric activity have been fruitful because the resulting research findings seem to hold quite generally, not just within the laboratory. Moreover, the problem of method specificity has been minimized in these fields. For hemispheric activity, similar convergent findings have been obtained for several separate procedures: EEG, relative blood flow, and perceptual asymmetries. These indices appear stable and seem to have minimal specificity problems. The data-production processes can be readily controlled. Thus, with major new protocols pertaining to basic natural processes, highly significant bodies of knowledge can be developed with minimal interference from specificity in the methods used to produce the data and findings. Especially in the early stages of such work, multiple approaches (Campbell 1969) and triangulation (Crano 1981) are fruitful strategies, with the strategy of "convergent operations" probably being more valuable later (Garner 1974; Garner, Hake & Eriksen 1956).

Basic behavioral processes can also be studied as they occur in naturalistic settings. Just look at behavior. This approach is often very difficult because it relies on the investigator's skill in determining when a basic process is occurring. Sometimes the investigator can set up fairly natural conditions and just let the behavior happen. For example, McClintock (1981) constructed a relatively naturalistic environment for rats and then recorded their mating behavior in the dark (using infrared illumination). She found that this behavior differed sharply from mating behavior in rats in small confining cages. Two other research programs of local colleagues have concentrated on naturally occurring behavior, one on casual conversations (Duncan & Fiske 1977) and one on experience as sampled by randomized beeper signals (Larson & Csikszentmihalyi 1983).

In a basic behavioral process, the task of adaptation is carried out. Such functioning can be studied without the difficulty of ascribing meaning to the information being processed. When the task is clear, the type of information and the kind of output or response are determined. What is consistent and replicable is the way the information is processed, regardless of its particular content in any given instance.

Fixing the Object of Inquiry

Progress in science is associated with pinning down exactly what we are trying to understand. One obvious step toward such delimitation is the recording of protocols. In this way, both the experimenter in the laboratory and the investigator studying naturalistic behavior can obtain more dependable data. Also, a permanent record can be analyzed and subdivided into small temporal units. The coding process can be examined and repeated to check on accuracy. Even more important, as new variables are developed, as new ways of conceptualizing the protocol are created, they can be applied to the permanent record and the resulting data compared to that from the former methods.

When a recorded protocol is used to generate data, the investigator can examine the data-producing process more carefully. There is no time pressure, as there is in the observing of on-going behavior. The process can be repeated with variations to determine the effects of components in the method. In addition, when a protocol is recorded, the investigator can usually specify fairly precisely the conditions under which it was obtained—the time, place, participants, and circumstances. He or she can then circumscribe the class of systems to which the empirical findings and conclusions can be applied with confidence (cf. Cronbach 1982, 65, and chap. 4 in this volume). The use of recorded protocols enables the investigator to assess more exactly the degree of homogeneity in a given set of protocols, an important concern discussed earlier. In his Nobel Laureate address, Wigner perceptively observes:

> It is often said that the objective of physics is the explanation of nature, or at least of inanimate nature. . . . It is clear that . . . physics does not endeavor to explain nature. In fact, the great success of physics is due to a restriction of its objectives: it only endeavors to explain the regularities in the behavior of objects. This renunciation of the broader aim, and the specification of the domain for which an explanation can be sought, now appears to us an obvious necessity. In fact, the specification of the explainable may have been the greatest discovery of physics so far. (1964, 995)

Social scientists have often had too high a level of aspiration. They have all too frequently set out to understand broad, vague things—intelligence, delinquency, and culture—as entities, rather than seeing them as topics or areas within which to explore. The areas where progress is being made are those where the protocols have been circumscribed and where "regularities in the behavior of objects" have been identified.

Regularity is an attribution made after demonstrating dependability. Dependability, another broad term, has three aspects. First there is the replicabiliy of observations, the extent to which independent observations of the same protocol agree. Second, there is representativeness, the extent to which the findings obtained in a research study agree with those for the populations of people, stimuli, and conditions to which the investigator wants to generalize. Finally, there is the reproducibility of conclusions, of evidence for or against conceptual propositions when the same fundamental proposition is empirically examined by work with different types of pertinent protocols. A high degree of reproducibility requires adequate representativeness, which in turn has to be based on sufficient replicability. Dependability by itself is a necessary but not a sufficient requirement for adequacy of protocols and of data. Some method effects can be highly regular. The first step in science, however, seems to be the identification of "regularities in the behavior of objects," as a base from which to compare systematic differences in sets of such regularities observed under differing conditions.

Regularity and dependability appear to be maximized when small objects are studied and when the protocol unit being measured is short. Advances in social science have come from examining parts and stages of behavioral and experiential processes: the stages of sleep, the subdividing of intelligent performance (as in mental tests) into components, the successive moments in face-to-face interaction, the sampling of experience by randomly signaling subjects with "beepers." Locating each observation in space is clearly necessary, but even more critical is subdivision into smaller and smaller temporal units. Behavior is change of action over time, and such change occurs very rapidly. When a protocol can be objectively divided into small units, the production of data about each unit can usually avoid many kinds of procedure specificity associated with processes in the data producers. A fruitful strategy is to select the smallest temporal protocol unit that makes a difference to the actor or the perceiver, that is, that conveys a piece of information. In dyadic interaction, it can be a perceptible action. In verbal content, the whole word is the smallest unit with information content.

Such dissection is rejected by many social scientists, especially those who prefer to work at higher, more abstract levels of analysis. They choose to work on such topics as the mental health of an individual or the efficiency of an organization. But they typically find that they have to break each topic down into subtopics. For example, part of mental health is the adequacy of the mental patient's functioning in personal interactions, and that can be further subdivided into functioning with spouse, with supervisor, or still further, to functioning with such a significant other under a specified condition. To find the answer to a scientific question, the investigator often has to restructure the problem into a set of more restricted questions.

Basic behavioral processes are rapid, each phase being of short duration. Interactions between persons and interactions between an organism and its environment involve very rapid actions and reactions. But social science is also concerned with larger entities, even within the functioning of the individual. A person forms impressions based on extended experiences. Attributions about other people are stored in long-term memory. When talking about others or when asked to judge others for research or administrative purposes, one retrieves these attributive impressions. They are, however, rather elusive and can be known by the investigator only when reported. Because of their adaptive importance, the forming of impressions and the products of summarizing, inferential processes continue to present challenges to social science. Once again, the problem of determining the meaning of specific content arises.

Controlling the Process of Producing Data

Much procedure specificity comes from inadequate control over the process of producing data. When the protocol is recorded, it is much easier to control that process: there is no problem of catching the behavior as it happens. Similarly, the behavioral protocol can be analyzed into smaller segments, a datum being obtained for each segment, rather than resorting to summary judgments. More generally, control is achieved by processing the protocol as directly as possible. The more direct the process, the more dependable the data and the more replicable the data. How public and explicit is that process? If the observing procedure is simple and direct, different data producers generate highly congruent, even interchangeable, sets of data. Moreover, the difficulties associated with delayed reports can be avoided.

Simple and direct procedures for generating data from protocols have another major advantage: They make it easier to analyze the procedure, to discover components in the process that affect the data. They help the investigator to know what is going on instead of being restricted to speculation. In this way, the constant components of the procedure for producing data can be identified and their effects on the data can be evaluated. The best technique is the classic one: change a component and observe the change in the data, as in the contrast between mating in a cage and mating in a free environment (McClintock 1981). Again, by comparing responses to various types of mental test items, Sternberg (1983) has identified components of the responding process that are general across tests but can vary with the individual, as well as components more specific to test content.

In addition to the constant components of data-producing methods, there are components that vary with each application. As noted earlier, much specificity of procedure is associated with specific observers, especially in cases where the observing/judging process is complex. Each observer or rater goes about the task in an individualistic way. The use of simple, direct observations minimizes these individualistic contributions. Where complex processes are unavoidable, the data can be made more dependable and replicable by training the raters—by providing feedback and discussing disagreements. The unreliability of the single rater making complex judgments is often hidden by the reliability reported for the mean of several ratings. Thus, when the mean of seven raters is given as .70, an apparently adequate value, the reliability of the single rater is only .25, an inadequate level for scientific observations.

SPECIFICITY IN RESEARCH ON SOCIETAL PROBLEMS

The preceding pages have emphasized what is important to the scientific subculture: basic research, social science knowledge for its own sake. That subculture is part of a larger culture to which social scientists also belong. Important for it are societal problems, such as matters of human welfare. In the investigation of such problems, specificity of method and the consequent specificity of knowledge are also endemic. A prime example is the study of psychotherapeutic effectiveness. Measures of effects of such treatments are relatively specific to the perspective of the person producing the judgments used as data. The views of the patient, of the therapist, of significant others, and of disinterested judges yield quite distinct appraisals. Within each perspective, the particular instrument can also contribute its own specificity (for examples, see Cartwright, Kirtner & Fiske 1963; Garfield, Prager & Bergin 1971). Even when judges identify the patient's target problems and rate improvements on each, there is very limited agreement between ratings from different sources (Bond, Bloch & Yalom 1979).

New protocols getting at significant behavioral processes are being generated in the area of mental health. Paul and his associates have shown that it is possible to develop highly controlled procedures for the direct, descriptive observation of patient behavior, methods that eliminate the contribution of the specific observer (Paul & Lentz 1977; see also *Journal of Behavioral Assessment* 1, no. 3 [1979]). Their methods have been demonstrated to have practical value in decisions about patient management and in predictions about subsequent adaptation.

The problem of a taxonomy for patients in terms of amenability to each available form of treatment has not been adequately resolved. It is conceivable that the development of more objective methods for classification and diagnosis may contribute to the solution, for example, the identification of perceptual or cognitive dysfunctions such as in eye-tracking (Lipton et al. 1983). Even more fundamentally, the specific body of knowledge about smooth-pursuit-eye-movement dysfunctions, together with other evidence, may lead to an understanding of a central nervous system factor producing vulnerability to functional psychoses (Holzman 1982).

The need for replicable and dependable diagnostic classification has its counterpart in the problem of dealing systematically with therapist insights into connections between patients' symptoms and experiences and with regularities observed by therapists in treatment hours (among countless examples, see those cited by Meehl [1983]). Therapists have minibodies of knowledge that may yet be integrated into parcels of knowledge on which not only clinicians but also some of the rest of us may reach consensus. One promising strategy is the study of short-term connections by means of transcripts of therapeutic sessions, as in the search for the immediate antecedents of symptom-onset, for example, psychosomatic symptoms (Luborsky, Docherty & Penick 1973) or momentary forgetting (Luborsky & Mintz 1974; Luborsky, Sackeim & Christoph 1979). Equally intensive, fine-grained study of the therapeutic process is still an open challenge; related is the less difficult task of developing standardized ways for describing the treatment a given patient actually receives.

SUMMARY

Social science has accumulated many diverse and discrete bodies of knowledge. Each body of knowledge has typically been generated by a particular method or set of methods for obtaining measurements. Since each method produces data that are more or less specific, it is a discriminable way of knowing. The term "method" refers to the protocol studied (the actual behavioral events and their setting) and also to the processes involved in the production of data. In addition to specificity associated with the particular setting, the measuring procedures contribute specificity from such sources as the diverse interpretations of words, the use of retrieved memories, and the specific observer, especially when the data production requires complex cognitive processes. As a consequence of method specificity, the multiple bodies of knowledge remain distinct and unconnected.

Social science progresses by controlling the process of producing data so as to overcome the obstacle of method specificity. New major protocols are being discovered. Basic behavioral processes with very brief phases are being identified. The objects of inquiry can be fixed by recording the protocols and by locating regularities, keeping variables at a low level of abstraction and applying them to small objects and to short units of protocols. Although research on such societal problems as mental health has encountered the difficulties associated with method specificity, it too is progressing by using those strategies.

Social phenomena have always been perceived and known in diverse ways. To such bodies of knowledge, social scientists have added many others, each with a perspective and with one or more methods for observing. Occasionally, one method and the body of knowledge it has generated are put aside in favor of a method that seems more fruitful, that produces some knowledge that is inherently more satisfying. The diversity, however, is certain to remain. Within and without the domain of social science research, there will always be many ways of knowing social phenomena, some more systematic than others. Each body of knowledge has served some purpose and will continue to do so. The recent history of social science, however, suggests that growth in depth of understanding comes primarily from reducing the pervasive effects of method specificity.

Notes

1. The discussion at the conference of the earlier form of this paper was valuable. In this revision, I have made use of that material without

attempting to give credit to each participant for their contribution. To all who helped me, my thanks! In addition, I am indebted to Laurence Chalip, Lee Cronbach, Alan Fiske, Barbara Fiske, Eugene Gendlin, and Werner Wothke for very useful comments on a still earlier version.

References

Aserinsky, E., and Kleitman, N. 1953. Regularly occurring periods of eye motility, and concomitant phenomena, during sleep. *Science,* 118: 273–74.

Bales, R. F. 1950. *Interaction process analysis.* Cambridge, Mass: Addison-Wesley.

Bhaskar, R. 1982. Emergence, explanation, and emancipation. In *Explaining human behavior: Consciousness, human action, and structure,* ed. P. F. Secord. Beverly Hills: Sage.

Bond, G.; Bloch, S.; and Yalom, I. D. 1979. The evaluation of a "target problem" approach to outcome measurement. *Psychotherapy: Theory, Research, and Practice* 16: 48–54.

Campbell, D. T. 1969. Definitional versus multiple operationalism. *et al.* 2: 14–17.

Campbell, D. T., and Fiske, D. W. 1959. Convergent and discriminant validation by the multitrait-multimethod matrix. *Psychological Bulletin* 56: 81–105.

Cartwright, D. B.; Kirtner, W. L.; and Fiske, D. W. 1963. Method factors in changes associated with psychotherapy. *Journal of Abnormal and Social Psychology* 66: 164–75.

Cook, T. D., and Campbell, D. T. 1979. *Quasi-experimentation: Design and analysis issues for field settings.* Chicago: Rand McNally.

Crano, W. D. 1981. Triangulation and cross-cultural research. In *Scientific inquiry and the social sciences: A volume in honor of Donald T. Campbell,* ed. M. B. Brewer and B. E. Collins. San Francisco: Jossey-Bass.

Cronbach, L. J. 1982. *Designing evaluations of educational and social programs.* San Francisco: Jossey-Bass.

Duncan, S., Jr., and Fiske, D. W. 1977. *Face-to-face interaction: Research, methods, and theory.* Hillsdale, N.J.: Erlbaum.

Ericsson, K. A., and Simon, H. A. 1980. Verbal reports as data. *Psychological Review* 87: 215–51.

Feldstein, S., and Welkowitz, J. 1978. A chronography of conversation: In defense of an objective approach. In *Nonverbal behavior and communication,* ed. A. W. Siegman and S. Feldstein, Hillsdale, N.J.: Erlbaum.

Fiske, D. W. 1978. *Strategies for personality research: The observation versus interpretation of behavior.* San Francisco: Jossey-Bass.

———, ed. 1981. *Problems with language imprecision.* New Directions for Methodology of Social and Behavioral Science, no. 9. San Francisco: Jossey-Bass.

———. In press. Measuring to understand and understanding measuring.

Garfield, S. L.; Prager, R. A.; and Bergin, A. E. 1971. Evaluation of outcome in psychotherapy. *Journal of Consulting and Clinical Psychology* 37: 307–13.

Garner, W. R. 1974. *The processing of information and structure.* Hillsdale, N.J.: Erlbaum.

Garner, W. R.; Hake, H. W.; and Eriksen, C. W. 1956. Operationism and the concept of perception. *Psychological Review* 63: 149–59.

Holzman, P. S. 1982. The search for a biological marker in the functional psychoses. In *Preventive intervention in schizophrenia: Are we ready?* ed. M. J. Goldstein. Washington, D.C.: U.S. Department of Health and Human Services.

Jaffe, J., and Feldstein, S. 1970. *Rhythms of dialogue.* New York: Academic Press.

Jones, M. B., and Fennell, R. S., III. 1965. Runway performance in two strains of rats. *Quarterly Journal of the Florida Academy of Science* 28: 289–96.

Kendon, A., and Ferber, A. 1973. A description of some human greetings. In *Comparative ecology and behaviour of primates,* ed. R. P. Michael and J. H. Crook. New York: Academic Press.

Kuhn, T. S. 1970. *The structure of scientific revolutions.* 2d ed. Chicago: University of Chicago Press.

Larson, R., and Csikszentmihalyi, M. 1983. The experience sampling method. In *Naturalistic approaches to studying social interaction,* ed. H. Reis. New Directions for Methodology of Social and Behavioral Science, no. 15. San Francisco: Jossey-Bass.

Levine, D. N. 1968. The flexibility of traditional culture. *Journal of Social Issues* 24: 129–41.

Lipton, R. B., Levy, D. L.; Holzman, P. S.; and Levin, S. 1983. Eye movement dysfunctions in psychiatric patients: A review. *Schizophrenia Bulletin* 9: 15–34.

Luborsky, L.; Docherty, J. P.; and Penick, S. 1973. Onset conditions for psychosomatic symptoms: A comparative review of immediate observation with retrospective research. *Psychosomatic Medicine* 35: 187–204.

Luborsky, L., and Mintz, J. 1974. What sets off a momentary forgetting during psychoanalysis? Investigations of symptom-onset conditions. *Psychoanalysis and Contemporary Science* 3: 233–68.

Luborsky, L.; Sackeim, H.; and Christoph, P. 1979. The state conducive to momentary forgetting. In *Functional disorders of memory,* ed. J. Kihlstrom and F. Evans. Hillsdale, N.J.: Erlbaum.

McClintock, M. K. 1981. Simplicity from complexity: A naturalistic approach to behavior and endocrine function. In *Generalizing from laboratory to life,* ed. I. Silverman. New Directions for Methodology of Social and Behavioral Science, no. 8. San Francisco: Jossey-Bass.

Meehl, P. E. 1983. Subjectivity in psychoanalytic inference: The nagging persistence of Wilhelm Fliess's Achensee question. In *Testing scientific theories,* ed. J. Earman. Minnesota Studies in the Philosophy of Science, vol. 10. Minneapolis: University of Minnesota Press.

Newell, A. 1973. You can't play twenty questions with nature and win: Projective comments on the papers of this symposium. In *Visual information processing*, ed. W. G. Chase. New York: Academic Press.

Paul, G. L., and Lentz, R. J. 1977. *Psychosocial treatment of chronic mental patients: Milieu versus social-learning programs.* Cambridge: Harvard University Press.

Pepper, S. C. 1981. Problems in the quantification of frequency expressions. In *Problems with language imprecision*, ed. D. W. Fiske. New Directions for Methodology of Social and Behavioral Science, no. 9. San Francisco: Jossey-Bass.

Pepper, S., and Prytulak, L. S. 1974. Sometimes frequently means seldom: Context effects in the interpretation of quantitative expressions. *Journal of Research in Personality* 8: 95–101.

Popper, K. R. 1959. *The logic of scientific discovery.* New York: Basic Books, 1959.

Shweder, R. A., and D'Andrade, R. G. 1979. Accurate reflections or systematic distortion? A reply to Block, Weiss, and Thorne. *Journal of Personality and Social Psychology* 37: 1075–84.

———. 1980. The systematic distortion hypothesis. In *Fallible judgment in behavioral research*, ed. R. A. Shweder. New Directions for Methodology of Social and Behavioral Science, no. 4. San Francisco: Jossey-Bass.

Smith, M. L.; Glass, G. V.; and Miller, T. I. 1980. *The benefits of psychotherapy.* Baltimore: Johns Hopkins University Press.

Sternberg, R. J. 1983. Components of human intelligence. *Cognition* 15: 1–48.

Sudman, S., and Bradburn, N. M. 1982. *Asking questions: A practical guide to questionnaire design.* San Francisco: Jossey-Bass.

Turner, C. F., and Krauss, E. 1978. Fallible indicators of the subjective state of the nation. *American Psychologist* 33: 456–70.

Vesell, E. S. 1967. Induction of drug-metabolizing enzymes in liver microsomes of mice and rats by softwood bedding. *Science* 157: 1057–58.

Wigner, E. P. 1964. Events, laws of nature, and invariance principles. *Science* 145: 995–99.

4 Social Inquiry by and for Earthlings

Lee J. Cronbach

Philosophers' "rational reconstruction" has created a legend of science as a transcendental activity, one that could best be conducted by sending teams of observers to hover over Earth.[1] Standing highest on the scale of being, said Kant, are "the most sublime classes of rational creatures, which inhabit Jupiter and Saturn" (see Toulmin & Goodfield 1965, 99); there, if anywhere, must the idealized scientist dwell. Saturn's inhabitants are not bent on exploiting Earth's resources, nor is their quest primarily for knowledge useful on Saturn. Hermann Hesse caught their spirit in his Bead Game: Ingenuity is testimony to one's own excellence and, like other art forms, an expression of reverence.

Because observations unordered cannot be an object of contemplation, an integrative story is the most valued product of science. Saturnians cherish retellings that capture most of what observers have reported and that can make sense of (or, better, foretell) observations yet to be made. The stories that have commanded greatest respect have always been incomplete, some of them have been contradicted by new observations, and there is always the possibility that some genius will rearrange a collage of peephole visions into a graceful gestalt. Saturnians therefore do not expect the Bead Game to end at some moment when clarion certainty is proclaimed.

But Beadmasters do have faith that the universe will yield its secrets to scientific method, as the bandits' cave was attuned to "Open Sesame!" Beings from Jupiter as well as Saturn might begin to play the Bead Game. Learning from the responses and rebuffs of Nature, these new players would become better and better at the game. If Jupiter's Beadmasters should happen to make Earth the object of inquiry, say the Saturnians, then their evolving model and the Saturnian model must come closer and closer to agreement.

Two atoms of hydrogen combine with one of oxygen. Attraction is inversely proportional to the square of distance. A Beadmaster believes that such statements would be supported if a time machine enabled us to observe the world of a million years ago or of a million years hence. That is why investigators from Jupiter, in another eon, can be expected to converge on Saturnian chemistry and celestial mechanics. For Saturnians, then, time has a boundless horizon. A line of inquiry started in one generation can be advanced endlessly. The cost of studying events that are rare or buried in noise can be spread over millennia by the patient Saturnian community.

Saturnians, with their timeless perspective, do not discount the future; a similar patience among earthly students of society would be irresponsible. Faith that solid theories will evolve in some future century, from whatever we now report, is insufficient to justify large investments in the many social science disciplines. Resources for social inquiry are necessarily limited, hence policies for deploying them are required. What should members of our disciplines be trying to accomplish, if the Saturnian ideal is not the appropriate one? The community needs and will continue to need richer ideas about ability, aging, aggression, attitudes, and all other topics in the *International Encyclopaedia of the Social Sciences,* and we should favor studies that promise to shed light on these topics for our generation and the next.

In saying this, I do not place a premium on ad hoc "applied" research. Challenges to social thought and practice, and new proposals, can arise from inquiry of almost any kind, from piecemeal technology to abstract philosophizing. Quite "basic" inquiries can alter thought about man and society—the work of Harlow and of von Neumann come to mind as examples. Targeted policy research does the same. Instead of "answering" the practical question toward which it was pointed, the targeted study usually contributes primarily by changing perceptions of a broad topic, according to recent studies of utilization (Weiss 1977). A good example is the origin of a social psychology of the workplace in the Hawthorne research, which began as an attempt at psychotechnology, an example to which I shall return.

WHY SATURNIAN IDEALS DO NOT SUIT SOCIAL INQUIRY

A "social physics" is an unlikely development. The Pill dates back less than one generation; widespread advanced education of women dates back less than two; about four generations back, in Western democracies, free public education spread; five generations back, the Industrial Revolution. Such rapid change severely limits generalization about social structures and relationships.

Much of the similarity in persons' actions comes from shared experiences, and customary behavior (hence an institution) is modified by a process of contagious reinterpretation of roles and goals. Traditional natural science encounters no irregularities of this character. Although particles are attracted to other particles, they don't fall in love. Within a troop of baboons, correlated changes in perception do account for the change in females' response to an aging male; but that is no counterpart of the way a culture uses language to define appropriate objects for sexual love. To explain conduct, a phenomenology—especially an appreciation of the nouns and verbs our subjects call upon to organize experience—is indispensable (see especially Geertz 1983, 58–68, on changes from culture to culture in the concept of "person" or "self").

The astronomer and zoologist do not talk to stars and starfish, so they can expect the same processes to operate before and after they produce a theory. Humans who investigate human affairs cannot pretend to be bystanders; social institutions and actions are notoriously reactive to the scribbler in the garret or at court (Gergen 1982). Social scientists define many of the terms by which community affairs are regulated. Census tabulations, for example, determine how much influence citizens of different backgrounds will have; introducing a census category such as "Hispanic-American" fosters political coalitions and conflicts that otherwise might never have been.

An Ideal in Personality Research

Today's widespread dissatisfaction within the social science community (Kruskal 1982) derives in large measure from our positivistic heritage and the consequent idolization of formal theory. It comes also from the fact that any stone can make a wrecking ball whereas well-shaped building stones are hard to come by. For us to place an exaggerated valuation on rigor and on "theory-choice" can be self-defeating (Merton 1975).

In the 1950s, a serious effort was made to bring rigorous evaluation to interpretations of psychological tests, particularly personality tests. Paul Meehl and I described how this rigor could be achieved in the light of philosophy of science as it stood just before Popper took over the lead (Cronbach & Meehl 1955).[2] Despite some complaint that our paper was insufficiently positivistic, its notion of "construct validation" has been popular and the ideals are still being relayed to fledgling researchers. Useful though the formulation was and in some ways still is, this movement has had a repressive effect.

The call for validation originated in an attempt at professional self-regulation, an attempt to bring to testing criticism stern enough to keep users aware of limitations yet gentle enough to encourage innovation in technique and theory. Our advice was upbeat: Sound ideas survive validation and the others are kept out of print, so each year's interpretations are sure to be better. Our paper even spoke cheerfully of the cloudy notions out of which orderly theories crystallize. Taken as a whole, however, the paper devalued conjectural interpretations. Some of our contemporaries went further, writing that a research report should be denied publication unless the test of a prespecified formal hypothesis implied a risk of type 1 error less than .001.

Unfortunately, the more explicit a proposition and the more rigorous the investigation of it, the more likely it is to be disconfirmed. Personality research in particular is now demoralized (Fiske 1974; Rorer & Widiger 1983). In the two decades prior to the enshrinement of construct validation, many personality variables had been conceived and means of measuring them proposed. After 1955, hardly anyone tilled those potentially fertile fields. A program of validation for any one construct could require at least a lifetime's work, so almost no one attempted it. Sustained cooperative concentration on some limited aspect of personality could shorten the work, but such effort is rare. "Motivation to achieve" is perhaps unique in having a fifty-year history of progressive elucidation by a community of scholars, yet that program of work examined just a tiny corner of the Murray system of concepts.

When each construct (and each proposed indicator of it) is expected to justify its existence from the outset by successfully predicting novel observations, ideas face an up-or-out decision much too early. Progress requires that we respect poorly formed and even "untestable" ideas. Open-mindedness can be carried too far, of course; a possible truth is a possible falsehood. The judgment that an idea may be viable should nonetheless be granted generously. We should be stern only where it would cost us much to be wrong (Putnam 1978, 90).

Not infrequently, a candidate notion in physical theory receives sympathetic attention for decades before it is stated in a defensible manner. Thus the most basic aspects of atomic theory were in dispute from 1800 to 1860. According to Glymour (1980b), Dalton's initial reports just after 1800 were "vague" and "conjectural" in places and incompatible with the contemporary data of Gay-Lussac on gases. Worse, Dalton put forward a calculus for determining atomic weights that was "wonderfully appealing . . . also plainly unsatisfactory." From 1826 to 1837, the prestigious M. Dumas published "apparently devastating criticisms"; yet the community persevered. During half a century, the arguments of the leading chemists ranged from tough-mindedness to open-mindedness to special pleading. Each investigator had his own list of atomic weights, accepting from a neighbor only procedures and results that advanced his preferred scheme. Somehow the chemists managed to encourage each other, through their years of disharmony, to stay with the puzzle.

Explanations for Capacities

Before looking further at typical social inquiry, I note that the Saturnian ideal probably does apply to the study of "capacities." Capacities are described in propositions about the conductivity of wires of various composition, for example, and in statements about the number of bits that can be held in short-term memory. A physical law is typically a statement of a capacity, dividing possibility from impossibilities. The gas law tells what volume a mole of a gas can (and must) occupy at a specified temperature and pressure. Capacities are the prime source of the "puzzles" to which Kuhnian normal science attends.

For scientists seeking to explain a capacity, the question is, How could this have come about? (Toulmin 1972). Why must it be this amount of hydrogen that combines with one mole of oxygen and not some other? Why must the ratio of round to wrinkled peas be three to one? Such a definite, solidly confirmed phenomenon should be explainable. One reason for the chemists' six decades of concentration on atomic weights was that the law of definite proportions described capacities that clamored for explication. Similarly, Toulmin tells how provocative for the science of optics was the discovery that Iceland spar produces a double image. There was nothing inherently or practically important about Iceland spar; its importance was that it posed a sharp challenge within the theory of its time.

Manicas (1982) foresees that part of psychology can become a hard science about capacities. Behavioral capacities, he suggests, can be explained in terms of physiology, and on this biological frontier, Saturnian ideals should apply. Physiology can in principle explain how this or that action is possible. Perhaps we have been insufficiently attentive to capacities of experiential or social origin. The German postwar economic miracle, the musical prodigy, the society without an incest taboo, the fakir on his bed of nails—these are capacities for which it seems reasonable to seek nonphysiological explanations.

Scientists often uncover an unrecognized capacity by establishing exceptional conditions: pure substances or strains, high temperatures, massive doses, extensive practice, and the like. Sometimes what has been thought impossible is brought about; thus what were once "inert gases" have been caused to enter chemical reactions. Akin to the Iceland-spar observation is the discovery of Hatano and Osawa (1983) that abacus experts remember very much longer digit strings than ordinary students can retain. (The experts store a visual-kinesthetic representation that is more efficient than auditory storage.)

Insofar as social scientists seek to account for capacities, they will combine historical research with retroduction and rational analysis. They can add manipulation and contemporary observation when the phenomenon recurs naturally or can be induced. One excellent example in psychology is the work by Simon (1979) and others on the skill of chessmasters. A bit less theoretical and less experimental is the political scientists' postmortem analysis of a pre-election survey that is contradicted by the actual vote. An explanation is likely to be time-and-place-bound; prediction of recurrence is not necessary.

Intriguing through the study of capacities may be, it is not the main business of social inquiry. The main thrust of inquiry has to concern itself with what people and institutions typically do and with how change occurs. With reference to abilities, aging, and so on, we can record single case histories or we can compile distributions of variables and changes in the distributions and the conditions associated with the variation. The information is thus idiosyncratic or probabilistic, and explanations must be correspondingly loose or underjustified.

LEVELS OF SOCIAL KNOWLEDGE

Social inquirers might seek knowledge of four types—descriptive and historical reports, concepts, generalized propositions, and systematic explanations. We are well able to produce the first two, and they should not be undervalued.

Historical Knowledge

To most present-tense questions about everyday behavior and society, a Saturnian study of Earth in 1800 would have given an answer different from that of a Jovian study in year 2000. Here are examples:

> In a certain polity, what kinds of persons have disproportionate influence on governmental policy?

> What are the "developmental tasks" whose successful accomplishment near such and such age is associated with mental health?

> Among American adults of similar age and income, what distinguishes those who save money from those who go into debt?

These local correlational questions are nontrivial. They are important for self-understanding, for evaluation of the society, and for suggesting how an individual or institution might intervene to some advantage.

The answers are historical findings. Each question could have been stated for an earlier year and studied by traditional historical method. The questions are no less historical for being studied in real time, because the answers are properly put in the past tense. To report on last week's data in the present tense is to assert: "I believe that today's situation differs in no important way from the situation observed."

Concepts

Investigators attempt to extend historical reports into propositions, and understanding is often identified with the number and power of the propositions. I would stress, however, the benefit that concepts confer when we are not prepared to specify their interconnections or even to define them sharply. A concept captures a line of thought and by its very existence points to an aspect of events that some thinker has considered important. The armatures of the research questions posed above are concepts: "influences," "developmental tasks," "saving." Concepts suggest first-order questions to investigate and aspects of a situation to be observed or put under research control. A concept such as "electricity" or "social class" has value even when, in its early days, it is a place marker for a possible building site rather than the keystone of a theoretical arch.

Generalizations

A general proposition links concept words in a present-tense sentence (or, in specifically historical scholarship, the past tense). Corresponding to the questions above are these beliefs, all of them important as sources of understanding and as heuristics:

> In a democracy, equal eligibility to vote does not imply equal influence.

> In any culture, mental health is conditioned in part by some set of accomplishments the culture expects at a given age.

> Economic behavior is conditioned by subcultural influences and personal psychological history.

Such propositions can be loosely knitted into networks, but for this discussion, single sentences can represent types of theory. A present-tense proposition in social science is unlikely to be at once definite, general, and dependable (Thorngate 1976).

Klein (1983) set out to persuade a nonspecialist academic audience that economists command lawlike knowledge. He offered many examples but went on to say that some of the propositions are no more than truisms arising from definitions or assumptions—mathematical idealizations rather than substantive summaries. Propositions such as the law of supply and demand describe, at best, "tendencies that prevail in the long run," Klein said. Because of inelasticity and restraints on trade, the variables can move contrary to the law—for a certain commodity, in a certain market, for some period of time. Because the average of trends across commodities or decades is fairly consistent with the law, it can be a point of departure for thinking. The escape clause "in the long run," however, makes the proposition incapable of falsification, so it is not the stuff of Saturnian theory.

Can We Hope for Theory?

Our propositional knowledge, such as it is, consists almost wholly of statistical associations found in a certain range of contexts; the range of our evidence is far less than the reach of almost all our propositions. It is doubtful that we will have explanatory networks of significant scope, at least during our era (this remark echoes Meehl 1978, 829; see also Putnam 1978, 62–66).

Putnam (1978) argues that realism is an empirical hypothesis, one that can be defended if we observe that a science converges. It has been traditional to assert that because convergence has occurred in physics and biology, similar convergence will occur in social science. That extrapolation one is free to believe or disbelieve. In my opinion, social science is cumulative, not in possessing ever-more-refined answers about fixed questions, but in possessing an ever-richer repertoire of questions.

The Difficulty of Bounding Generalizations

Saturnian science constructs if-then statements about a system, that is, about a set of objects so bounded that the objects move and metamorphose in essentially the same manner no matter what is going on outside the system. The challenge is to devise or discover boundaries across which transactions are few or effectively constant. When Darwin began on Galapagos he bagged finches and described each one without recording where the capture was made. He made no progress in explaining the variety of finches as long as he regarded the entire archipelago as a system. The hunch that the islands had distinct populations led him to keep records of locale. He might never have achieved his great synthesis had he not stumbled upon a natural laboratory where life on one island proceeds indepedent of life on the next. On the mainland, the greater number of competing populations and their overlapping ranges obscure the patterning of the distribution.

An object of social inquiry is more like the mainland than like one of Darwin's island. The economy, the family, and the ideology of Middletown change because dollars, people, and messages zip across town lines and state lines and even across oceans. Our norms, regression coefficients, and so on, describe how often persons or other objects in a named category make a kind of response under incompletely specified conditions. The category rarely represents a system. An experimenter tries to wall off a subsystem and is likely to ignore the larger system when he puts his conclusion into words. Actually, the so-called independent variable is the conjunction of the manipulated variable with all the other features of the system.

Brownell and Moser (1949) conducted a particularly admirable educational experiment in which it might seem as if each classroom was a system and the teaching method the independent variable, but that view is naive (as they showed). Brownell and Moser randomly assigned dozens of third-grade classrooms to four specified methods of teaching subtraction. The borrowing technique, taught meaningfully, was far superior to the alternatives. The substantial residual variance was largely explained by pupils' past history. Only the pupils whose earlier teachers had stressed meanings profited from the meaningful lessons on borrowing. Pupils whose past teachers had emphasized practice (and ignored meaning) succeeded with rote instruction and not with explanatory instruction; these pupils could make nothing of the explanations. The question initially posed, "Which subtraction lessons produce the best outcome?" was unanswerable. The combination of subtraction technique and teaching technique and pupils' past history was what mattered.

Social scientists have overemphasized the kind of quantitative summary that is contingent on a time-bound mix of events in the sample. The only way to give a magnitude for "effect size" in the Brownell study was to average over the distribution of pupil histories. Whether a similar result will be found in another place and time depends on the larger system that influences the instructional style of primary teachers. With probabilistic information, we can identify only a part of a sufficient condition for an outcome (Mackie 1974). No matter how much information on contingencies is compiled, the summary is likely to remain inexact and the fully sufficient explanation beyond reach. (Physics is less troubled by its probabilistic events than we are; a tiny amount of matter consists of a great number of particles or microfields; hence at a very low level of aggregation, probabilities approach 1.00 or .00.)

EVALUATING DIRECT CONCLUSIONS

Information collected by specific procedures in specific places leads to statements of three types: about *uto*, *UTO*, and **UTO*. The symbols *U*, *T*, and *O* refer to aspects of the study plan *UTO*—respectively, to the sort of unit-treatment combination identified as the target and the proposed operations for observing and for processing data (Cronbach 1982). The units are from a certain time and place, hence variation associated with the setting or cultural-context is confounded with choice of units. The investigator recruits subjects, observes them under chosen circumstances (perhaps specially created), and records and tabulates what happens; this generates a particular *uto* combination. She may report on *uto* or she may generalize to the class *UTO*, but she and those who follow her will almost always extrapolate to a domain **UTO* that differs from *UTO*.

Any investigation is first of all a case study. The historical record

on *uto*—of what was done to produce data and of the data themselves—is noninferential; there is no issue of sampling error or of
bias in the experimenter's perception or of the "meaning" of the
facts. The only inference stems from the reader's need to assume
that the investigator did not lie and did not suppress information
she knew would change the story.

The *u* of the study are a subset of the population *U* identified for
investigation. The units may be, for example, individuals, families,
clinics, communities. Likewise, because the plan for observing and
analyzing (*O*) is capable of being carried out in many ways, the
actual procedures (*o*) are to be regarded as an unsystematic sample
of the observations, codings, and so on, that would be consistent
with the plan. The conditions to which a given subject is exposed
constitute a realization *t* of treatment plan *T*. That plan specifies
much, but by no means all, of what will be done. In psychotherapy
of a stated kind, for example, the treatment events vary from person to person; each realization is a sample of what the treatment
description implies.

Accepting a Claim to Reproducibility

The actual *uto* is thus one among the many on which investigators
supplied the plan *UTO* might have reported. Typically an investigator generalizes, claiming that the findings in her *uto* would have
appeared (within a stated margin of error) in other studies under
the plan. The plan *UTO* constitutes the more or less operational
definition needed to guide a replicator. The firmer the plan, the
greater the reproducibility of both procedures and (uninterpreted)
findings.

Any reader accepting the generalization to *UTO* relies on many
assumptions, usually tacit ones. Acceptance implies confidence, for
example, that the sampling plan for *U* was carried out so that *u* fits
the statistical model. Thus if twenty-five students were taught by
the same teacher, and the analyst based the error estimate on an *N*
of twenty-five, she has assumed that the teacher does not matter,
that the variability of scores would be the same if the twenty-five
students had come from twenty-five classes. Another assumption is
that the particular observers gave much the same data as other
representatives of the class *O* would have given; controls such as
blind scoring make that assumption more credible. Essentially, acceptance of the argument leading from *uto* to *UTO* rests on a
thought experiment. When the reader imagines a contemporary

and entirely independent replication guided only by the verbal specification of *UTO,* does he expect it to yield essentially the same regression coefficient or effect size or other result?

A principal advantage of the social sciences and history over other sources of social ideas is the reproducibility that reports at the operational levels *uto* and *UTO* can claim. A discipline learns a great deal about how to make studies reproducible, hence about how to anticipate whether a study will be reproducible. The limitations of particular techniques are searched out and controls are devised; a technology of investigation develops. When observations are guided by such expertise, a contradictory outcome in a companion study is as enlightening as a confirmation, if not more so.

EXTRAPOLATIONS AND THEIR ACCEPTANCE

Ellipsis and abstraction are necessary for communication, so a finding is almost never reported in the operational language of *UTO.* A broader statement is made: "Meaningful instruction produced better performance of subtraction than rote instruction." The user of the information goes further, shifting to the present tense and possibly ignoring specifics, as in "Meaningful instruction works better than rote." Any proposition that is not explicitly about the historical *uto* or the *UTO* it sampled refers to a **UTO;* the asterisk indicates a change in *U, T,* and/or *O.* The proposition about **UTO* is in effect an extrapolation, a prediction about what will be observed in a study where the subjects or operations depart in some respects from those of the original study.

In a clinical judgment where a probabilistic finding about a class of persons is brought to bear on a new case, **UTO* is narrower than the original *UTO.* One way to reduce inferential risk is to collect data in the immediate local situation. The physician, knowing that drug X often cures disease Y, takes that generalization as a fallible prior for the next case; he finds both the "go" and "no go" decisions defensible, and when he opts to use the drug, he monitors closely the response of the particular patient. The virtues of such efforts are unquestionable; the chief perplexity is just how much to invest in close-coupled monitoring of a given application.

Often the risk of generalization and abstraction simply has to be taken. A particularly common form of ellipsis is to say that the treatment had such and such effect. The asymmetric emphasis on the treatment as the cause, rather than on the combination of treatment, units, setting, and so on, arises from the intent of social scientists to aid in the manipulation of human affairs (Cook & Campbell

1979, 25–28). The elliptical conclusion becomes even less replicable and harder to justify when a generic treatment name is substituted for the specification of T and the description of t; yet only a statement at the conceptual level can guide further inquiry or practical actions.

The Brownell-Moser lesson materials were particular, and no logic warrants extrapolating to other materials on subtraction or to other topics in arithmetic; but the label "meaningful" does point to a characteristic of stimuli that often has made a difference. The concept "meaningful" obviously is crude. Psychologists have done a great deal to sharpen it as it applies to syllables and word strings, and someday its application to lessons will be elaborated. Documenting just which lesson plans or, better, lesson realizations have led to the positive result in any one study is a starting point for that elaboration.

An investigation carried out under reproducible but highly specific conditions is not usually of great value in itself. It is in combining with other reports and with beliefs from other sources, into interpretations mediated by concepts, that a finding is helpful (Lindblom & Cohen 1979; Geertz 1983; Mook 1983). Nearly every reader of social research uses the original accounts and the secondary accounts for "enlightenment" (Weiss 1977). Though a study of a social service may have been motivated by uncertainties about its adequacy, only its operators are likely to fixate on information specific to it. Policymakers use each month's news from research primarily to reshape their broad perspectives and to note factors to bear in mind in the future. Likewise, a psychology textbook is mainly extrapolation from the corpus of research. In writing such a book, I look for concepts and questions that students will find useful in future contexts; the specifics of a study come in, not for their own sake, but to "vivify" the point (Gergen 1982).

The Role of Beliefs

The grounds for accepting or doubting a proposition about UTO are primarily methodological. The grounds for accepting a proposition about $*UTO$ are primarily substantive. That is, one judges whether the changes from UTO to $*UTO$ matter. Where data are projected to conditions not yet observed, readers must be skeptical if the model neglects a variable they consider relevant.

Coleman, Hoffer, and Kilgore (1982) allegedly found private schools more effective than public schools (according to certain measures on a certain sample). The United States is considering

policies under which more children, including more children from
poorer families, would go to private schools. Is it safe to infer that
more chidren would be better educated under the proposed policy? To judge that extrapolation, one must speculate about causal
processes. Coleman, having some evidence that the private schools
had superior discipline, gives that as a reason for their past success
and future promise. A critic can respond that when a private school
acquires a wide-range student body, its discipline will deteriorate
(James & Levin 1983). Anyone who finds the criticism sensible
must doubt Coleman's optimistic extrapolation.

Each of us decides which extrapolations to store in mind. A
statement is accepted to the degree that it and the accompanying
explanation are compatible with the hearer's store of beliefs. Rationalists protest this emphasis on audience response, because acceptance depends on the rhetorical skill and sometimes the
prestige of advocates. "Objective" knowledge, we are told, should
dominate over beliefs and impressions. The counterargument is
that our general propositions are weak and our networks gappy, so
a rigorous defense for an extrapolation is usually beyond reach. To
deal with uncertainties, it is rational to call upon cultural tradition
(Campbell 1975) and personal empathy; both are empirically
grounded. Not surprisingly, undisciplined sources of belief are especially influential in personal-social areas (Lindblom & Cohen
1979).

Admitting that loose thinking is characteristic of everyday coping, can we not refuse a proposition the status of "knowledge"
when a multiply anchored and convincing argument is lacking?
That ideal has to be discarded. As Lakatos (1978) pointed out,
"hard" scientists, to get on with their work, have to commit themselves to beliefs that reach beyond available evidence and perhaps
beyond conceivable evidence. For example, Toulmin and Goodfield (1965, 264) comment that, for all we know, the value of
Planck's h has been changing over time; if so, ideas about the galaxy
derived from Hubble's red shift are wrong. Most of the tacit assumptions behind interpretations of physical data are derived from
previous scientific findings, or at worst, the heuristic fruitfulness of
an assumption has been demonstrated in many contexts. The social
scientists' plight is much worse, as the underpinnings of our arguments are usually as much in question as the issues on which the
research centers (Meehl 1978; Cook & Campbell 1979, 25).

Those who believe that social research is already converging
counsel patience, confident that dependable theoretical networks

will be the reward of assiduous sciencing. That pietism—the pie being in the sky by and by—does not face up to our chief mission; scholars ought to offer tenable interpretations today and tomorrow. In Mary Hesse's words,

> I suggest that the proposal of a social theory is more like the arguing of a political case than like a natural-science explanation. It should seek for and respect the facts when these are to be had, but it cannot await a possibly unattainable total explanation. It must appeal explicitly to value judgments and may properly use persuasive rhetoric. No doubt it should differ from most political argument in seeking and accounting for facts more conscientiously, and in constraining its rhetoric. . . . Here the inheritance of virtues from the natural sciences comes to the social scientist's aid, and I hope that nothing I have said will be taken to undermine these virtues. (Hesse 1978, 16)

Pluralism

No one, I think, would question the need to have a population of concepts in circulation, so that some new ideas can win adherents and enter the main stream of thought (Merton 1975; Toulmin 1972, 1981). It is reasonable for different persons to accept different interpretations, and unreasonable to hope that empirical research can (or should) resolve all the conflicts among conceptualizations. A conception that some audience finds stimulating should be entertained unless and until it is proved untenable. We allow a work of art to throw new light on events without expecting the interpretation to be the whole and only truth; indeed, we value art because its practitioners offer alternative interpretations (Putnam 1978, 87ff.). Shaffer's *Amadeus* has impact just because Shaffer violates the expectation of Mozart-the-man the audience brings to the theater. For anyone who accepts Shaffer's portrait as a possible, partial truth, the show is more than a pastime; it advances a thesis: "Goodness has nothing to do with art." Interpretations arising out of scholarship ought to be afforded the tolerance afforded to art, and fortunately they sometimes are. For example, it was as artistic portrayal that Murray's list of needs and presses made its contribution. Murray offered, not a set of propositions intended to displace all competitors, but an alternative vocabulary for talking about persons, incentives, and gratifications.

Many a realist wants concepts to name entities that exist in nature quite apart from man's construing. Social inquiry, I think, would be better off without that aspiration. To be sure, interpretations must be compatible with observations; Shaffer's story can command respect only because it is consistent with letters and other documents from Mozart's life. But when we ask our theories to "cut Nature closer to the joint," we ask too much. In physical nature, systems are disjoint; there are conspicuous gaps between galaxies, between molecules, between muons. Though carbon atoms are not the little black balls of my high-school chemistry, we have no reason to doubt that carbon enters physical events as if it consists of coherent units built round twelve or fourteen protons. Few targets of social inquiry function as lasting entities, and such entities as we have are not classifiable into categories as "real" as those for atoms and plants. There is no reason to think that any one "structure" for personality or for social groups is more real than another. Rather, alternative conceptualizations highlight particular aspects of behavior and feeling and so suit particular purposes. To speak of "the structure" of a family or a classroom is no more justified (and no less) than a sculptor's reference to "the structure" of his sitter's face.

Because their information is limited, interpreters have to rely on what Vico called *fantasia* and what the Germans called *Verstehen*. Dilthey and his colleagues were right to assign a central role to the *gestaltende Kraft* we bring to explanations. Murray's analysis of Satan (1962) is an example to set alongside Shaffer's Mozart. Concepts from psychology, glosses of theological writings in their historical context, and fantasia combine to make this an impressive *tour d'élan*.

A scholarly community has a great talent for generating plural explanations that are consistent with much the same premises. Each interested person attaches subjective probabilities to rival statements. Further inquiry, critical analysis, and debate can bring the members of the community more nearly to agreement, or can show the value of dialectical alternation. Members of a discipline identify the types of faulty extrapolation their brand of inquiry is likely to inspire and can alert their professional successors to all such lines of criticism. Each specialty knows of specific pitfalls to bear in mind; that is where the power of a discipline lies.

We can rarely see a topic in proper perspective if our inquiry employs resources from only one discipline (Toulmin, in Kasschau & Cofer 1981, 268ff.; and in Brewer & Collins 1982, 33). With regard to problems I have worked on, someone with a disciplinary base far from my own has often supplied a relevant framework my analysis had missed. Social science profits from interdisciplinary task forces or institutes and from reviews of proposals by broadly constituted study sections. We need additional mechanisms for bringing multiple perspectives to bear. How often, for example, is a paper in sociology referred by a psychologist or an economist? This is but one of many possible devices by which a person working within one speciality can develop a more profound view. Bring in anthropology, political science, or history, and a vision emerges of a powerful and constructive machinery for developing interpretations. Interdisciplinary contacts will have their greatest benefit when each participant individually makes colleagues' idioms part of his or her own thinking. Schultz quotes two apt sentences from Hayek: "Nobody can be a great economist who is only an economist. . . . An economist who is only an economist is likely to become a nuisance if not a positive danger" (in Kruskal 1982, 129).

How Narrowly Should Inquiry Be Targeted?

A recurrent issue in research planning is concentration versus diversification, standard conditions versus representative conditions, justification versus discovery.

Three Strategies

When heterogeneous situations interest us, one strategy is to draw a large and representative sample and report an overall statistic. That can be useful if we will thereafter apply the knowledge to aggregates whose makeup matches the present one. But a statistical summary may misrepresent underlying relations; recall Estes' 1956 demonstration that the composite learning curve based on a group average differs in shape from the individuals' curves. If the individual curves are similar in some respect, one can of course represent that similarity by a composite statistic; but the formula for compositing is to be determined after the common pattern is perceived. A purely statistical study is a case study manqué.

Instead of aggregating diversity, we can narrow the target, studying a more homogeneous subclass of situations. That works fine when we care about the subclass and will encounter future instances of it. The price is continued ignorance about situations outside the subclass. To limit investigation to animals of a single strain makes a study powerful and informative so long as every other strain would lead one to the same conclusion. That assumption is risky until theory is well advanced, as is demonstrated by a historic dispute among psychologists that arose when Tolman's rats at Berkeley exhibited "latent learning" and Iowa rats did not. The

battle died down unresolved. When, two decades later, someone
ran rats from the Iowa and Berkeley strains side by side, the data
replicated the inconsistency! (Jones & Fennell 1965). Tolman
would not have discovered latent learning if he had unluckily
stocked his colony with the Iowa strain.

A third strategy will often be advisable, though it does not promise firm and replicable conclusions. A program of investigation can
divide resources over many subcategories or small collectives, attending to them separately. The data are comparatively thin, and
any contrast identified post hoc to account for variation is suspect.
The rule of parsimony discourages such shredouts; when in doubt,
it says, act as if the null hypothesis were true. But variation observed in shredouts is valid information at the level of local history.
Even "errors of observation" are facts that have causes. It is wrong
to ignore the variations and wrong to describe them in present-
tense conclusions; rather, like other historical facts, they ought to
be recorded as reminders of possibilities.

The Hawthorne Research

A notable example of effective investigation is found in *Management and the Worker* (Roethlisberger & Dickson 1939). Its power to
stimulate is evidenced by the controversy that continues to this day
(Bramel & Friend 1981, 1982; Sonnenfeld 1982). Fault-finding (in
the best sense as well as the worst) is to be expected when a study
deals with important matters, and that study touched a nerve.

The Western Electric investigators adopted an empirical, quantitative, experimental paradigm, yet they followed the third of my
strategies.[3] They knew what factors influenced productivity (they
thought) and set out to show just what level of illumination, timing
of work breaks, and so on would maximize output. Worker morale
turned out to be the salient influence, so much so that adverse
physical conditions arranged for test purposes did not impair output. What was conceived as a study of worker-as-machine became a
report on interpersonal relations.

Among many things Roethlisberger and Dickson did right, two
seem most noteworthy. They modeled the situation that interested
them with considerable realism, and observers remained on the
scene, ready to record prespecified variables plus anything else of
interest. I speak of modeling. The test room was artificial, to facilitate manipulation and observation, but a team of workers worked
real shifts with real tasks over many weeks. Roethlisberger and
Dickson, like Darwin, found themselves in a situation where com-

plex processes were isolated just sufficiently for important effects to come to attention.

It is easy to imagine what could have happened if, at the outset, Western Electric had solicited bids for a project to determine the trend relating output to illumination. The successful proposal would very likely have included the test room, the programmed change in lighting, and the measurement of output. But to hold down costs and compete successfully, the bidders might have turned the execution over to machines. The inquiry can be reduced to a routine: collect volunteers, divide at random, ring the changes on illumination, keep score, fit a curve. Here, as in the actual experiment, there might have been no difference between the experimental group and the controls. We cannot believe that illumination is irrelevant to assembly work, but the automated investigation would have nothing to say about why the results defied common sense.

The Western Electric investigators were not taken aback by their no-difference result because they had left themselves open to experience. They not only kept a fine-grain, worker-by-worker record of output, but they listened to conversations and made notes on the life of the group. Their report brought the test room alive for readers, which added greatly to the acceptance of the post hoc explanation. Not everyone has agreed with that interpretation, and—significantly—it is on the basis of the detailed volume that the critics make their case for alternative readings.

The "Search" in Research

To recommend that investigators try to see what is going on must seem like a trivial restatement of the obvious. An experienced investigator might be expected to do that almost as second nature. But the apprentice is positively discouraged from wide-eyed unstructured observation, and many investigators seem never to throw away the crutches supplied in the first year of graduate school.

In the quantitative branches of social science, preoccupation with formal hypothesis testing dominates course work, the doctoral dissertation, summaries of past research, and much of methodological doctrine (e.g., Cohen 1982). In evaluation research, for example, methodological recommendations are generally tilted toward the controlled testing of prespecified hypotheses—toward the formal, the replicable, the confirmatory (Cronbach 1982). In truth, many past evaluations were influential, not because of the controls imposed by the design, but because variation that was not controlled proved informative. In randomized experiments (Brownell's among them), it often has been information from uncontrolled variables or unplanned contrasts that influenced subsequent thought.

The formalities of testing null hypotheses and fits to models are geared to justification, which is a culminating step in a scientific effort. The function is to convince oneself and others that an interpretation developed out of less formal observation and retroduction is worth taking seriously. Much investigation has to precede a formal test to reach a hypothesis that warrants such an investment. Investigators free to do so should sniff round the phenomenon and probe unsystematically for a long while before they mount a wrap-up study intended to "establish" what they have perceived.

In the social sciences, virtually any study should be exploratory, even one that centers on a fixed hypothesis. The Roethlisberger-Dickson study was, after all, confirmatory, with an excellent formal design and quantification. The famous conclusion about the social side of worker response took off at an angle oblique to the initial hypotheses when those were disconfirmed. Detective work can be equally important in studies after a hypothesis is supported, particularly in elucidating cases that depart from the main trend.

We cannot be reminded too often of the way R. A. Fisher himself treated quantitative data in an experiment within a partly social system:

> He had a fine criterion, yield of wheat in bushels per acre. He found that after he controlled variety, and fertilizer, there was considerable variation from year to year. This variation had a slow up-and-down cycle over a seventy-year period. Now Fisher set himself on the trail of the residual variation. First he studied wheat records from other sections to see if they had the trend; they did not. He considered and ruled out rainfall as an explanation. Then he started reading the records of the plots and found weeds a possible factor. He considered the nature of each species of weed and found that the response of weed varieties to rainfall and cultivation accounted for much of the cycle. But the large trends were not explained until he showed that the upsurge of weeds after 1875 coincided with a school-attendance act which removed cheap labor from the fields, and that another cycle coincided with the retirement of a superintendent who made weed removal his personal concern. (Quoted from Edwards & Cronbach 1952, 58; based on Fisher 1920)

Enriching the Record of Observation

Conventional publication of full accounts is impractical with today's research volume and today's costs. Fortunately, technology is rushing to our aid. The computer has brought us a long way forward in the distribution of files of raw quantitative data, allowing secondary analyses and meta-analyses to capitalize on the initial investment. The computer has also encouraged historians to code documentary archives for statistical analysis.

These possibilities have crept up on us; so far we have reflected very little on their strengths and limitations. I am enthusiastic about reuse of old data, having repeatedly found it a stimulating and economical way to develop new ideas and sometimes to shatter conclusions I had strongly believed (e.g., Cronbach & Webb 1975). Still, it is difficult to make sense of data that we come to from a distance. In any single structured study, descriptive information influences the interpretation of the calculated result. The currently popular meta-analysis of quantitative summaries is impoverished; to understand the material, analysts would have to go back to descriptive information (particularly, information on atypical cases).

An antidote for the decontextualization that goes with computerizing may well be found in the microfiche and similar technologies that make permanently available much qualitative information that could interest later interpreters, subject to whatever denaturing protects subjects' rights. (I do not suggest saving every scrap of paper for posterity; investigator judgment is as important here as in deciding originally what data to collect.)

CONCLUDING REMARKS

Planning inquiry cannot be the subject of prescriptions because planning is the art of recognizing tradeoffs and placing bets (Cronbach 1982). The tradeoffs have to do with the breadth of an inquiry, the time scale of the undertaking, the appeal of each rival hypothesis, the degree of control imposed on events and observers, the form the report is to take, and many other considerations (Cook & Campbell 1979). Once outright blunders in a plan for a single investigation or for a community effort have been corrected, further improvement requires giving up some desideratum. Making an investigation more reproducible, for example, narrows its scope and makes broad interpretations riskier.

The style and procedures preferred for one inquiry can be ill-suited for another topic or at another stage in the evolution of knowledge or for an investigator in different circumstances. With that caveat, I recapitulate a few preferences I have suggested: for more exploratory work, for less emphasis on the magnitude and statistical significance of "effect sizes," for more effort to record concomitant and intermediate events that help explain local variation, for more discussion of research plans and interpretations with peers having disparate backgrounds. Each piece of research should be an effort to give an unimpeachable and reasonably full account of events in a time, place, and context. Multiple interpretations of information already in hand will often be more instructive, at less cost, than additional data gathering. I have encouraged critical analysis of research methods and their further development, along with substantive criticism of extrapolations. To advocate pluralistic tolerance of alternative accounts is in no way to advocate tendermindedness.

I have expressed doubt about professional ideals that would keep social "sciences" walled off from each other and from "nonscientific" attempts to observe, describe, and explain. We can enthusiastically endorse "Do your damnedest with your mind" without claiming that social science is the only profession approaching human affairs in that way. To grapple with loosely bounded problems—that is, with almost any problem that connects up with community concerns—we need to blur lines that separate "values" from "facts," "humanities" from "sciences," and "quantitative" from "qualitative" or "applied" from "basic" research (cf. Almond & Genco 1977; Geertz 1983; and Toulmin 1977).

If such suggestions are followed, will social knowledge "progress"? My answer is an emphatic "Yes, but. . . ." The progress will not be toward the theory of which Saturnians dream. It will be the kind of progress seen in architecture, music, and philosophy. Each of these fields has become richer in each century, the contributions of the past remaining a resource for the present. We are better off for having Descartes and Kant, Beethoven and Bartok, Piranesi and Le Corbusier. We do not store up truths or laws. What social scientists mostly harvest are additional concepts and inquiry skills, along with careful records of events observed. Rather than disparaging such inquiry as unproductive, we should cherish its power to nourish the culture. Mary Hesse put it nicely: "What progresses is the ability to use science to *learn* the environment. That learning is ever to be done afresh, day by day and generation by generation" (1978, 4; emphasis added).

Notes

1. My retelling of the legend, intended to be provocative as well as evocative, is not an entirely fair representation of the view of any philosopher living, dead, or present at this conference. In treating social inquiry, I echo many writers, notably Gergen, Meehl, Putnam, and Toulmin. I cannot hope that my arguments will be endorsed by all those I borrow from. Denis Phillips heads the list of Stanford friends to whom I am indebted for supportive suggestions and timely reproof.

2. Insofar as the paper reflected accurately the prevailing philosophy, Meehl deserves the credit. I was senior author only because Meehl wanted to encourage his student in that way. Although the metatheory of science has been greatly enriched since 1955, Meehl and I believe that the 1955 argument would stand, after some softening of language to recognize changes in rationalist thinking (see Glymour 1980a, and the appended discussion; Cronbach 1985). The more important question is whether our proximate goal should be to produce elaborated arguments of the kind to which the rationalists' criteria apply (Toulmin 1977).

3. My account confabulates Pennock's early studies on lighting with the later studies of rest pauses and incentives. The only public report of Pennock's work appears to have been that of Roethlisberger and Dickson.

References

Almond, G. A., and Genco, S. J. 1977. Clouds, clocks, and the study of politics. *World Politics* 29: 489–522.

Bramel, D., and Friend, R. 1981. Hawthorne, the myth of the docile worker, and class bias in psychology. *American Psychologist* 36: 867–78.

———. 1982. More Harvard humbug. *American Psychologist* 37: 1399–1401.

Brewer, M., and Collins, B., eds. 1982. *Scientific inquiry and the social sciences.* San Francisco: Jossey-Bass.

Brownell, W. A., and Moser, H. E. 1949. *Meaningful versus mechanical learning: A study in Grade III subtraction.* Duke University Research Studies in Education no. 8. Durham, N.C.: Duke University Press.

Campbell, D. T. 1975. On the conflicts between biological and social evolution and between psychology and moral tradition. *American Psychologist* 30: 1103–1126.

Cohen, P. 1982. To be or not to be: Control and balancing of Type I and Type II error. *Evaluation and Program Planning* 5: 247–54.

Coleman, J. S.; Hoffer, T.; and Kilgore, S. 1982. *High school achievement: Public, Catholic, and private schools compared.* New York: Basic Books.

Cook, T. D., and Campbell, D. T. 1979. *Quasi-experimentation: Design and analysis issues for field settings.* Chicago: Rand McNally.

Cronbach, L. J. 1982. *Designing evaluations of educational and social programs.* San Francisco: Jossey-Bass.

———. 1985. Construct validity after thirty years. Paper presented at the symposium "Intelligence: Measurement, Theory and Public Policy," Urbana, Illinois, 1 May.

Cronbach, L. J., and Meehl, P. E. 1955. Construct validity in psychological tests. *Psychological Bulletin* 52: 281–302.

Cronbach, L. J., and Webb, N. 1975. Between-class and within-class effects in a reported Aptitude x Treatment interaction: Reanalysis of a study by G. L. Anderson. *Journal of Educational Psychology* 67: 717–24.

Edwards, A. L., and Cronbach, L. J. 1952. Experimental design for research in psychotherapy. *Journal of Clinical Psychology* 8: 51–59.

Estes, W. K. 1956. The problem of inference from curves based on group data. *Psychological Bulletin* 53: 134–40.

Fisher, R. A. 1920. Studies in crop variation. *Journal of Agricultural Science* 11: 107–35.

Fiske, D. W. 1974. The limits of the conventional science of personality. *Journal of Personality* 42: 1–11.

Geertz, C. 1983. *Local knowledge.* New York: Basic Books.

Gergen, K. J. 1982. *Toward transformation in social knowledge.* New York: Springer-Verlag.

Glymour, C. 1980a. The good theories do. In *Construct validity in psychological measurement,* ed. A. P. Maslow and R. H. McKillip. Princeton: Educational Testing Service.

———. 1980b. *Theory and evidence.* Princeton: Princeton University Press.

Hatano, G., and Osawa, K. 1983. Digit memory of experts in abacus-derived mental computation: A further support for the "mental abacus" model. Paper presented to American Educational Research Association.

Hesse, M. 1978. Theory and value in the social sciences. In *Action and interpretation: Studies in the philosophy of the social sciences,* ed. C. Hookway and P. Pettit. Cambridge: Cambridge University Press.

James, T., and Levin, H. M., eds. 1983. *Public dollars for private schools: The case of tuition tax credits.* Philadelphia: Temple University Press.

Jones, M. B., and Fennell, R. S., III. 1965. Runway performance in two strains of rats. *Quarterly Journal of the Florida Academy of Sciences* 28: 289–96.

Kasschau, R. A., and Cofer, C. E., eds. 1981. *Psychology's second century: Enduring issues.* New York: Praeger.

Klein, L. R. 1983. Some laws of economics. *Bulletin of the American Academy of Arts and Sciences* 36: 21–45.

Kruskal, W. K., ed. 1982. *The future of the social sciences.* Chicago: University of Chicago Press.

Lakatos, I. 1978. *The methodology of scientific research programmes.* Ed. J. Worrall and G. Currie. Cambridge: Cambridge University Press.

Lindblom, C. E., and Cohen, D. K. 1979. *Usable knowledge.* New Haven: Yale University Press.

Mackie, J. L. 1974. *The cement of the universe: A study of causation.* Oxford: Clarendon Press.

Manicas, P. T. 1982. The human sciences: A radical separation of psychology and the social sciences. In *Explaining human behavior: Consciousness, human action, and social structure,* ed. P. F. Secord. Beverly Hills: Sage.

Meehl, P. E. 1978. Theoretical risks and tabular asterisks: Sir Karl, Sir Ronald, and the slow progress of soft psychology. *Journal of Consulting and Clinical Psychology* 46: 806–34.

Merton, R. K. 1975. Structural analysis in sociology. In *Approaches to the study of social structure,* ed. P. M. Blau. New York: Free Press.

Mook, D. G. 1983. In defense of external invalidity. *American Psychologist* 38: 379–87.

Murray, H. A. 1962. The personality and career of Satan. *Journal of Social Issues* 28: 36–54.

Putnam, H. 1978. *Meaning and the moral sciences.* London: Routledge and Kegan Paul.

Roethlisberger, F. J., and Dickson, W. J. 1939. *Management and the worker.* New York: Wiley.

Rorer, L. G., and Widiger, T. A. 1983. Personality structure and assessment. *Annual Review of Psychology* 34: 431–63.

Simon, H. A. 1979. *Models of thought.* New Haven: Yale University Press.

Sonnenfeld, J. 1982. Clarifying critical confusion in the Hawthorne hysteria. *American Psychologist* 37: 1397–99.

Thorngate, W. 1976. Possible limits on a science of social behavior. In *Social psychology in transition,* ed. L. H. Strickland et al. New York: Plenum.

Toulmin, S. 1972. *Human understanding.* Princeton: Princeton University Press.

———. 1977. From form to function: Philosophy and history of science in the 1950s and now. *Daedalus* 106: 143–62.

———. 1981. Evolution, adaptation, and human understanding. In *Scientific inquiry and the social sciences,* ed. M. B. Brewer and B. E. Collins, San Francisco: Jossey-Bass.

Toulmin, S., and Goodfield, J. 1965. *The discovery of time.* Chicago: University of Chicago Press.

Weiss, C. H., ed. 1977. *Using social research in public policy making.* Lexington, Mass.: D. C. Heath.

5 Science's Social System of Validity-Enhancing Collective Belief Change and the Problems of the Social Sciences

Donald T. Campbell

INTRODUCTION

The conclusions of this paper may seem old-fashioned and scientistic: There are social, psychological, and ecological requirements for being scientific that are shared by successful physical sciences and unsuccessful social sciences. The relative lack of success of the social sciences, as well as possibilities for improvement, are understandable in terms of these requirements. Yet these conclusions come from a point of view that shares most of the assumptions of the avant-garde and humanistic wings of our conference: antipositivism (if not antiscientism);[1] antifoundationalism; epistemological relativism; historicism (recognition of the historically dialectic indexicality of all scientific concepts); and the acceptance of the paradigm-laden presumptiveness of judgments of scientific progress, the theory-ladenness of scientific "facts," and the discretionary nature of theory choice.

I am self-consciously using the physical sciences as the model for the social sciences. But as I hope the following discussion of hermeneutics makes clear, I am borrowing from physics the social system of belief change, not the materialism, atomism, wholistic field theory, quantified measurement, laboratory experimentation, or mathematical theory. I leave it open as to whether or not the social science will eventually find these useful. Some of them do facilitate the social process described, but only if referentially appropriate.

I believe that there are fields in which science can be practiced but in which it could not have autonomously developed. Meteorology may be one, rainmaking by cloud seeding another, long-term ecological effects of industrial chemicals still another. This group probably also includes psychology and the social sciences. Successful science in these areas must be achieved by a cultural colonization in which the social norms and social system of science are successfully transferred. Success experiences are required to sustain such colonies.

COUNTERPOINT ON HERMENEUTICS

The concept of hermeneutics appears throughout this volume. I join those who assert the relevance of hermeneutics for the social sciences. The hermeneutic principles that attract me are those emerging from communities of scholars persisting over several generations and achieving what they regard as improved interpretations of specific texts: principles such as the hermeneutic circle (cycle, spiral), part-whole iteration, the principle of charity (assumption of the text producer's corationality), contextual coherence, extension of context, thick description, contrast indexicality, a dialectic of guess-and-criticism, and so on. Habermas identifies this tradition as "hermeneutic objectivism" and offers an antifoundationalist version that might better be called "validity-seeking hermeneutics," merging with his "hermeneutic reconstructionism" (1983, 251–61, n. 8). What I join him in rejecting is the currently fashionable hermeneutic nihilism, in which validity of interpretation is rejected as a goal. Like the nihilists, I applaud the achievement of radical interpretations, but only because I see these as the inevitably wasteful route to a potential future consensus on a more valid interpretation. The sociology of science that I attempt in what follows is hermeneutic in almost all of Habermas's senses, emphasizing intentional communicative acts and intentional interpretative efforts and presuming the rationality and communicative intent of the communicators. More clearly than Habermas, I emphasize that the physical sciences have also been hermeneutic communities, more successful for reasons of referential ecology than for reasons of method. My title for this paper could refer equally well to "scholarship's" social system of validity-enhancing belief change" as to "science's."

Hermeneutics arose out of philology, out of Homeric and classical Greek as well as biblical studies. While biblical studies currently represent a hermeneutic community successfully achieving what are perceived to be better and better interpretations, there is a sense in which Homeric studies would have been a less misleading basis. Biblical scholars of Schleiermacher's day had, in addition to the goal of interpreting the text's original meaning, the additional burden of believing that the texts were both divinely inspired and eternally relevant. Each generation of preachers used the same old texts to speak to the changing religious needs of its day. This is probably an important background motive for Bultmann's historical-ontological relativism (1956), in which the "true" interpretation differed for each generation of interpreters. From this developed a still more "sophisticated" epistemology denying the goal of truth. Of course, Bultmann and his followers have instead emphasized the changing historical, contextual, presumptive, interpretive frame unique to each generation of interpreters (paradigm-embeddedness à la Kuhn 1962). But granting this predicament, the goal of understanding the original meaning need not have been given up. This ontological relativism now dominates social scientists' and philosophers' use of hermeneutics. Paradoxically, the community of biblical translation and interpretation has continued to focus on the intended meaning in the original context. They testify to a collective experience of successful progress plausibly based upon a cumulative tradition with increasing breadth of context and range of articulated alternative interpretations.

One of the major contributions of this volume may turn out to be in helping unify the "hard" and "soft" methodologies now being recommended to the social sciences. A useful tactic may be to recognize convergences of efforts in postpositivist methodology from the hard-science camp, on the one hand, and central themes in the hermeneutic tradition on the other. For this purpose, I will extend my discussion of hermeneutics a little further, focusing on the joint rejection of the atomistic-foundationalist component of empiricism. This was the claim (implicit or explicit) that the validity of derived knowledge and theory could never be greater than the individual data upon which they were based, imputing incorrigibility to the data in the process. Let me begin with two quotations:

> A scholar is deciphering an archaic text. On first reading he gets only fragmentary hunches which he forces into a guess at the overall direction of the message. Using this, he goes over it again, decoding a bit more, deciding on plausible translations of a few words he has never encountered before. He repeats this hermeneutic cycle or spiral again and again, revising past guesses and making new ones for previously unattempted sections. If he is being successful, and has extensive enough texts to properly probe his translation hypotheses, he arrives at such a remarkable confidence that he can in places decide that the ancient scribe made a clerical error, and that he, the modern, knows better what that ancient intended than

what the ancient's written text records. I believe such things happen, and often validly so. It well illustrates this holistic dependence on fallible elements, since any part of the text could have been a clerical error. (Campbell 1977, 97–98)

Both psychology and philosophy are emerging from an epoch in which the *quest for punctiform certainty* seemed the optimal approach to knowledge. To both Pavlov and Watson, single retinal cell activations and single muscle activations seemed more certainly reidentifiable and specifiable than perceptions of objects or adaptive acts. The effort in epistemology to remove equivocality by founding knowledge on particulate sense data and the spirit of logical atomism point to the same search for certainty in particulars. These are efforts of the past, now increasingly recognized to be untenable, yet the quest for punctiform certainty is still a pervasive part of our intellectual background. A preview of the line of argument as it relates to the nostalgia for certainty through incorrigible particulars may be provided by the following analogy. Imagine the task of identifying "the same" dot of ink in two newspaper prints of the same photograph. The task is impossible if the photographs are examined by exposing only one dot at a time. It becomes more possible the larger the area of each print exposed. Insofar as any certainty in the identification of a single particle is achieved, it is because a prior identification of the whole has been achieved. Rather than the identification of the whole being achieved through the firm establishment of particles, the reverse is the case, the complex being more certainly known than the elements, neither, of course, being known incorrigibly. (Campbell 1966, 82)

My own most concrete success in a now-seen-to-be-hermeneutic enterprise (Campbell 1964) comes from work on cultural differences in optical illusions (Segall, Campbell & Herskovits 1966). In this study, the comprehension checks were formally similar to the measurement items, differing only in degree. In the language of the title, there was no formal way of "distinguishing differences in perception from failures of communication." Yet using what I now recognize as the hermeneutic principle of charity, assuming a basic human similarity, we not only demonstrated cultural differences in perception but also measured their direction and extent. Had the differences been too large, we could not have distinguished them from failures of communication. Hollis (1967) uses a remarkably similar argument for the problem of cross-cultural understanding of ritual language.

RELATIVIST SOCIOLOGY OF SCIENCE

Any theory of how science could produce beliefs of improved "truth," or competence in reference, will have to be sociological in considerable part and will have to be epistemologically relativistic. Both scientific method and the moral cultures of scientific communities will have to be seen as products of cultural evolution, rather than (or in addition to) being the products of an exercise in pure logic. Scientific method and the "proper" norms of science will have to be seen as empirically based, empirically winnowed, quasi-scientific hypotheses; that is, they have the status of contingent truths rather than (or in addition to being) analytic truths. Even if there were analytically certain rules for the transmission of validity from beliefs to derived beliefs, they could only be discovered by a biological trial and error of genes controlling brain development or by a comparably presumptive, non-clairvoyant winnowing of individual and socially transmitted hunches. The persisting debates over what it is to be rational or logical support such a view. Recognizing that both the primary and secondary qualities are "constructed by the brain/mind" does not ipso facto render them invalid if natural selection has operated to give us a well-winnowed subset of many competing constructions (Campbell 1974, 1984). Similarly, to see the explicit rules and implicit norms of science as socially constructed processes does not preclude their validity. To hypothesize their validity, however, requires the specification of the winnowing processes operating over them and competing social constructions in such a manner as to plausibly select for validity.

An impressive new movement has been started by the vigorous young school of sociologists of science centered in Britain and Western Europe designated by Bloor (1976) and Barnes (Barnes & Bloor 1982) as "the strong programme" (see Shapin 1982, for a convenient review), by Collins (1981a) as the "empirical programme of relativism," and by Latour and Woolgar (1979) and Knorr-Cetina (1981) as "social constructivist." Many of the slogans of this movement are ones with which I fully agree.

1. Social-causal analyses of belief adoption, belief retention, and belief change are just as necessary and appropriate in explaining why past scientists adopted beliefs their science now regards as true as for adoptions of beliefs now regarded as false. The new relativists, as I shall call them, rightly criticize Mannheim for exempting the physical sciences and mathematics from his sociology of

knowledge and rightly criticize those sociologists of science (if any) who have found sociological analysis only appropriate for "deviant" science, exempting the "valid" changes in theory.[2]

2. The Quine-Duhem observation on the equivocality of "factual" (experimental, observational) falsifications or confirmations of theoretical predictions is an unavoidable predicament in all scientific belief change and allows for extrascientific beliefs and preferences to influence the inevitably discretionary judgments involved. No certain proof, logical or observational, is ever available or ever socially compelling.

3. In explaining why scientists in the past adopted a belief currently regarded as true, sociologists of science cannot legitimately use this "truth" of the belief as an explanation of why it was adopted. (This argument follows from the preceding point and from the acknowledgment by the scientific community that the best theories are only transiently true.)

4. Political power within the scientific community, based on prestigious professorships, journals, funding committees, placement networks, power in the larger society, and so on, often leads one scientific theory to gain or retain acceptance over equally plausible theories. Similarly, social-ideological commitments (national, political, religious, economic self-interest, etc.) often influence the discretionary choice involved in scientific belief in "facts" or theory, unconsciously if not consciously.

5. Scientists do not live up to the so-called norms of science, for example, of neutrality, objectivity, and sharing of all information.

6. When one looks closely at the laboratory culture in which beliefs about scientific facts are produced, the view of the laboratory as revealing nature in any direct way becomes less tenable the closer the inspection. Social persuasion and selection processes are involved that are grossly underrepresented in published articles, scientific text books, the popular imagery of successful science, and even practicing scientists' image of the certainty of science in general (if not of their own and competing laboratory work on problems currently in doubt).

7. Sociology of science should be pursued in union with the sociology of knowledge, not as an independent, unrelated tradition.

8. Sociology of science should focus on scientific belief and belief change, rather than relegating these to the scientists, beyond the purview of the sociologists of science.

I am ambivalent about one claim of the new relativists and disagree with another. The first is that the sociologist and anthropologist of science, like the sociologist and anthropologist of religion, should be agnostic as to the truth of the beliefs and the optimality of the belief-change system that is studied. One should not be a believer or a prejudiced disbeliever. History and current practice in both astronomy and astrology should be studied with equal trust and respect. This view is also accepted by some leading historians of science. For the scientific sociology of science, this principle exemplifies the Mertonian scientific norm of neutrality.

My own point of view on this issue is ambivalent (Campbell 1979, 1985a, 1985b). On one hand, I approve this point of view for the study of religion. On the other, I must confess to being a believer in the superiority of the social processes of science for validity-enhancing belief change to those of religion, governmental politics, and cultural evolution more generally. But I do not believe that the unique and epistemologically relevant aspects of the social processes of science have been adequately described or that "the scientific method" has been adequately formulated. Furthermore, from such fragments of theory of science as I have, I judge that the development of this social theory of science will be furthered by vigorous disagreements with agnostic sociologists of science. Harry Collins provides a convenient example. In a triumphant summary of the premises, achievements, and conclusions of his school, he asserts that "the natural world has a small or non-existent role in the construction of scientific knowledge" (1981a, 3). In his own empirical work, he has documented how far from the ideal of replication and cross-validation the actual practice of science is. Such studies discipline my own efforts at a social theory of scientific competence by challenging the dependence I and my predecessors place upon the successful replication of experiments.

Moreover, I feel that sociologists of science who are active disbelievers in science (who endorse the nonexistent role in Collins's statement above) can play an important part in disciplining a competent theory of scientific competence if, despite competing perspectives, they remain in detailed communication with each other, their refutational effort accompanied by acceptance of the hermeneutic "principle of charity": "They too are intelligent dedicated scholars like us, dedicated to not deceiving themselves or others." If some of them, such as Feyerabend (1975), affect the clown's role, it is only in the service of a more profound honesty, insight, and understanding. If they deny the goal of "truth," it is only because of the higher truth that no such goal is possible.[3]

With almost complete unanimity (for a partial exception, see

Gieryn 1982, 1983), my friends in the new sociology of science reject the task of elaborating the "epistemologically relevant internalist theory of science" ("ERISS," Campbell 1981) that I have on my agenda. What I see as needed are speculations, mutual criticisms, and theory-probing investigations on what sort of social system of belief communication among scientists would optimally foster belief change to adequately reflect the referents of the belief were there to exist an external world independent (or partially independent) of such beliefs. Epistemological relativists who stop short of ontological nihilism should be able to speculate and assemble arguments on this issue. Ontological nihilism as a systematic position would seem to undermine curiosity and the motivation to persuade others of the errors in their beliefs. But the new relativists are too agnostic (or too busy and successful in their present undertakings) to undertake the ERISS agenda (Campbell 1981). Their agnosticism extends to an atheoretical positivist asceticism that allows no speculation about unobservables.

For those of us coming from the naturalistic epistemology tradition, those of us still concerned with a theory of science that shares an agenda with the older philosophy of science, those of us fascinated by past successes of science, the ERISS agenda seems to me unavoidable. We must meet the challenge of the relativists by making it plausible that some version of the social processes of past (and perhaps current) science would lead to validity-enhancing belief change. In doing so, we must take seriously what sociology and anthropology have taught us about belief-transmitting communities of all types and what sociologists of knowledge and science have taught us about the more specialized and dependent subgroups and institutions identified as scientific.

To refer back to the quote from Collins above, those sociologists of science who tentatively judge that "the natural world has [at least] a small . . . role in the construction of scientific knowledge" need sociological (as well as psychological) explanations as to how that partial role comes about. Scientific knowledge is a social construction by scientists, even in those aspects where the natural world plays a role in the construction. Once one has begun on this sociology, it does not increase the ontological assumptions to ask under what social system of belief communication and target characteristics the role of the natural world would be maximized. Such theory will be fallible, corrigible, presumptive, and contingent, as all science is. None the less, most postpositivists in the theory of science have already made the assumptions required. It is on the basis of fragments of such a theory that I hope to compare the physical and social sciences.

Here is a more specific illustration in a setting already used by the new sociologists of science: MacKenzie and Barnes (1975, 1979) have described how the Batesonian-Mendelians wrested dominance within the biological community in Britain from the Galtonian-Pearsonians around 1910. Their explanation is primarily in terms of ideological class and clique membership in the larger society. They mention many instances of mutual scientific criticism in correspondence, public presentations, and publications, but they do not explicate the sociology of these processes or raise the question of the role of social communication about purported observations of specimens and experiments in the social persuasion process. Without denying the relevance in many theory preferences of membership in the larger community's competing cliques, I feel we also need an internalist sociology of scientific belief change. Such a sociology would focus more on the case of Darbishire, assistant and student of the influential Professor Weldon, Pearson's major ally (MacKenzie & Barnes 1975; see also Provine 1971). After humiliating cross-examination by Bateson about his data, Darbishire converted to the still relatively powerless Mendelian position against all self-interest (unless an estimate as to the eventual "correctness" of theory is credited with providing an element of self-interest to the belief-exchange/belief-change processes). What sociological conditions permitted this humiliation? Why were the upstart Mendelians allowed to participate? Was a partial toleration of minority points of view a factor? What strange sociology lay behind Darbishire's presentation of data that could be interpreted as showing recessive factors and F_2 variability greater than F_1? (For F_2 "segregation" and the phenomena explicable by dominant and recessive traits, the Pearsonian model offered no explanation.) Was it mere stupidity or social norms that kept him from editing his data so as to eliminate this discrepant outcome? (Probably a rationalizable discarding of only 5 or 10 cases out of his possibly 100 or so F_2's would have done it.) What sociology and psychology led him to be influenced by the unpredicted outcome of his own research? Was the socially evolved ritual of experimentation something more than the sanctification of an already determined belief? Did his social indoctrination within the larger society and within science provide some role for the outcome of the experiment in belief change, in spite of the indubitable availability of Quine-Duhem cop-outs?

The case of another convert (reported on by Provine 1971) provides an interesting contrast. In the chaotic setting of American universities of the time, T. H. Morgan made an impressive early career as an anti-Mendelian. There were no dominant theorists to whom he needed to defer for the sake of his career. Then he became a vigorous pro-Mendelian, a move that in no way jeopardized his prestige or tenure. Indeed, it turned out to be a very opportune move in terms of salary, influence, and fame. But it was not opportunistic in terms of the contemporary scientific establishment and its beliefs. Given, however, a social system employing experimental replication in its persuasion process, the F_2 variability that he found in his early research may well have convinced him that it was a dependable phenomenon that he could count on others replicating, and thus it could contribute to a self-serving career of intellectual leadership, which he would be denied if he persisted in anti-Mendelian arguments. (A more complete constructivist social psychology of science will also eventually include the joys of "discovery" and the gratification of assertions believed to be "true.")

Nils Roll-Hansen (1983) has provided an important reanalysis of MacKenzie and Barnes's presentation of the victory of Mendelism in terms of a rationalist sociology of scientific knowledge. He concludes that Pearson's personal enmities and overemotional commitment to continuous variation and no unobserved entities blinded him to the facts and arguments of the Mendelians that were sufficient to convert the younger biometricians. Pearson's behavior represented a distinct deviation from the current norms of science. My own analysis does not overlap Roll-Hansen's but is one with which he would probably concur.[4]

While I welcome Roll-Hansen's contribution, I do not want to identify myself with it. For one reason, I am fully committed to epistemological relativism. For another, my position is "rationalist" only if the competence-enhancing processes of mutation and natural selection, or avoidance conditioning in animals, can be regarded as "rational." Rather than focusing the issue on rationalism versus relativism, I prefer to hinge it on hypothetical ontological realism versus positivist antirealism, which in extreme form becomes ontological nihilism. Roll-Hansen, while accepting much of the relativists' contribution, concludes, "It is the general claims about scientific knowledge as a product of 'social construction' that I find unreasonable and lacking in evidence" (1983, 511). In contrast, I identify my own position as completely "constructivist" and go on to posit fallibly that to some degree the social winnowing processes characterizing science lead to the selective propagation of those few social constructions that refer more competently to their presumed ontological referents. I prefer to let rest the question whether belief-change processes that supposedly provide an opportunity for Nature herself to contribute to the differential retention of some social constructions are to be regarded as "rational."

In Karen Knorr-Cetina's *The Manufacture of Knowledge* (1981), as in Latour and Woolgar's *Laboratory Life: The Social Construction of Scientific Facts* (1979), the production of scientific belief assertions or truth claims is shown by participant observation and ethnographic research to be a process in which order is imposed upon a chaotic welter of inconsistent and inconclusive observations through quasi-conspiratorial social negotiations. Thus when life in the scientific laboratory is examined in detail, the factual proof that might be expected never appears. Ambiguity, equivocality, and discretionary judgment pervade. A point at which Nature intrudes and says yes or no to theory is never encountered. This research experience increases doubts about the reputed objectivity of science.

Just as a study of the microprocesses of vision failed to encounter dependable truth-transmitting links and thus led to a revival of skepticism in seventeenth-century epistemology, so too an examination of the social microprocesses of science leads to a skepticism as to how it can be a source of competent belief. For scientific beliefs, validity must come from the contribution of the referent of belief to the selection processes (in addition to, or in spite of, all the other belief-selection processes). The case studies of Latour and Woolgar and also Knorr-Cetina were done in applied biology laboratory cultures dominated by the experimentalists' distrust of "the theorist." To reconcile their reports with the possibility of Nature herself participating in the belief selection, one might attend to the hundred or so instances reported (by implication, a sampling from thousands) in which ideas, procedures, and strategies are proposed and rejected because they "won't work." This not-working is often decided by thought and argument and often by laboratory efforts. Some of the rejections no doubt involve blind social conformity to locally preferred belief, but probably only a small proportion can be so dismissed. We need an expanded, still more "microprocess," sociology of idea winnowing.

While the main line sociology of science in the United States is much less focused on belief change than are the new relativists, a great deal of it is epistemologically relevant. Zuckerman's "Deviant

Behavior and Social Control in Science" (1977) directly addresses the problem raised by Hull's sociobiology of scientists, (1978) that is, the social system explanation of how some degree of mutual trust and honesty among scientists is possible. Merton and Gieryn (1982) argue that the threat of the loss of public support by a profession can lead to intraprofessional monitoring for honesty. Merton's analyses (1973) of the norms of science and of the reward systems of science are all relevant. There are also a considerable number of philosophers who have undertaken the beginnings of similar ventures. My own premature fragments offered here are not to be taken as representing this literature (see Campbell 1985b for references).

Disputatious Communities of "Truth" Seekers

The title of this section denotes one sociological feature of scientific belief exchanges. I use it to introduce my version of the ideology of the scientific revolution. However, I have yet to integrate it with the history of the scientific revolution or with Habermas's concept of an ideal speech community, with which it probably has considerable communality (Habermas 1970a, 1970b; McCarthy 1973).

The ideology of science was and is explicitly antiauthoritarian, antitraditional, antirevelational, and individualistic. Truth is yet to be revealed. Old beliefs are to be doubted until they have been reconfirmed by the methods of the new science. Persuasion is to be limited to egalitarian means, potentially accessible to all, that is, to visual and logical demonstrations (note how much of proof in Euclid is based upon dependably shareable visual judgments). The community of scientists is to stay together in focused disputation, attending to each others' arguments and illustrations, mutually monitoring and keeping each other honest until some working consensus emerges (but conformity of belief per se is rejected as an acceptable goal). Note how the ideology explicitly rejects the normal social tendency to split up into like-minded groups on specific scientific beliefs, but at the same time it requires a like-mindedness on the social norms of the shared inquiry. Sociologically, this is a difficult ideology to put into practice. Merton (1973) has described the requirement as "organized skepticism." Both features of the term are required, yet "organized" and "skepticism" are inherently at odds. Societal and institutional settings in which organized skepticism can be approximated are rare and unstable. Nonetheless, it may be regarded as a viable sociological thesis about a system of belief change that might, were it to exist, improve beliefs about the physical world (including the not-directly-observable physical world).

In making this assertion, I am invoking the "historically dialectic indexicality" (Campbell 1982) of ideological statements on the issue of respect for tradition. Variation, selection, and retention are all three necessary for any fit-increasing process, and variation is at the expense of retention (see, e.g., Campbell 1974a, 1974b). To so stress variation and selection and neglect retention in the official ideology would be adaptive only if, at a particular historical period, retention were grossly overemphasized in the general cultural ideology and practice. At the time of the scientific revolution, retention had gotten entirely out of hand insofar as beliefs about unobservable physical processes and competence in negotiating with the physical world were concerned.[5] An antitraditional counteremphasis was adaptive at that time, as it still is for much of science, as long as it does not jeopardize a tradition-conserving practice within the domains of scientific belief (there the 1 to 99 doubt/trust ratio must hold and must include ordinary beliefs about observables [Campbell 1977, 1978]). With such plausible apologies for aspects that in the seventeenth century did not need underscoring, I believe we should seriously consider the ideology of the scientific revolution as a useful, albeit contingent, thesis in an epistemologically relevant sociology of science.

From my perspective, the ideology and norms of science are not clearly distinguished from "scientific method." Scientific method is also to be seen as a product of cultural-evolutionary process on the part of a bounded belief-transmitting subsociety of many generations. With Feyerabend (1975), I would agree that new criteria of method are developed as new choices provoke new arguments. Like religious commandments, the "rules" may be mutually incompatible in the sense that if any one were to be followed with complete loyalty, it would interfere with compliance with the others. Each is dialectically and historically indexical, a shorthand interpretable only against a background of prior and current norms and practices. While historically both methods and ideology have fed on concrete successes, it is convenient to regard the ideology and practice of cooperative truth seeking as coming first and method as a rationalized summary of successful usage in the community. This is more obviously so for the hermeneutic methods, but I believe it also holds for Mill's canons of cause and Fisher's analysis of variance.

Visual Demonstration and Assent to Facts

Just as Stegmuller (1976) in his formalization of Kuhn revives a version of theories being checked against facts-laden-with-other-theories, so I believe sociology of science will find some version of the fact/explanation or fact/theory distinction essential. In the paradigmatic instance, the "facts" are visually supported beliefs shared by the community and visual demonstrations introduced in a persuasive process. In the early stages of physics, chemistry, and experimental biology, the terms "demonstration" and "experiment" have much the same referent. I believe the persuasive role of demonstrations to fellow scientists (and initially to lay audiences) provides a more important connotation than "experiment" for understanding the social grounding of scientific belief, even though demonstrations are minimally practiced in current experimental science. "Facts" were originally theoretical inferences supported by processes built into the nervous system by both natural selection and learning—ontological assumptions built into neural information-processing channels.[6] At a more mature stage, facts may be microtheories no longer controversial within the scientific community.

Referential Ecology

A successful science has to be able to achieve assent on some considerable store of agreed-upon facts (many implicit) and has to be able to demonstrate new facts frequently. The persistent difficulty of the social sciences in achieving agreement upon facts is certainly a major source of its failure to achieve scientific status. Much of this is a referential-ecology predicament that is unavoidable since it is intrinsic to social science topics. Some of the problem, however, is a larger societal ecology-of-support issue. Were social scientists to limit their work to topics on which factual assent could be readily achieved, it might be that society would not support their research, nor students attend lectures limited to their findings, because of their banality. This needs thorough exploration. But some of the fact-assent problems might be alleviated through structural and ideological changes in the social science community, in publication practices, reward systems, funding priorities, and the like.

Replicability of Fact

A crucial part of the egalitarian, antiauthoritarian ideology of the seventeenth-century "new science" was the ideal that each member of the scientific community could replicate a demonstration for himself. (Whether or not we end up regarding experimental alchemy as protochemistry, we must recognize that its ideology of secrecy was an anathema to scientific exchange.) Each scientist was to be allowed to inspect the apparatus and try out the shared recipe. Collins's sociological studies showing the absence of replication in current physics (1975, 1981b) are to be taken very seriously. Nonetheless, the early study of electricity will show hundreds of Leyden jars, Voltaic piles, and static electricity wheels generating sparks in hundreds of labs, almost none reported in publication (in that sense they are replication or teaching and not "research") but playing an overwhelming role in the social persuasion process. A healthy community of truth seekers can flourish where such replication is possible. It becomes precarious where it is not. Those undergraduate chemistry laboratories in which students must fake their results to meet the course requirements are a degenerate form of persuasive demonstration and a threat to the precarious social system of validity-enhancing belief change.

Replication is available in astronomy, in historical studies where multiple relevant sources and texts are available, and is an ever-present, if rare, potential in public opinion surveying. Replications can be attempted, but too frequently fail, in the most exciting fringes of experimental social psychology (a referential-ecology problem, at least in part). Perhaps as a result, social psychology has the custom (atypical of successful science) of trusting a single dramatic study in going on to the next experiment without explicit or implicit replication. The effort and cost of replications within a social system that regards them as unpublishable and of low prestige contribute to their absence. The lack of replications greatly weakens the essential social control on opportunistic selection from proliferated small-sample studies, on overediting of data to achieve a publishable paper, or on partial faking of data. Thus experimental social psychology lacks the social control that exists in those sciences in which replication is feasible and regularly succeeds (Campbell 1979).

In general, the absence of the norms and practices of replication and of the possibility of replication for historical or cost reasons are major problems for the social sciences. From the standpoint of an epistemologically relevant sociology of science, this absence makes it theoretically predictable that the social disciplines will make little progress. Can planned changes in science policy (in universities, journals, professional associations, and funding agencies) change the situation?

The achievements of disputatious communities in the fields of history and hermeneutics have been at the level of facts, of historically and contextually singular facts (including those about historically specific "meanings" and theory-laden facts involving culturally shared theories of human nature). Moreover, the scrupulous mutual monitoring of such communities in the humanities has often led to an explicit distrust of theory because theory is seen as a source of distortion and disregard of facts. Historians have used Spengler, Teggart, and Toynbee as bad examples in teaching the evils of theoretical pretensions. The Boasian anthropologists have used Bastian, Spencer, Lang, Tyler, Frazer, and Westermarck for the same purpose.

The Ecology of Explanations and Anticipations of Facts

It is our ontological predicament that the events and stabilities we come to know lie at the intersection of innumerable forces, restraints, and causal processes, most of them unmapped at any given stage. This is true both of the biological evolution of sensing and predictive machinery and of culture or science. The survival value of perception and memory lies in those ecologies in which the highest order interactions of all of the variables are not significant, in which *ceteris* are approximately *paribus*. Similarly, the growth of science has required, not only the accumulation of facts, but also the achievement of successful approximative theory relating facts to facts. This is most possible in those ecologies where powerful, oversimplified *ceteris paribus* laws can be invented (that they "work" makes this subset of inventions also discoveries) to sustain the group's feeling of progress until the shared corpus permits more complex theories with more detailed explanations and increased precision of prediction.

Success in this regard must often be a matter of the referential ecology. Take, for example, the attitude-change research epitomized by dissonance theory in experimental social psychology. In most respects, the participants acted correctly in terms of my tentative sociology of successful science. The generally recognized collective fatigue and search for other models (documented by Gergen 1982) was in my judgment due to referential ecology. Major effects were replicated far beyond chance, but unevenly and with no emergence of dependable laws as to why and when. Some critics I respect believe that the waning interest was due to faint-heartedness, boredom, and careerist topic changes and that we now have for dissonance theory dependable interaction laws quite sufficient to support a major scientific edifice. But these loyalists do not agree on which dependable laws result.

Degrees of Freedom and Historical/Contextual Uniqueness

Classic theories of physics and chemistry sought laws in which historical date and provincial location could be disregarded. Whether or not physics can ever quite achieve this, the biological and social sciences are much less likely to be able to do so and if they did would be shifting to a different set of scientific puzzles than they have at present undertaken (cf. Cronbach, chap. 4, this volume). This difference in referential ecology rightly motivates social science methodologists and metatheorists to be wary of borrowing uncritically a theory of science based solely on the physical sciences. The methods of the humanities appropriately become attractive alternatives to be considered. But it is intrinsic to understanding (or interpretation, explanation, prediction, or theory) that the principles invoked are to some extent transtemporal and transcontextual, however conditionally hedged. Complete situational and historical uniqueness eliminates not only theory but also any grounds for "understanding" or shared "meaning."

Insofar as the disputatious communities of scholars dispute about theory, they are likely to generate plausible rival hypotheses and to enter into arguments in which mutual persuasion becomes possible only where there exist degrees of freedom sufficient to make possible cross-validation (using that concept as a metaphor for those arguments of ad hoc-ness, undisciplined choice from innumerable equally plausible interpretations, capitalizing on chance in a Znanieckian search for a complete explanation of all details with a grab-bag of the thousands of explanatory concepts implicit in ordinary language). Such degrees of freedom can come only from attempting generalization across instances, persons, provinces, times, or the like. Of course, we do not want to accept rejection of the "one-shot case study" (as in Campbell & Stanley 1963), but instead we want to join my later recognition (Campbell 1975) of the degrees of freedom available in a case study that come from ability to check some multiple implications of a theory in that setting. Yet until we have successful cases of mutual persuasion converging upon an agreed-upon theory achieved by such methods, we should continue to regard the problem as serious.

This issue is not at all specific to the humanistic methodologies. It exists in extreme degree for quantitative economics. It seems to me that economists have made the wrong choice in focusing on national economies, where only short runs of thirty or forty "comparable" years are available, rather than on the economics of, for example, neighborhood laundries, where degrees of freedom for testing hypotheses on not-yet-used samples abound.

Eliminating Rival Hypotheses through Discretionary Ramification Extinction

The social crux of science, so it seems to me, is the ability to render implausible rival hypotheses. This focus, exemplified in the quasi-experimental tradition (Campbell & Stanley 1963; Cook & Campbell 1979), seems to me now more central than experimental isolation or experimental control. Insulated laboratory walls, controlled atmospheres, and lead shielding are all secondary and historically specific means for rendering implausible the rival hypotheses that the current generation of disputative colleagues have effectively raised. Randomized assignment to treatments does not prove the hypothesis under test, nor disprove rival hypotheses, but instead renders many rival hypotheses improbable. Unlike experimental isolation in which explicit rival hypotheses guide the design, randomized assignment may seem to rule out a totality of unspecified rival hypotheses. But careful inspection of the degrees-of-freedom problem for multiple hypothesis testing will probably show this conclusion to be unjustified. The narrowing of experimental comparisons by specialized control groups clearly illustrates the role of the current contents of the disputatious dialogue. In early studies of the effects of specific brain-region ablations, the community regarded surgical shock as a plausible rival explanation of some effects, and thus the sham-operation control group was orthodox for a while. But soon the observed and predicted effects were so specific that surgical-shock effects became implausible, and the sham-operation control group was dropped. In contrast, in pharmaceutical research, placebo effects remain very plausible, and double-blind drug trials remain orthodox.

The Quine-Duhem equivocality of any experimental result is a very real problem for any community of scholars. It can only be resolved by discretionary judgments of plausibility. Nonetheless, scientific communities often achieve working consensus, often against the interests of the established and powerful. The central mode of argument involved is closer to the hermeneutic methods than to some idealizations of scientific certainty. The strategy of trusting most of the fabric of corrigible benefits while you challenge and revise a few (the 1 to 99 doubt/trust ratio) is central. Within that general strategy, ramification extinction of rival hypotheses is ubiquitous. Each of the Quine-Duhem type alternatives not only provides an explanation of the fact in focus but also makes many other predictions. When the competing persuaders make them explicit and follow them up, these other implications often turn out to greatly reduce the plausibility of the rivals and lead even the most committed doubters to adopt the new theory. It was thus (as Moyer 1979 has so well described) that the British community of astronomers and physicists changed between 1915 and 1925 from overwhelming faith in Newtonian gravitational theory to complete acceptance of general relativity, prodded by their 1919 eclipse observations and the ensuing several years of debate. Something similar is described by Clausner and Shimony (1978) for ten years of testing of Bell's theorem. Each particular experiment was flawed, but through ramification extinction of the alternative explanations these flaws permitted, even the hidden-variable theorists who motivated the experiments are for the most part convinced that such theories are ruled out by the experimental outcomes.

Insulation of the Social System of Science from that of the Larger Society

Thomas Kuhn says of the physical sciences that

> there are no other professional communities in which individual creative work is so exclusively addressed to and evaluated by other members of the profession. The most esoteric of poets or the most abstract of theologians is far more concerned than the scientist with lay approbation of his creative work, though he may be even less concerned with approbation in general. That difference proves consequential. Just because he is working only for an audience of colleagues, an audience that shares his own values and beliefs, the scientist can take a single set of standards for granted. He need not worry about what some other group or school will think and can therefore dispose of one problem and get on to the next more quickly than those who work for a more heterodox group. Even more important, the insulation of the scientific community from society permits the individual scientist to concentrate his attention upon problems that he has good reason to believe he will be able to solve. Unlike the engineer, and many doctors, and most the-

ologians, the scientist need not choose problems because they urgently need solution and without regard for the tools available to solve them. In this respect, also, the *contrast between natural scientists and many social scientists proves instructive. The latter often tend, as the former almost never do, to defend their choice of a research problem*—e.g., the effects of racial discrimination or the causes of the business cycle—*chiefly in terms of the social importance of achieving a solution. Which group would one then expect to solve problems at a more rapid rate?* (Kuhn [1962] 1970, 164; emphasis added)

Since scientists have to live in the larger society and are supported by it in their scientific activity, it becomes probable that science works best on beliefs about which powerful economic, political, and religious authorities are indifferent (Ravetz 1971). Thus static electricity (rubbing cats' fur on amber) and magnetism were optimal foci of scientific growth. However, it follows from the psychology of discretionary judgment that visual demonstrations vary greatly in clarity and persuasiveness, and those produced in research on magnetic and static electricity were often dramatically convincing. If convincing enough, demonstrations can even overcome political relevance. For example, the successful predictions of lunar and solar eclipses have historically been so compelling that demonstrable competence in this regard led Chinese emperors to replace their well-entrenched court astronomers (despite their political importance in public auguries of royal fate) with powerless Italian astronomers (Sivin 1980, 25–26). But the combination of perceptually unclear demonstrations with highly important political beliefs, such as is found in the applied social sciences, is on these a priori theoretical considerations unlikely to produce belief change in the direction of increased competence of reference (for a more detailed and less pessimistic analysis, see Campbell 1984a).

Critical Mass and Success Experiences

There are sociological requirements that must be met for sustaining communities of truth-seeking belief exchangers. A critical mass and the appearance of progress (collective success experiences) are among them. In the natural sciences, fad phenomena in the choice of problems to work on, with a concomitant enthusiasm and intensity of informal communications, are characteristic. For focal problems, these mobilized concentrations of effort supply the critical mass, mutual monitoring, cross-validation, and sometimes sustained perceptions of progress. Without perceived breakthroughs into further problem areas, interest dwindles and experimental energy becomes available for new perceptions of hot problems and promising techniques.

Certainly there are many areas of the social sciences that lack critical mass at the mutual monitoring level. Pressures in problem choice exist in both directions: A strong preference for working in an area with no competitors would certainly dominate were it not for the risk that fellow scientists would pay no attention. Sociology-of-science studies might well ask scholars in various fields about a specific publication "If you are wrong about this, who will notice? Who will try to check by replicating? Who will publish (or informally publicize) their disagreement? Who will let you know privately about a successful or unsuccessful replication or other data that support or weaken your position?" These studies should focus both on the level of fact and on the level of theory (a distinction that in practice can be made, even though we epistemological relativists recognize all facts as theory, or as theory-laden). Without having such studies available, let me nonetheless hazard some opinions.

There exist mutually monitoring communities in religious hermeneuties for such issues as who borrowed from whom in the New Testament gospels and the proper translation of crucial verses in the Old and New Testaments. There have in the past and may still exist such communities in Homeric scholarship. It might thus be reasonable for practitioners to claim that cumulative progress had been made.

In anthropological ethnography, no such communities exist, Lewis (1951), Bennett (1946), Holmes (1957), Freeman (1983), Firth (1983), and Brady (1983) notwithstanding. Instead, one seeks a region as yet unstudied on one's special topic and, once successfully published, may jealously try to prevent others from allegedly needless replication of one's work. The field's shortage of investigators and the genuine collective interest in describing all vanishing cultures before they disappear provide justification. Mutually monitoring communication networks seem better realized in anthropological linguistics and in the theory of the origins of city-states as tested by archaeology.

Contrast the ethnomethodology movement within sociology with the behavior-modification movement within psychology. Both are proud, self-conscious deviations from the mainstream of their disciplines. Both have social-solidarity needs that press for the inhibition of internal divisiveness, and hence for the inhibition of mutual criticism, in order to shore up intramovement morale against the neglect or attacks of the dominant paradigm. The behavior modifiers withdraw to their own journals and within them pursue vigorous internal disputation. The ethnomethodologists, on the contrary, produce isolated illustrations of their method and theory but, owing to their lack of numbers and embattled status, never disagree with each other about matters of fact. Insofar as they disagree about matters of theory, they tend toward further sectarianism and reduced communication rather than mutual monitoring. The same can be said of those social scientists practicing ethogenics in the Harré tradition and those who identify their method and theory with *Verstehen,* hermeneutics, critical-emancipatory theory, dialectical materialism, phenomenology, and symbolic interactionism (except for its atypical labeling theory). Mutual monitoring fails, not only within these movements, but to too great an extent also in their roles vis-à-vis their parent disciplines. These are all movements of great actual or potential value for mainstream social science as penetrating criticisms and suggestions for revision. But this effect can only be achieved if both the radical critics and the mainstream scholars remain within a common communication network and listen seriously to each other. Indeed, this exchange is now developing in the behavior-modification movement in relation to mainstream learning theory.

IMPLICATIONS FOR SOCIAL SCIENCE POLICY

If we had an epistemologically relevant sociology of science, and if under the guidance of that theory we had a competent study of current practice in the social sciences instead of the impressionistic sketches I have offered in the last few sections, we would have a basis for recommendations to the social science funding community. The central goal would be to establish and maintain a disputatious scholarly community for each problem area. Perhaps each grant and contract application should answer, for previous and proposed research, questions like those suggested above (e.g., "If you are wrong about this, who, if anyone, will notice?"). Given limited funds, this might lead to a decision to fund fewer problem areas more generously. Where promising developments emerge, independent participants should be funded rather than allowing one research team to maintain a monopoly.

This conference and others like it show a great enthusiasm for ethnographic, hermeneutic, participant-observer, ethnomethodological, and phenomenological approaches. This testimony is so impressive that the social science community should respond with generous funding for the application of some of these approaches to some problem areas, so that the kind of community we need is created. Such funding should avoid further extension of isolated, uncontested illustrations. Even though the epistemology of some versions of these movements deny the relevance, there should be replication efforts and sequential studies guided by rival interpretations of prior studies. I join D'Andrade (see chap. 1, this vol.) in affirming my faith that these approaches have much to offer the validity-seeking social sciences that is not precluded by their relevance for other epistemologies and goals.

Effective communication has been greatly facilitated by journals specifically dedicated to critique and rebuttal, such as *Current Anthropology* and *Behavioral and Brain Sciences*. These are expensive to run and require subsidies. It seems to me of highest priority to create many more of these journals, perhaps with narrower scopes, and some that cross disciplinary boundaries (Campbell 1969). Funding priority should be given to studies designed to help choose among well-articulated alternatives emerging from confrontations. Annual problem-centered conference series have in some areas produced similar benefits. Funds for visiting other laboratories working on the same problems are also of value.

Innovation, validation, and cumulative growth in a research tradition are intrinsically incompatible goals, in that too much of one jeopardizes the others. Thus policy advice depends upon a judgment of current balance. I judge the social sciences to have a surfeit of brilliant theories, inadequately sifted. Promising lines of growth are often abandoned because of boredom on the part of funders or scholars. But the detailed sociology of our past and current practice on which such a judgment should be based has not been done. My policy recommendations (particularly the following one) are contingent on the validity of my estimate of the current imbalance.

Funding policy should place greater stress on replication. Grant awards should specify that the central findings of the research being built upon be replicated as a part of the extension. These and other replications should be "heteromethod" insofar as theory does not specify method. Their outcomes should be published no matter how confusing. They should be made available for literature review and meta-analysis through subsidized retrieval systems (such as *Selected Documents in Psychology* and *Dissertation Abstracts*). *Psychological Abstracts* and *Sociological Abstracts* should be subsidized so that they can include abstracts of unpublished and semipublished research, including dissertations.

The sociology of science offered in this paper (see also Polanyi 1966; Campbell 1969) suggests that underdeveloped areas for science should be colonized first at the fringes that overlap thriving scientific communities. For pure science, this would be my recommendation. For applied social science, the mutual monitoring community of experts must be achieved in other ways. I have spelled out elsewhere the possibilities as I see them (Campbell 1984). I reject the one-decision/one-research model of program evaluation. For locally replicable programs, I recommend a contagious cross-validation model. For big-unit programs, I suggest more artificial efforts to achieve replication and to create a consensual validational community, for example, splitting the study into two parallel contracts and legitimizing intrastaff criticism.

CONCLUSIONS

There are social, psychological, and ecological requirements for being scientific that are shared by successful physical sciences and unsuccessful social sciences. The relative lack of success of the social sciences, as well as possibilities for improvement, are understandable in terms of these requirements.

Notes

1. In "Convergent and Discriminant Validation by the Multitrait-Multimethod Matrix" (1959), Fiske and I struck one of the first public blows in psychology against logical positivism as epitomized in the "operational definition" of theoretical terms. We were promptly scolded by logical positivists for this heresy (see Bechtoldt [1959], speaking for the philosopher Gustav Bergmann as well as himself; rebuttal by Campbell [1960]). Bechtoldt also scolded Cronbach and Meehl (1955) for giving some standing to "construct validity" as a fourth alternative to operationally defined "predictive," "concurrent," and "content" validities. However, even for construct validity, Cronbach and Meehl tried to be loyal logical positivists by asserting that the meaning of such constructs was defined by their place in a nomological net that linked them to "directly" observed, operationally defined terms. The earlier MacCorquodale and Meehl distinction (1948) between hypothetical constructs and intervening variables would have been more clearly postpositivistic had they concluded that typically all terms in all sciences were hypothetical constructs.

In contrast, in the multitrait-multimethod matrix paper, we announced that all psychological measures had to be validated against other imperfect measures, also of unknown validity. There were no foundational measures to start with. Note that we did this by claiming greater loyalty to general scientific practice and denying logical positivism's validity if used as a description of the scientific method even for the physical sciences. We did not do what most recent social science critics of positivism have done, that is, reject for personality research the physical science model of what it is to be scientific.

2. Note that as Gieryn (1982) and Roll-Hansen (1983) remind us, Merton had announced this socialization of validity-enhancing belief change as a characteristic of sociology of science beginning in the 1930s, and certainly by 1945.

3. Roll-Hansen (1983) has proposed focusing disputation on specific episodes in science as a way of alleviating the futile selective citation of differing episodes in the history of science by theorists of opposing views.

4. Readers should be warned that my analysis involves none of the research in primary sources that characterizes MacKenzie and Barnes's and Roll-Hansen's work.

5. I am indebted to Laudan (1981) for this emphasis.

6. Latour (1982) shows the current importance of visual demonstration in his studies of graphs and pictures as persuasive "inscription devices," often of a rhetorically exaggerated or overclarified nature.

References

Barnes, B., and Bloor, D. 1982. Relativism, rationality, and the sociology of knowledge. In *Rationality and relativism*, ed. M. Hollis and L. Lukes. Oxford: Blackwell.

Bechtoldt, H. P. 1959. Construct validity: A critique. *American Psychologist* 14: 201–38.

Bennett, J. W. 1946. The interpretation of pueblo culture. *Southwestern Journal of Anthropology* 2: 361–74.

Bloor, D. 1976. *Knowledge and social imagery*. London: Routledge and Kegan Paul.

Brady, I., ed. 1983. Speaking in the name of the real: Freeman and Mead on Samoa. Contributions by A. B. Weiner, T. Schwartz, L. Holmes, and B. Shore. *American Anthropologist* 85: 908–47.

Bultmann, R. K. 1956. *History and eschatology*. Edinburgh: Edinburgh University Press.

Campbell, D. T. 1960. Recommendations for APA test standards regarding construct, trait, or discriminant validity. *American Psychologist* 15: 546–53.

———. 1964. Distinguishing differences of perception from failures of communication in cross-cultural studies. In *Cross-cultural understanding: Epistemology in anthropology*, ed. F. S. C. Northrop and H. H. Livingston. New York: Harper and Row.

————. 1966. Pattern matching as an essential in distal knowing. In *The psychology of Egon Brunswik,* ed. K. R. Hammond. New York: Holt, Rinehart, and Winston.

————. 1969. Ethnocentrism of disciplines and the fish-scale model of omniscience. In *Interdisciplinary relationships in the social sciences,* ed. M. Sherif and C. W. Sherif. Chicago: Aldine.

————. 1974a. Unjustified variation and selective retention in scientific discovery. In *Studies in the philosophy of biology,* ed. F. J. Ayala and T. Dobzhansky. London: Macmillan.

————. 1974b. Evolutionary epistemology. In *The philosophy of Karl Popper,* ed. P. A. Schlipp, LaSalle, Ill.: Open Court.

————. 1975. "Degrees of freedom" and the case study. *Comparative Political Studies* 3: 178–93.

————. 1977. Descriptive epistemology: Psychological, sociological, and evolutionary. William James Lectures, Harvard University. Mimeograph.

————. 1978. Qualitative knowing in action research. In *The social contexts of method,* ed. Michael Brenner, Peter Marsh, and Marylin Brenner. London: Croom Helm.

————. 1979. A tribal model of the social system vehicle carrying scientific knowledge. *Knowledge: Creation, Diffusion, Utilization* 2: 181–201.

————. 1981. ERISS Conference. *4S Newsletter* (Society for the Social Studies of Science) 6: 24–25.

————. 1982. Experiments as arguments. *Knowledge: Creation, Diffusion, Utilization* 3: 327–37.

————. 1984. Can we be scientific in applied social science. In *Evaluation Studies Review Annual,* vol. 9, ed. Ross Conner, David G. Altman, and Christine Jackson. Beverly Hills: Sage.

————. 1985a. Science policy from a naturalistic sociological epistemology. *PSA 1984,* vol. 2. Philosophy of Science Association.

————. 1985b. Toward an epistemologically-relevant sociology of science. *Science, Technology, and Human Values* 10: 38–48.'

Campbell, D. T., and Fiske, D. W. 1959. Convergent and discriminant validation by the multitrait-multimethod matrix. *Psychological Bulletin* 65: 81–105.

Campbell, D. T., and Stanley, J. [1963] 1966. *Experimental and quasi-experimental designs for research.* Chicago: Rand McNally.

Clausner, J. I., and Shimony, A. 1978. Bell's theorem: Experimental tests and implications. *Reports on Progress in Physics,* 41: 1881–1927.

Collins, H. M. 1975. The seven sexes: A study in the sociology of a phenomenon, or the replication of experiments in physics. *Sociology* 9: 205–24.

————. 1981a. Stages in the empirical programme of relativism. *Social Studies of Science* 11: 3–10.

————. 1981b. Son of seven sexes: The social destruction of a physical phenomenon. *Social Studies of Science* 11: 33–62.

Cook, T. C., and Campbell, D. T. 1979. *Quasi-experimentation: Design and analysis for field settings.* Chicago: Rand McNally.

Cronbach, L. J., and Meehl, P. E. 1955. Construct validity in psychological tests. *Psychological Bulletin* 52: 281–302.

Feyerabend, P. K. 1975. *Against method.* London: NLB Press.

Firth, R. 1983. Review of Derek Freeman's *Margaret Mead and Samoa. RAIN* 57: 11–12.

Freeman, D. 1983. *Margaret Mead and Samoa.* Cambridge: Harvard University Press.

Gergen, K. J. 1982. *Toward transformation in social knowledge.* New York: Springer-Verlag.

Gieryn, T. F. 1982. Relativist/Constructivist programmes in the sociology of science: redundance and retreat. *Social Studies of Science* 12: 279–97.

———. 1983. Boundary-work and the demarcation of science from non-science: Strains and interests in professional ideologies of scientists. *American Sociological Review* 48: 781–95.

Habermas, J. 1970a. On systematically distorted communication. *Inquiry* 13: 205–18.

———. 1970b. Toward a theory of communicative competence. *Inquiry* 13: 360–75.

———. 1983. Interpretive social science vs. hermeneuticism. In *Social science as moral inquiry,* ed. Norma Haan, Robert N. Bellah, Paul Rabinow, and William M. Sullivan. New York: Columbia University Press.

Hollis, M. 1967. Reason and ritual. *Philosophy* 43: 231–47. Reprinted in *Rationality,* ed. Brian R. Wilson. New York: Harper and Row, Harper Torchbooks.

Holmes, L. D. 1957. The restudy of Manu'an culture: A problem in methodology. Ph.D. diss., Northwestern University.

Hull, D. L. 1978. Altruism in science: A sociobiological model of cooperative behaviour among scientists. *Animal Behaviour* 26: 685–97.

Knorr-Cetina, K. D. 1981. *The manufacture of knowledge: An essay on the constructivist and contextual nature of science.* Oxford: Pergamon.

Kuhn, T. S. 1970. *The structure of scientific revolutions.* 2d ed. Chicago: University of Chicago Press.

Latour, B. 1982. Inscription devices in science. Presentation at the meetings of the Society for the Social Studies of Science, Philadelphia, 29 October.

Latour, B., and Woolgar, S. 1979. *Laboratory life: The social construction of scientific facts.* Beverly Hills: Sage.

Laudan, L. 1981. *Science and hypothesis.* Dordrecht: D. Reidel.

Lewis, O. 1951. *Life in a Mexican village: Tepoztlan restudied.* Urbana: University of Illinois Press.

MacCorquodale, K., and Meehl, P. E. 1948. On a distinction between hypothetical constructs and intervening variables. *Psychological Review* 55: 95–107.

MacKenzie, D. A., and Barnes, B. 1975. Biometrician versus Mendelian: A controversy and its explanation (in German). *Kolner Zeitschrift fur Soziologie und Sozialpsychologie* 18: 165–96.

———. 1979. Scientific judgment: The biometry-Mendelism controversy. In *The natural order: Historical studies of scientific culture,* ed. B. Barnes and S. Shapin. Beverly Hills: Sage.

McCarthy, T. 1973. A theory of communicative competence. *Philosophy of the Social Sciences* 3: 135–56.

Merton, R. K. 1973. *The sociology of science.* Ed. N. W. Storer. Chicago: University of Chicago Press.

Merton, R. K., and Gieryn, T. F. 1982. Institutionalized altruism: The case of the professions. In *Social research and the practicing professions,* ed. R. K. Merton. Cambridge, Mass.: Abt Books.

Moyer, D. F. 1979. Revolution in science: The 1919 eclipse test of general relativity. In *On the path of Albert Einstein,* ed. Behram Kursunoglu, Arnold Perlmutter, and Linda F. Scott. New York: Plenum Press.

Polanyi, M. 1966. The message of the Hungarian revolution. *American Scholar* 35: 261–76.

Provine, W. 1971. *Origins of theoretical population genetics.* Chicago: University of Chicago Press.

Ravetz, J. R. 1971. *Scientific knowledge and its social problems.* Oxford: Clarendon Press.

Roll-Hansen, N. 1983. The death of spontaneous generation and the birth of the gene: Two case studies of relativism. *Social Studies of Science* 13: 481–519.

Segall, M. H.; Campbell, D. T.; and Herskovits, M. J. 1966. *The influence of culture on visual perception.* Indianapolis: Bobbs-Merrill.

Shapin, S. 1982. History of science and its sociological reconstructions. *History of Science* 20: 157–211.

Sivin, N. 1980. Science in China's past. In *Science in contemporary China,* ed. L. A. Orleans. Stanford: Stanford University Press.

Stegmuller, W. 1976. *The structure and dynamics of theories.* New York: Springer-Verlag.

Zuckerman, H. 1977. Deviant behavior and social control in science. In *Deviance and social change,* ed. Edward Sagarin. Sage Annual Reviews of Studies in Deviance, vol. 1. Beverly Hills: Sage.

6 Correspondence versus Autonomy in the Language of Understanding Human Action

Kenneth J. Gergen

Some years ago, I became absorbed with the problem of historicity in human action. There seemed good reason to contend that patterns of human conduct are subject to continuous alteration across time. If this assumption is justified, certain limits seemed to be placed over the capacity of the sociobehavioral sciences to accumulate knowledge in the traditional sense (Gergen 1973, 1978a, 1982). Although continued attention to this problem is surely warranted (see especially chaps. 2 and 4, this volume), it is to another related set of issues that I shall address my remarks. During the course of studying the historicity problem, I became increasingly struck with what appeared to be a very loose relationship between language and the patterns of conduct to which language ostensibly refers. Commonly we take the language of social description to stand in some roughly correspondent relationship to discriminable patterns of action. Thus, whether in science or daily life, description is assumed to be informative about actions independent of it. Yet common experience provides numerous instances in which such assumptions are contradicted. For example, an individual might be described as "intelligent," "warm," or "depressed," and all the while his bodily movements are undergoing continuous alteration. His actions are protean, elastic, multiplicitous, but the description remains static. Similar discrepancies can be discerned on the professional level. In psychoanalysis, for example, practitioners demonstrate an uncanny ability to apply a restricted descriptive vocabulary to an immense range of life patterns. Regardless of the vicissitudes of one's life trajectory, for analytic purposes, it can be characterized by a relatively narrow range of descriptors. If one turns to the psychological laboratory, one continues to find investigators capable of retaining a given theoretical account regardless of the range of data brought to bear. I can think of no psychological theory that has yet been abandoned for reasons of clear observational challenge.

The concern of this chapter, then, is the problem of the relationship between descriptive language and the world it is designed to represent. The problem is of no small consequence, for as philosophers of science have long been aware, it is primarily in the degree to which there is correspondence between theoretical language and real-world events that scientific theory acquires utility in the market of prediction and control. If scientific language bears no determinate relationship to events external to the language itself, not only does its contribution to prediction and control become problematic, but scientific theory becomes closed to improvement through observation. The hope that knowledge may be advanced through continued, systematic observation is rendered problematic. More generally, one would be moved to question the fundamental objectivity of scientific accounts. If such accounts are not grounded in observation, then what furnishes their warrant? The question is critical as it is this claim to objectivity that has furnished the chief basis for the broad authority claimed by the sciences over the past century.

It is in these many respects that early philosophers of science have been keen to establish a close relationship between language and observation. At the heart of the logical positivist movement, for example, lay the "verifiability principle of meaning"; to wit, the meaning of a proposition rests on its capacity for verification through observation. As it was argued, propositions not open to corroboration or emendation through observation are unworthy of further disputation. The problem was, however, to account for the connection between propositions and observations. Schlick (1934) argued that the meaning of single words within propositions must be established through ostensive ("pointing to") means. In his early work, Carnap (1928) proposed that thing-predicates represented "primitive ideas," thus reducing scientific propositions to reports of private experience. For Neurath (1932), propositions were to be verified though "protocol sentences," which were themselves to refer to the biological processes of perception. As all such statements are thus reducible to the language of physics, Neurath argued, there was a fundamental unity among all branches of science. From yet another vantage point, Russell (1924) proposed that objective knowledge could be reduced to sets of "atomic propositions," the truth of which would rest on isolated and discriminable facts.

Yet such attempts to establish secure and determinate relationships between words and real-world referents eventually came
under heavy attack. Were the propositions entering into the verifiability principle themselves subject to verification? If not, in what
sense were they meaningful? Propositions appear to have meaning
over and above the referential capacity of the words that make
them up. How is such meaning to be understood? Are propositions
subject to verification, or only single terms? Is verification a state of
mind, and if so, in what sense are states of mind themselves verifia-
ble? On what grounds are the basic facts to which descriptors refer
to be established? How can rules for linking predicates with particulars be constructed when the terms of the rules themselves remain
meaningless until defined by further linking rules? These and
other nettlesome questions have remained recalcitrant to a broadly
compelling solution. Today it is generally agreed that the manner
in which objectivity in meaning is achieved, along with a specification of the rules for when it is not, remains unsatisfactorily explicated (cf. Fuller 1983; Barnes 1982).

At the same time, other lines of argumentation have been
emerging, the implications of which are substantial. In each of
these cases, a significant question has been raised concerning the
relationship between word and object, or theory and evidence. In
each case, the arguments grant such substantial autonomy to theoretical discourse that major revisions seem demanded in the traditional account of science. Certain of these arguments are of
particular significance to the formulation of metatheory for the
sociobehavioral sciences. They emerge from differing (although
sometimes congenial) intellectual contexts, and their contours are
not always distinguishable. Thus I will initially attempt to bring
four of these positions into clear focus. After examining the implications of these arguments for the sciences more generally, we
can move to consider a variety of major functions to be fulfilled by
theories of human action.

THE CONTEXTUAL DEPENDENCY OF MEANING

The initial line of argument is one that has wended its way through
several philosophic debates and has subsequently had a marked
impact on microsociological thought. As we have seen from the
logical empiricist perspective, critical descriptive terms at the theoretical level should correspond to specifiable or delimited observations. The ideal situation would be one in which discrete
particulars at the level of observation would stand in a one-to-one

relationship with mathematical integers at the theoretical level. The attempt of correspondence theorists is thus to establish foundations of knowledge that are context free. That is, the linkage between theoretical terms and observations (or the objective meaning of propositions) should remain stable across varying contexts both at the theoretical and at the observational level. If context invariance is not maintained, then the potential for scientific prognostication is severely threatened; one would be unable to specify what facts would be predicted by the theory as theoretical and historical contexts were altered. The possibility for empirical test is further impugned because one would be unable to specify what observations would count as confirmations or disconfirmations of a theory across varying contexts.

Wittgenstein's *Philosophical Investigations* was one of the first significant works to challenge the possibility for context-free correspondence. As he proposed, the meaning of words (or sentences) is achieved through their use in the carrying out of various life forms. Such uses may be viewed as so many language games, each subject to its own particular rules. The precise boundaries of the rules cannot be explicated, as the terms of explication will themselves be context (or "use") dependent. "There are countless . . . different kinds of use of what we call 'symbols,' 'words,' 'sentences.' And this multiplicity is not something fixed, given once and for all; but new types of language, new language-games, as we may say, come into existence, and these become obsolete and get forgotten" (1963, 11e). Essentially this means that any scientific term derives its meaning from its context of usage, which can also include the syntactic conventions governing its use. To illustrate, in the case of psychology, a term like "aggression" derives its meaning from the many contexts in which it is employed. There are also many different contexts of usage, thus giving the term a far different meaning depending on whether one is speaking about soldiers at war, tennis players, investment policies, woodchopping, or weed growth in the spring. To specify the conditions of use in any precise way is also problematic, as the terms of specification are themselves embedded in differing word games. In effect, anything said about aggression, or any other phenomenon, cannot be cut away from the historically situated context of concept usage.

Wittgenstein's doubts concerning the capacity of language to render context-free description are extended in the work of Quine (1951, 1960). As Quine demonstrates, the attempt to define even a single word in terms of empirical referent is problematic. In partic-

ular, the contexts in which single terms are employed are apt to be
so many and varied that there is no strictly ostensive means of securing word-object identities. The term "rabbit," for example, may
figure in many different linguistic, social, and environmental contexts. As a result, it is virtually impossible to determine through
observation the truth value of propositions containing the term.
There simply is no stimulus event (or class of events) to which the
term is unambiguously wedded.

Concern with the contextual dependency of "what is true" has
also reverberated throughout the social sciences. One of the most
significant manifestations is reflected in the ethnomethodological
movement (see especially Garfinkel 1967). As ethnomethodologists
maintain, descriptive terms within both the sciences and everyday
life are fundamentally indexical; that is, their meaning is free to
vary across divergent contexts of usage. Descriptions index events
within situations and are devoid of generalized meaning. The essential defeasibility of descriptive terms is demonstrated by wide-
ranging studies of how people go about determining in various
situations what counts as a psychiatric problem or as suicide, juvenile crime, gender, states of mind, alcoholism, mental illness, or
other putative constituents of the taken-for-granted world (see
Garfinkel 1967; Atkinson 1977; Cicourel 1968; Kessler & McKenna 1978; Coulter 1979; McAndrew 1969; Scheff 1966).

When writ large, the contextualist arguments suggest that descriptive and explanatory schemas within the sciences remain mute
with respect to prediction and empirical evaluation until linked to
referents. However, rules as to how such linkages are to be constructed are generally unexplicated (and indeed there are principled impediments to establishing such rules). Thus descriptive
and explanatory constructions are fundamentally free to vary in
their empirical content or implications across context of usage. By
extension, this is to say that any behavioral theory may in principle
be applied to (used to describe or explain) virtually any human
action. The constraints over such application lie chiefly within the
social process through which contextual linkages are forged. Thus
almost any theory (Freudian, Skinnerian, social learning, role-rule,
cognitive) should be capable of absorbing all empirical outcomes so
long as there are communities of scholars capable of negotiating
the meaning of theoretical terms across divergent context.

THE SOCIAL CONSTRUCTION OF REALITY

In the preceding discussion, the semantic link between word and
object was weakened by taking into account the contextual depen-

dency of linking practices. A second threat to incorrigibility of meaning has been nurtured in different soil, namely, that of rationalist and idealist philosophy. Debate over the origin of abstract ideas has had a long and vigorous history. Empiricists such as Locke, Hume, and the Mills have argued, on the one hand, that such ideas are derived from sensory input, while on the other, rationalist/idealist thinkers such as Kant, Spinoza, Schopenhauer, and Nietzsche have demonstrated the manifold weaknesses in such a position. As they proposed in various ways, the mind functions as a generative source of ideas. In effect, the mind generates the conceptual basis for interpreting and understanding (and some will argue, perceiving) the world. The implications of this latter position for a theory of meaning, or semantic linkages, are far-reaching. To the extent that the mind furnishes the categories of understanding, there are no real-world objects of study other than those inherent within the mental makeup of persons. There are no objects save those for which there are preceding categories. The result is that semantic linkages do not derive from a conjoining of independent realms—object and category—tied through linking definitions. Rather, in the act of comprehension, object and concept are one; objects reduce to the mental a priori.

In the present century, this tradition has manifested itself in numerous ways. Several are especially pertinent to our proceedings. First, within the philosophy of science, the reduction of object to percept occurs, though in muted form, in Kuhn's influential work (1970). In his most radical moments, Kuhn raises serious doubts over the cumulativeness of scientific knowledge. Scientific anomalies are not generally viewed by Kuhn as contradictions to the assumptions of normal science. Rather, they are orthogonal to it. Thus when a new theory is articulated to render the anomalies coherent, this theory is not so much an improvement over the old as it is essentially a different theory, designed to account for different data, to ask different questions. As Kuhn argues, scientific revolutions are akin to "Gestalt shifts"; one simply sees the world through a different theoretical lens. Kuhn's closet rationalism gives way to a more complete assault in Hanson's widely credited *Patterns of Discovery* (1958). As Hanson proposes, what we take to be elementary facts (observables) are determined in significant degree by the conceptual systems we bring to bear upon them. Visual experience is a product of conceptual or theoretical invention.

> The infant and the layman can see—they are not blind. But they cannot see what the physicist sees; they are blind to what he sees.

> We may not hear that the oboe is out of tune, though this will be
> painfully obvious to the trained musician. . . . The element of the
> visitor's visual field, though identical with those of the physicist, are
> not organized for him as for the physicist; the same lines, colours,
> shapes are apprehended by both, but not in the same way. (Hanson
> 1958, 17)

Just as contextualism as a philosophic orientation is reflected in substantive inquiry.in the social sciences, the rationalist orientation has also manifested itself in a variety of important ways. Highly influential has been the social phenomenology of Alfred Schutz (1962–66). As Schutz maintained, understanding of others is predicated upon a system of preconceptualization: "I bring into each concrete situation a stock of preconstructed knowledge which includes networks of typifications of human individuals in general, typical human motivations, goals, and action patterns" (1964, 29). Thus the identification of others' actions is essentially prefigured.

For Schutz, as well as for Kuhn and Hanson, the assumption is implicit but incompletely elaborated that such prefigurations are derived from social interchange. This assumption is a pivotal one in that it enables the thorny problem of innate ideas to be avoided. The view that people bring to situations cognitive sets, frameworks, or orientations that are genetically rather than environmentally induced has had a long and rather unpleasant intellectual history. To lodge the frameworks of social understanding within social process largely insulates against the accumulated criticism. It is the social basis of the phenomenological fixing that comes to play a critical role in the broadly influential work of Berger and Luckmann (1966). As they reason, Schutz's work forms the basis for a sociology of knowledge concerned with the ways in which knowledge both emerges from and serves to order social process. The individual "internalizes" the objective order and typically employs such internalized representations to recreate the social order.

This form of social constructionism is broadly apparent in recent social psychological writings. For example, extending Schachter's labeling theory of emotions (1964) in a sophisticated and compelling way is the work of Averill (1983) on the social construction of anger. Here anger is removed from psychology as an object of study. There is no independent process to be interrogated. Rather, there are historically contingent, culturally specific constructions of emotional worlds. In a similar vein, Sabini and Silver (1982) have discussed in piquant detail the ways by which people determine what counts in social life as envy, flirtation, anger, and the like. Inquiry has also been opened on the social functions of causal accounting in human affairs (Harré 1981; Lalljee 1981; Gergen & Gergen 1982). Mummendey and her colleagues (1982) have attempted to demonstrate how aggression is not a fact in nature but a label used by people for social purposes. Similar arguments have been mounted in the case of the self (Gergen 1977). The implications of this orientation for science become more fully explicated in the work of Latour and Woolgar (1979) on the social construction of scientific facts. They undertake a close examination of the various social "microprocesses" through which biological researchers attempt to generate incorrigible facts from manifest disorder.

As we see, although the intellectual origins differ, both the contexualist and the constructionist reach similar conclusions. Social actions, as matters of common concern, owe their existence to the social process whereby meanings are generated and events indexed by these meanings. There are no independently identifiable, real-world referents to which the language of social description is cemented.

DECONSTRUCTIONISM AND THE FIGURATIVE BASIS OF HUMAN UNDERSTANDING

As we have seen, the contextualist approach emphasizes the situational dependence of meaning, while the constructionist emphasizes the social origins of meaning within situations. In both cases however, the deployment of a descriptive term is determined less by the features of the object, action, or event to be described than it is by extraneous processes. A third line of argument threatens the empirical dependence of theoretical description in an entirely different way. Rather than directly challenging the connection between theory and event, the attempt has been to demonstrate how much what is communicated about events is determined, not by the character of events themselves, but by linguistic figures or forms. To the extent that description and explanation are dependent on such figures or forms, what science tells us about the "thing in itself" is rendered suspect. Although the threat to the semantic link is thus an indirect one, the implications for correspondence assumptions are nevertheless powerful.

To appreciate more fully the force of this line of argument, one must take into account the structuralist movement, to which deconstructionism is largely a response. Structuralism as an intellectual endeavor has largely been given to a dualistic conception of communicative acts, one that discriminates between surface actions and underlying meaning. Following Saussure's distinction (1959) between the "signifier" (or word) and the "signified" (or the underlying concept the word represents), it is assumed that the sprawling, ephemeral, and variegated acts of communication may be expressions of more fundamental, structured sets of principles, dimensions, conceptual templates, or the like. A penetrating examination of the spoken or written word might thus reveal the more latent, possibly unconscious structure that lies beneath, structure that may serve as the ultimate basis for human understanding itself. In this view, for example, Lévi-Strauss (1963) has proposed that wide-ranging cultural forms and artifacts can be traced to a fundamental binary logic. Chomsky (1968) has attempted to locate a "deep" grammatical structure from which all well-formed sentences may be derived. Lacan's persistent concern (1978) has been with the structural features of the layers of the mind.

In spite of the immense and optimistic challenge furnished by the structuralist movement, mounting criticism combined with the steady accumulation of competing accounts of the "hidden structures" have left the movement crippled. For one, the hermeneuticist writings of Gadamer (1975) and Ricoeur (1974) may be singled out for their debilitating implications. As argued by Gadamer, the interpretation of texts (i.e., the apprehension of underlying meaning) is largely dependent on historically situated conventions. Thus what a text "means" can only be determined within the contemporary "horizon of understanding." Whether this understanding coincides with that of the initial author is essentially indeterminant. Although differing from Gadamer in important respects, Ricoeur echoes this concern in his argument that texts serve as means of "opening up" possible existences. Interpreting a person's words is not a matter of determining with clarity their precise underlying structure. Rather, words have a social career that escapes the finite horizon lived by the writer. The critical implications of this line of reasoning for structuralist thought are clear enough: to the extent that interpretations of the "underlying realm" are dependent on historically based conventions, such interpretations give more insight into contemporary practices of accounting than they do into underlying structure. Or, to put it another way, the constraints over what may be said about such underlying structures are not furnished by the structures themselves so much as they are by the acceptable practices of rendering interpretation.

These implications are amplified in the works of deconstructionist writers such as Derrida (1977), Hartman (1975), and deMan (1979). Here the recurrent concern is with the literary figures (tropes, metaphors, and other rhetorical stratagems) that dominate the process of interpretation. If one chooses to interpret or describe, such interpretations must abide by the rules governing interpretation itself. As certain literary forms are selected and others abandoned, not only will the resultant work (whether literary, philosophic, or scientific) be delimited, but the object of interpretation will be deconstructed. Thus, in adopting a given literary form, the form itself comes to dominate description in a way that obliterates or masks from view the object of description. If one attempts to interpret the "underlying intention" of a given author (or actor), the literary form intrinsic to interpretation itself will obscure and replace the object of concern. In Derrida's terms, "Il n'y a pas de hors texte" (There is nothing outside the text). Or to bring the matter closer to home, behavioral description possesses an autumy of its own. Once a descriptive form is adopted, it carries on an independent existence and the referential implications are obscured. For example, to use the metaphor of the computer to "describe" mental functioning is to restrain the descriptive enterprise in significant ways. Concepts of creativity, imagination, and unconscious cease to be matters of major concern. In effect, once the metaphor has been selected, the actual processes at stake are circumscribed. Whatever their properties, they will be replaced by constituents of the metaphor.

Behavioral scientists have increasingly come to share these concerns with the figurative basis of theoretical accounts (cf. Leary, in press; Sampson 1983). In particular, a keen interest has developed in recent years over the dominant metaphors guiding theoretical construction in psychology. Much of this discussion has been inspired by Pepper's analysis (1972) of world hypotheses. Following Pepper, many analysts have criticized mainstream psychology of the present century for its virtually exclusive reliance on a mechanistic metaphor (Hollis 1977; Shotter 1975). Such criticisms often revolve around issues of the value biases implicit in the metaphor. However, from the present perspective, we see that once a theorist is committed to the metaphor of the human as machine, the particular activities of the person cease to play a central role in the process of theoretical description and explanation. Regardless of the character of the person's behavior, the mechanist theorist is virtually obliged to segment him from the environment, to view the environment in terms of stimulus or input elements, to view the person as reactive to and dependent on these input elements, to view the domain of the mental as structured (constituted of interacting elements), to segment behavior into units that can be coordinated to the stimulus inputs, and so on. Other metaphors exist as alternatives to the mechanistic. For example, the organismic, the marketplace, the dramaturgical, and the rule-following metaphors have all played a significant role in psychological research of the past decades (see Overton & Reese 1973; Thibaut & Kelley 1959; Sarbin & Scheibe 1983; and Harré & Secord 1972). Each carries with it certain advantages and limitations, each commits itself to certain value positions, and, most important for present purposes, each acts so as to imply an ontology. Once the terms of this ontology are explicated, the precise actions of the individual so "described" cease to be significant. They primarily serve to set the context for exercising the favored metaphor.

FROM ACTION TO LINGUISTIC AUTONOMY

Although thinkers in the deconstructionist vein furnish an indirect threat to assumptions of semantic mapping, one final line of argument must be considered. In this case, a principled challenge is launched more directly against the relationship between word and entity. To appreciate the force of this challenge, we must turn the clock back to late nineteenth-century Germany and the intense debate over the character of the specifically human sciences (*Geistenwissenschaften*) as opposed to the natural sciences (*Naturwissenschaften*). Dilthey, Weber, Rickert, and many others argued that the study of human behavior was centrally concerned, not with the objectivity given behavior of persons, but with the underlying meaning of behavior to persons. The understanding of human conduct thus required a penetration into the subjective life of individuals, into their intentions, motives, and reasons. A similar line of argument was later adopted by Collingwood in his characterization of historical study: "Unlike the natural scientist, the historian is not concerned with events as such at all. He is concerned with those events which are the outward expression of thoughts and is only concerned with these so far as they express throughts" (1946, 217). Peter Winch's influential *The Idea of a Social Science* (1958) elaborates further on this thesis. As Winch maintains, the objects of natural science study have an existence independent of the concepts used to understand them. However, in the case of human action, the concepts of understanding essentially establish the ontological foundations. For example, the occurrence of something that we term "claps of thunder" is independent of the concept of thunder; however, in the case of human action, without a concept of "command" or "obedience," such "events" simply do not exist.

This thinking wends its way into contemporary study in the form of antibehaviorist thinking. Most important in this instance, Charles Taylor (1964), among others, has distinguished between human behavior (bodily movements caused by forces or elements over which the individual has no control) and human action (movements of the body resulting from intentionality or reasons). Human study, on this account, is not principally concerned with the former (such as the velocity of a free-falling human body), but is vitally absorbed with the latter. The understanding of human action requires that one take into account the precipitating reasons (motives, intentions), and most of our terms for describing human conduct are essentially wedded to the assumption of underlying reasons or intentions. That is, when an individual is described as aggressive, the assumption follows that he or she must have intended to be so. If one had no such intention, then the descriptor would simply be inappropriate. In the same way, the logic of our language does not permit us to say that one "reads a book," "writes a speech," "takes a plane to Chicago," or even "criticizes others" without any intention of doing so. In effect, the common language is a language of reasons rather than causes.

The argument that the language for describing human conduct is largely an intentional one is broadly compelling. A rationale for why such language is required is spelled out elsewhere (Gergen 1982). However, in the present context, we must inquire into the implications of this view for the problem of semantic linkages. Essentially we find ourselves in the following condition: The language of person description is not linked to, defined by, nor does it refer to spatiotemporal particulars as such. Rather, its referents seem largely to be psychological conditions (intentions, meanings, motives, etc.). When we speak of a person being aggressive, helpful, obedient, conforming, and the like, we are speaking, not of the overt movements of the body, but of psychic dispositions. Yet if this conclusion is accepted, we then confront the problem of grounding the semantic linkage between person description and psychological state. How is one to recognize the occurrence of one form of intention or motive as opposed to another?

A variety of answers to this question have been posed over the centuries, and there is simply not space and time enough for a review of these proposals and their difficulties. However, that there are difficulties has become most apparent in recent hermeneutic debate. The problem is generally cast in terms of accuracy of interpretation. When confronted with competing accounts of the interpretation of a text, how are judgments to be rendered regarding relative accuracy? How can one interpretation be judged as "missing the author's point" (meaning, intention) and another deemed accurate? Again, attempts have been made to answer this question positively (Habermas 1983; Hirsch 1967), but none of these arguments has yet commanded broad agreement. Furthermore, the specter of cultural and historical relativism remains robust. We have already touched on the work of Gadamer and Ricoeur in this respect.

In my view, there are principled reasons for indeterminacy of interpretation. In particular, it appears that all attempts to clarify or determine with accuracy the intent of a given action are subject to infinite regression. As we have seen, behaviors are indexed by intentional language (e.g., aggression, dominance, helpfulness). In effect, the label commits one to assumptions about a psychological state that is not itself made transparent by the movements of the body. If clarification is then desired concerning the actual motive or intention, we must rely on other behavioral indicators (e.g., utterances, movements). Yet the description of these indicators is subject to the same problem as the initial interpretation; the descriptor commits one to still further assumptions about psychological dispositions. For example, interpreting a given action (e.g., delivering shock to another subject) as aggression, is in itself without objective warrant. The experimenter does not truly know what the subject was intending when he pressed his fingers on the button. For clarification, the subject might then be asked what he was "trying" to do. Yet his utterance (e.g., "He had it coming") itself stands in need of interpretation (are these words expressing anger, moral duty, a need for reciprocation, a need to fulfill the experimenter's expectation?). Whatever conclusion is drawn rests on the same quicksand as the initial interpretation. It commits one to yet another objectively unwarranted conclusion, as would all further attempts to clarify or "shed further light" through observation.

This analysis leaves us confronting the possibility that the language of person description (and explanation) is generated, elaborated, extended, or cast aside in relative independence of the activities it is designed to describe. In principle, its life is essentially autonomous from and orthogonal to the life for which it accounts. This is not to say that we cannot reach agreement (even rapidly) regarding the adequacy of behavioral description. Rather, it is to venture that adequacy in description is not engendered by the character of the acts in question but by the exigencies of social practice. For example, we may readily agree that a person is "dominating a conversation," but with the proper negotiation of terms, the same actions could be viewed as "submissive," "loving," "inquiring," "lazy," and so on. The necessity of shifting from one description to another does not derive from the character of the actions themselves; the actions are identical across descriptions. Rather, they depend on the skills or abilities of the interlocutors to navigate successfully the existing language conventions.

Given the relative autonomy of descriptive activity, the way is open for considering the origins, forms, potentials, and pervasiveness of accounting practices. In effect, one is sensitized to the possibilities for ethnographic analyses of person description (ethnopsychology, ethnosociology, etc.) with reflexive ramifications for the relevant disciplines. Such work is already well underway in anthropology and cross-cultural psychology. Analyses have focused, not only on the particular system of psychological description in various primitive cultures (Heelas & Lock 1981; Lutz 1982), but as well on potential generalities across cultures (cf. Shweder & Bourne 1982; White 1980). The implications of such work also play a critically reflexive role for the behavioral scientist. For example, concerted inquiry has demonstrated how common linguistic conventions can serve to fashion what are taken to be scientific facts about personality (Shweder & D'Andrade 1980; Shweder 1982). Of more general significance, recent attempts have been made toward systematizing the common-sense suppositions upon which all such knowledge must be grounded if one is to "make sense" (and not "nonsense") within contemporary Western culture. In this regard, Smedslund (1978) has attempted to isolate common-sense theorems that underlie psychological theories such as social learning theory. Ossorio (1978) has outlined a discrete set of parameters that appear to guide the description of persons. My own attempt (Gergen 1984) has been to demonstrate that virtually all that may be said about a given activity (e.g., "aggression") is already given in the linguistic rules governing the terms in question. Through a procedural unpacking process, it is possible to elucidate the grammatical scaffolding.

DESCRIPTIVE LANGUAGE: CONSTRAINED AND FREE

This analysis has explored four contemporary threats to the kinds of dependencies on semantic languages required for a progressive, empirically based science. Let us consider their implications for the possibility of observational constraints over description and then move to examine the implications for the future of the sociobehavioral sciences.

The contextualist arguments hold that descriptions of the world are in themselves uninformative about the nature of things. Such descriptions may be constrained by observation, but a continuous process of ostensive grounding is necessitated as environmental and linguistic circumstances are altered. The same descriptive term may have multiple referents (or none at all) depending on what language game one is playing at a given time. So long as one is committed to a particular game, then, a certain degree of constraint or "objective meaning" is possible. From the scientific perspective, observation may thus play an important role in the constraining of theory; however, its constraining power is lodged within social process. Within particular scientific subcultures at specific periods, localized agreement over concept application ("what counts as what") can be reached, and this does seem to be the case for most natural science explanation (see Campbell, chap. 5, this volume, for a discussion of the social processes generating such agreements).

From the constructionist vantage point, we find that descriptive languages are not derived from observation; rather, such languages operate as the lenses or filters through which we determine what counts as an object. As argued, it is problematic to extend the metaphor of the lens to the domain of perception. The argument that language determines the way events are registered on the senses is badly flawed. It seems more promising to argue that the forestructure of the descriptive language will have a strong determining effect on the account to be rendered of the world. Whatever one's observations, they must be recreated within the sensemaking devices at our disposal. Thus it is not the observation that produces the chief constraint over description; it is the form of descriptive discourse itself that constrains. The origins of these forms may, again, be traced to the sphere of social interchange. Is this to obviate fully the process of systematic observation within the sciences? It would not appear so. So long as it is possible for scientists to agree on how to employ the filter or the lens in a given setting, then it should be possible for observed variations to correct or sustain a given theory. If what we term measures of "the earth's rotation" were to undergo rapid change, certain questions would undoubtedly be raised concerning current astronomical theorizing. The conventions of discourse might determine how sense was made. Nevertheless, the constructed events could then stand as a goad to theoretical activity.

Much the same result emerges when we take into account the deconstructionist orientation. Here it may be argued that scientific description is strongly influenced by the linguistic figures (metaphors, tropes, etc.) selected for communication. Once the figure has been selected (and it is unclear how such determination could be induced from observation), certain descriptive practices are virtually required. The language itself functions continuously without dependence on the particulars of the world to be described. Yet observational constraint can be secured in much the same way as in the contextualist and constructionist cases. Localized social agreements can be reached regarding the proper metaphor or other literary figure to apply to certain observable events. Once such semantic linkages are conventionalized, then observation may inform one as to when the figure is relevant, correct, or inaccurate, and when it is not. In the same way, mathematical systems possess their own internal logic; yet once agreement is reached over how various mathematical integers index various observables (e.g., what counts as "three" as opposed to "four" entities), there may be little subsequent ambiguity over applying this system to events. For all of these arguments, then, we may surely agree with Quine's contention that scientific theory is grossly underdetermined with respect to observation; and we may agree with Kuhn that what we term advances in science are highly dependent on social negotiation practices among scientists. Yet when lodged within certain social practices, empirical observations do retain at least the capacity to constrain theoretical description.

It is the fourth line of argument, which stresses the language of action, that poses the most radical challenge to traditional correspondence views. In this case, we find that terms of behavioral description cannot in principle be linked in a definitional sense to observed patterns of human activity. By and large, the language of human action simply has no recognizable spatiotemporal coordinates. Nor, given the practical obstacles to cementing static, linguistic integers to an ever-changing pattern, does such an outcome seem possible. Theoretical description and explanation may thus proceed in relative independence of behavioral observation. This latter threat to semantic linkage may also demarcate the study of human action from the study of many natural phenomena. Although language conventions in both domains enjoy far greater autonomy than suggested by early correspondence enthusiasts, it does seem possible through social practice to link language and observation in the natural science case in a way that does not seem possible in the case of human action.

As we thus see, traditional empiricist and postempiricist accounts of behavioral science practices are placed in severe jeopardy. The present arguments suggest that the assiduous application of empirical method, combined with sophisticated logic, will not yield the kind of knowledge of human affairs optimistically promised in various logical empiricist (and critical rationalist) writings. Such systems of understanding would not appear to be derived from, guided by, or ultimately corrected by the world of observation. They seem quintessentially products of human interaction—communal artifacts, the major functions of which must be traced to their function within a social process. For the traditional empiricist or the security-seeking scientist, such conclusions will be found pessimistic, even nihilistic. However, they are so only if one remains glued to past conceptions of the scientific enterprise. When properly extended, this line of argument suggests that the potential of sociobehavioral study has scarcely been tapped. This study may be of enormous consequence to society, but traditional scientific practices of the craft have virtually ensured that its potential will not be realized.

Whither the Science of Human Action?

To appreciate the unrealized potential of behavioral inquiry, it is useful to return to Austin's concept of performative utterances (1962), that is, utterances that do not describe or report anything about the world, that can neither be verified or falsified, but that themselves constitute significant forms of social action. For example, utterances such as "I vow," "I promise," or "I am obligated" are not reports on real-world states of affairs. However, they often play an immensely important role in social affairs. In a major sense, the forms of theoretical description and understanding generated within the sociobehavioral sciences may be considered performative in character. They appear to describe events in the real world, but closer examination reveals no spatiotemporal coordinates. Nevertheless, such descriptions are integral to the broader social process in which the sciences are embedded. Scientific explanations and descriptions serve in the same way as "vows," "promises," and other performatives. They operate as actions with significant social consequences. Again in Austin's terms, they carry with them a considerable degree of "illocutionary force," that is, the capacity to invoke patterns of social action. We must, then, consider the performative uses to which language is put within the culture. As the inventors, purveyors, and elaborators of language—and specifically, languages about people—the sociobehavioral scientists can serve a critical role within the culture, both intellectual and societal. Three of these functions deserve special attention. In each case, we will consider the implications for the field of mental health, a focal domain throughout this volume.

Societal Reproduction and Transformation

For human populations, language constitutes perhaps the major form of communal or coordinated social action. When people are actively engaged in linguistic interchange, they are carrying out intricate interdependent activities—much like dancing or fencing. Further, because language is used to "describe" or explain people's internal states (e.g., intentions, affects, plans), it is a major vehicle of social influence. The description of a people's internal states may dramatically alter others' actions toward them—including the giving and taking of life. To attribute a person's failure to his "motivation" has far different implications than pointing to his lack of genetic endowment; to attribute achievement to motives of self-aggrandizement is to imply a different treatment of the actor than to see such achievement as an act of altruism; to say that a killing was accompanied by "malice aforethought" is to threaten the actor's life in a way that an attribution of temporary insanity would not. As language users with a high degree of visibility in the culture, sociobehavioral scientists are positioned to have enormous influence on the dominant theories of society and thus on its social patterns and institutions.

In recent years, critics of the science have become increasingly concerned over such influences. As they have pointed out, the sciences treat their descriptions and explanations as if they were neutral accounts of the facts. Yet they are far from neutral in their effects. As Gouldner (1970) has shown, for example, structural-functional theory in sociology serves to maintain the existing state of society's major institutions. It favors the status quo and militates against revolution. Social change agents are, within its framework, to be distrusted. Similarly, mechanistic accounts of human activity, because of the emphasis placed on manipulation of environmental stimuli, tend to favor those who have the power in society to control these stimuli (Argyris 1975). Most psychological theory, with its explanatory focus on the internal workings of mind, places the blame for undesirable actions (crime, unemployment, drug consumption) on the individual. Theories holding "principled decision making" superior in moral matters implicitly favor a male-dominated culture (Gilligan 1982). Women, as it is said, prefer a more contextually based form of moral decision making. Many additional examples could be supplied.

Most existing analyses of the implicit value biases of scientific theory have taken the scientist to task for such biases. The scientist is criticized for masking "ought" statements, or visions of the good, behind seemingly neutral descriptions. My arguments do not detract from the importance of these attacks. However, it is also clear that the theorists who are attacked are not misguided in their expression of value commitments. They can do little else. If they can be blamed at all, it is perhaps for their failure to appreciate the significance of such commitments. Rather than searching for means of cleansing scientific discourse from prescriptive implication (which itself would act as a process of mystification), scientists should seek to gain as much sophistication as possible regarding the forms of descriptive and explanatory discourse that will best enable them to achieve their valued goals for society. They should improve their skills in creating "images of the good" rather than seeking escape.

The present arguments also give special importance to the sciences as forces for societal transformation. Not only can the understandings developed and disseminated by the sciences re-create (or destroy) social organization, they may also help to transform that organization. For example, implicit in each of the above critiques is a vision of alternative social arrangements (change as opposed to the status quo, a redistribution of power, communal institutions, etc.). These implicit commitments carry the same prescriptive significance as the theories under attack. To attack a theory for its support of the status quo is to favor forms of change. To criticize forms of explanation for their bias toward person-blame is to simultaneously suggest that systems, not persons, are generic causes. However, it also seems clear that criticism of existing understandings is only one means of using the science to transform the culture. Theories may insinuate themselves into social life in other ways as well. For one, various social groups whom scientists believe to be disenfranchised or oppressed may require the kinds of language forms that would give them a sense of unity and rationale for collective action. It is this sort of theoretical work in which Marxist theorists have often excelled and that today has galvanzied the feminist movement into a vital social force. In addition to critique and the articulation of rationales, the scientists may also perceive a need for theoretical accounts that can favor certain forms of institution more generally. For example, critics may be justified in attacking the individualistic bias of psychological theory. However, there remains the difficult task of creating descriptive and explanatory forms that would render communitarianism both intelligible and desirable.

What implications does this line of reasoning have for inquiry into mental health? At the outset, it is clear that prevailing theories of mental illness and health have been of enormous social consequence within the culture. The incarceration of non-normal persons within this country has depended in large measure on the pervasive ethnopsychology. That is, if the non-normal are viewed as "ill," "unreasonable," "controlled by unconscious and uncontrollable forces," then locked wards seem reasonable. If the same symptoms are explained in terms of normal psychological functioning, reasonable and functional within their context and under voluntary and socially accessible control, then forced segregation is injurious if not immoral. In most cases, theories of mental or emotional well-being are transparent prescriptions for the good life. However, theorists in this domain seldom seem self-reflexive in these pronouncements. Images of the good are made to appear as by-products of careful empirical inquiry. In this sense, almost all such accounts are not only designed to mystify, but they lack thoughtful appraisal of the potential assets and liabilities of the kinds of ideal types championed by the theories. An important goal for future theoretical work in the mental health arena is the development of probing rationale for the kinds of action patterns and social institutions that may be achieved through favored theoretical positions.

Critique and the Transcendence of Ontology

Mention has been made of the use of critique within the sciences for purposes of social transformation. However, there is a second and less ideologically restricted sense in which critique should come to occupy a central role within the sciences. In this case, critique serves as a major means of escaping the strangulating effects of one-dimensional ontologies. As we have seen, descriptions of persons may be elaborated, extended, or abandoned without regard to the actual activity of persons to which they have putative reference. Yet despite its lack of spatiotemporal coordinates, the language is deployed as a referential device. As the descriptive language is put into action, the interlocutors make an implicit commitment to a world of events that is independent of the language. Simultaneous to language use is its objectification; an ontology of intangibles is created. As an inadvertent by-product of communication, a powerful world of impalpable particulars springs to life.

Required, then, is a process whereby the science can continuously demystify the realities it serves to create. The scientist is invited to carry out the kind of intellectual work that will enable the culture to transcend the pervasive ontology of the time, to reach beyond and to appreciate both the advantages and shortcomings of the dominant world view. As Stolzenberg has proposed in the case of mathematics, "We need to adopt an activist policy concerning the invention and following of procedures that entail the undoing of accepted beliefs and habits of thought; and we ought to regard the invention of such procedures as one of the fundamental means by which scientific knowledge may be increased" (1978, 229). The process of person description seems virtually inevitable; indeed such description serves many valuable functions in social life. As we have seen, the scientist can enrich and potentiate that language. However, because any tool constrains as it liberates, the scientist seems optimally positioned to monitor, critique, and cast necessary doubt on the use of his own implements.

Within the mental health domain, this kind of critique has demanded a certain degree of attention. Particularly in regard to psychotherapeutic aims and techniques, a keen, self-conscious attitude has developed. Much less has been done to monitor the hidden agendas underlying diagnostic, mensurational, and experimental psychopathology research programs. What does the most recent edition of the *Diagnostic and Statistical Manual of the American Psychiatric Association* (DSM-3) tell us about contemporary culture and the valuational commitments of its authors? What social patterns are favored by tests that place a strong value on believing one controls one's own outcomes, living under low stress, or being cognitively differentiated? If research results are interpreted in such a way that biological as opposed to cognitive processes are held primarily responsible for schizophrenia, what are the likely repercussions for institutions of family, school, and treatment centers? Such analyses should become a normal part of the research process, ideally preceding rather than following the mounting of large-scale research programs.

Enhancing Symbolic Resources

One may justifiably lament the loss of security implicit in this analysis. The belief that theoretical systems may be corrected through observation has been a long-standing source of optimism in the sociobehavioral sciences. Yet I do not simultaneously disparage the companionate conception of scientific progress. Advancement in the understanding of human conduct, not only is a possibility within the present framework, but may indeed be considered a central concern of scientific work. Such progress derives from the development and elaboration of conceptual systems. In their performative capacity, concepts of human conduct operate much as tools for carrying out relationships. Any given set of tools both enables and constrains. It facilitates certain lines of action while restricting others. Advancement in understanding largely derives, then, from the development of new forms of discourse. With the emergence of new language frames, the potential for effective human action is augmented. To view social life as an exchange of reinforcements is both fascinating and rich in evocative potential—but ultimately delimited. Greater efficacy can be achieved if one has at one's disposal lenses through which social life may be seen as sets of rituals, theatrical presentations, economically determined patterns, power dynamics, dialectic transformations, and so on. In effect, the sociobehavioral sciences stand in an optimal position to contribute to the symbolic resources of the culture.

This contribution may be best served by what I have termed "generative theory," that is, theoretical views that are lodged against or contradict the taken-for-granted world of daily life (whether within the sciences or without) and that open new vistas of intelligibility (Gergen 1978b). As any given theoretical system is elaborated and its general intelligiblity is increased, it becomes objectified. It acquires the mystique of real-world representation. The invitation to sustain such common-sense formulations is virtually irresistible; failure to do so risks ridicule and social isolation. Yet it is just this mantle of apparent madness that must be donned if conceptual progress is to be achieved. In effect, some of the greatest conceptual strides are to be made when the theorist can bracket the accepted realities and fumble toward the articulation of the absurd. It is precisely this capacity that elevates the work of such theorists as Freud, Jung, Skinner, and Goffman. Each has succeeded, in varying degrees, to make uncommon sense.

In terms of future inquiry in the mental health domain, a special premium is to be placed on such generative theorizing. For example, the most popular theories of depression today trace its roots to environmental causes (e.g., uncontrollable circumstances and esteem-lowering communications). In this sense, depression appears to be an inescapable, innately determined reaction to particular events in the world. Such theories feed the common belief that people are victims of depression much as they are victims of war or earthquakes. A generative theory in this case might be one that reframed depression as a voluntary act over which people could exert control if they so desired. Rather than a society of victims, one might thus help to create a culture in which depressions were voluntarily used (or not) by people to serve their ends. Many other forms of "mental illness" are similar to depression in their mechanistic structures and are equally ripe for unseating. (See Shweder's essay, chap. 7 this volume, for further discussion of mental health theory and the creation of culture.)

The status of empirical work in the development of fundamental understanding is clearly diminished by this account. Rather than furnishing a warrant for theoretical statements, as traditional science would have it, such work largely serves a rhetorical function. It becomes a means for enhancing the objectification process. In particular, it enables the scientist to translate the abstract and typically rarefied language of the theoretical account into a more general or lay language (the language of methodology and scientific procedure) and thereby increase the intelligibility of the former. Research thus continues to serve an important function, but one that is quite secondary to the development of symbolic resources. There are other than rhetorical functions for empirical research. Particularly in the field of mental health, there may be a special need for certain kinds of actuarial prediction. Ascertaining the number of persons seeking therapeutic help, using heavy amounts of debilitating drugs, taking their lives, seeking divorce, experiencing rape or physical abuse, and so on, along with studies of major predictors, could do much to improve mental health policies and services. The attempt in this case is, not the objectification of theory, but merely the kind of counting and prediction that makes for more effective utilization of physical resources.

SUMMARY

This chapter attempted, first, to examine several lines of argument that together pose a major threat to the belief that precise linkages can be forged between theories and evidence, propositions and particulars, or words and things. This analysis suggests that whatever the relation between these domains, it is both ambiguous and dependent on social convention. Further, in the case of describing human action, we confront the possibility that theory is fundamentally closed to empirical evaluation. Within this context, we then examined the possibilities for a positive program in the social sciences. It was proposed that the sciences chiefly be viewed as sources of intelligibility or vehicles for the conceptual construction of reality. From this vantage point, the sciences can play a pivotal role in transforming or sustaining patterns of social conduct. Further, there is a critical need for conceptual work that can enable people to transcend or escape the taken-for-granted realities in which they are often enmeshed. In effect, the social sciences can make an immeasurable contribution to the symbolic resources of the culture. This is a challenge that traditional empiricist epistemology has largely obscured; it is also a challenge of immense and exciting proportion.

References

Argyris, C. 1975. Dangers in applying results from experimental social psychology. *American Psychologist* 30: 469–85.

Atkinson, M. 1977. *Discovering suicide: Studies in the social organization of sudden death.* London: Macmillan.

Austin, J. L. 1962. *How to do things with words.* New York: Oxford University Press.

Averill, J. 1982. *Anger and aggression.* New York: Springer-Verlag.

Barnes, B. 1982. Social life as bootstrapped induction. Manuscript.

Berger, P. L., and Luckmann, T. 1966. *The social construction of reality.* Garden City, N.Y.: Doubleday.

Carnap, R. [1928] 1967. *The logical structure of the world.* 2d ed. London: Routledge & Kegan Paul.

Chomsky, N. 1968. *Language and mind.* New York: Harcourt, Brace and World.

Cicourel, A. V. 1968. *The social organization of juvenile justice.* New York: Wiley.

Collingwood, R. 1946. *The idea of history.* Oxford: Clarendon Press.

Coulter, J. 1979. *The social construction of the mind.* New York: Macmillan.

deMan, P. 1978. The epistemology of metaphor. *Critical Inquiry* 5: 13–30.

Derrida, J. 1977. *Of grammatology.* Trans. Gayatri C. Spivak. Baltimore: Johns Hopkins University Press.

Fuller, S. 1983. The "reductio ad symbolum" and the possibility of a linguistic object. *Philosophy of the Social Sciences* 13: 129–56.

Gadamer, H. G. 1975. *Truth and method.* Ed. G. Barden and J. Cumming. New York: Seabury.

Garfinkel, H. 1967. *Studies in ethnomethodology.* Englewood Cliffs, N.J.: Prentice-Hall.

Gergen, K. J. 1973. Social psychology as history. *Journal of Personality and Social Psychology* 26: 309–20.

———. 1977. The social construction of self-knowledge. In *The self, psychological and philosophical issues,* ed. T. Mischel. Oxford: Blackwell.

———. 1978a. Experimentation in social psychology: A reappraisal. *European Journal of Social Psychology* 8: 507–27.

———. 1978b. Toward generative theory. *Journal of Personality and Social Psychology* 36: 1344–60.

———. 1980. Toward intellectual audacity in social psychology. In *The development of social psychology,* ed. R. Gilmour and S. Duck. London: Academic Press.

———. 1982. *Toward transformation in social knowledge.* NewYork: Springer-Verlag.

———. 1984. Aggression as discourse. In *The social psychology of aggression,* ed. A. Mummendey. Heidelberg: Springer-Verlag.

Gergen, K. G., and Gergen, M. M. 1982. Form and function in the explanation of human conduct. In *Explaining social behavior: Consciousness, human action, and social structure,* ed. P. Secord. Beverly Hills: Sage.

Gilligan, C. 1982. *In a different voice.* Cambridge: Harvard University Press.

Gouldner, A. 1970. *The coming crisis of Western sociology.* New York: Basic Books.

Habermas, J. 1983. Hermeneutics and critical theory. Paper presented at Bryn Mawr College, 19 February.

Hanson, N. 1958. *Patterns of discovery.* London: Cambridge University Press.

Harré, R. 1981. Expressive aspects of descriptions of others. In *The psychology of ordinary explanations,* ed. C. Antaki. London: Academic Press.

Harré, R., and Secord, P. F. 1972. *The explanation of social behavior.* Oxford: Blackwell.

Hartman, G. 1975. *The fate of reading and other essays.* Chicago: University of Chicago Press.

Heelas, P., and Lock, A. 1981. *Indigenous psychologies.* London: Academic Press.

Hirsch, E., Jr. 1967. *Validity in interpretation.* New Haven: Yale University Press.

Hollis, M. 1977. *Models of man.* London: Cambridge University Press.

Kessler, S., and McKenna, W. 1978. *Gender: An ethnomethodological approach.* New York: Wiley.

Kuhn, T. S. 1970. *The structure of scientific revolutions.* 2d ed. Chicago: University of Chicago Press.

Lacan, G. 1978. *The four fundamental concepts of psychoanalysis.* Ed. J. Jacques-Alain Miller. New York: Norton.

Lalljee, M. 1981. Attribution theory and the analysis of explanations. In *The psychology of ordinary explanations,* ed. C. Antaki. London: Academic Press.

Latour, B., and Woolgar, S. 1979. *Laboratory life: The social construction of scientific facts.* Beverly Hills: Sage.

Leary, D., ed. In press. *Metaphors in the history of psychology.* Cambridge: Cambridge University Press.

Lévi-Strauss, C. 1963. *Structural anthropology.* New York: Basic Books.

Lutz, C. 1982. The domain of emotion words on Ifaluk. *American Ethnologist* 9: 113–28.

McAndrew, C. 1969. On the notion that persons given to frequent drunkenness are suffering from a disease called alcoholism. In *Changing perspectives in mental illness,* ed. S. Plog and R. Edgerton. New York: Holt, Rinehart and Winston.

Mummendey, A.; Bonewasser, M.; Loschper, G.; and Linneweber, V. 1982. It is always somebody else who is aggressive. *Zeitschrift für Sozialpsychologie* 13. 341–52.

Neurath, O. [1932] 1959. Protocol sentences. In *Logical positivism,* ed. A. J. Ayer. Glencoe, Ill.: Free Press.

Ossorio, P. 1978. *What actually happens.* Columbia: University of South Carolina Press.

Overton, W., and Reese, H. 1973. Models of development: Methodological implications. In *Life-span developmental psychology: Methodological issues,* ed. J. R. Nesselroade and H. W. Reese. New York: Academic Press.

Pepper, S. C. 1972. *World hypotheses.* Berkeley: University of California Press.

Quine, W. V. O. 1951. Two dogmas of empiricism. *Philosophical Review* 60: 20–43.

———. 1960. *Word and object.* Cambridge, Mass: MIT Technology Press.

Ricoeur, P. 1974. *The conflict of interpretation: Essays in hermeneutics.* Evanston, Ill.: Northwestern University Press.

Russell, B. 1924. Logical atomism. In *Contemporary British philosophy,* ed. J. H. Muirhead. New York: Macmillan.

Sabini, J., and Silver, M. 1982. *The moralities of everyday life.* London: Oxford University Press.

Sampson, E. E. 1977. Psychology and the American ideal. *Journal of Personality and Social Psychology* 35: 767–82.

———. 1983. Deconstructing psychology's subject. *Journal of Mind and Behavior* 4: 135–64.

Sarbin, T. R., and Scheibe, K. E. 1983. *Studies in social identity.* New York: Praeger.

Saussure, F. de. 1959. *Course in general linguistics.* Trans. Wade Baskin. New York: Philosophical Library (Original in French, 1916).

Schachter, S. 1964. The interaction of cognitive and physiological determinants of emotional state. In *Advances in experimental social psychology*, vol. 1, ed. L. Berkowitz. New York: Academic Press.

Scheff, T. J. 1966. *Being mentally ill: A sociological theory*. Chicago: Aldine.

Schlick, M. [1934] 1959. The foundation of knowledge. In *Logical positivism*, ed. A. J. Ayer. Glencoe, Ill.: Free Press.

Shotter, J. 1975. *Images of man in psychological research*. London: Methuen.

Shutz, A. 1962–66. *Collected papers*. Vols. 1–3. The Hague: Martinus Nijhoff.

Shweder, R. A. 1982. Fact and artifact in trait perception. In *Progress in experimental personality research*, vol. 11, ed. B. A. Maher and W. B. Maher. New York: Academic Press.

Shweder, R. A., and D'Andrade, R. G. 1980. The systematic distortion hypothesis. In *Fallible judgment in behavioral research*, ed. R. A. Shweder. New directions for methodology of social and behavioral science, no. 4. San Francisco: Jossey-Bass.

Shweder, R. A., and Bourne, E. 1982. Does the concept of the person vary cross-culturally? In *Cultural conceptions of mental health and therapy*, ed. A. J. Marsella and G. White. Boston: Reidel.

Smedslund, J. 1978. Bandura's theory of self-efficacy: A set of common sense theories. *Scandinavian Journal of Psychology* 19: 1–14.

Stolzenberg, G. 1978. Can an inquiry into the foundations of mathematics tell us anything interesting about mind? In *Psychology and biology of language and thought: Essays in honor of Eric Lenneberg*, ed. G. A. Miller and E. Lenneberg. New York: Academic Press.

Taylor, C. 1964. *The explanation of behavior*. London: Routledge and Kegan Paul.

Thibaut, J., and Kelley, H. 1959. *The social psychology of groups*. New York: Wiley.

White, G. 1980. Conceptual universals in interpersonal language. *American Anthropologist* 82: 759–81.

Winch, P. 1958. *The idea of a social science and its relation to philosophy*. New York: Humanities Press.

Wittgenstein, L. 1963. *Philosophical investigations*. Trans. G. Anscombe. New York: Macmillan.

7   Divergent Rationalities

Richard A. Shweder

One thing that bothers some observers of the social sciences is that the foundations of the field seem to be "essentially contestable" (to borrow an expression from Gallie 1964).[1] Diverse schools of thought, each identified with some founding father (Freud, Marx, Darwin, Skinner, Piaget, Adam Smith) or rebellious progeny (Jung, Sullivan, Rogers, Kohut), conceptualize mind, motivation, society, and nature in somewhat different ways. The basic concepts and "root metaphors" (Pepper 1972) of each school are difficult to coordinate or translate; and if one school makes the rare effort to coordinate viewpoints and succeeds (from its point of view) in translating into its own terms the concepts of the other school (for example, Dollard and Miller's 1950 translation of Freud into learning theory), that other school is quick to complain that something essential has been lost in the translation. Within the social sciences, there seem to be so many perspectives and no detached way to choose among them (each school, of course, trains its own partisan advocates), and those diverse perspectives seem neither to be perspectives on exactly the same thing nor perspectives on entirely different things.

Some observers are reminded by this diversity of Kuhn's preparadigmatic stage of science (1970), and the social sciences are sometimes described as science in its youth. But that does not seem quite right. Social thought has been around for a long time; it is not as if each of the several schools of thought is pressing for that notable scientific achievement or crucial experiment in the wake of which the diversity will disappear, a unifying paradigm will emerge, and real science will begin. Of course, there may well be a continuing competition for political domination and unification of the field (control of editorships of journals, etc.), but at the higher levels of intellectual activity, things are essentially multiparadigmatic or pluralistic. The diversity somehow is endemic, and the shift from one school of thought to another is much like a move across "ideological regions," a radical change in conceptual reference points.

Being an anthropologist, I have from time to time moved across ideological regions, having lived in worlds—among Zinacanteco shamans in Mexico, Oriya temple priests in India (Shweder 1979; Shweder & Bourne 1982; Shweder & Miller 1985)—where an empathic shift in conceptual reference points has produced in me a somewhat different sense of what's real and what's unreal. I'm not sure which requires a greater alteration of consciousness: moving into a Hindu temple town in India—where it is thought that ancestral spirits return home every day to be fed; that souls transmigrate; that the womb is hell; that nature, through its unequal distribution of health, wealth, and status, punishes vice and rewards virtue; and that at least some dreams are really communications received over a noisy channel from gods, goddesses, and spirits—or attending a seminar at the Institute for Psychoanalysis or the Institute for Marxist Studies or the Radical Behaviorist Institute or the Institute for a Market Mentality. In both excursions across cultures and across cults, what looks from the outside like superstition, ideology or supernatural belief, looks from a different perspective, the inside point of view, like an objective inquiry founded, not on supernatural principles, but rather on a different theory of natural law. What appears from the outside like a faith, a fiction, or a fantasy comes to feel from the inside like a rational enterprise. Certain readings in history can have the same effect; they challenge any easy contrast between science and religion, reason and superstition, objectivity and subjectivity, between what's seen and what's unseen, what's real and what's unreal.

Cornelius Loos had a hard time getting his book published in 1592. The thesis of the book was that the devil did not exist, that there were no such things as witches, and that all those confessions by women throughout Europe stating that they had flown through the night to an orgiastic Black Sabbath were nothing more than products of their imagination. Loos's book was never published; instead he was widely viewed as an enemy of reason and was denounced, imprisoned, and forced to recant. It is sobering to read Trevor-Roper's brilliant account "The European Witch-Craze of the Sixteenth and Seventeenth Centuries" (1967). For one comes away feeling that it was the promoters of the witch-hunts and the witch-burnings who were the guardians of reason and science, while it was the skeptics who seemed to shy away from the reasonable implications of their own conceptual reference points.

Widely accepted during those two hundred years, one conceptual reference point of the time was that the devil, fallen from heaven, had established his own kingdom and that the Church was engaged in a mortal struggle against Satan's attempts to regain his lost empire. Rational inquiry was not necessarily incompatible with belief in the "doctrine of the kingdom of Satan"; and as Trevor-Roper documents, many of the promoters of witch-hunts were the leading intellectuals of their time, who knew all about the canons of scientific objectivity and logical consistency and applied them to the evidence at hand. A powerful scientific case was developed in defense of the witch-hunts.

The evidence at hand was a corpus of detailed confessions by women all over Europe, which was scrutinized for its objectivity. Confessions in Scotland were found to converge with confessions in distant Prussia, and certain common themes were identified: a secret pact with the devil to help him recover hegemony, anointment with the fat of a murdered child (so-called devil's grease), an aerial night journey to a sabbath ground, worship of the devil, dancing, macabre music, cold and tasteless food, and a promiscuous sexual orgy. Aware of the seriousness of a witchcraft accusation, some defenders of the witch-hunts examined the alternative "subjectivist" hypothesis and dismissed it; for if the confessions were all delusions, induced by some subjective state like melancholia, then why should there be such convergence in reported accounts from all corners of Europe? The consistencies or common elements in the stories of confessed witches, stories from women who spoke different languages and came from different countries, lent credence to the accounts.

Some defenders of the witch-hunts also entertained the alternative "method effect" hypothesis and dismissed it. The skeptics had argued that the common elements in the confessions of witches could be explained by reference to the use by inquisitors of certain standard leading questions and techniques of torture. Skeptics argued that it was the identity of the elicitation procedures, not the identity of the experience with the devil, that explained the similarities in the contents of the confessions. Upon examination, the skeptics turned out to be wrong. Many confessions were voluntary, torture was not used in every country, and even without leading questions the same story unfolded: a pact with the devil, a night flight, a Black Sabbath.

In the face of this onslaught of reason and evidence, the skeptics remained for two centuries on the defensive. For two hundred years, the best they could do was advance some wildly speculative claims about the living conditions of the devil (for example, that he had been locked up in hell and could not possibly intervene in human affairs) or else about methodological and procedural issues like the cruelty of torture or the possibility that some innocent people might be convicted. As Trevor-Roper notes, "To the last the most radical argument against the witch-craze was not that witches do not exist, not even that the pact with Satan is impossible, but simply that the judges err in the identification" (1967, 149).

"Malpractice" claims of that sort do not pose a serious threat to the underlying rationality of an ideological region, for they presuppose the conceptual reference points in question. A case in point is reported in *Sudan Notes and Records* (1920, 245–59). Parents and villagers in a Nubian district of Sudan stand by and watch a female child cease to live while a native healer, by lashing, beating, and choking tries to cast out of the girl a possessing devil, a "jinn." At the subsequent trial, the healer claims to have been contacted in a dream and empowered to use his tampura (a mandolinlike instrument) to drive out afflicting demons: "Each devil has its special note. When it is struck the devil speaks, and makes his demands for what he wants, which has to be provided by the friends of the patient, when he is satisfied and leaves the patient." The healer claims that in this case, the devil's requests were refused by the family, and when that happens, the jinn is likely to "break the neck of the afflicted person." The healer claims to have entered into physical battle with the demon in the girl's body. "My jinn and her jinn entered on a struggle for mastery. Mine in me was throttling hers in her and vice versa. . . . Her jinn overcame my jinn. . . . Hers killed her because its demands were refused. Mine would do the same to me if I refused its demands."

At the trial, it is apparent that for the Nubians involved, if not the colonial court, this is a potential case of malpractice, which is understood by the participants within the framework of a well-established Islamic theory of satanic beings that no one has reason to doubt. Appearing as a witness is another native healer, a woman, who had originally been consulted by the dead girl's parents: "Azab and Medim brought me their daughter and stayed two nights. Then I told them I could not put her right. They were no ordinary devils (*dsātir*) but malicious jinns who had made her make water on my bed clothes." And the witness tells the court that when the accused healer first appeared on the scene and started beating the girl, the witness had said to the girl's father, "There is no medicine for jinns; if you are going to have treatment of this kind [beatings] take her away from my zariba." The witness also reveals that, at the time, the accused healer had told her that the devil was a foreign Christian devil that the witness did not know how to treat.

The father of the girl is cross-examined by the court: "Why did you not stop this cruel treatment?" The father replies, "He told me it would effect a cure and I believed him." A farmer, who observed the beatings, is examined: "How could you stand there and see a girl throttled?" He replies, "It was our ignorance. . . . [The healer] said, 'Don't say anything. The more you object the more you encourage devils and handicap me.' " The farmer reveals that he himself had tried to tell the healer that if he wanted to drive out devils, there was a way of writing holy passages and a way of smoking demons out of the body. (For a detailed ethnographic account of Islamic theories of satanic beings and jinns, and also of various contemporary South Asian conceptions of illness and therapeutic practice, see Kakar 1982).

A striking feature of the trial is that while objections are raised about the competence of the healer, his particular diagnosis, and the procedures used, Nubian theories of illness and cure left open the possibility, and no rational Nubian had reason to doubt, that the girl might have been possessed by a spirit—just as no rational European in the sixteenth and seventeenth centuries could coherently or credibly raise doubts about the existence of the devil (if God exists then so must the devil). When in 1592 Cornelius Loos tried to raise such skeptical doubts, he was punished as a reckless enemy of reason and forced to recant.

A comparable situation today might be that of an evolutionary biologist trying to prevail upon the secular academic community that the evolution of biological forms does not occur by a process of natural selection. He might, for example, try pointing to the lack of "transitional forms" in the fossil record or to the difficulty of plausibly explaining how highly integrated biological systems or subsystems—which, please note, require complex integration among diverse parts to function at all—could exist in incomplete transitional states or be the product of a piecemeal, intermittent, or random process. One imagines the biologist suggesting that the facts of natural history are not inconsistent with the idea that all that neatly organized yet increasing complexity is the product of invention and foresight and that it is high time to start searching for a possible designer of biological organisms—perhaps a visitor from another galaxy. One wonders what sort of reception this would receive from colleagues!

Anthropologists are sometimes accused of being "soft on superstitition"; of refusing to say of those peoples of the world who believe in witches, ghosts, jinns, dreams, transmigrating souls, and visitors from distant worlds that they are deluded, wrong, confused, irrational, or misinformed; of refusing to interpret intellectual change as the history of a never-ending battle between reason and superstition. Like most half-truths, the accusation is wrong but not entirely misguided. What is wrong with the accusation is that anthropologists, like most other people, hold deep convictions about what's fantasy and what's reality, what's subjective and what's objective, what comes from inside the skin and what comes from outside the skin, what's part of the experience or representation of a thing and what's the thing itself (as seen from "nowhere in particular," Nagel 1979). At least for some anthropologists, those convictions have a decisive influence on their analyses of alien beliefs.

Murdock, for example, sounding somewhat like Cornelius Loos, expresses a now common twentieth-century view:

> There are, for example, no such things as souls, or demons, and such mental constructs as Jehovah are as fictitious as those of Superman or Santa Claus. Neither ghosts nor gods exert the slightest influence on men and their behavior. But men can and do influence the behavior of one another, and the ideas they hold can have a serious bearing on how they behave. The Crusades, the Inquisition, and Hitler's "holocaust" illustrate, not strictly the power of ideas, but the influence that can be exerted by men who hold particular ideas. (1980, 54)

The point is forcefully reiterated by Schneider; at least when it comes to the question of the existence of demons and ghosts, there is agreement between Schneider and Murdock:

> There is no supernatural. Ghosts do not exist. Spirits do not in fact make storms, cause winds, bring illness or effect cures. The gods in the heavens do not really make the stars go around, and neither do they decide each man's fate at his birth. Since there are no real ghosts, spirits, gods, and goddesses, it follows logically (as Durkheim showed so clearly) that their real and true nature cannot decisively shape man's beliefs about them or the social institutions related to them. Man's beliefs about ghosts and spirits must be wholly formed by man himself. Whatever unity there is to man's

beliefs about the supernatural derives, therefore, from the nature of man himself and not from the nature of the supernatural. (1965, 85–86)

Schneider, in later writings, sharply distinguishes between the question of the reality of ghosts as "cultural constructs" (as elements in what Freud would have referred to as "thought-reality" or "psychical reality") and the question of the reality of ghosts as elements in external or physical reality (1968, 2–3). Although claiming that "a good deal of empirical testing" has proved that ghosts do not exist in external reality, he argues that the question of whether one can actually go out and capture a ghost is irrelevant for understanding the meaning and significance of ghosts as constructs in the psychic reality of the native. He argues for a "symbolic" interpretation of cultural constructs.

Spiro, however, raises an important objection to Schneider's attempt to totally separate the meaning of cultural constructs from the question of their existence in external reality (Spiro 1982, 53–54, 63; Spiro 1984). He points out that a primary meaning of religious constructs as cultural constructs is that they are thought by the native to represent external reality, and the beings and entities of religion—ghosts, spirits, goddesses—are thought by the native to exist independently of psychic reality. The native who believes in spirits is hardly indifferent to such external-reality oriented questions as What makes spirits angry? Can they invade a person's body? How can invading spirits be exorcised? And those people who believed in the kingdom of Satan did go out hunting for witches and roasted them alive when they found them. Pressing forth a logic implicit in Schneider's own earlier Durkheimian analysis, Spiro argues that it is precisely because ghosts, spirits, and goddesses do not in fact exist except as cultural constructs that the main significance of religious beliefs is that they are delusional systems like dreams and other hallucinations, in which "stimuli originating in the inner world are taken as objects and events in the outer world." He tries to explain these delusional ideas in terms of irrational motives and childhood wishes and fantasies concerning dependency on superior beings—parental figures.

I think it is somewhere around there in the argument, with the conclusion that religion is fantasy confused with reality, that some anthropologists turn "soft on superstition." The reason is not that the world is free of delusion, ignorance, confusion, irrationality, or error; there's plenty of that around (see, for examples, Tversky & Kahneman 1974; Shweder 1977, 1980; Nisbett & Ross 1980; Spiro

1983, 1984). One reason they turn soft is the suspicion, well-expressed by Horton, that the goals of "religious thought" may not be unlike the goals of scientific thought "to explain and influence the workings of one's everyday world by discovering the constant principles that underlie the apparent chaos and flux of sensory experience" (Horton [1964] 1979, 250). The doctrine of the kingdom of Satan provided people in the sixteenth and seventeenth centuries with a powerful explanation of illness and suffering, and as noted earlier, the doctrine was constantly being tested against "reality." It is conceivable that the sense of objectivity invested in religious beliefs is not fundamentally different from the sense of objectivity invested in scientific beliefs, and that to describe other peoples' beliefs as religious or supernatural and our own as scientific is merely to disguise a prejudice in favor of our own conception of natural law over theirs. This is perhaps not unlike what goes on when a radical behaviorist dismisses the entities and forces of psychoanalysis, or when a classical economist finds it difficult to see anything of value in the Marxist account of social formations. Why is it that only other people have ideologies or supernatural beliefs?

A second reason that some anthropologists are soft on superstition has to do with the fascinating distribution of some so-called superstitious beliefs around the world. Murdock (1980), for example, has examined the distribution of theories about the causes of illness across a worldwide sample of 139 societies. He discovered that there are very few societies in the world where the causal categories of Western medical science (infection, stress, organic deterioration, accident, etc.) are thought to provide important explanations for illness; and he discovered that those causal categories that are thought to be important (for example, sorcery, witchcraft, soul loss, retribution for violation of moral injunctions) cluster in six broad geographical regions and remain relatively constant across societies belonging to the same linguistic families. Thus, for example, explanations of illness by reference to a special class of people called witches who are endowed with the propensity and power for evil predominate among those in the circum-Mediterranean region of the world (including the descendants of those sixteenth- and seventeenth-century promoters of witch-hunts) and among the speakers of three large linguistic phyla (including the Indo-European languages), while in sub-Sahara Africa (not including Sudan), the same illness event is most likely to be explained as nature's punishment for the violation of a taboo, and not by reference to a witch.

The existence of geographically contiguous and linguistically bounded "ideological regions" of the type discovered by Murdock suggests the diffusion through communication and contact of a conceptual scheme or theoretical point of view. Given the existence of such broad regions of perception, it becomes increasingly diffi- cult to argue that ideas such as "witches cause illness" are the prod- uct of irrational or delusional processes, for what we know about the worldwide distribution of irrational and delusional processes, which admittedly is not very much, does not suggest a distribution paralleling linguistic phyla or such vast areas as the circum-Medi- terranean or sub-Sahara Africa. Some irrational processes may well be universal (Tversky & Kahneman 1973; Shweder 1977; Kahne- man, Slovic & Tversky 1982). Other irrational processes seem to be generated within the context of a family or even perhaps a whole society (Whiting 1977; Spiro 1965, 1983). What seems unlikely and implausible is that irrational or delusional processes cluster around geographical regions and linguistic phyla, especially since the so- cieties within each of Murdock's ideological regions differ from each other in terms of exactly those factors that might be expected to explain the occurrence of irrational thought; that is, they differ in family organization, educational institutions, child-training prac- tices, and so on. As Murdock, Wilson, and Frederick argue, if irra- tional or delusional processes were primarily responsible for the genesis of such beliefs as the kingdom of Satan, then "one would expect considerably more diversity than actually occurs among the societies of a region and considerably less average difference be- tween regions" (1978, 457). In fact, they advance that criticism against the well-known and important hypothesis of Whiting and Child (1953) that child-training practices create irrational response tendencies in children that later give rise, through defensive pro- jection, to illusory theories about the causes of illness. Within any one ideological region, as Murdock and his associates note, cultures with variant child-training practices seem to adopt similar theories of illness.

We seem to have carved out for ourselves a rather unfortunate set of choices. One is to argue, along with Murdock, Schneider, and Spiro, that the things to which ghosts, souls, witches, and demons refer do not exist, that ghosts and souls exist solely as elements in psychic reality, and that the idea of a ghost or a soul is totally sub- jective. The problem is that to argue this way is to transform re- ligious concepts into either "symbols" (Schneider) or "delusions" (Spiro), despite the fact that the native does not use his idea of a witch or demon as though it were arbitrary, conventional, or a marker of something else; nor does he apply his ideas irrationally. The only alternative seems to be to argue that religious concepts are objective. But to argue that way is to risk the reception received by Cornelius Loos—to be branded an enemy of reason, denounced and forced to recant: "Do you really think ghosts exist?!"

Faced with two unacceptable alternatives, one can only reject them both. I want to argue that ghosts, spirits, demons, witches, souls, and other so-called religious or supernatural concepts are, in some important sense, real and objective, and that if we understood the meaning of those concepts properly and learned how to apply them to experience, we would see that there exist things to which ghosts, demons, witches, and souls refer, things that can be interpreted using those concepts. However, I want to add quickly that to speak of those concepts as real and objective is to raise the question, In what sense are they real and objective, and how is that sense to be described? Certainly not, I shall argue, by radically opposing subjectivity to objectivity.

Spiro is undoubtedly right. A remarkable feature of the entities of religious thought is that they are thought to be external, objective, and real. But, it seems to me, it is precisely that feature that marks a point of strong resemblance with scientific concepts, for one of the features of scientific thinking is that "representations" of reality are typically treated as though they were real, and unseen ideas and constructs are not only used to help interpret what is seen but are presumed to exist externally, behind or within that small piece of reality that can be seen. Indeed, it seems to me worth considering the possibility raised by Horton (1967) that religious thinking is a variety of scientific thinking and that both inevitably require leaps beyond the evidence at hand to a world of imagined entities whose postulated existence is used to make sense of that which meets the senses.

Kuhn, in his moderate postscript to *The Structure of Scientific Revolutions* (1970, 206–7), makes an indirect case for the similarity of religion and science by distinguishing between the "ontological development" of a theory (the types of things, entities, or forces postulated by a theory) and its "instrumental development." What Kuhn argues is that as an instrument for puzzle solving, Einstein's theory of relativity is superior to Newton's mechanics, which in turn is superior to Aristotle's physics. But he goes on to remark, "I can see in their succession no coherent direction of ontological development. On the contrary, in some important respects, though by no means in all, Einstein's general theory of relativity is closer to

Aristotle's than either of them is to Newton's." Kuhn abandons the idea of "correspondence with reality" as a criterion for judging the progress of a scientific theory: "There is, I think, no theory-independent way to reconstruct phrases like 'really there'; the notion of a match between the ontology of a theory and its 'real' counterpart in nature now seems to me illusive in principle." The rub here seems to be that the mind has no way of getting beyond the skin. Thus, any ideas we might have about what is hidden, "two steps removed," so to speak, behind an external world of objects and events is highly inferential, even conjectural. It becomes impossible, in principle, to separate what is mind and what is reality, to say how things would look from "nowhere in particular," or to guarantee that all minds will conjecture in the same way or that any one description of what is out there is the only way to make sense of that which arrives at the surface of the skin. (For a critique of the idea that theories can be judged by reference to their "correspondence with reality," see Goodman 1968, 1984; Putnam 1981; also Gergen, chap. 6, this volume.)

Hesse makes a cognate point about the divergencies in thinking in modern physics. She points out that the description of real-world essences in modern physics has been neither cumulative nor convergent: "The succession of theories of the atom, and hence the fundamental nature of matter, for example, exhibits no convergence, but oscillates between continuity and discontinuity, field conceptions and particle conceptions, and even speculatively among different typologies of space" (1972, 281–82). It is hard to overlook here the analogy to "ideological regions" (is it witchcraft, transgression, or infection that causes illness?) and to the endemic diversity among social science schools of thought. More important, it is hard to overlook the implication that ontological diversity is not a mark of intellectual immaturity; nor is it necessarily an impediment to progress in a discipline. Indeed, it begins to seem as if, in the "mature sciences," where just like everywhere else there is no theory-independent way to determine what is really lurking out there, it is just as difficult to draw a sharp distinction between what is subjective or theory dependent and what is not; and in the mature sciences, just like everywhere else, there is more than one conceptual reference point from which to construe what unseen forces are really there.

Goodman, who has argued that the real world "is as many ways as it can be truly described," that "there is no such thing as *the* way the world is" (1968, 6), and that it is not meaningful to talk about

anything in particular existing apart from our "version" of it or our
theoretical attempt to understand it, recommends for modern science, and for modern physics in particular, a policy of "judicious
vacillation":

> The physicist flits back and forth between a world of waves and a
> world of particles as suits his purpose. We usually think and work
> within one world-version at a time—hence Hilary Putnam's term
> 'internal realism'—but we shift from one to the other often. When
> we undertake to relate different versions, we introduce multiple
> worlds. When that becomes awkward we drop the worlds for the
> time being and consider only the versions. We are monists, plu-
> ralists and nihilists not quite as the wind blows but as befits the
> context. (1984, 278)

Adopting the philosopher's equivalent to the mythical role of the
"trickster," seeking to embarrass our received categories and oppositions, Goodman puts it wryly: "One might say that there is only
one world but this holds for each of the many worlds."[2]To ask
whether the knowledge one has permits or encourages useful encounters with the world may be quite separable from the assumption that the postulated forces and entities of one's theory exist
independently of one's conceptual reference point (see Cartwright
1983).

The postulation of our own mental constructs as unseen external forces seems to be a central and perhaps indispensable feature
of scientific thought. Horton aptly notes that to construct a scientific theory is to elaborate "a schema of forces or entities (of a limited number of kinds and governed by a limited number of general
principles) operating 'behind' or 'within' the world of common-
sense observation" (1967, 51). With the exception of a few radical
and flawed attempts (like "operationalism") to eliminate everything
unseen from a scientific discourse, Horton's definition seems to
capture a characteristic feature of scientific thought. The difficulty
here seems to be that the postulation of unseen forces or entities
operating behind the world of our senses is an indispensable yet
highly discretionary act of interpretation only weakly constrained
by sense experience (see Gergen, chap. 6, this volume). If the
"hard" data of experimental physics leave scientists free to choose
between several different basic conceptions about the nature of
matter, it hardly seems surprising that the facts about illness do not
settle the question whether or not those who suffer are the victims
of a witch. There is a soft side to all hard data, or perhaps the
crucial point is that without the soft side there is no hard side. All

features of a world, as Goodman has argued (1984, 279), are creatures of some version of it. Unfortunately, given our dominant mythic idealizations of science, the idea that all objects are subject
dependent is not one we readily accept.

The mythic idealizations of science in our culture typically focus
on the physical or natural sciences. It is the natural sciences that
have an elevated position in our culture, and it is the physical world
that is often taken as a model of the social world, not the other way
around. More than a few social scientists are busy at work searching
for a periodic table of social elements, many more have been fascinated by physical metaphors (forces, energy, mechanisms, computers, etc.), and the organization of knowledge in physics and
chemistry (for example, the specification of automatic and highly
general laws of nature) is often adopted as the ideal for social understanding. It is perhaps worth noting that modern physics, since
at least the work of Niels Bohr, has moved away from mechanistic
imagery and the idea of objective predetermination and toward
what has aptly been labeled the physics of possibility, ambiguity,
and uncertainty. It would seem that our mythic idealizations of science change quite slowly (see Matson 1964, 147–55).

Of course, in some non-Western cultures, it is quite the opposite
(Fortes 1959; Smith 1961; Durkheim & Mauss 1963; Horton 1968;
Pepper 1972). In those cultures, much of the intellectual action is
in the area of social thought. The social order or human order is
taken as a model for the natural order, and nature is personified
and viewed as capable of being influenced through prayer, sacri-
fice and offerings, and righteous or heroic conduct. It is animism,
not mechanism, that dominates the intellectual scene. But that is
another story. The point I wish to make here is that the mythic
idealization in our culture of the physical or natural sciences may
have led us to draw an all-too-sharp contrast between what is hard
and what is soft, between what is objective and what is subjective.

It is noteworthy that in our culture the term "natural" has come
to be restricted to those disciplines that study physical things devoid of subjectivity. At least in the West, Mother Nature has lost her
animus, and at least in recent times, animistic or, more accurately,
human or subjective properties such as intentionality, belief, desire, meaning, feeling, self-awareness, value, and purpose have
been actively driven out of the nature studied by those "natural
sciences" from which many social scientists have drawn their ideas
about what kinds of things are really real and really out there, and
how to go about finding them. Today, in the received view, what

"is" has nothing to do with what "ought to be." Matters of fact are unrelated to matters of value. Particles in motion do not think, feel, or have intentions. While metaphorically speaking there may be natural "selection," Mother Nature does it without a purpose in mind. For the social sciences, the problem with this image of nature is that human beings do think, feel, intend, wish, desire, and believe, and one of the most characteristic things studied by social scientists is human subjectivity—mind, self, and emotions. Thus two questions inevitably arise: Is an objectivity-seeking science of subjectivity possible? Does an objectivity-seeking science necessarily presuppose a dehumanized conception of nature, a conception of knowledge free of subjective perspective, and an idea of "reality" independent of conceptual scheme?

The representation of scientific ideals in the natural-physical sciences has had an inordinate influence on thinking about the possibilities for a social science. There is one representation in particular that I have in mind. I am not sure where the representation originated, and it may be outdated and overworked, but it continues to have its influence, and the news that it is outdated has not yet arrived in all circles. In this idealization of scientific thinking, the key notion is "transcendent objectivity" (Nagel 1979): a world of objects devoid of subjective properties and a set of scientific methods and procedures free of subjective judgments for gaining knowledge of how those objects would appear if viewed from "nowhere in particular." Associated with this image of scientific ideals is an image of nature as a scene of objects and events displaying regular and automated, or mechanical, connections. There is also the idea that there are general procedures, techniques, and methods for discovering truths about nature, that a perspective-free (literal?) transcript of nature is, in principle, possible, and that if individual scientists systematically apply certain general knowledge production procedures for discovering truths about nature, there will slowly accumulate a complete, objective, and unified description of nature, the way it "really" is—and the way it is is regular, automated, and lawlike.

That idealization of what science is like is widely invoked in discussions about the possibility of a social science, and it has provoked two reactions. Given this account of what science is about, some—let us call them "hermeneuticists" (Ricoeur 1970, 1974; Spence 1982)—would treat social science as a humanity, hang on to human subjectivity (emotions, beliefs, desires, values, etc.), but abandon the science. Others—let us call them "positivists"—would treat social science as a physical-natural science, leave human subjectivity to the humanists, hermeneuticists, and common sense, and restrict the domain of social science inquiry to those nonsubjective social phenomena, for example, brain asymmetry, hormone regulation, demography, or visual perception, where automatic, lawlike connections can be discovered.

"Positivisim" is a complex epithet in hermeneutic circles, and "hermeneutics" is a complex epithet among positivists. Yet hermeneuticists and positivists share more than reciprocal insults. They share that idealized, and perhaps outmoded, conception of objective science in which there is no place for a science of subjectivity. That conception can be crudely reiterated by reference to what I shall call "the standard dichotomies," a parallel series of oppositions beginning with the opposition between the objective versus the subjective and ending with the opposition between the natural sciences versus the humanities. The series runs as follows: objective versus subjective, seen versus unseen, outer versus inner, public versus private, controlled versus free, reliable versus unreliable, systematic versus unsystematic, automatic (mechanical) versus willed (purposive), explanation versus understanding, prediction versus understanding, explained-by-reference-to-causal-law versus understood-by-reference-to-intentions, general versus context-specific, regular versus irregular, discovered versus constructed, value-free versus value-saturated, formal versus informal, materialist versus idealist, one versus many, instrumental versus symbolic, motion versus action, science versus humanity.

Both reactions, the hermeneutic and the positivist, signal an end to social inquiry as we know it. From the perspective of the hermeneuticist and positivist, there are only two kinds of things in the world: subjectivity devoid of matter (culture) and matter devoid of subjectivity (nature). The first is the realm of the humanist. The second is the realm of the natural scientist. There is no third realm.

There is, however, a third reaction to that idealization of objective science discussed earlier. I will call it the science-of-subjectivity reaction, even though the expression "science of subjectivity" is a contradiction in terms from the perspective of either hermeneutics or positivism. The basic idea is that we must revise our conception of ideal scientific practice and our conception of the relationship between nature and culture, objectivity and subjectivity. The idea is that as we have learned more from historians and historically oriented philosophers about the actual workings of science (Kuhn 1970; Feyerabend 1975; Lakatos 1970; Hesse 1972, 1980; Barnes

1973; Hanson 1958), objectivity-seeking science has come to seem inherently subject dependent. And, as we have learned more from linguists, sociologists, anthropologists, and psychologists about the workings of human subjectivity, including the organization of lexical meanings (Berlin & Kay 1969), folk beliefs (Sahlins 1976; D'Andrade 1976), emotional response (Osgood, May & Miron 1975), and everyday inferencing (Tversky & Kahneman 1974; Kahneman, Slovic & Tversky 1982), human subjectivity has come to seem more objectlike than imagined. The real world, it seems, is populated with subject-dependent objects and objectlike subjectivity, two types of phenomena for which there is no place in the mutually exclusive and exhaustive realms of the symbol-and-meaning-seeking hermeneuticist and the automated-law-seeking positivist. From the point of view of the science of subjectivity, there is no neat boundary line separating these two realms. Subjective phenomena can be studied objectively, and objective study always extends beyond the evidence in hand to the unseen and is never free of a subjective perspective. Thus, for example, the contents of subjectivity can be thought of as causes, and causes need not be widely generalized to be lawlike, although they may be. As Edelson remarks, "Not all hypotheses of interest to a scientist are universal generalizations (1984, 28). From the perspective of a science of subjectivity, knowing what follows what in the world of physical objects is not fundamentally different from knowing what follows what in the world of semantic objects (Hesse 1972) or from determining the patterns and constraints that constitute such phenomena as "natural" languages, which are objective and subjective at the same time.[3] An important implication of this deliberate blurring of the boundaries between objectivity and subjectivity is that other conceptions that rest on a neat and clean contrast between what's objective and what's subjective ought to be revised, which means, to say the least, we may have to rethink for a bit our conception of "rationality" and our conception of "meaning."

A science of subjectivity requires a broadened conception of rationality. Within the positivist idealization of science, rational thinking is equated with deductive logic (syllogistic reasoning, the predicate calculus) and inductive logic (Mill's principles of experimental reasoning, Bayes's principles of statistical inference, etc.). In the positivist's quest for transcendent objectivity and a literal transcript of nature, the rational mind seeks to "mirror" the object world and the lawlike connections among objects (Rorty 1979). Inductive logic is valued because it is the mind's device for detecting true connections. Deductive logic is valued because it is the mind's device for preserving those truths and generating their logical implications. Thinking not guided by inductive or deductive logic is viewed as nonrational and unlikely to result in a reliable and valid picture of the object world.

The positivist conception of rational thought is probably too narrow for a science of subjectivity. We certainly would not want to do without inductive and deductive logic; they are our precious inheritance. Nevertheless, inductive and deductive logic cannot account for every example of systematic, constrained thinking, and there are many examples of impersonal constraints that are not logical rules—not the least of which are the rules of language. Consider a type of example analyzed by Paul Grice (1975) and cited by George Miller (1981). Rick says to Don, "I have a headache. Do you have an aspirin?" Don says to Rick, "There's a store around the corner." Hearing that exchange of words, most competent speakers of English feel that Rick "must" conclude that "the store around the corner sells aspirin" and "the store around the corner is open." It's what any rational person would conclude. Yet this is not a case of logical implication. As Grice and Miller point out, there is no way that "Rick needs an aspirin and there is a store around the corner" can logically imply "the store around the corner sells aspirin" and "the store around the corner is open." Still, that is what we "must" conclude. Grice calls the "must" a conversational implicature instead of a logical implication. He posits that there are systematic, general, rational, but nonlogical rules that constrain our conversation. One rule of conversation is "make what you say relevant." Such nonlogical constraints have also been called "pragmatic implications."

The positivist-hermeneutic conception of rationality has strained under the weight of evidence from research on pragmatic implications.

> Our alternatives seem to be these: Either (1) we deny that there is any rational (logical, grammatical) constraint over the "pragmatic implications" of what we say—or perhaps deny that there *are* any *implications,* on the ground that the relation in question is not deductive . . . ; or else (2) we admit the constraint and say either (a) since all necessity is logical, the "pragmatic implications" of our utterance are (quasi-) logical implications; with or without adding (b) since the "pragmatic implications" cannot be construed in terms of deductive logic, there must be some "third sort" of logic; or we say (c) some necessity is not logical. (Cavell 1969, 10)

I think what we have come to realize is that if rational thought is restricted to inductive and deductive logic, we will have very little of a rational sort to say to each other. No presuppositions. No analogies. No semantic or pragmatic implications. As Miller puts it, "Strictly speaking, formal logic cannot even go from 'Fido is a poodle' to 'Fido is a dog,' because the relation between these sentences depends on their meaning, not their form. Logic can go from 'All poodles are dogs' and 'Fido is a poodle' to 'Fido is a dog,' but it makes for dull conversation" (1981, 136). Yet if rational thought requires a "third sort" of logic or a nonlogical necessity, it is not the kind of constraint that anchors us to a unitary external world of objects. It is more like the kind of thing that makes it possible for two Marxists, two psychoanalysts, two radical behaviorists, two Muslim fundamentalists to have rational discussions within their respective versions of reality but not across them. Rationality seems to have that peculiar bounded quality; it requires deductive and inductive logic, but deductive and inductive reasoning goes on within the framework of a third sort of logic that is bound to something neither uniform nor unitary. What we seem to need is a concept of divergent rationality.

In defining the concept "divergent rationality," it is useful to consider a minitaxonomy of the processes underlying subjective experience. These processes can be grouped in a rough-and-ready way into those that are rational, nonrational, and irrational. A rational process is a self-regulating process controlled by, or at least guided by, impersonal criteria, reason, and evidence. It can be distinguished, on the one hand, from nonrational processes, where reason and evidence are irrelevant to subjective experience. The processes that account for tastes, preferences, likes or dislikes in food are prototypical examples of nonrational processes. On the other hand, rational processes can be distinguished from irrational processes, where there is a breakdown or degradation of the capacities that support rationality. Examples from our own culture include the loss of voluntary control, the failure to distinguish self from other or to discriminate past, present, and future.

Some rational processes are universally distributed across our species. As far as we know, all peoples respect certain elementary logical principles (negation, the law of the excluded middle) and adopt certain common patterns of hypothetical reasoning, means-ends analysis, causal analysis, and experimental reasoning. Things that vary together are connected by the human mind. So are things that are contiguous in time and space, and so on.

At the same time, there are certain rational processes that are not universal. These include, for example, the presuppositions and premises from which a person reasons; the metaphors, analogies, and models used for generating explanations; the categories or classifications used for partitioning objects and events into kinds; and the types of evidence that are viewed as authoritative—intuition, introspection, external observation, meditation, scriptural evidence, evidence from seers, monks, prophets, or elders. The version of reality we construct is a product of both the universal and the nonuniversal rational processes, but it is because not all rational processes are universal that we need a concept of divergent rationality.

For example, there are several hundred million people in that "ideological region" known as South Asia who believe in the transmigration of the soul and the continuity of identity across lifetimes (see Shweder 1985). Let us try to step inside their world for a moment. Perhaps one reason for the near universal acceptance of the idea of the soul is that it helps conceptualize the intuitive experience of what we in our secular culture call the "self," that direct contact we all have with our own "observing ego." In South Asia, among Hindus, that observing ego is conceptualized as a soul or spirit, and all sorts of searching questions are asked about where it came from, where it's going, and why it is now occupying the body it happens to occupy (Sivananda 1979). It is at this point in the reflective process that the concept of a reincarnating soul is postulated to exist behind or within experience, and the concept is used to explain or make sense of various facts of life.

Stevenson (1977) has itemized some of the facts of life that can be explained with the concept of reincarnation and the idea of the identity of the soul (self) across lifetimes, and I have added to his list other facts that call out for explanation. The explanation by reference to reincarnation is especially powerful for those who are willing to accept as evidence the pervasive intuitive experience of one's own observing ego and for those who have already adopted a conceptual reference point from which souls exist, for whom reincarnation and the transmission of prior experiences across lifetimes is at least a theoretical possibility. Fact: Identical twins reared together not infrequently display marked differences in personality; for example, one but not the other may become schizophrenic. Fact: The personalities of siblings who grow up in the same family are no more similar to each other than random pairs of people drawn from different families. Fact: Children often have fears or phobias that cannot be accounted for by any known trauma and are not shared by any other members of their family. Fact: Children sometimes have skills or talents, for example, mathematical or musical abilities, unlike those of their relatives, abilities that could not have been learned through imitation or instruction. Each of these facts seems resistant to either genetic or environmental explanations or else requires a good deal of hand waving by genetic or environmental advocates. But if the qualities of the self and the record of individual experience in prior lives were preserved over rebirths, the facts could be consistently explained (for example, by reference to musical accomplishment in a former life). Add to these facts several not insignificant questions: Why do I feel like I've met this person before? (Perhaps you did, long long ago!) Why are some people born into wealth, health, and status and others born poor and sickly? (Perhaps it's a reward or punishment for conduct in a former life.) What are we to make of those cases where a child claims to have a memory of a former life in another family at another time and many of the details in the child's account of that family turn out to be accurate? (See Stevenson 1960 for the documentation of several such cases.) For the believer, the concept of reincarnation is not without explanatory appeal, and within certain communities in South Asia, rationality and objectivity are not inconsistent with its use.

Concepts about dreaming provide a second illustration of "divergent rationality." In our culture, dreams have all but lost their place in our lives, and we treat the events in our dreams as either unreal or fanciful. Interestingly, there is cross-cultural developmental evidence that suggests that even in cultures where adults believe in the reality of dream events, children become disillusioned with their dreams and, by age ten or so, come on their own to view them as fantasies (Kohlberg 1966, 1969; Laurendeau & Pinard 1972; Shweder & LeVine 1975). Yet despite that universal subjectivism of late childhood, there are many cultures in the world where adults believe in a spiritual world. In those cultures, the reality of dream events is revived for the disillusioned child through exposure by adults to various theories of soul wandering during sleep (Gregor 1981), communications from guardian spirits (Wallace 1972), visions into the netherworld, or recollections of past lives. Among the Iroquois, for example, dreams were viewed as either expressions of the wishes of the dreamer's soul or as the expressed wishes of some superior spiritual being, and the Iroquois felt under considerable obligation to fulfill those wishes and feared the consequences if they did not (Wallace 1972, 69). Iroquois practices were organized (the "Society of the Masks".) so as to make it possible to realize that obligation.

It's not all that hard to convert a dream into a perception; sharing a dream will do it. O'Flaherty, in a discussion of the phenomenological status of dream events, analyzes the idea of a shared dream and relates an example from a short story, "The Brushwork Boy," written by Rudyard Kipling:

> A young boy dreamed again and again of a girl with whom he rode on horseback along a beach until a policeman called Day awakened him. He grew up and joined the cavalry in India, where he drew a map of the place in his dream. When he returned to his parents' home in England, he heard a girl singing a song about the sea of dreams, the city of sleep and the policeman Day; he recognized her as the girl in his dreams. When he told her of his dream, she told him of the boy she had always dreamed of, in the same dream. (1984, 71–73)

Imagine you had a very detailed dream, a specific cast of characters, a specific location and setting, and a specific sequence of events. The next day you meet someone for the first time whom you recognize as a character in your dream, and she recognizes you as a character in her dream of the night before and accurately describes, in detail, all the dream events. I suspect it is an experience of that magnitude that would be required to convince the Western skeptic that dream events might sometimes originate from without and not from within. But even that experience might be dismissed as insufficient, coincidental, or just uncanny. Yet for those peoples for whom nature is populated with spirits, gods, and goddesses capable of communication from a world beyond (or, in more mystical cultures, from a world within), evidence of that sort is not required, and it seems eminently reasonable to interpret dream images as blurry perceptions or degraded signals received over a noisy channel. There is nothing irrational about the idea that dream events are real. Most people who believe that dream events are real are quite able in other contexts to distinguish fact from fiction, reality from fantasy, and they themselves, as children, probably once believed that dreams were unreal.

The science of subjectivity not only requires a broadened concept of rationality; it also requires a broadened concept of meaning (D'Andrade 1984). According to the "standard dichotomies," subjectivity is free-willed, unreliable, idiosyncratic, private, and personal. It is not the stuff out of which to build an objective, impersonal, reliable science of nature. Indeed, for a positivist, one of the distressing things about natural language is that expressions that refer to the same external object (my father, the old man, the wise man) can have different meanings, and the language is full of concepts that seem to refer to things that cannot be seen (ghosts, gods, unicorns, and demons). Consistent with their goal that language mirror reality, positivists insist that the meaning of a scientific concept or term be restricted to that which is most objectlike, public, reliable, impersonal, and the same for all observers, namely, things one could point at in nature. For positivists, concepts and terms are designed to mirror or correspond to things as they are in external reality; what a concept means is the thing that it identifies or, preferably, the operations or procedures that can be used to identify a something as a something. The meaning of a concept is equated with its object reference and wrested from the evocative, connotative, personal, unbounded, and fluctuating realm of subjectivity. From the positivist point of view, if we cannot do away entirely with the words and meanings of natural language, at least we can nail the meanings down to something fixed and stable, things you can point at, weigh, and measure. The positivist wishes to eliminate all subjectivity from the meaning of concepts, and thus, from that objectivist stance: "An utterance has meaning by virtue of corresponding to a state of affairs," and we study language "by analyzing how the structures of utterances correspond systematically to the states of affairs they describe" (see Winograd 1980, 225, for a discussion of objectivist and subjectivist approaches to the study of language).

Curiously, hermeneuticists seem to agree with positivists that natural-language utterances are personal, subjective, and fluctuating, and many hermeneuticists in fact promote the idea that there is no "right meaning" to a natural-language utterance or text, "only a meaning for a particular person at a particular moment in a particular situation" (Winograd 1980, 225; see also Hirsch 1967, 1976; Gadamer 1975; Ricoeur 1974). Where the positivist wants to reduce the meaning of a concept to a single thing that can be pointed to in external objective reality, the hermeneuticist wants to argue that the meaning of any one thing in external reality is the totality of all the interior subjective associations it elicits in you and me.

It would seem that a middle position is possible, and that once again a radical contrast between what's objective and what's subjective does not serve us well. The objective meaning of something is whatever that something implies to those who understand it, as discussed above with the pragmatic implication of "There's a store around the corner." There is a sense in which it makes sense to talk about the objective meaning of natural-language utterances, and correspondence with reality has little to do with it. There is also a second class of meanings that include each meaning of something to someone. The meaning of something to someone is whatever that something suggests to whoever experiences it. That, with some distortion, might be called its subjective meaning. The meaning of the term "father" (used to refer to a kinsman) is related to such implications as "male adult" and "ought to care about the safety of his children," and if you do not understand that, you do not understand. To some people, however, the term suggests or elicits a broader propositional content, for example, "that person who wants to castrate me." That's not the objective meaning of the term "father," but that is what it means to some people. The study of meaning in its broadest sense includes both types of meaning—the objective meaning of something and the meaning of something to someone. It is the study of both implications (including pragmatic implications) and suggestions (Hirsch 1967, 1976). As it turns out, even the so-called subjective meanings, the suggestions, are not always, or even typically, fluctuating, personal, or unconstrained.

It is now widely recognized that the meanings of nonreferential terms in natural language can be orderly, reliable, impersonal, and shared (see, e.g., D'Andrade 1976, 1984). Even what something means to someone, what it suggests, its subjective meaning, can be systematic, general, and objectlike. Whorf presents us with a simple yet powerful example (1956, 217). He points out that the nonsense sound pattern "QUEEP" affects consciousness in the same way the world over. "QUEEP" has the following connotations: fast (vs. slow), sharp (vs. dull), narrow (vs. wide), light (vs. dark). Our subjective reaction to "QUEEP" is a panhuman reaction; "QUEEP" as a nonsense sound elicits the same subjective reaction from all peoples regardless of race, climate, or culture. It is a general or universal subjective response. It is not a subjective state that we will or choose to occur—it is more like an automatic subjective happening, and it is a highly systematic response. Indeed, Osgood, May, and Miron (1975) have demonstrated that connotative meanings of the type mentioned above systematically vary along three general and universal parameters: pleasantness, strain, and excitement, or alternatively, evaluation, potency, and activity.

Whorf then asks us to consider the sound pattern "DEEP."

"DEEP" is phonetically similar to "QUEEP," and indeed it elicits the same set of subjective reactions (fast, sharp, narrow, and light) from all peoples, except speakers of English. For English speakers, however, "DEEP" is not a nonsense sound; it is sound with a meaning of its own. And that meaning, a historically constrained subjective fact, totally overrides and alters our consciousness of its sound properties. For English speakers, and for English speakers only, "DEEP" is slow, dull, wide, and dark.

Whorf's example of "QUEEP" and "DEEP" illustrates three points. First, subjective states can have objectlike properties; they can be structured, automatic, reliable, and constrained. Second, subjective states are not always or even typically idiosyncratic and personal. They are stabilized and patterned at various levels of generality from the personal to the cultural to the universal. Third, the meaning of things, a fact about our subjectivity, can be decisive for how we respond.

The recognition of divergent rationality, of subject-dependent objects, and of a third sort of logic or nonlogical necessity is bound to lead to a shift in our understanding of research findings in various areas of the social sciences. I'd like to illustrate this point briefly by reference to research on the development of moral reasoning and moral understandings, an area in which I am currently conducting cross-cultural research (Shweder, Turiel, & Much 1980; Shweder 1982a; Shweder & Miller 1985).

The most influential scheme for studying moral development is the one proposed by Kohlberg (1969, 1971, 1981). The scheme is premised on a provocative contrast between subjectivity and objectivity. Kohlberg identifies three major levels in the attainment of moral understandings; each level is divided into two stages. Kohlberg argues that, in the earliest or lowest, the "preconventional," level (stages 1 and 2), the meaning of "rightness" is defined entirely by reference to the subjective feelings of the self. At that level, the only thing that defines right versus wrong conduct is one's personal perspective and personal preferences; what's virtuous is whatever avoids punishment or brings reward to you. If the self likes it, it is right; if the self doesn't like it, it's wrong. In the second or intermediate, the "conventional," level of the scheme (stages 3 and 4), Kohlberg argues that the meaning of "rightness" is still defined by reference to subjective feeling, but now it's the subjective feelings of others that matter. What's virtuous is defined as whatever agrees with, or conforms to, the subjective preferences of authority figures (parents, legislatures). If the group likes it, it is right; if the group doesn't like it, it is wrong.

In the third or higher, the "postconventional," level (stages 5 and 6), Kohlberg argues that the meaning of "rightness" is defined by reference to objective standards detached or decentered from the subjective feelings of either the self or the group. What's virtuous is defined in terms of universalizable principles of justice, natural rights, and a humanistic respect for all persons regardless of sex, age, ethnicity, religion, and so on. It is only at the postconventional level that people attain what might be called a genuine moral orientation, in which they recognize that there are obligations in the world that any rational person is objectively bound to respect.

One of the most striking research findings using Kohlberg's scheme is that very few people are postconventional thinkers. On a worldwide scale, perhaps less than five percent of all responses are pure stage 5 or higher. If one accepts Kohlberg's interview methodology and the underlying logic of his scheme, then one must conclude the incredible; that almost all adults in almost all cultures define virtue as conformity with the subjective preferences of the group and never attain the idea that there are objective obligations that take precedence over the wants and desires of the self and the group.

But, of course, one need not accept either the methodology or the underlying logic of Kohlberg's scheme. His interview methodology requires that subjects produce moral arguments and talk like a moral philosopher. Several researchers have relaxed the demand characteristics of the moral development interview situation, requiring only that subjects be discriminating and consistent in their responses to direct probes about the impersonality, alterability, and relativity of rules (Turiel 1979, 1980; Nucci & Turiel 1978; Nucci 1981; Smetana 1982; Shweder, Turiel & Much 1980; Shweder 1982a). What they have discovered is that even young children have a grasp of the idea of objective obligations and recognize that moral rules (the prohibition on stealing) cannot be altered by majority vote or the preferences of the group.

A second reaction, a reaction relevant to our discussion of the false contrast between subjectivity and objectivity, is to reject the underlying logic of Kohlberg's scheme. What the scheme seems to lack is the idea of divergent rationality. One reason that so few people around the world are postconventional thinkers may be that

most people reject the particular conceptual reference points from
which Kohlberg has constructed his notion of objective ethics. It is
important to recognize that rejecting Kohlberg's post conventional
level of thinking is not necessarily the same as defining morality as
subjective preferences, for there may well be other conceptual reference points from which to construct an objective ethic.

Several features of Kohlberg's postconventional level of moral
thinking do seem to be expressive of particular conceptual reference points associated with Western liberal thought (see Shweder
1982b; Shweder & Miller 1985). Thus, in addition to certain formal
or logical principles such as "treat like cases alike and different
cases differently," which are not peculiar to our own historical tradition, the criteria of postconventional thinking include a cluster of
ideas associated with Western liberal democracy: a belief in equal
and universal natural rights; allegiance to "humanity" in general
over one's tribe, community, or nation; a proneness to overlook the
differences between people (in sex, age, intelligence, religion, ethnicity) and emphasize their likenesses; a secular (not religious) belief that life on earth is sacred; and a renunciation of power and
force in getting others to accept your views.

Kohlberg's postconventional level is certainly one possible objectification of morality, but not the only possible objectification. For
the past two years, I have been conducting research with Hindu
Brahmans in the temple town of Bhubaneswar, Orissa, where a
shift in conceptual reference points produces a very different sense
of one's objective obligations. I think there can be little doubt that
my Oriya Brahman informants view their moral obligations in impersonal, objective terms. When they argue that it is wrong for a
widow to remarry, eat fish or meat, or wear brightly colored saris,
that it is wrong for a menstruating woman to enter the kitchen or
sleep in the same bed as her husband, or that it is right to arrange a
marriage or to forbid Untouchables from entering the temple, they
are not simply expressing their likes or preferences; rather they are
describing what they view as the impersonal requirements of natural law. Being objective obligations, they are not thought to be
changeable by majority vote, and they are thought to be universally
binding on all those to whom they apply (see Shweder & Miller
1985).

The idea of divergent rationality is quite helpful in comparing
Hindu and American moral codes, for one finds that the moral
sensibilities of Oriya Brahmans and American secular humanists
are virtually independent of one another. There are certain areas

of agreement, for example, that it is wrong to break a promise, engage in arbitrary assault, destroy the personal possessions of others, discriminate against someone on the basis of irrelevant criteria, engage in incest, or cut in front in a line. But there are also many cases where what is a serious moral breach in one culture is not a breach at all in the other culture. For example, in Orissa, but not in America, it is a serious moral breach if one of your family eats beef or if a woman asks her husband to massage her legs or eats at the same time with her husband's elder brother. And in America, but not in Orissa, it is a serious moral breach if a married son, by virtue of his sex, is given a lion's share of the family inheritance and the married daughter receives very little, or if a husband beats his wife for repeatedly going to the movies without asking his permission. Notably, within both cultures, there are "argument structures" or "cultural rationales" that objectify those moral judgments (LeVine 1984), and within each culture there are sophisticates or virtuosos who are extremely adept at applying those argument structures in defense of their practices (see Shweder & Miller 1985). Thus, for example, in India it is thought to be objectively right to have arranged marriages: "A marriage is something that affects so many people, relatives, and friends, in serious ways. How can you possibly leave it up to one person, blinded by lust or passion, to make the decision?" It is thought to be natural for a married son to inherit most of the father's estate and for a married daughter to inherit little: "Parents live with their married sons, not their married daughters. It is the son who must care for the parents in their old age. He must bear the financial burden and arrange the funeral rites. Married daughters have received a dowry and left the family. The needs of the son are greater." And for Oriya Brahmans, reason demands that insubordinate wives receive punishment, for the family is a corporate group, like an orchestra or military unit, with differentiated and clearly defined roles. Is it unreasonable to punish a private in the army who leaves camp without permission? And isn't physical punishment more humane—for it only hurts in the place where you are hit, whereas other forms of punishment attack the soul and hurt a great deal more.

I cannot here go into detail about Oriya practices or the conceptual reference points, metaphors and analogies, sources of evidence, cultural rationales, and argument structures that lend them rational support. To an outside observer, however, what is striking is that these argument structures are elaborated from conceptual reference points that, not only are discrepant with our own, but

seem to suggest fundamentally different starting points in the conception of self, society, and nature. Oriya Brahmans construct their
objective obligations from the premise that people have souls that
transmigrate, that nature is just, and that the differences between
people, especially differences in health, wealth, and status, are
there for a reason—as just desert for conduct in former lives.
Given such a premise, the multifarious differences between people,
for example, in sex, birth order, lineage, are not only not overlooked, but are emphasized. Whereas Americans tend to view the
"individual" as an autonomous unit and the fundamental building
block of the social order, with relationships to other individuals,
and indeed society itself, being established only through discretionary choice (the myth of a "social contract"), Oriya Brahmans view
the social order as part of the natural order, stress the priority of
the social whole and the interdependence of hierarchically arranged roles. Given such a premise, the emphasis is on natural duties, not natural rights, and a primary objective obligation of life is
to live up to the duties of one's various roles (as a son, a father, a
householder, etc.). The fate of one's soul depends upon it (see
Shweder & Miller 1985). The idea of divergent rationality helps us
see that there may be more than one conceptual reference point
from which to construct an objective ethic. Indeed, without the
idea of divergent rationality, we might have been misled into equating moral thought with the premises implicit in Kohlberg's scheme,
and we might have been tempted to follow Kohlberg (1981, 25–27,
76, 136–38) in doubting the rationality of those whose practices
and beliefs differ from our own.

CONCLUSION

Several years ago, I read the voluminous three-year (1931–34) correspondence and debate between J. B. S. Haldane, the eminent
evolutionary biologist, and Arnold Lunn, a rather formidable "cre-
ationist" (Lunn & Haldane 1935). Lunn tried to convince Haldane
that the facts of natural history were more consistent with the inference of a designer or inventor than with the idea of evolution by
mutation, cell recombination, and natural selection. Haldane tried
to convince Lunn that his ideas of design were part of an outmoded
religious way of thinking that science had replaced. In my view, the
debate ended in a stalemate. Both men were educated and informed. Both men engaged in extraordinary feats of deductive
and inductive reasoning. By the end, I was convinced that there
was nothing in the universal aspects of reason shared by the two

men that could settle the issue, that religion and science were not quite as different as I had supposed, and that the convergence of belief is not the sine qua non of rationality.

In this essay, I have tried to find a way around symbolic and irrationalist interpretations of intellectual diversity. I have pointed out that theories, doctrines, and concepts often classified by outside observers as symbolic, delusional, ideological, supernatural, or religious, not only are viewed as reasonable, natural, and objective to the insider, but are also sufficiently explained by reference to processes legitimately classified as rational. To support that claim, I have introduced the notion of "divergent rationality"—not every rational process is a universal process—and I have sought to erode the boundary line between subjectivity and objectivity. The object world, I have argued, is subject dependent. Subjectivity is objectlike. Rationality is compatible with diversity. The emergence of schools of thought, cults, and cultures is to be expected—perhaps even encouraged. Reality is not independent of our version of it (Goodman 1968, 1984). Within any version there is a distinction to be made between what's real and what's unreal, but not necessarily the same distinction.

The counterpoint is that not every version of reality is livable, and there is much to be learned by examining the difference between those speculative ontologies, conceptual reference points, and root metaphors that we can live by and those that we can't. Despite the fact that they may seem alien, strange, or irrational to outsiders, the cultures studied by anthropologists are, with some few exceptions, examples of versions of reality that one can live by. They are functioning examples of divergent rationalities. By understanding better those cultures, we may come to better understand the endemic diversity of intellectual "cults" and schools of thought within our own science. Indeed, until we come to understand *that* better, there is little point in being troubled that we all cannot agree on what mind, self, and society are all about.

Notes

1. I wish to thank Donald W. Fiske, Jerome Kagan, Julius Kirshner, Arthur Kleinman, and Frank Richter for their stimulating comments on an earlier version of this chapter.
2. Ibid. See Geertz (1983) on the anthropologist as trickster.
3. Given its liminal status, it is perhaps not too surprising that from the

perspective of the science of subjectivity, it is natural language that is so frequently used as a model for nature (Tyler 1969; Kessing 1972; Casson 1981). Psychosomatic medicine and the placebo phenomenon are additional examples of things that cannot easily be classified as either subjective or objective—they are both.

References

Barnes, B. 1973. The comparison of belief-systems: An anomaly versus falsehood. In *Modes of thought*, ed. R. Horton and R. Finnegan. London: Faber and Faber.

Berlin, B., and Kay, P. 1969. *Basic color terms: Their universality and evolution.* Berkeley: University of California Press.

Cartwright, N. 1983. *How the laws of physics lie.* New York: Oxford University Press.

Casson, R. W. 1981. *Language, culture, and cognition.* New York: Macmillan.

Cavell, S. 1969. *Must we mean what we say?* New York: Charles Scribner.

D'Andrade, R. G. 1976. A propositional analysis of U.S. American beliefs about illness. In *Meaning in anthropology,* ed. R. Basso and H. Selby. Albuquerque: University of New Mexico Press.

———. 1984. Cultural meaning systems. In *Culture theory: Essays on mind, self, and emotion,* ed. R. A. Shweder and R. A. LeVine. New York: Cambridge University Press.

Dollard, J., and Miller, N. E. 1950. *Personality and psychotherapy.* New York: McGraw-Hill.

Durkheim, E., and Mauss, M. 1963. *Primitive classification.* Chicago: University of Chicago Press.

Edelson, M. 1984. *Hypothesis and evidence in psychoanalysis.* Chicago: University of Chicago Press.

Feyerabend, P. 1975. *Against method.* Atlantic Highlands, N.J.: Humanities Press.

Fortes, M. 1959. *Oedipus and Job in West African religion.* Cambridge: Cambridge University Press.

Gadamer, H. G. 1975. *Truth and method.* New York: Seabury Press.

Gallie, W. 1964. *Philosophy and the historical understanding.* New York: Schoken.

Geertz, C. 1983. Anti-anti-relativism. Distinguished lecture, American Anthropological Association meetings, Chicago, Illinois.

Goodman, N. 1968. *Languages of art.* New York: Bobbs-Merrill.

———. 1972. *Problems and projects.* New York: Bobbs-Merrill.

———. 1978. *Ways of worldmaking.* New York: Bobbs-Merrill.

———. 1984. Notes on the well-made world. *Partisan Review* 51:276–88.

Gregor, T. 1981. "Far, far away my shadow wandered . . . " Dream symbolism and dream theories of the Mehinaku Indians of Brazil. *American Ethnologist* 8:702–20.

Grice, H. P. 1975. Logic and conversation. In *Syntax and semantics*. Vol. 3: *Speech arts*, ed. P. Cole and J. C. Morgan. New York: Academic Press.

Hanson, N. 1958. *Patterns of discovery*. London: Cambridge University Press.

Hesse, M. 1972. In defense of objectivity. *Proceedings of the British Academy* 58:275–92.

———. 1980. *Revolutions and reconstructions in the philosophy of science*. Brighton: Harvester Press.

Hirsch, E. D. 1967. *Validity in interpretation*. New Haven: Yale University Press.

———. 1976. *The aims of interpretation*. Chicago: University of Chicago Press.

Horton, R. [1964] 1979. Ritual man in Africa. In *Reader in comparative religion*, ed. W. A. Lessa and E. Z. Vogt. 4th ed. New York: Harper and Row.

———. 1967. African traditional thought and Western science. *Africa* 37:50–71 (part 1), 159–87 (part 2).

———. 1968. Neo-Tylorianism: Sound sense or sinister prejudice? *Man* 3:625–34.

Kahneman, D.; Slovic, P.; and Tversky, A., eds. 1982. *Judgment under uncertainty*. London: Cambridge University Press.

Kakar, S. 1982. *Shamans, mystics, and doctors*. Boston: Beacon Press.

Kessing, R. M. 1972. Paradigms lost: The new ethnography and the new linguistics. *Southwestern Journal of Anthropology* 28:199–232.

Kohlberg, L. 1966. Cognitive stages and preschool education. *Human Development* 9:5–17.

———. 1969. Stage and sequence: The cognitive-developmental approach to socialization. In *Handbook of socialization theory and research*, ed. D. A. Goslin. New York: Rand McNally.

———. 1971. From is to ought: How to commit the naturalistic fallacy and get away with it in the study of moral development. In *Cognitive development and epistemology*, ed. T. Mischel. New York: Academic Press.

———. 1981. *The philosophy of moral development*. San Francisco: Harper and Row.

Kuhn, T. S. 1970. *The structure of scientific revolutions*. 2d ed. Chicago: University of Chicago Press.

Lakatos, I. 1970. Falsification and the methodology of scientific research. In *Criticism and the growth of knowledge*, ed. I. Lakatos and A. Mesgrave. Cambridge: Cambridge University Press.

Laurendeau, M., and Pinard, A. 1972. *Causal thinking in children*. New York: International Universities Press.

LeVine, R. A. 1984. Properties of culture. In *Culture theory: Essays on mind, self, and emotion*, ed. R. A. Shweder and R. A. LeVine. New York: Cambridge University Press.

Lunn, A., and Haldane, J. B. S. 1935. *Science and the supernatural*. London: Eyre and Spottiswoode.

Matson, F. W. 1964. *The broken image: Man, science, and society*. New York: Braziller.

Miller, G. A. 1981. *Language and speech*. San Francisco: W. H. Freeman.

Murdock, G. P. 1980. *Theories of illness: A world survey*. Pittsburgh: University of Pittsburgh Press.

Murdock, G. P.; Wilson, S. F.; and Frederick, V. 1978. World distribution of theories of illness. *Ethnology* 17:449–70.

Nagel, T. 1979. Subjective and objective. In *Mortal questions,* ed. T. Nagel. Cambridge: Cambridge University Press.

Nisbett, R., and Ross, L. 1980. *Human inference: Strategies and shortcomings of social judgment*. Englewood Cliffs, N.J. Prentice-Hall.

Nucci, L. 1981. Conceptions of personal issues: A domain distinct from moral or societal concepts. *Child Development* 52:114–21.

Nucci, L., and Turiel, E. 1978. Social interactions and the development of social concepts in pre-school children. *Child Development* 49:400–407.

O'Flaherty, W. D. 1984. *Dreams, illusions, and other realities*. Chicago: University of Chicago Press.

Osgood, C. E.; May, W. H.; and Miron, M. S. 1975. *Cross-cultural universals of affective meaning*. Urbana: University of Illinois Press.

Pepper, S. C. 1972. *World hypotheses: A study in evidence*. Berkeley: University of California Press.

Putnam, H. 1978. *Meaning and the moral sciences*. London: Routledge and Kegan Paul.

———. 1981. *Reason, truth, and history*. Cambridge: Cambridge University Press.

Ricoeur, P. 1970. *Freud and philosophy*. New Haven: Yale University Press.

———. 1974. *The conflict of interpretations*. Evanston, Ill.: Northwestern University Press.

Rorty, R. 1979. *Philosophy and the mirror of nature*. Princeton: Princeton University Press.

Sahlins, M. 1976. *Culture and practical reason*. Chicago: University of Chicago Press.

Schneider, D. M. 1965. Kinship and biology. In *Aspects of the analysis of family structure,* ed. A. G. Coale et al. Princeton: Princeton University Press.

———. 1968. *American kinship: A cultural account*. Englewood Cliffs, N.J.: Prentice-Hall.

Shweder, R. A. 1977. Likeness and likelihood in everyday thought: Magical thinking in judgments about personality. *Current Anthropology* 18:637–58.

———. 1979. Aspects of cognition in Zinacanteco shamans: Experimental results. In *Reader in comparative religion,* ed. W. Lessa and E. Z. Vogt. 4th ed. New York: Harper and Row.

———. 1980. Rethinking culture and personality theory. Part 3: From genesis and typology to hermeneutics and dynamics. *Ethos* 8:60–94.

———. 1982a. Beyond self-constructed knowledge: The study of culture and morality. *Merrill-Palmer Quarterly* 28:41–69.

———. 1982b. Liberalism as destiny. Review of *Essays on moral development*. Vol. 1: *The philosophy of moral development* by Lawrence Kohlberg. *Contemporary Psychology* 27:421–24.

———. 1985. Menstrual pollution, soul loss, and the comparative study of emotions. In *Culture and depression: Towards an anthropology of affects and affective disorders*, ed. A. Kleinman and B. J. Good. Los Angeles: University of California Press.

Shweder, R. A., and Bourne, E. J. 1982. Does the concept of the person vary cross-culturally? In *Cultural conceptions of mental health and therapy*, ed. A. J. Marsella and G. White. Boston: Reidel.

Shweder, R. A., and LeVine, R. A. 1975. Dream concepts in Hausa children: A critique of the "Doctrine of Invariant Sequence" in cognitive development. *Ethos* 3:209–230.

Shweder, R. A., and Miller, J. G. 1985. The social construction of the person: How is it possible? In *The social construction of the person*, ed. K. Gergen and K. Davis. New York: Springer-Verlag.

Shweder, R. A.; Turiel, E.; and Much, N. C. 1980. The moral intuitions of the child. In *On the development of social cognition in children*, ed. J. H. Flavell and L. Ross. New York: Cambridge University Press.

Sivananda, Swami. 1979. *What becomes of the soul after death?* Shivanandanagar, India: Divine Life Society.

Smetana, J. 1982. *Concepts of self and morality: Women's reasoning about abortion.* New York: Praeger.

Smith, H. 1961. *Accents of the world's philosophies.* Publications in the Humanities No. 50. Cambridge: Department of Humanities, Massachusetts Institute of Technology.

Spence, D. 1982. *Narrative truth and historical truth.* New York: Norton.

Spiro, M. 1965. Religion as a culturally constituted defense mechanism. In *Context and meaning in cultural anthropology*, ed. M. Spiro. New York: Free Press.

———. 1982. Collective representations and mental representations in religious symbol systems. In *On symbols in anthropology*, vol. 3, ed. J. Maquet. Los Angeles: University of California Press.

———. 1983. *Oedipus in the Trobriands.* Chicago: University of Chicago Press.

———. 1984. Some reflections on cultural determinism and relativism with special reference to emotion and reason. In *Culture theory: Essays on mind, self, and emotion*, ed. R. A. Shweder and R. A. LeVine. New York: Cambridge University Press.

Stevenson, I. 1960. The evidence for survival from claimed memories of former incarnations. *Journal of the American Society for Psychical Research* 54:51–117.

———. 1977. The explanatory value of the idea of reincarnation. *Journal of Nervous and Mental Diseases* 164:305–26.

Two murder trials in Kordofan. 1920. *Sudan Notes and Records*, 245–59. Transcripts.

Trevor-Roper, H. R. 1967. The European witch-craze of the sixteenth and seventeenth centuries. In *Religion, the Reformation, and social change*, ed. H. R. Trevor-Roper. London: Macmillan.

Turiel, E. 1979. Distinct conceptual and developmental domains: Social convention and morality. In *Nebraska symposium on motivation, 1977*, ed. C. B. Keasy. 25: Lincoln: University of Nebraska Press.

————. 1980. Domains and categories in social cognitive development. In *The relationship between social and cognitive development*, ed. W. Overton. Hillsdale, N.J.: Erlbaum.

Tversky, A., and Kahneman, D. 1974. Judgment under uncertainty: Heuristics and biases. *Science* 185:1124–31.

Tyler, S. 1969. *Cognitive anthropology*. New York: Holt, Rinehart and Winston.

Wallace, A. F. C. 1972. *The death and rebirth of the Seneca*. New York: Random House.

Whiting, J. W. M. 1977. A model for psychocultural research. In *Culture and infancy: Variations in human experience*, ed. P. H. Leiderman, S. R. Tulkin, and A. Rosenfeld. New York: Academic Press.

Whiting, J. W. M., and Child, I. 1953. *Child training and personality*. New Haven: Yale University Press.

Whorf, B. L. 1956. *Language, thought, and reality*. Cambridge, Mass.: MIT Press.

Winograd, T. 1980. What does it mean to understand language? *Cognitive Science* 4:209–41.

8 Explanation in the Social Sciences and in Life Situations

Paul F. Secord

> The skills of an applied and a pure scientist are characteristically different. . . . The pure scientist . . . deliberately excludes, whereas the applied scientist seeks always to accommodate, the effects of intervening levels of reality.
>
> —ROY BHASKAR, 1975

Roy Bhaskar's quote concerning the nature of applied social science follows directly from his realist view of the philosophy of social science (1975, 1978, 1979, 1982). Bhaskar's synthesis rests on many sources, including those associated with the Kuhnian view as well as those of its critics. Contributing most directly to the new synthesis is the work of Harré (1970, 1972) and of Harré and Madden (1975). This new philosophy of science has profound implications for the social sciences, as described by Manicas and Secord (1983). Unlike most other critiques of positivist approaches to science, the greatest strength of this realist view lies in its constructive nature. In this paper, I will emphasize this aspect, especially as applied to solving social problems. Let me hasten to add that, as in any philosophical analysis, no specific methodological prescriptions are given for how to do research. Nevertheless, Bhaskar's analysis is highly suggestive of new ways of interpreting research and provides a way of structuring the relationship between the social sciences and applied problem situations.

Most behavioral scientists explicitly or implicitly see their discipline within what has been called the "standard view of science" (Scheffler 1967; Manicas & Secord 1983). Under this view, psychologists see individual behaviors as a function of a multiple set of variables or conditions, and their task as that of identifying these determining variables. Just as a machine functions in a certain way under certain conditions, persons behave according to their present physical and psychological state and the stimulus context in which they are situated. This leads immediately to a dilemma. If the behavior of individuals is subject to variation in the presence of myriad different conditions, it is easy to see that the set of conditions quickly reaches a point beyond which they cannot be dealt with. Logically, the conditions that control behavior would extend to include the entire universe. Thus it seems a hopeless task to try to specify such conditions in any detail. Worse yet, statisticians readily recognize that the interpretation of multiple regression designs involving more than just a few variables are extraordinarily prone to guesswork and error (Blalock 1982).

Bhaskar's new synthesis mutes the effect of this dilemma. He points out that this kind of thinking results from the following misconceptions of the nature of science:

1. Universal laws expressed in terms of regular concomitances between events are the basis of all science.

2. Explanation of a particular phenomenon is accomplished through deduction from universal laws that are applicable to the phenomenon.

3. Causal sequences are inferred from regular concomitances of antecedents and their consequences.

4. The main task of the behavioral sciences is to discover the regularities in behavior.

These propositions sound reasonable, but each of them can be demonstrated to create both logical and practical problems for scientists. Key elements of Bhaskar's contrasting view of science include the following.

1. The standard view of science misconceives the world, which is radically open. Closed systems rarely occur, and then only in the laboratory.

2. The standard view of science confuses observable regularities with the abstract entities of science.

3. Laws are about behavioral tendencies of entities that stem from their nature. They operate in both closed and open systems, although their effects may not be observable in open systems. Laws do not describe the patterns or legitimate the predictions of kinds of events. Rather they set limits and impose constraints on the types of action possible.

4. The task of science is to discover the nature of entities, their powers, liabilities, and effects. Powers and liabilities can be attributed to entities even though these properties may never be expressed.

5. Causes are found in the nature of things, in their structural

properties that create powers or liabilities. Locating causes in the nature of entities greatly attenuates the problem of generalizing from closed systems to open systems. Their nature remains the same but is often not evidenced or activated in the open world. Clearly (in our everyday experience) we are able to identify causes operating in open systems, because our actions depend upon this ability. These notions of causal powers suggest that the task of science must be sharply separated from the task of explanation in the open world.

6. Social phenomena are stratified; they consist of complex objects having different levels. Because of the complexity of the internal structure of persons, an antecedent state description does not enable prediction of behavior: persons may behave differently in the same external circumstances because of being in different internal states.

The radical nature of this critique of conventional science, as well as its constructive features, is apt to be missed unless I concentrate on several vital points. Scientific laws are to be conceived as causal principles or tendencies rooted in the natures of the relevant entities and not as reflecting regular concomitance between *events*. The Humean regularity conception of cause is replaced with the notion of causal powers that have their origins in the dynamic structures of the entities under study. And finally, a radical distinction is drawn between the open world of everyday life and the closed system in the science laboratory.

SCIENCE AS UNIVERSAL LAWS BASED ON REGULARITIES

Much of the recent lament concerning the lack of progress in the social sciences during the twentieth century takes as its evidence an invidious comparison with the natural sciences. None of the critiques, however, take a hard look at the natural sciences; usually only physics is considered, and the other natural sciences are ignored. More appalling is that not even physics is fairly represented. Usually the field to be held up as a model is Newtonian physics. Indeed, it is not uncommon to identify only a single characteristic of that field—its universal laws—as the chief characteristic of the natural sciences in general! This is sometimes a background assumption, taken for granted, and sometimes explicitly put forward. With that assumption, the progress of the human sciences is evaluated in terms of the extent to which they have managed to establish universal laws. The conclusion follows neatly: obviously the social "sciences" have failed to achieve real status as science.

Before accepting that conclusion, the line of possible argument should be examined more carefully. What is sometimes not noted is that Newtonian physics applies to a closed system; moreover, laws are taken to be best exemplified in terms of the regular associations between events, for example, the regular movements of heavenly bodies in relation to one another. We can legitimately ask whether this kind of science constitutes an appropriate model for the social sciences. If this doubt is not shared, we can turn to a far more important consideration. Almost any physicist will tell you that despite its preeminence in history and in the popular mind, Newtonian physics is an anomaly—other areas of physics have little resemblance to it. Consider the variety in just a few illustrative areas, such as atomic or particle physics, plasma physics, atmospheric physics, molecular physics, the physics of structural materials, of surface tension, and so on. What the appropriate science model is for these areas is by no means clear, and it could be argued that the model is apt to bear little resemblance to that for Newtonian physics.

Doubt concerning the appropriate natural science model increases by an order of magnitude when we turn to the other natural sciences. Biology, in particular, may readily be conceived of in terms of an alternative model based on causal powers. Bhaskar follows Harré and Madden in conceiving of scientific laws as causal principles or tendencies rooted in the natures of the relevant entities and not as regular concomitance between events. What is emphasized, in direct contrast to Humean skepticism concerning the reality of cause, is the idea that the structures and properties of an entity, under the appropriate conditions, give it the power or capacity to act in particular ways. Glass shatters easily because of its particular crystalline structure; dynamite explodes when detonated because of its physicochemical structure. In this view, expounded in detail by Harré and Madden (1975), causes are natural necessities and not mere logical necessities or psychological illusions. Following this view, the essence of scientific investigation is tracing the actions of entities (whether material objects or living organisms) to their origins in the natures of the entities and the prevailing conditions of action.

CAUSAL POWERS

The following brief report of a decade-long research program on cancer metastases conducted by Isaiah Joshua Fidler and his colleagues nicely illustrates the concept of causal powers in the realist account of science discussed here. The report is abridged and paraphrased from a longer one (Rodgers 1983). The objective of the program was to obtain a better understanding of how and why tumor cells metastasize and to find a way to combat this process. In this account, I italicize all of those words that fit the realist view— words associated with generative mechanism, causal powers, and the origins of these processes in the nature of the entity.

Metastasis is a well-known phenomenon: cells originating in a tumor travel to other parts of the body and *destroy* normal cells in those parts. Yet of cancer cells injected in mice, only .1 percent survive. Survival could be some sort of random process in which all cells have equal survival chances, but this seemed unlikely to Fidler, who set out to prove that the cells that survived had a special *nature*. His hunch was supported when he took cells from a metastatically generated tumor and injected them. These cells *produced* eighty times more metastases than did cells from the original tumor. Fidler concluded that cells in a tumor are incredibly diverse and that there is *something special* about cells that successfully metasta-size—they have different *natures*.

To test his hypothesis, Fidler grew a tumor in the laboratory and split it in two. One half was left to grow in the original culture. From the other half, seventeen individual cells were isolated and cloned to produce seventeen different lines of cells, each line con-taining identical ones. The effects of the cells taken from the origi-nal culture were compared with the effects of the cloned cells by injecting them into laboratory animals. Cells from the original culture tended to *produce* about the same number of metastases— they were roughly equal in their *power* to *produce* tumors. But, as anticipated, the cloned cells were much more varied in their effect. One set of identical clones might *produce* very few tumors, while another set of different identical clones were all highly effective in *producing* tumors. This supported Fidler's hypothesis that cells with the *capacity* to metastasize had special *properties*. Other research sup-ported this idea. Metastatic cells from the same cancer were found to vary enormously in their *sensitivity* to drugs used to treat cancer; some were remarkably *resistant* and had the capacity to *adapt*.

These findings suggest that current methods of treating cancer, aimed at *killing* a majority of the cancer cells with *radiation* and *chemotherapy*, is misguided. Such treatment is apt to be ineffective if the cells with the *capacity* to metastasize are resistant. In further research, Fidler worked with macrophages, white blood cells that specialize in *engulfing* and *digesting* bacteria, trying to find a way to *turn them on* so that they would *attack* and *destroy* cancer cells. At this point he has had partial success in *activating* macrophages.

I present this account, not as evidence to support the realist view

202 PAUL F. SECORD

and its causal language, but rather to illustrate how such language is apt to play a crucial role in the way the scientist thinks. Scientists do not approach a problem by starting with an established universal law from which they can make deductions; they are much more apt to think in terms of active causal mechanisms and their enabling conditions. The essential concepts guiding this sort of research, which is certainly not atypical or unusual, are that living organisms have certain active powers or capacities that must be recognized and described. But doing that is only the first step—a kind of promissory note. What follows is the effort to specify what structures in the organism's nature account for that power, along with the specification of internal states and external conditions that enable and activate the power.

Interwoven throughout this account are cause-and-effect relationships, notions of actions and mechanisms that produce particular effects. Notice that Fidler has recognized the distinctive behavior of metastatic cells and has moved directly to finding ways of combating them. The realist view described here, however, would require as an ultimate goal that the physicochemical nature of these cells be specified in a manner that explains their special powers. Again, this account is not presented as supportive evidence but merely as illustrative of the uses of the concept of causal powers. It could be argued that this particular account is of discovery rather than confirmation or that other scientists do very different sorts of things. But it illustrates nicely the particularistic nature of science in contrast to the ideal of universalism constructed by philosophers.

More needs to be said about causal powers, as argued in detail by Harré and Madden in their book on the topic (1975). The concept is a radical departure from views prevailing in the philosophy of science during the past two centuries, views largely originating with David Hume (1748). This paper is hardly the place to review these arguments; rather, my aim is to make clear how differently science may be approached from this causal perspective. Causal powers are not merely inferred from regular concomitances of antecedents and consequents; instead, through appropriate experimentation, the scientist sees that the structure of the substance or entity or process under investigation, along with certain necessary conditions, accounts for the power or capacity to perform or behave in the observed fashion. Instead of being content with recording the antecedents that precede certain consequences, the scientist zeroes in on the nature of the active substance or agent that, under the right conditions, accounts for the performance. This shifts the causal focus to the structural natures of entities or processes with contextual conditions as a background factor.

Capacities are not necessarily activated in the open world; it is clear that they may be present for years even though the individual does not enact them. One of the great advantages of this focus on causal powers as stemming from the nature of a person is that it allows knowledge to be cumulative. The idea that the structural properties of an entity endow it with certain capacities makes it possible for focused inquiry to accumulate a data base and gradually to gain a better understanding of phenomena. Research programs can collect more and more information concerning the conditions under which a particular capacity is facilitated or activated, as well as those conditions inhibiting or constraining its exercise.

An extensive independent analysis of psychological explanation provides considerable insight into how the notion of causal powers might be applied to psychology. Cummins (1983) notes that the received doctrine for scientific explanation is subsumption under law, as exemplified in the covering law model, and further, that this doctrine has been more influential in psychology than anywhere else, even though in his opinion psychological explanation makes little sense as subsumption. He treats psychological phenomena as manifestations of capacities that are explained by analysis and contrasts several forms of analysis with subsumption under law.

Cummins observes that changes in the state of a system are most often explained in terms of subsumption under causal laws, but that such explanations are often inadequate. He identifies this kind of law as a transition law and differentiates it from causal laws that seek to explain the properties of a system (as opposed to the transition of the system). But in addition to causal laws, other laws that are not causal statements are of great importance in science and are often crucial to explanation. These include the following:

1. *Nomic correlations.* An example is the law correlating thermal and electrical conductivity. Nomic correlations are predictive rules but have no explanatory role.

2. *Nomic attributions.* These are lawlike statements to the effect that all entities of a certain kind have a certain property.

3. *Instantiation laws.* These are lawlike statements indicating how a property is instantiated in a particular type of system.

4. *Composition laws.* These are lawlike statements that describe patterns or compositions of a specified system.

The last three types of laws enter into explanatory analyses that are common in science. Cummins identifies what he calls property theories and describes the strategy for explaining the properties of a system. He calls attention to the fact that many scientific theories are intended, not to explain changes of state, but to explain properties. Whereas covering law explanations may seem plausible for dealing with changes of state, they produce only banalities if they are used to explain properties. Property theories are not intended to explain the acquisition by system S of a property P (e.g., how did organisms acquire the capacity to pass on traits to offspring?) but rather what it is about system S that accounts for its displaying that property (e.g., what is there about S that enables it to pass on traits to offspring?).

The strategy for answering such questions is succinctly stated by Cummins: It "is to construct an analysis of S that explains S's possession of P by appeal to the properties of S's components and their mode of organization" (1983, 15). When the property is complex, a prerequisite step to explanation involves the analysis of a system into discrete properties, which in turn can be explained through componential analysis. Although the principle is intuitively obvious when a very simple property is explained, the analysis of more complex properties (e.g., a personality disposition) can be very complicated, and Cummins takes pains to point out some of the confusions that might be engendered.

Among the most important stipulations is the necessity for independently specifying the elemental components of the property being explained; that is, no use may be made of the property itself in explaining how the components function to produce the property. The explanation hinges on knowledge of the properties of the components of the property to be explained and of the way in which these components are organized. These components must be identified through nomic attributions, "lawlike statements to the effect that all x's have a certain property P" (ibid., 7). It is this latter requirement that provides force to the explanation. In explaining a complex property, it may be necessary to analyze the properties of the components into still simpler properties; however, an infinite regress is avoided because at some level only nomic attributions are required.

Explanation through instantiation should not be thought of as necessarily reductive. The property to be explained is often not to be identified with the components of the property as, say, in reducing chemistry to physics. Reduction of psychological properties typically fails because these properties can be realized or instantiated in more than one way, just as adding up numbers can be one kind of process in a mechanical calculator and another in a computer. The analysis of a property into its components does not always provide an adequate explanation of the property. The componential or compositional analysis often is not sufficient to explain more complex properties. The most interesting properties are dispositions or capacities, and to explain them, what Cummins calls "functional analysis" is used. A functional analysis does not provide a complete explanation of a disposition. For this, the details of how the disposition is instantiated in a larger system must be known. The greater the contrast between the capacity to be explained and the elemental units entering into the functional explanation, the more powerful the explanation.

A form of functional explanation central to cognitive psychology is termed "interpretive analysis." We might think of the input and output of a computer program at a low, descriptive level involving the electronic signals occurring. In contrast, at the interpretive level, input and output are described symbolically. Here the gap between the symbolic level and the electronic level is very great, and it becomes difficult to see how specification of more elemental properties constitutes explanation. Cummins argues that only when some isomorphism of structure between the information-processing program and some program couched in descriptive terms can be spelled out do we have an adequate explanation. This example reveals the difficulty and complexity of functional analysis, but also suggests that, when successful, it has great explanatory power.

Both material objects and persons can readily be regarded as having causal powers. Dynamite has the power to explode, seeds have the power to germinate, and persons have the power of speech. Harré and Madden regard the concept as useful for both the natural and social sciences, although unfortunately their book is almost exclusively devoted to natural science examples. At the same time, however, the concept does provide an important point of differentiation between the natural and social sciences. This difference lies in how the powers or capacities of inanimate and animate objects are conceptualized and identified. To make the distinction, the doctrine of "actualism," the idea that "nothing ever has the power to do what it does not actually do," must be refuted (Ayers 1968, 89). Ayers argues successfully that the necessary conditions for actualizing a potentiality are different from the necessary conditions for the existence of a potentiality. The potentiality,

capacity, or power of a thing depends upon its nature, and it must
be sharply separated from extrinsic or situational conditions. An
automobile designed and constructed to go one-hundred miles per
hour has the capacity to do this, whether or not it has a driver and a
road to drive on.

The difference between inanimate and animate objects is this:
when all of the extrinsic conditions required by material objects are
met, their powers are invariably actualized in performance. The
necessary conditions are sufficient to produce the action; it is not
possible for the automobile to do otherwise. Not so for the human
case. From the fact that an individual has the capacity and opportunity to act, we cannot predict that he or she will act. Opportunity
cannot be assimilated to external circumstances as in the case of a
thing. Many of the confusions in the arguments over determinism
stem from the failure to make this distinction. Moral character is
sometimes conflated with capacity. This is a mistake; moral character is irrelevant to what a person can do. The possibilities of action are logical ones that stem from a person's capacities, and of
course they may run counter to moral character. All but the most
helpless invalid are capable of committing murder, although only a
few will ever exercise that capacity. To say "He is not capable of
committing murder; it's not in his character" only appears to be a
statement about capacity. In reality, it is a statement about character and motivation, a way of saying that he's not likely to commit
murder.

The rejection of actualism is not a mere abstract idea; it has
important implications for social psychological experimentation
and for the concept of attitude. Many social psychological studies
yield results describing "normative" behavior; that is, they ask the
question "How do most of the subjects behave under the experimental conditions?" Confusion arises if the experimenters take
their results to predict what subjects will do in nonlaboratory circumstances. The only legitimate way that they can be taken is to
conclude that subjects have the capacity to behave in the way that
was demonstrated under the laboratory conditions. Moreover,
from Bhaskar's realist perspective, the well-conducted experiment
warrants the inference that they also have this capacity in the nonlaboratory world. Thus the demonstration in an experiment that
the presence of a gun among other objects causes aroused subjects
to behave more aggressively in the laboratory certainly demonstrates that the sight of a gun can lead individuals to behave more
aggressively, but it does not warrant the conclusion that individuals

will be more aggressive when a gun is visible (Berkowitz & Donnerstein 1982; Secord 1982, 1984). How could it? Clearly a gun
pointed at you and held by a robber is more likely to frighten you
and lead to compliance with his demands, although some foolhar-
dy individuals might grapple for the gun.

Attitude has been a central concept in the history of social psychology, but from time to time it has been attacked on the grounds
that attitudes have low correlations with behavior. Such assertions
typically are supported by empirical studies yielding low or zero
correlation between attitude scale measures and behavioral criteria.
But the requirement that attitudes be expressed or activated in actual behavior falls into the trap of actualism. The demand for direct correlations is sheer nonsense: an employee can dislike his boss
and yet continue to behave courteously toward him because he
likes his work and wants to keep his job. Powers or capacities need
not be expressed to be valid, and their exercise depends upon the
presence of certain activating conditions, of both an internal and
external kind.

Similarly the famous experiments by Stanley Milgram (1974)
demonstrate clearly that individuals can be induced to behave in a
surprisingly cruel fashion toward an innocent victim, but the extent
to which they would behave similarly outside of the laboratory is
far from clear. Nevertheless, these experiments have value; they
extend our knowledge of the limits of human behavior beyond
what might be thought credible. Yet, by themselves, they do not
enable us to predict behavior in the social world.

SOCIAL PHENOMENA AND CETERIS PARIBUS CLAUSES

One difference between physical science and social science theories
is that physical theories specify the conditions under which relationships hold, whereas social theories have open *ceteris paribus*
clauses. This has happened largely under the aegis of logical
positivism and is a chief reason why much psychological and social
theory is vacuous. Making the psychological experiment central to
psychology as a science has also played a central role. Why this is
the case needs discussion. In their desire to develop psychology as a
real science, psychologists chose the experiment as their principal
method because they rightly saw that the experiment was central to
the success of the physical sciences. Why, then, didn't psychology
achieve the same success?

In a limited sense, the tens of thousands of experiments carried out during the century-long history of experimental psychology did produce a science. The sagacity of our foremost experimental psychologists led them to limit their efforts to certain kinds of experiments, experiments that did indeed produce a large amount of valid psychological knowledge. But this knowledge is subject to severe limitations (Manicas 1982). Critical views of psychology from outside the profession and self-criticism within it zero in on its limited usefulness for understanding or controlling behavior in the social world. The hard-earned knowledge from experiments is difficult to apply. Why application is more difficult in the social than in the physical realm needs elaboration.

Central to the explanation of this problem is Bhaskar's idea that a radical distinction must be made between the (partially) closed world of the experiment and the radical openness of the natural world. To the extent that the scientist succeeds in controlling relevant variables, the experiment can be viewed as a closed system that enables testing hypotheses or propositions. But the outside world is an open system, stratified into different levels or structures that intersect in unpredictable ways. Although there is a gap between laboratory and nonlaboratory phenomena in the natural world as well, the gap is far greater in the social sciences.

One of the contrasts is between the behavior of material objects, structures, and processes of the natural sciences and the behavior of living organisms. In the physical sciences, the difference between the behavior of material objects in the laboratory and outside of it is less radical than in psychology and the social sciences. In many instances, the behavior of a material object in the laboratory and outside of it is the same. Critical problems of application arise when conditions prevailing in the laboratory cannot be created outside of it; nevertheless, in the natural sciences, this becomes an engineering problem that is usually solvable with sufficient effort. Some applications are immediate, while others require considerable work. It took a long time to produce the first atomic bomb even though the theoretical principles of producing energy by splitting the atom were well known. In large part, this was because of the technical problems of creating the unusual conditions under which atoms would split. A key reason why application is possible in the natural sciences is that, there, the *ceteris paribus* clause is spelled out. That is, all of the relevant conditions under which the target reaction will occur are known and their parameters specified. Often effects occur only within the limits of certain parameters, and typically the experimenter takes care to control the conditions accordingly. Because of this, it becomes technically possible for engineers to attack the problem of creating the parametric conditions outside of the laboratory.

Psychology and the social sciences have not been approached in the same way, and the reasons why are instructive. Despite repeated assertions to the contrary, it is not that human behavior is more complicated than physical processes. Consider, for example, the enormous complexity of organic chemistry, whether it be analysis of some complex substance or whether it be discovering a method of synthesizing some natural substance. Neither psychology nor the social sciences currently deal with phenomena that match this complexity. They do not have theories that are of comparable complexity in their abstract structures. In the few instances where such theories have been generated, the theories fail to make any connection with behavior. Similarly, the gap that must be bridged between theory and observation in particle physics is awesome compared to psychological and social phenomena. So it seems that difficulties in applying behavioral science knowledge lie elsewhere than in complexity.

A central factor is that experiments in psychology use *ceteris paribus* clauses differently from the natural sciences. Typically, psychologists use them to state in a more general form a relationship demonstrated only under conditions that prevailed in the laboratory; an "other things being equal" clause is simply added or just implied. Unlike physicists, behavioral scientists do not specify what these conditions are; they remain unknown. Since many parameters are unknown, "control" is often achieved through such means as randomized "equivalent" groups. In effect, this requires the use of statistics with error terms that in part represent unmeasured parameters.

There are, however, good reasons for this difference. Physics deals with material objects and their structures, while the behavioral sciences deal with living organisms. By and large physics is generalizable outside of the laboratory because physical objects seldom change appreciably under laboratory conditions (obviously there are exceptions). This is so because physical objects are much less responsive to environments than organisms. But a rat, pigeon, or human is confronted with vastly different environments in laboratory and in life situations. When this is combined with the lack of specification of relevant parameters, the upshot is that experimental psychologists have no warrant for extending their results to behaviors outside of the laboratory. They can, however, as noted earlier, legitimately assume that capacities demonstrated in the laboratory potentially extend to the everyday world.

Consider the century that has been spent in laboratory research on learning and learning theory. And, to take just one example, consider further how little of this huge output contributes to an explanation of how children learn in a classroom. That classroom learning remains largely unexplained should not be a surprise. Throughout most of its history, experimental research on learning has been conducted on rats and pigeons as often as on humans and, with humans, has mainly used nonsense syllables and individual words. The experimental paradigm, moreover, has forced subjects to behave in a less-than-human, unnaturally constrained manner. Thus only knowledge of more primitive learning capacities has been acquired. Participants in such experiments, including rats and pigeons, have not been allowed to use their native intelligence and pragmatic skills. So it follows that we could learn very little of how these higher-level learning capacities are employed in the classroom or in other, freer situations. This traditional approach to studying the learning process has guaranteed that how parameters affect learning outside of the laboratory will simply remain a mystery.

Actually, experimental psychologists have unwittingly followed the realist paradigm in their selection of topics for laboratory study. Perception, learning, and cognition in general are powers or capacities that lend themselves to experimental study. In this respect, the approach parallels that of natural scientists, who study the powers of material objects. But there is a critical difference here. The powers of material objects remain much the same inside and outside of the laboratory, and for many physical processes, but not all, controlling the conditional parameters is not outrageously more difficult outside than inside the laboratory. Controlling the behaviors of living organisms inside and outside of the laboratory is vastly different, however, and it is this which makes application to life situations difficult. I have already called attention to the mistaken doctrine of actualism, which in one sense denies that generalization is a problem. One factor accounting for differences in laboratory and nonlaboratory behavior is motivational, and I will discuss this shortly. But first, let's look briefly at an ecological perspective.

The work of James J. Gibson (1979) and his colleagues (Shaw & Bransford 1977) is especially congruent with the realist view of science outlined here, although his notion of direct realism should not be confused with our realist view. His work can be seen as focusing on the characteristics of the environment that enable organisms to activate their perceptual powers. Certain types of visual perceptions are made possible by the presence of invariances in the environment. Visual perception is especially dependent on the invariances to be found in ambient light. As long as laboratory studies were limited to visual discriminations not involving ambient light, the laboratory approach could not discover these vital "external" conditions. Gibson's concept of "affordances" attempts to extend this thinking beyond the visual senses (for an application to social behavior, see McArthur & Baron 1983). Affordances refer to properties of the environment that play a vital role, not only in visual perception, but in influencing a wide variety of behaviors. Certain types of objects "afford" particular behaviors; for example, a chair affords sitting, a swimming pool invites swimming. The idea is not unlike Kurt Lewin's concept of "valence" or "demand characteristics" (1935), although Gibson's emphasis is more on the objective properties of objects that account for the affordance. His work can be seen as a search for the external conditions that enable or activate the exercise of powers.

ORDINARY LANGUAGE AND THE USE OF ACCOUNTS

The use of ordinary-language accounts of behavior is essential to applying the social sciences to life situations. Two major issues arise concerning everyday language. One is the use of ordinary language to describe behavior, and the other, the use of ordinary language in accounting for one's own behavior. Rosenberg (1983) has called attention to the problem created by the dependence of social science on the use of ordinary language in the description of social phenomena—one of the prominent controversies in the massive philosophical literature on the topic. In essence, he sees ordinary language as hopelessly subjective and as unsuitable for science, and this is one of the reasons why he looks to sociobiology as a possible way out. At the same time, he notes correctly that sociobiology, like the other social sciences, states its aims concerning human behavior in a way that implies the use of ordinary language, and he hopes that this will somehow be corrected.

My position, however, is quite different. Following Harré and Secord (1972), I argue that any application of social science must necessarily involve ordinary language. Harré and I see several types of languages as essential to a fully developed social science. The natures of organisms are described in a mix of physiological and psychological terms, but their behaviors or actions must be described in ordinary-language terms simply because there is no other language. Although ordinary language is occasionally enriched by adopting established psychological terms, no comprehensive scientific language for describing behavior has emerged. The dismal record of stimulus-response language, popular in psychology at one time, dampens further any enthusiasm for such a language. That a scientific language could be developed is not inconceivable, although it is unlikely. But the point is that even then, in order to communicate with the users of applied research, it would be necessary to translate behavior descriptions into ordinary language. Social problems are described in ordinary-language terms—at least the behavioral aspects of the problems are (cf. Fiske, chap. 3, this volume). The very fabric of society, as well as the meanings of our everyday behaviors, is woven into ordinary language, and it is this feature of language that makes it "subjective." But it also makes it relevant. It is difficult to see how a "scientific" language could avoid this involvement and still describe the same behavior in the same social context.

Closely related here is the question of whether reasons can be causes, another controversy producing volumes of philosophical literature. During the last two decades, this has shaken down and a moderate consensus has been achieved on the conclusion that reasons can be causes. In Bhaskar's scheme (1979), they are usually proximate causes. Nothing in this way of thinking precludes a search for antecedent causes that account for the person having the reason; character dispositions, early experiences, and so on, are not excluded as more remote causes. But often such searches are fruitless in the face of the massiveness of every individual's experiences and the paucity of biographical data. Moreover, some kinds of reasons are in a sense "explanation stoppers," such as the statement "I don't know why I like that painting, I just like it!"

The underlying issue here is that of consciousness or reflective awareness. Individuals can sometimes give valid accounts of their behavior, and social science is enriched if such accounts constitute a part of the research data. This is not to say that individuals cannot be wrong in the accounts they give for their actions, nor is it to say that investigators are always right in their version of accounts given by clients. It is only to argue that knowledge is incomplete in the absence of such accounts. Social scientists interested in application can scarcely afford to ignore accounts; if they do, they risk making fools of themselves. Psychological investigations involving interviewing or other techniques of obtaining personal accounts, when competently done, contribute legitimate knowledge to understanding human behavior.

At the same time, it is important to recognize that this type of application, for example, in psychotherapy, takes the behavioral scientist far afield, compared to laboratory research. But it is worth emphasizing that there is no way of bridging the gap; the chasm is there because that's the way the world is. The applied scientist must be more than a scientist. He or she must have considerable knowledge and experience relevant to the application, and must draw upon biographical, historical, and contextual knowledge if the application is to be effective. This is true because of the nature of our world, and not because of the immaturity or wrongheadedness of social science.

Tacit Knowledge and Unconscious Motivation

Accounts often include intentions and motives of various sorts; indeed, reasons are often motives. But few would dispute that we often do not have an explanation of why we behave as we do, and that much of our knowledge is tacit and often our own motives are not accessible to us. These are serious problems, especially for psychologists, and Bhaskar's realist theory does not provide any special assistance here. To the extent that motives are biologically based, they fit well into the realist scheme, which emphasizes different levels and structures interacting to produce particular effects. But capacities or powers are only a part of the story; beliefs and feelings are important to understanding behavior. The recent explosion of cognitive psychology overemphasizes cognition at the expense of feeling, as Zajonc (1980) has noted.

Capacities can be affected by motives and feelings. A commonplace symptom of neurosis is an inability to exercise one's capacities, and sometimes this incapacitation may be so severe as to totally camouflage their existence. Within this realist scheme, such incapacities are as important as capacities and are termed "liabilities." In this instance, the emotional disturbance constitutes an internal condition preventing the exercise of one's capacities. In connection with either powers or liabilities, it is helpful to think of enabling and constraining conditions. Some conditions facilitate the exercise of powers, and others constrain them. Liabilities appear mainly to be a function of internal conditions that constrain the capacity from being exercised or that facilitate the activation of a capacity that is potentially damaging (e.g., drug abuse). Elsewhere I have suggested that, in effect, what behavior therapists do is to manipulate constraining and enabling conditions in order to change behavior, and that their beloved concept of "reinforcement" is often incoherent when applied to the situations in which they work (Secord 1977). The systematic study of enabling and constraining conditions in connection with the exercise or facilitation of capacities or the elimination of liabilities would seem to hold promise for bringing about changes in behaviors. Recently I have been impressed by the extensive use made by golf professionals in their tutoring and writing of very explicit, specific instructions to take certain actions (e.g., keeping your left arm straight), as well as various cognitive schemes (e.g., imagine a straight line from the ball to the target, consider the ball only as an object that gets in the way, think of swinging *through* the ball not *to* the ball). I do not know how effective these techniques are, but because they are widely used in golf instruction, I suspect that they have some merit. No doubt there are similar enabling conditions for other types of capacities or skills, including psychological or social skills, and systematic research on both enabling and constraining conditions for various social behaviors might well pay off (cf. Cronbach Chap. 4, this volume).

A natural tendency is to think of powers or liabilities as biologically based and, indeed, some certainly are. But possibly some capacities are psychological in the sense of having been established through experience, and certainly some liabilities are acquired in that way. It is easy to see Sigmund Freud's thinking as very compatible with an interpretation of science in terms of causal powers and liabilities. Glymour (1974) has argued that Freud's use of case studies is very much like scientific thinking, in this case like the use of Kepler's laws of astronomy! But Freud's analysis of incapacities can very readily be assimilated to the realist scheme. Freud traces certain types of liabilities—guilt complexes, obsessions, compulsions—to certain types of characteristic experiences accompanied by standard sets of conditions that trip off certain types of reactions in persons. Thus he seems to provide some good examples of psychologically based liabilities. Finally, tacit knowledge, unconscious motivation, and enabling and constraining conditions have important links to social structure, and that topic is discussed next.

SOCIAL STRUCTURES

Any attempt to apply psychology to a social problem is apt to fail if it does not take the social setting or context into account. Social

structures play an important role in maintaining or changing behavior. Recent contributions from Bhaskar (1982), Giddens (1976,
1982), and Manicas (1980) have clarified some of the persistent
complexities concerning social structures. They are fundamentally
different from natural structures, in that they are constituted by
the active doings of persons and thus do not exist independently of
the agents' conceptions of what they are doing. Yet at the same
time, agents do not necessarily grasp what the social structures are.
Moreover, social structures are real in that they have real effects.
They precede the individual, they are outside of the individual,
and they are external facticities; thus they have coercive power
over individuals.

The fact that "social structures are both constituted by human
agency and yet at the same time are the medium of this constitu-
tion" (Giddens 1976, 121) has often led social scientists to choose
either persons or structures as primal causal agents. Thus, Max
Weber (1947) has emphasized voluntarism and agency in creating
social structure: insofar as social structure affects behavior, it does
so because it has a subjective reality in the minds of the actors. This
in a sense subordinates structures to their construction by persons
(Berger & Luckmann 1967) and robs them of any independent
causal status. Emile Durkheim (1951), on the other hand, gave primacy to social structure. His most famous example concerned the
effect of anomie in a society on suicide rates, and he emphasized
that this relationship did not require psychological analysis of the
individuals who took their own lives.

The resolution of this apparent dilemma lies in the key insight
that although individuals do indeed influence social structures by
their actions, these structures are partly independent in that they
precede the individual; moreover, they are rarely shaped by rational means. Virtually all structures result at least in part, and
sometimes wholly, from the unintended consequences of human
actions. For example, the activities of a great many different individuals and agencies in the service of their own needs may create a
complex structure that we refer to as economic recession. None of
these individuals or other units intended to create this structure,
yet it establishes certain constraints on their lives. It is important to
see that social structures can have causal efficacy and yet to not
deny similar efficacy to the actions of individuals. Structures precede the entrance of individuals into society, and individuals act
within them as a medium. The example of a recession depends
upon a preexisting economic structure within which the actions of

individuals and other units take place, even as these actions inadvertently bring about changes in the structure itself.

The concept of social structure is often used in an empirical, descriptive sense. Thus social institutions are often thought of as structures. It is important to recognize, though, that only structures that are abstract and theoretical have any explanatory power. Conceptually, they are forms of relationships among people, and it is their form that gives them explanatory force. As Giddens (1976) observes, institutions are not structures, but they have structures. An example that distinguishes the empirical from the conceptual is the use of size as a structural variable. The size (of a group, for example) is an empirical measure and is not in itself a structural component. Groups of different sizes, however, may have real structural differences in virtue of their difference in size, as when, for example, communications among members assume different structural patterns in the differently sized groups.

Types of Structures

The realist position outlined here suggests that we need much more theoretical development concerning the nature of behavioral and social structures and the ways in which they persist or change. It may well be, as Cummins (1983) suggests, that the dominance of the covering law model of science has inhibited the development of alternative forms of psychological theory. Certainly the focus of psychologists on the experiment is in part responsible for the inattention to structure. Experiments are typically limited to short duration and deal with behaviors taken out of their natural context. In any case, it seems apparent that concepts of time and succession, as well as structural relations between persons, are poorly developed in the behavioral and social sciences.

Psychologists and other social scientists have at times emphasized the structure of relations among people, although ideas proposed so far have seldom had a lasting impact on social science theory. Nevertheless, it is quite possible that sufficient theoretical development and more sophisticated technology would produce structural theories of lasting value. We do know that many relationships among people are extraordinarily stable, and that other relationships change in systematic ways. An adequate structural language for describing these relationships and their changes would advance our science. Worthy of emphasis is the point that we need concepts for many forms of structure. One is temporal, as, for example, in the beginnings and endings of episodic relationships (Albert & Kessler

1976). Other structures might be described as different forms of "connectedness" in relationships among people. Although we might expect a great variety of such forms, one hopes that only a small finite set of these will prove important to social science.

APPLYING SOCIAL SCIENCE TO LIFE SITUATIONS

Because of the radical openness of social phenomena, which contrasts markedly with the controlled nature of scientific investigation, the behavioral sciences are only partly applicable to real-world problems. But this should not be misunderstood. Under the new perspective, application is easier in one sense, although the limitations of application are more clearly recognized. Application is easier because, instead of requiring universal laws, which are impossible to achieve, its laws are tendencies based upon the natures of persons and of social structures that underlie behavioral relationships. These natures account for the causal powers of persons or of social structures. Persons are a mix of physiological and psychological attributes that generate powers under the relevant extrinsic and intrinsic conditions.

This emphasis on causal powers makes generalization from the laboratory easier because powers and liabilities may be presumed to be potentiated by the same conditions whether inside or outside of the laboratory. This does not mean that they will necessarily be manifested outside of the laboratory, for other overriding conditions may prevent their occurrence. It is this last proviso that identifies the task of applied psychologists: they must identify the extralaboratory conditions that are relevant to the exercise of the powers identified through laboratory study. Emphasizing causal powers also sharpens the task of both the pure and the applied scientist: their investigations can be more focused and can exclude an enormous variety of irrelevant considerations. The traditional requirement that science be couched in terms of universal laws, on the other hand, involves the scientist in the dilemma of *ceteris paribus* clauses and the difficulty of generalizing from the laboratory.

The realist perspective gives direction to applied research by underscoring the importance of gaining knowledge of the participants and the social context. Application cannot be a wholly scientific procedure, and the basic scientific knowledge that is used in application must be augmented by competent human judgments. These judgments concern the biographical history of the participants and relevant subjective features of the social context. There is no substitute for the wise use of such judgments in solving social problems. Again, lest I be misunderstood, I am not arguing against the use of psychometric instruments to gain some understanding of persons, but simply indicating that by themselves they are not enough. Moreover, so little progress has been made in assessing social structures (e.g., in organizational settings) that global judgments by behavioral scientists experienced in application must be heavily used in appraising and solving social problems.

Of further importance for applied social science is that both persons and social phenomena are stratified into many different levels. They can be seen as having physical, biological, psychological, and sociological levels, for example, although of course other categorizations are possible. Because persons are complex entities with internal states, they must be treated holistically; moreover, they behave within a set of complex social structures. These properties of the world demand that application be interdisciplinary—no one discipline can aspire to explaining social behavior in real-world settings.

The interconnectedness of social life means that various behaviors are facilitated or discouraged by social structural factors that must be taken into account. If they are not dealt with in the process of attempting to bring about social change, the effort is largely wasted. Examples are legion. Consider the case of individual psychotherapy. Hundreds of thousands of people are seeing psychotherapists who limit their contacts to the troubled individual despite the fact that most social behaviors, including undesirable ones, are supported by the significant other people with whom the patient interacts. Worse yet, insufficent attention has been given to developing systematic theory as to how to change such support systems, either through dealing with the patient or with significant others.

Attempts to bring about social change on a larger scale often suffer in a similar way from a narrowness of vision. For example, educational research firmly established that one of the most important factors in the educational achievement of children is the quality of the peers that surround them in the classroom. From this conclusion, the inference was made that busing low-performing black children to better schools would improve their performance. Such a conclusion is unfortunately a simple-minded extension of a valid social science discovery, because it does not take into account the ramifications of the action intended to create social change. These include the attitudes and behaviors of the peers toward the newcomers, the reaction of the bused children to their new situation, the actions of white parents in withdrawing their children from such schools by moving to the suburbs, the opposition or support provided by government officials or community leaders, and so on.

Again it is important to reiterate that applied scientists must be more than scientists, they must have considerable knowledge and experience relevant to the application and must draw upon biographical, historical, and social structural knowledge if the application is to be effective. They need to obtain probing accounts of how the affected individuals see the projected social change, they need to understand how these accounts support the behavior that is to be changed, and they must grasp how existing social structures relate to the target behavior. It is easy to see how an adequate application requires the efforts of psychologists and sociologists and sometimes anthropologists, political scientists, or economists, in addition to the wisdom gained through intimate knowledge and experience with the situation in which social changes are to be brought about. The major role in all of this for social science itself is the development of social theory as it pertains to the involvement of social structures and individuals in the process of social change. Just as physicists, in order to make possible the creation of an atomic bomb, had to spell out in precise detail the conditions under which an explosion would occur, and then engineers had to find practical ways to create those conditions, social scientists need both to be able to describe the social structures and individual changes in behavior necessary to produce a planned change and to find a way to create those structures and changes.

In conclusion, the social scientist wishing to deal with an applied problem must search for and describe the structural enablements and constraints that play a part in creating the problem, and he must find a way of transforming these elements to create the kind of situation desired. Often there will be little guidance from social science in general, for each applied problem has many unique features. In fact extensive experience in similar settings may well provide more guidance than the formal body of social science knowledge. Progress in social science toward a better understanding of structures will eventually alleviate the situation, but applied research will inevitably and always require knowledge and experience of the particular target situation that goes beyond theoretical knowledge.

References

Albert, S., and Kessler, S. 1976. Processes for ending social encounters: The conceptual archeology of a temporal place. *Journal for the Theory of Social Behavior* 6:147–70.

Ayers, M. R. 1968. *The refutation of determinism: An essay in philosophical logic.* London: Methuen.

Berger, P. L., and Luckmann, T. 1967. *The social construction of reality.* London: Allen Lane.

Berkowitz, L., and Donnerstein, E. 1982. External validity is more than skin deep: Some answers to criticisms of laboratory experiments. *American Psychologist* 37:245–57.

Bhaskar, R. 1975. *A realist theory of science.* Leeds: Leeds Books. (An edition published in 1978 by Harvester Press contains a postscript clarifying Bhaskar's use of the term "law.")

————. 1978. On the possibility of social scientific knowledge and the limits of behaviorism. *Journal for the Theory of Social Behavior* 8:1–28.

————. 1979. *The possibility of naturalism.* Brighton: Harvester Press.

————. 1982. Emergence, explanation, and emancipation. In *Explaining human behavior: Consciousness, behavior, and social structure,* ed. P. F. Secord. Beverly Hills: Sage.

Blalock, H. M., Jr. 1982. *Conceptualization and measurement in the social sciences.* Beverly Hills: Sage.

Cummins, R. 1983. *The nature of psychological explanation.* Cambridge: MIT Press.

Durkheim, E. 1951. *Suicide.* Translated by J. A. Spaulding and G. Simpson, edited and introduced by G. Simpson. Glencoe, Ill.: Free Press.

Gibson, J. J. 1979. *The ecological approach to visual perception.* Boston: Houghton Mifflin.

Giddens, A. 1976. *New rules of sociological method.* London: Hutchinson.

————. 1982. On the relation of sociology to philosophy. In *Explaining human behavior: Consciousness, human action, and social structure,* ed. P. F. Secord. Beverly Hills: Sage.

Glymour, C. 1974. Freud, Kepler, and the clinical evidence. In *Freud: A collection of critical essays,* ed. R. Wollheim. Garden City, N.Y.: Doubleday.

Harré, R. 1970. *The principles of scientific thinking.* Chicago: University of Chicago Press.

————. 1972. *Philosophies of science.* Oxford: Oxford University Press.

Harré, R., and Madden, E. H. 1975. *Causal powers.* Totowa, N.J.: Littlefield Adams.

Harré, R., and Secord, P. F. 1972. *The explanation of social behavior.* Oxford: Blackwell.

Hume, D. 1748. *Enquiry concerning human understanding.* London.

Lewin, K. 1935. *A dynamic theory of personality.* New York: McGraw-Hill.

Manicas, P. T. 1980. The concept of social structure. *Journal for the Theory of Social Behavior* 10:65–82.

———. 1982. The human sciences: A radical separation of psychology and the social sciences. In *Explaining human behavior,* ed. P. F. Secord. Beverly Hills: Sage.

Manicas, P. T., and Secord, P. F. 1983. Implications for psychology of the new philosophy of science. *American Psychologist* 38:399–413.

McArthur, L. Z., and Baron, R. M. 1983. Toward an ecological theory of social perception. *Psychological Review* 90:215–38.

Milgram, S. 1974. *Obedience to authority: An experimental view.* New York: Harper and Row.

Rodgers, J. E. 1983. Catching the cancer strays. *Science83* 4:42–51.

Rosenberg, A. 1983. Human science and biological science: Defects and opportunities. In *Scientific explanation and understanding,* ed. N. Rescher. Lanham, Md.: University Press of America.

Scheffler, I. 1967. *Science and subjectivity.* New York: Bobbs-Merrill.

Secord, P. F. 1977. Making oneself behave. In *The self: Psychological and philosophical issues.* ed. T. Mischel. Oxford: Blackwell.

———. 1982. Comment: The behavior identity problem in generalizing from experiments. *American Psychologist* 37:1408.

———. 1984. Determinism, free will, and self-intervention: A psychological perspective. *New Ideas in Psychology* 2:25–33.

Shaw, R., and Bransford, J., eds. 1977. *Perceiving, acting, and knowing.* Hillsdale, N.J.: Erlbaum.

Weber, M. 1947. *The theory of social and economic organization.* New York: Free Press.

Zajonc, R. B. 1980. Feeling and thinking: Preferences need no inferences. *American Psychologist* 35:151–75.

9 Some Uses and Misuses of the Social Sciences in Medicine

Arthur Kleinman

There are a number of distinctive social sciences in and of medicine: medical anthropology, sociology, psychology, geography, political science, economics, history, and ethics. I will discuss examples of their effective use and point out areas where their appropriate application would yield even more significant results. I will also describe barriers to the use of social science in the domain of health and health care—some that exist in the health professions, other in the social sciences themselves. Since clinical experience gives ample evidence that every effective intervention has potential and actual untoward effects—even placebos after all exert nocebo effects—it should not surprise us that social science applications in medicine have had their share of side effects. I will direct our attention to several misuses and abuses that have not helped instill confidence in health professionals and laymen that social science has a significant contribution to make. I do not hesitate to expose the misadventures because from personal experience, I am convinced that the successes are noteworthy and much more numerous.

Since I am an anthropologist and a physician, my priorities will lead us along a very particular route, one that I will not necessarily claim to be the royal road, but one that I feel fairly certain is not the proverbial garden path either. I will argue that in reciprocity for the uses of social science in medicine, the health domain offers the social sciences an especially important testing ground for the construction of theory and the development of methodologies, a domain in which the practical relevance of social science is beyond dispute. In this sense, medicine has uses in the social sciences.

The social sciences in medicine are still regarded by health professionals as a "new direction," but in fact the relationship is an old one. Take for example the interaction between anthropology and medicine. Physicians were among the nineteenth-century founders

222

of anthropology: Paul Broca in France, W. H. R. Rivers in Great
Britain, Rudolph Virchow in Germany. Medical anthropology
counts among its founders both anthropologists (e.g., Clements)
and physicians (e.g., Ackerknecht). For over a quarter of a century,
medical anthropology has made significant contributions to public
health in non-Western societies and to studies of cultural influence
on illness and health care in our own society. The classic sociological studies of the professionalization of physicians were conducted in the 1950s. Since that time, medical sociology has become
a central component of health services research and of epidemiology. The study of stressful life change, of social supports
and illness onset, is a field dominated by social scientists.

Behavioral medicine is present in one form or another in most
of the major medical schools. When I began medical school more
than twenty years ago, behavioral science courses had already become an established if not very large domain in the medical school
curriculum of most schools. Since that time, all American medical
students are examined in behavioral science as part of the national
board examinations. Schools of public health, medicine, and nursing have had sociologists, anthropologists, and psychologists on the
faculty for several decades, and in the past decade, large social science research and teaching programs have been developed in both
private and state schools of the health professions. Increasingly,
political scientists and economists are shaping the discourse on policy issues in health and health care.

In spite of these and many other illustrations of the long-term
contributions of social science to medicine, however, the folk view
in the health professions perennially is that social science is "new"
to medicine, the implication being that the social sciences are marginal to and not fully legitimated in medicine. The same ambivalence that greeted social science teaching and teachers at
Stanford Medical School in 1962, when I was a medical student,
greets social science teaching and teachers today at the Harvard
Medical School, where I am myself a teacher of medical social science. Doubtless, much of this resistance to social science undeser-
vedly spills over from the larger society, but the on-the-ground
reality simply is that social science and social scientists have had a
very limited influence on the ethos of health science schools. The
situation is somewhat better in nursing schools and somewhat
worse in medical schools and teaching hospitals; schools of public
health fall somewhere in between. Increasing demands on limited
funding for research projects and teaching appointments have

made the situation a bit more difficult over the past several years. Ironically, psychiatry, long the most open of the medical specialties to social science, has responded to the current climate with less interest in social science, while the primary care fields (especially family medicine) have begun to give social science and social scientists more attention.

Later I will examine some of the barriers within medicine to the application of the social sciences. Here I merely register the problems. Medical sociology, for example, which arguably has gained greater entrée into medicine than any other social science, was the subject of a study by Petersdorf and Feinstein (1981) that demonstrated both considerable ignorance among chairmen of departments of internal medicine, pediatrics, and family medicine about the nature and potential contributions of sociology and lack of application in these clinical disciplines. Internal medicine faculty demonstrated the least interest in medical sociology and use of it in teaching, family medicine faculty the most.

Excluding psychology, one would be hard pressed to demonstrate any major influence of social science concepts on the clinical practice of psychiatry; and surprising as it may seem, it is my impression that, psychoanalytic, behavioral, and developmental models to the side, most of psychological theory is neither taught to nor understood by psychiatrists. In fact, few health science students or faculty have had enough experience reading social science literature to become comfortable with the concepts and methods of social sciences. This, by the way, is the obverse of their experience in biochemistry, genetics, and neurosciences, fields in which they are taught to become critical readers of the literature. But in the practice of contemporary health care, it can be easily shown that social science is more relevant to day-to-day problems than are these biological sciences (Katon, Kleinman & Rosen, 1982).

OBSTACLES TO THE SOCIAL SCIENCES IN MEDICINE

Why do the social sciences remain marginal in medicine in spite of their obvious relevance? First, there is the inherent bias of the still dominant biomedical paradigm in medicine. For all the writing about the bio-psycho-social approach to illness and holistic medicine, the discourse of professional medicine remains empiricist and materialist. In this stratigraphic view, fundamental reality is biological; psychological and social dimensions of sickness are epiphenomenal layers to be quickly stripped away in order to expose bedrock. Unless a problem or intervention can be specified in biological terms, it is suspect. Reductionism, which has contributed so importantly to the revolution in molecular biology but is seen as woefully inappropriate in evolutionary and ecological branches of biology (Mayr 1982), is unabashedly regarded in medicine as the fundamental task of medical science and practice (Hahn & Kleinman, in press; Latour & Woolgar 1979). The working philosophy of medicine is much closer to that classical logical positivism now discredited in the philosophy of science than to the consensus on neorealism that characterizes the contemporary discourse in the history and philosophy of science.

In anthropological perspective, this scientific and clinical world view constructs a particularly narrow definition of disease that separates it from social sources and consequences and studies it as a discrete abnormality in biological structure and functioning. This is the archetypal disease of scientific medicine. Gonorrhea is an infection by a bacterium, the rest is flummery and artifact! The therapeutic side of this is the well-known technical fix. The treatment of gonorrhea is an antibiotic, that's all. This tendentious professional world view is oriented principally to treatment, not prevention, and the more narrowly conceived and technique-laden, the better. The psychosocial dimensions of care are relegated to the "art of medicine." In Harrison's widely used *Textbook of Internal Medicine,* the "art" is covered in a few pages, while the remaining one thousand and more pages cover the "science." That this approach is an inadequate basis not only of practice but also of how to do clinical science is perhaps something medical educators may agree to over sherry with academic colleagues from outside of medicine or in a seminar on bioethics, but the ethnographic reality is that this is the functioning epistemology of day-to-day medical pedagogy. As both a card-carrying medico and a social scientist, I regret to tell you that social science has had no significant impact on this cultural epistemology.

Second, there is substantial bias against social scientists, which doubtless reflects societal values, but to my mind occurs in exaggerated form in medicine. This is shown by the ideological rhetoric of the "return-to-our-medical-roots" movement in psychiatry, which is a simplistic biological revanchism, as much anti-social science as pro-biology.

Third, preprofessional educational requirements for health science students and the criteria for admission to health science schools push students away from social science courses and provide them inadequate exposure to social science concepts and methods.

Hence they enter medical school with little knowledge of social science or conviction that it is relevant to medicine. What they then receive is too little, too late. Moreover, the premedical social science major has not been the darling of medical school admissions committees.

Fourth, for health science students, there are few role models of either social scientists with strong clinical interests or clinicians trained in social science. Since the great majority of students will in fact enter practice after training ends, the lack of clinical role models is especially significant.

Fifth, compared with physicians and biologists, social scientists make up a very small portion of medical school faculties and command much more limited resources and teaching hours than their non–social science colleagues. As Starr (1983) convincingly discloses, this continuing limitation derives from institutional decisions and constraints and is not the result of the relative relevance of social science to health and health care. It is important to recognize in this regard that between fifty and seventy-five percent of clinical practice in primary care (the major component of medical practice) is taken up with psychological and social aspects of sickness (Katon, Kleinman & Rosen 1982). Hypertension is the second most common disorder in primary care, depression the first (Kleinman & Katon, in press). The single most frequent diagnosis in primary care is "nonsickness"—a rather pathetic but nonetheless mischievous euphemism for stress, somatization, and a host of important social and personal problems that contribute to demoralization and are articulated in a bodily idiom of distress that leads to medical help seeking (Chrisman & Kleinman 1983; Kleinman 1982). In spite of this epidemiological reality, psychosocial aspects of care and those who teach them are routinely stigmatized by biomedical scientists and clinical teachers as "soft," in contrast to biology, which, relevant and useful or not, is "hard." Students are "taught" to avoid the "soft" and follow the "hard," notwithstanding the preponderance of "soft" problems in medical care and the well-known negative consequences of "hard" interventions. Surely here we are identifying a mischievous and misleading societywide ideology, as dangerous for America's medicine as for her politics and diplomacy.

Although other reasons for the marginality of the social sciences in medicine can be adduced, I will mention only a final and tacit obstacle. Anthropology, as an example, has been appropriately named the "uncomfortable" science by one of its greatest practitioners, Raymond Firth. That is to say, anthropological investigation leads (or should lead) the researcher and the reader of his work to juxtapose conflicting value orientations, to query the meanings and norms that guide common-sense decision making in the practical world, to examine covert dimensions of social life, and to view the wider context of sociopolitical and economic constraints on microclinical behavior. This task of configuring medical problems as social problems is the obverse of medical work, which can be thought of as the configuring of social problems as discrete biomedical ones. Medical educators, researchers, and practitioners are made to feel uncomfortable by social science, and many of them resent and avoid it because it calls into question core assumptions and values.[1] Since I believe this questioning is both an appropriate and a positive contribution of social science to medicine, I mention the medical reaction, not to suggest that social science relinquish this role, but to point up the opposition it creates.

Social science is marginal to biomedicine because of their very different paradigms of practice. To expand significantly the role of social science in medicine requires a transformation (but not necessarily a radical one) of the paradigm of practice, primarily that of medicine, but to a lesser extent that of social science as well. This is already happening in nursing and public health, but it is only beginning to occur in medicine. Not surprisingly, behavioral medicine is leading the way in this expansion, especially as it has been recast to complement biomedical research and practice as a rather narrowly applied, technology-oriented practice. A language of behavior is now legitimated in the house of medicine, alongside a language of biology. The languages of experience, relationships, and meaning are not yet fully legitimated and neither are the sciences that study them. The final obstacle of different value hierarchies in medicine, then, can be conceived as the most fundamental of all. The fact that there are medical social sciences and scientists within the professional institutions of medicine, however, demonstrates that this can be overcome. But to overcome it, there must be negotiations of the uses (practical and moral) of social science as viewed by social scientists and physicians, a point I will return to later.

OBSTACLES IN SOCIAL SCIENCE

Until very recently, there was no training offered young medical social scientists in how to teach and research in health science settings. This has led to predictable problems in personal and professional adaptation, repeated case by case and worsened by uncertain career paths and reward systems. There is still little in the way of an organized monitoring of the social science literatures to identify and assess concepts and methodologies that might be useful in the health sciences and translate them systematically into practical research strategies. Most of what is done in the way of translation is what a particular social scientist might do as part of a particular research project. As a result, major social science ideas circulate as atomized terms cut off from their theoretical bases, and for this reason, they diffuse poorly and are improperly understood.

Closely related to this problem is the tendency of the medical social sciences to deemphasize theory. This tendency surely is abetted by the empiricist orientation of medicine. But there are other important reasons. Funding for the medical social sciences is chiefly in the form of support for highly focused projects that are attempts to answer practical questions posed by health professionals. Hence these projects rarely test major theoretical positions or encourage theory building. Social science consultation on medical research projects is usually centered on statistical, research design, and questionnaire issues. The absence of a cadre of physicians systematically trained in social science assures that the focus will be very narrow, because the social scientist does not have a medical collaborator who understands the conceptual questions behind the research. For these reasons, and also because of the lower status accorded applied social scientists within their own disciplines, the health field has not attracted the most conceptually innovative and theoretically sophisticated social scientists.

Another set of obstacles has to do with social science stereotypes of medicine. Like those held by physicians about social scientists, these tend to be negative, demeaning, and extreme. Hence the romantic, reverse ethnocentrism of some in medical anthropology that accords positive virtues to folk healers and their opposite qualities to biomedicine or the view of psychiatrists as jailors that has emanated from certain groups of sociologists. A Marxist notion has been mischievous here: it holds that teaching physicians to recognize psychosocial problems and provide more effective and sensitive care for them is a way of contributing to medicalization, as well as a means of providing physicians with greater power over patients and of shoring up an ineffective capitalist institution that it would be better to allow to fall to the ground so that it could be replaced (once the revolution comes) with a better one (Taussig 1980). Ideologically based stereotypes such as these do not promise improved communication between social scientists and physicians.

It is all too easy to understand, however, how social scientists in medicine have come to find these views congenial in the face of marginal status, prejudice, and the absense of an audience. The alternative response of angry withdrawal has been equally unavailing, but much more common. We might call this reaction identifying with the aggressor. Here the social scientist comes to accept the biomedical stereotypes and relinquishes his own intellectual and professional autonomy. To my mind, much of health services research is a good example of this response. We see, not major reformulations that are linked to sophisticated social science theory, but rather somewhat mindless surveys of uninteresting questions that carry the advantage of being fundable. In medical anthropology, an earlier generation of investigators took up posts in health science schools and, as handmaidens of biomedicine, practiced a kind of toothless anthropology in which an autonomous cultural critique of biomedical categories and practices was abandoned and virtually no theory was generated (Kleinman 1980).

Something of this sort is going on at present in the various clinical and faculty-scholars programs in medical schools that are intended to provide academic physicians with knowledge of the social sciences and in which social scientists are recruited as teachers. We teach them a bit of research design, some statistics and a hodge-podge of mid-range concepts without ever exposing them in depth to the critical discourse in social science over major conceptual questions. That is, we fail to teach them to think as social scientists or to take a scholarly approach to their work. It is no surprise, then, that these physicians, whose future responsibility will include social and behavioral research and teaching in medicine, are "scholars" in name only and are largely unprepared to function as facilitators of social science in medicine. These physicians are not trained in the right environment—in centers of excellence where they can learn social science as a basic science away from the ethos of medicine. Nor have we developed for them career paths and reward systems. In the late nineteenth and early twentieth centuries, physicians who obtained much more substantial training in biological science became the critical cadre that built contemporary biomedical science. This should be a model for our work with academic physicians, but in my experience, it is not an accurate description of how we educate even that very small group of physicians who are interested in our fields.

Perhaps these individual strands can be woven into a larger theme. The social sciences in medicine by and large have failed to articulate a vision of how social science might or should function in the medical domain either as the chief source of health policy alternatives or as one of the two sources (biology being the other) of health science education and research. Few today would quarrel with the notion that the social sciences have some role to play in the health sciences, but what that role will be depends to a greater extent than social scientists have heretofore recognized on how they themselves articulate what it could be. It is understandable that social scientists, recognizing the underdeveloped state of their science and the marked difficulties of validly and reliably applying laboratory paradigms to heterogenous groups in complex real-life situations, have hesitated to articulate such a vision. That the absence of a coherent and compelling vision, however, feeds back to drive a vicious circle of marginal expectation and fragmented efforts leading to marginal and fragmented effects is equally understandable and frustrating.

USES OF SOCIAL SCIENCE IN AND FOR MEDICINE

We can point to literally hundreds of examples of the successful uses of social science in and for medicine. I will review some examples from my own field, medical anthropology, that hold importance for clinical research and practice. The illness focus and clinical emphasis, as I have already noted, reflect my own orientation and are not meant to deny the importance of the other paradigmatic orientation of the medical social sciences: the perspective of health policy and public health from which one could write a very different review.

Medical anthropology has advanced a technical distinction between "illness" and "disease." Illness is defined as socially learned and culturally shared ways of perceiving, labeling, experiencing, and reacting to symptoms. This includes most notably the personal and interpersonal problems illness creates or intensifies, as well as the processes by which these illness problems are handled by the patient and his social network (see Kleinman 1982, 1983). Most usually, illness is first experienced by patients in the context of family. Most illness appears to be monitored, normalized, consulted upon, and treated entirely within the patients' social network in what has been called the popular health care arena of local health care systems. This makes the family the major source of health care in society, an empirical finding that has yet to receive the attention it deserves (see Chrisman & Kleinman 1983; Demers et al. 1980; Hulka, Kupper & Cassel 1972; White, Williams & Greenberg 1961; Zola 1972, 1973).

When patients visit physicians, their discourse is initially about illness and illness problems in particular. Practitioners then recast these problems in terms of their theoretical perspectives, and in this way "disease" is socially constructed (Blumhagen 1982; Helman 1985; Kleinman 1980).

The illness/disease distinction provides medical social scientists with both an autonomous subject matter that has been virtually unstudied in medicine—the nature of illness experiences and problems—and a powerful framework for studying the work of doctoring as the cultural construction of clinical reality. The social epidemiology and phenomenology of illness is in its infancy, but it could and should become a major field of social science research in medicine. For example, the amplification of chronic illness behavior owing to the influence of psychosocial and cultural variables has in the past few years attracted key contributions from medical psychologists, sociologists, anthropologists, economists, political scientists, and historians (Alexander 1982; Figlio 1982; Mechanic 1980; Pennebaker & Skelton 1978; Plough 1981; Stewart & Sullivan 1982; Stone 1979a, 1979b; Yelin, Nevitt & Epstein 1980). This research is a crucial complement to biomedical studies of disease etiology and treatment, to which social scientists also contribute. The difference is that the study of illness presents social science with an alternative way of configuring health problems that emphasizes their social and psychological dimensions, a configuration that complements and corrects the limitations of the biomedical model and that opens up substantial theoretical and practical therapeutic and preventive themes for research. While some labeling approaches to this subject have rightly been criticized for paying no attention to biological constraints on illness, more recent research has attempted to examine biosocial interactions, thereby linking this field of research to psychosomatic and stress research. Such linkages are essential to foster theory construction and interdisciplinary research. In chronic pain and other disability problems, social science approaches of restricting illness limitation and improving patient functioning in family, work, and health care systems are rapidly replacing the biomedical paradigm of disease cure, which is repeatedly found to be inappropriate and even harmful for chronic pain patients.

An especially important aspect of this subject for medical anthropology is cross-cultural comparison of illness behavior. For example, we have conducted studies of styles of somatization in psychiatric and medical disorders in Chinese and American populations with particular concern for the way social relationships and cultural norms shape physiologically based symptoms and cognitive and affective processes (Kleinman 1982).[2] This research has practical significance with respect to the development of clinical strategies to better recognize and manage these ubiquitous primary care problems in different cultural settings (Katon & Kleinman 1981; Katon, Kleinman & Rosen 1982). For example, in China and in the United States, somatization may result from demoralization owing to job dissatisfaction or underemployment, unsanctioned anger in an intolerable family relationship, or unavoidable political or economic failure. Some of these social sources are technically remedial, others are potential foci for innovative social change, but all are worthy of definition. Where somatization is maintained or worsened owing to the leverage it gives the chronically ill to manipulate the sick role for their own gain (conscious or not), recognition of its role in altering patterns of access to family or work resources may help in cost containment as much as in rehabilitation. The definition of such problems and negotiation of intervention are based on social science ideas and furthered by social science methods. Elsewhere I have also suggested that this problem framework enables social science to contribute to the development of clinical theory and methods in family medicine, primary care internal medicine, and primary care nursing practice (Kleinman 1983).

Among other clinically applied contributions of medical anthropology and medical sociology to health care are descriptions of the help-seeking process, including determinations of variations in different ethnic groups (Harwood 1981); more detailed and sophisticated analyses of doctor-patient communication, including sociolinguistic discourse analysis (Mishler 1985); comparisons of indigenous healing systems and biomedical care that assess universal and particular aspects of healing; and a new generation of studies of biomedical practitioners and their practices that examine how the social institutions of biomedicine and its professional norms influence the work of doctoring and of medical research (Hahn & Gaines in press; Bosk 1981; Latour & Woolgar 1979).

More central uses of social science in medicine have undoubtedly resulted from the application of survey research techniques and statistical innovations to epidemiology, biostatistics, and health services research. It is all too easy to forget the difficult and laborious work that went into the development of these scientific methods over the past three decades of social scientific progress; in my personal experience, both the provenance for the innovations and the history of the struggles to develop them are either ignored by or unknown to the medical scientists who currently use them.

Limitations of space prevent me from reviewing many key contributions of psychology to medicine and psychiatry, such as more refined models and methodologies to assess cognitive and affective dimensions of psychopathology; the health consequences of the interaction between stressful life events, coping styles, and social supports; and ways of measuring psychophysiological and sociophysiological processes that link changes in social environment to alterations in autonomic nervous system, neuroendocrine, immunological, and endorphin systems. On the treatment side, behavioral interventions to help manage pain and chronic illness behavior, psychotherapeutic approaches to reduce somatization, and various attempts to improve health status by treating family problems and changing life-style patterns have contributed importantly to health care. Each of these areas offers an illustration of both appropriate current use of social science and of efforts to develop a long-term relationship between social science and clinical care programs.

Alongside these effective uses of social science *in* medicine are examples of significant contributions of social science *for* medicine. That is to say, social scientists working outside the institutional frameworks and structures of relevance of medicine have provided valuable studies of the social determinants of health and forceful critiques of the social forces shaping the institutions of health care and the dominant approaches to the major health care delivery problems of our time. The provocative studies of sociologists like Freidson (1970) and Starr (1983), of historians like Foucault (1965,1973) and Rothman (1971), and of many economists and political scientists doubtless could not have been conducted within a narrow institutional framework of professional medical interest. While these contributions tend to be articulated as macrosocial discourse, work is increasingly being conducted that illuminates the dynamic relationship between macrosocial variables and microclinical events. Among many examples, there are Stone's analyses (1979a, 1979b) of the function of illness tests in American distributive politics, the determination by Yelin and others (1980) that local work conditions are better predictors of return to work among workers on disability leave than medical variables, Luft's research on the economic causes and consequences of specific kinds of health problems (1978), Labov and Fanshel's sociolinguistic parsing of how cultural symbols and social relations affect psychotherapy (1977), and Estroff's ethnographies of the street lives of the chronic mentally ill (1981, 1982). This orientation has been transported within medical institutions themselves in Bosk's studies of the moral training of surgeons (1981), Zerubavel's analysis of the social organization of time in the hospital (1979), Plough's review of crises of legitimation in renal dialysis programs (1981), in the better-known writings of more senior participant-observers of medicine (e.g., Renee Fox), and in the new anthropology of biomedicine (see Hahn & Kleinman 1983).

Elsewhere my colleague Noel Chrisman and I (1983) have reviewed a very large body of social science studies of the non-biomedical components of local health care systems, studies that challenge the inattention of health planners to social network and family settings of care. Hundreds of social science studies of health maintenance practices, of the major social contributions to disease causation and to the failure of public health programs, especially in the developing world, and of self-care and the family contribution to illness onset and health care, to mention only a few relevant topics, offer an independent social science perspective to the biomedical one that predominates in epidemiological and health services research.

Given all of these useful contributions of social science to medicine, the reader might well wonder why its influence has been so limited. The reasons are not difficult to discern. The actual number of useful studies (though impressive when viewed by itself) becomes quite small in relative terms when diluted with the tens of thousands of health science studies conducted in the health field each year. These studies, moreover, are most often published in the social science literature where they exert a greater influence on social scientists than on health scientists, administrators, planners, or practitioners, who do not routinely read this literature. All too infrequently are their conclusions translated into practical strategies for practice or planning or for setting the problem frameworks and solution frameworks for medical research. In fact, so cut off from the rest of the medical science literature are the medical social sciences that these conclusions are most often not brought to the attention of relevant medical personnel, and hence they usually exert an insignificant influence on biomedicine. Even more important, there has been relatively limited uptake of these contributions into political decision making on health issues, including health research.

Part of the problem is the political structure of policymaking, which has emphasized certain of the social sciences (economics and political science) over others (psychology, sociology, anthropology) and which has excluded from the policy forum alternative concepts and data that are deemed politically unacceptable. But there can be little doubt that another part of the problem is the failure of the medical social sciences to articulate their work effectively as viable policy alternatives. A glaring and tragic example of this is in the psychotherapy field, where increasing evidence of the very real value of psychotherapy for certain classes of medical patients in primary care who somatize treatable psychiatric disorders and psychological problems has not been effectively presented in the national policy debate on the costs of health care (cf. Follette & Cummings 1967; Cummings & Follette 1976; Lowy 1975). That failure is visible, not only in the recent cutbacks in health insurance coverage for psychotherapy, but also in the disappointingly little attention given to psychotherapy of medical patients as a strategy of the new cost containment programs. Perhaps a more ominous failure of policy articulation of social science research is the absence of effective public policy opposition to the corporate takeover of health care by for-profit business, a rapid development that many social science students of health care privately fear. The deafening silence has much to do with an absence of relevant research findings, a point I will return to further on.

This question of the lack of significant influence of social science studies on the health field leads naturally to a less congenial but, for all its frustrating examples, no less instructive subject: the misuses of social science in medicine. Before we take up this vexing account, it is worth recalling David Rothman's warning about the history of reforms of the asylum in American society (1971): that with the intention always of making things better, almost invariably things were made worse. Since it is quite apparent, fortunately, that this cannot be said of the social sciences in medicine, we can embark on a brief review of this troubling subject without too much trepidation.

SOME MISUSES AND ABUSES OF SOCIAL SCIENCE

For several years I observed a multidisciplinary chronic illness service in a hospital that functioned as a tertiary care referral site for patients with chronic medical disability who were referred by their physicians because they had failed to respond to routine biomedical interventions. This clinical service included, as well as traditional biomedical treatment interventions, a program of behavioral therapy run by clinical psychologists. I attended the weekly in-patient rounds where anesthesiologists, rehabilitation medicine physicians, psychologists, psychiatrists, nurses, social workers, physical therapists, and occasionally orthopedic surgeons and neurosurgeons discussed patients who were actively receiving diagnostic assessment or treatment. As an ethnographer, I was particularly interested in the way these health professionals talked about patients, how quite distinctive therapeutic discourses gave rise to alternative, and at times conflicting, cultural constructions of clinical reality, how these particular constructions were negotiated into a unified treatment plan, and how alternative constructions and the process by which they were negotiated shaped treatment expectations.

After attending these meetings for several years, I came away with the disturbing impression that (at least on this service) the behavioral construction of chronic illness and disability, though frequently of therapeutic value (especially in the short run), was more demeaning and dehumanizing of patients than the biomedical model, which is so often and appropriately the recipient of these negative descriptors. As assessed by these behavioral clinicians, especially the younger ones, many patients sounded like criminals and malingerers, though few in fact actually were, and many families sounded like hotbeds of deviance propagating immoral and illegal behaviors aimed at creating havoc with the medical system. Although there was no technical reason why the operant-conditioning paradigm should lead to such a value-laden and cynical discourse on patients, that is what it amounted to. Patients were stripped of the protection of the sick role and left in a liminal no-man's-land where neither they nor their caregivers could tell if they were morally or even legally culpable for their behavior. Once the medical category of "patient" had been undermined, these individuals, even if they had been surreptitiously labeled "crocks" by their physicians, were designated in staff-to-staff communication in a more damaging and denigrating way as "con men," "sociopaths," "deadbeats," and even worse, as faceless automatons whose headaches, backaches, and weakness were the direct and sole result of environmental operants. Needless to say, the therapeutic discourse was no more sensitive, and you can well imagine that there was a flourishing black humor turning on the term "extinguish."

Now, lest I be misinterpreted, I am not contending that this is the general contribution of behavioral medicine (heaven help us!), but that the discourse these particular behaviorists shaped was more starkly inhuman and as narrowly technical as the biomedical discourse on disease. Furthermore, I think this can be seen as a misuse and abuse of a potentially powerful social science intervention in the health field that may not be limited to this program alone; properly applied, this intervention could and should lead to more person- and context-oriented, humane, and even more therapeutically effective treatment intervention.

What happened in the unfortunate instance I am recounting? The individuals involved were committed clinicians, careful clinical researchers, decent human beings. Their clinical construction of reality was influenced by the not-so-covert values of the biomedical discourse, by the gallow's humor that journeymen in health care develop to manage the anxieties and frustrations they experience in the exigent difficulties of their trade, and by institutional demands for technical efficiency and insurance demands that the intervention be technologized for purposes of reimbursement. I think this appalling distortion can happen wherever social science formulations function as the handmaidens of biomedicine, as merely technical applications rather than as alternative configurations of human miseries in their contexts of particular meanings, norms, and power (Kleinman 1980), or when social scientists fail to be critical of their potentially untoward effects.

Care is moral praxis. Social scientists who enter this arena as practitioners or as clinical researchers carry the same therapeutic mandate borne by other health professionals. The Hippocratic maxim so often quoted yet infrequently followed by physicians, "First do no harm," signals the complexities of an almost always ambiguous domain within which simply to be present and listen is to act and engender psychophysiological and ethical consequences. Social science in this arena is no longer simply science; it is part of clinical practice, the other parts of which are biological science, clinical experience, and a vast uncharted territory of action. Here probabilistic reasoning based on populations must be translated into highly inaccurate predictions about an individual. This clinical realm is like the portion of medieval European maps to the east of the last known city that carried the warning "From here, lions!" Social scientists are more comfortable charting this domain than working in it. But as social science increasingly becomes part of clinical science and even of practice, it is subject to the same misuses and abuses that affect other components of the clinical world: quackery, charlatanism, economic and sexual exploitation, ethical and legal offenses, and so forth.

There are current questions of major importance in the health field that have attracted little social science research, even though such research is clearly crucial to their assessment. Examples include, among many others, hospice care for the terminally ill, which has just become an official component of the American health care system but for which there are virtually no studies evaluating its effect on the dying patient, his or her family, or the community; description of the changes in health care services when they are organized within for-profit institutions; assessment of the therapeutic efficacy and dangers of the literally hundreds of alternative therapies practiced by modern folk healers and laymen, including the estimated million or so lay psychotherapists in the United States. I regard as a misuse of medical social science the avoidance of such large-scale, salient problems. These are messy and difficult real-world problems, but they can be, and must be, researched. They are sidestepped for several reasons besides their complexity and the consequent technical difficulties, though this problem certainly discourages some serious scholars. These include the absence of major funding sources for such questions; their marginal relationship to the structure of relevance developed in the particular medical social sciences; their immediate and unavoidable policy implications; the lack of substantial medical social science research centers with broad-based longitudinal research programs on large-scale interdisciplinary topics—like healing, death, and dying and the social organization of health care—instead of single cross-sectional studies in a number of unrelated fields. Closely related to the last point is the limited number of medical social scientists who have made career commitments to the study of such large-scale questions. The fragmentation of social science studies along single-discipline lines also has not improved this situation.

Another misuse of the social sciences in medicine relates to their failure to take themselves seriously enough in the health field. For example, in the field of mental disorders, some of the best epidemiological and phenomenological studies have been conducted by social scientists (e.g., George Brown's work on depression: Brown & Harris 1978). Yet it is surprising that social scientists have neither leveled a systematic critique at the third edition of the *Diagnostic and Statistical Manual of the American Psychiatric Association* (DSM-3) or the ninth edition of the World Health Organization's *International Classification of Disease* (ICD-9) nor set forth alternative classificatory schemes. DSM-3 is doubtless a big advance over

DSM-2, but we are all aware of its enormous problems. I hardly need review them, but a few of the more notable are the classification of symptoms as disorders (e.g., conversion disorder), the reliance on the wastebasket category "atypical" to handle substantial cross-cultural and cross-class differences in symptomatology (e.g., culture-bound disorders or the case of major depression disorders in non-Western societies, which often lack dysphoria, low self-esteem or guilt), the crude reification of personality disorders, the lack of validity and reliability for much of the somatoform disorders section, the blaming of the victim implicit in the middle-class value orientation of sociopathy, and so forth. Surely a major project for the medical social sciences is to effectively critique DSM-3 to set the groundwork either for a much improved DSM-4 or for alternative diagnostic systems. The silence on this question is an embarrassment to social science; it reflects a remarkable willingness to work within the marked limits of a problem framework set by psychiatry and is not helpful to the advancement of psychiatric science.

Psychological anthropology is a case in point. This field has been of remarkably little help to cross-cultural psychiatry. It is not just that we are still a long way from obtaining basic cross-cultural data on cognitive, affective, and behavioral norms, but anthropological research has almost totally disregarded these tasks. That is to say, for all the funding of anthropological field research in the past by the National Institute of Mental Health, few anthropologists have attempted to devote careers either to studying cross-cultural norms needed to establish limits of normal functioning or to studying cross-cultural aspects of psychopathology. In the World Health Organization's International Pilot Study Of Schizophrenia (1973), the key finding was that outcome of schizophrenia varies inversely with the social development of the society. This finding should have elicited at least a few substantial anthropological studies of possible cultural and social determinants of a major difference in outcome. But in fact anthropologists have contributed hardly at all to the research being conducted on this topic, which is formulated in a biomedical framework that both fails to examine potentially crucial cultural and social factors and studies a few rather simplistically formulated social and cultural variables in a manner that most anthropologists find inadequate. In a field in which hypotheses are infrequently tested, it is saddening that when descriptive data are available to develop sophisticated hypotheses concerning a substantial cross-cultural difference in the course of major mental illness, none are being formulated. Similarly, in the case of child psychiatry, which is in desperate need of a relevant data base, we have the disappointing example of outstanding research by behavioral scientists on perceptual and attentional processes in childhood with findings that are not applied by them or by colleagues concerned with pathology to the study of childhood disorders. That this connection has not been made is in striking contrast to the application of molecular genetic research to medical disorders.

Given the scientific stage of the medical social sciences, I realize that I am making more substantial demands on social science research in medicine than have heretofore been made or are probably warranted. But it strikes me that if the social sciences in medicine are to demonstrate their potential use, they must take on salient practical problems and must enter into long-term interdisciplinary collaborations with the relevant medical sciences.

POSTSCRIPT

As I view it, social science is not simply another field of science; it is a particular kind of human science. In contrast to biomedicine, which is mute on the subject, social science queries the relationship between meanings, norms, and power, on the one side, and between health, illness, and care on the other. Biomedicine offers the medical social sciences the advantage of more precisely determining the sociophysiological integrations that mediate this relationship. But social science offers biomedicine access to a more rigorous and discriminating understanding of the human side of illness and care. This access extends self-reflexively to biomedical categories and practice itself. That is to say, social science contributes to metatheory in medicine, a subject that has been woefully and dangerously underdeveloped in our time.

This theme has personal meaning for me because the study of anthropology liberated my thinking from the narrow conceptual framework of biomedicine and helped me to rethink illness and healing from a rather different perspective. I believe this perspective is one of the great contributions of anthropology and of the other social sciences. It is an experience that l have been trying for the past decade to reproduce for the medical students, resident physicians, and practitioners whom I teach. I have no doubt in my mind that this is a most important use of social science, though I still remain uncertain and unskilled in achieving the desired effect.

It is not a one-way street: biomedicine offers anthropology a field of inquiry and powerful methodologies. Furthermore, in the biomedical domain, it is apparent that the materialist and idealist models that anthropologists employ are far less availing than interactionist models (Hahn & Kleinman 1983); hence biomedicine has the potential of contributing to theory development in anthropology. Somehow the relationship between social science and medicine needs to be conceived in terms of this creative dialectic. It is one of the continuing disappointments of my academic experience to recognize that it usually is not so regarded. If this relationship is to be fostered, it is not only funding for research collaboration and teaching and the other obstacles that I have reviewed that must be addressed; we must discuss as well the best ways of advancing theory in this still poorly explored intellectual borderland between medicine and social science. Thus far, critical analysis of bridging ideas between social science and medicine has received far too little attention. Indeed, the modus operandi of most collaborations is to avoid such questions for fear they will make collaboration more difficult. The result is a missed opportunity to advance both disciplines and to contribute to one of the great potentials of current intellectual life. Such theoretical labor would bring intellectual excitement to a subject that all-too-frequently fails to attract the best students and young investigators because it strikes them as somewhat superficial and insubstantial. It would help revivify cognate fields in medicine—social medicine, public health, psychiatry, bioethics   that are in hard times, passing through conceptual doldrums. There is recognition today that paradigms are changing, that interdisciplinary questions are overshadowing disciplinary interests, that the language we use to configure problems is inadequate, that we are entering a new period of intellectual change but with great uncertainty how best to proceed. It is unfortunate that the climate of funding is such that we tend to disregard these broader concerns in order to keep our individual ships afloat. But this should not be an excuse for a failure of intellectual nerve. The relationship between social science and medicine will prosper as much from the development of the kind of intellectual bridges I am describing as from infusion of monies. We should be establishing the agenda for theoretical debate that will set the foundations for those bridges. I meant this earlier when I said that a serious obstacle to the effective use of social science in medicine is lack of a vision of what the role of social science could be; that obstacle is even greater in medicine. It is important, then, that we get the debate started from which such a vision can emerge.

Notes

1. When it comes to the life world of patients, there is a kind of hubris in medical education that is in stark contrast to the humility accorded the biological world. Perhaps some degree of hubris is needed for healers to engage in the incredibly complicated and uncertain psychosocial world that embeds illness experiences. Social science offers systematized, rigorous, uncommon knowledge about this world that challenges both the common-sense view and the hubris of the medical educator and practitioner. Perhaps the latter feel that they will be overwhelmed and paralyzed by uncertainty if they once assume toward the meanings and relationships of patients' life worlds the scholarly and critical stance that they take when assessing physiology. Whatever the reasons for it, this behavior is rightly upsetting to social scientists and helps to make them feel uncomfortable in medicine. It is most disheartening to see this behavior in psychiatric educators, who frequently seem to act as if they are behavioral scientists but clearly have not explored the subject in any depth or breadth. This must be one of the reasons social scientists are threatening to medical educators. It also offers an illustration of the work social scientists have cut out for them in the health professions. Not only do health science students require education in the relevant social science concepts and data, but so do their teachers, who may well find (as I did) that social science can liberate them from an intellectual framework that can be overly narrow and inflexible and can open up for them alternative ways of construing medical problems. But first this lack of scholarly humility toward the day-to-day world of personal experience and relationships must be, with empathy, confronted and critiqued.

2. "Somatization" is the presentation of psychological and interpersonal problems in a bodily idiom of distress and a pattern of medical help seeking. It can result from psychophysiological arousal in acute stress reactions and psychiatric disorders, from the amplification of symptoms of physiological pathology in chronic medical and psychiatric disorders, or from amplification and mislabeling of normal physiological processes. In these conditions, personal, interpersonal, and cultural variables systematically dampen affective complaints and exaggerate bodily ones. Somatization represents a major illustration of the influence of personal and family coping style and communicative processes, cultural norms and meanings, and social relations and institutional constraints on illness behavior. For example, it illustrates key differences in the phenomenology of mental illness cross-culturally and across social classes (Katon, Kleinman & Rosen 1982; Kleinman & Katon, in press; Kleinman 1977, 1980, 1982, 1984). Styles of somatization—exhaustion weakness, pseudo-neurological, chronic pain, gastrointestinal pain, semen loss, fright and soul loss, cosmetic preoccupation, head preoccupation, pseudoangina-hyperventilation—both

differ in content in different sociocultural contexts and convey distinctive meaning in those contexts. The translation between overt discourse on symptoms and covert discourse on power relationships in family, work, and community is a contribution of social sciences' hermeneutics of suspiciousness to medicine, as well as a powerful opportunity to deploy that interpretive method in a real-world situation. Herein also lies a problem, for social science reveals that some and perhaps many sources of somatization reside in the sociopolitical and economic structure and are medically intractable. This is a message that clinicians sometimes regard as nihilistic, though it need not be so.

References

Alexander, L. 1982. Illness maintenance and the new American sick role. In *Clinically applied anthropology*, ed. N. Chrisman and T. Maretzki. Dordrecht: D. Reidel.

Blumhagen, D. 1982. The meaning of hypertension. In *Clinically applied anthropology*, ed. N. Chrisman, and T. Maretzki. Dordrecht: D. Reidel.

Bosk, C. 1981. *Forgive and remember: Managing medical failure.* Chicago: University of Chicago Press.

Brown, G., and Harris, T. 1978. *The Social Origins of Depression.* New York: Free Press.

Chrisman, N., and Kleinman, A. 1983. Popular health care and lay referral networks. In *Handbook of health, health care, and health professions*, ed. D. Mechanic. New York: Free Press.

Cummings, W. A., and Follette, W. T. 1976. Brief psychotherapy and medical utilization: An eight-year follow-up. In *The professional psychologist today*, ed. H. Dorken et al. San Francisco: Jossey-Bass.

Demers, R., et al. 1980. An exploration of the depth and dimensions of illness behavior. *Journal of Family Practice* 11: 1085–92.

Estroff, S. 1981. *Making it crazy: An ethnography of psychiatric clients in an American community.* Berkeley: University of California Press.

———. 1982. Long-term psychiatric clients in an American community. In *Clinically applied anthropology*, ed. N. Chrisman and T. Maretzki. Dordrecht: D. Reidel.

Eisenberg, L., and Kleinman, A., eds. 1981. *Relevance of social science for medicine.* Dordrecht: D. Reidel.

Figlio, K. 1982. How does illness mediate social relations? Workmen's compensation and medical-legal problems, 1890–1940. In *The problems of medical knowledge*, ed. P. Wright and A. Treacher. Edinburgh: University of Edinburgh Press.

Follette, W. T., and Cummings, W. A. 1967. Psychiatric services and medical utilization in a prepared health plan setting. *Medical Care* 5:25–35.

Foucault, M. 1965. *Madness and civilization.* New York: Mentor.

———. 1973. *The birth of the clinic.* New York: Pantheon.

Freidson, E. 1970. *Profession of medicine: A study of the sociology of applied knowledge.* New York: Dodd and Mead.

Hahn, R., and Gaines, A., eds. In press. *Physicians of western medicine: Anthropological approaches to theory and practice.* Dordrecht: D. Reidel.

Hahn, R., and Kleinman, A. 1983. Biomedical practice and anthropological theory. *Annual Review of Anthropology.* 12:305–33.

———. In press. Biomedicine as a cultural system. In *The encyclopedia of the social history of the biomedical sciences,* ed. M. Piattelli-Palmarini. Milan: Franco Maria Ricci.

Harwood, A., ed. 1981. *Ethnicity and medical care.* Cambridge: Harvard University Press.

Helman, C. 1985. Pseudo-angina and magical illness: A case history. In *Physicians of western medicine: Anthropological approaches to theory and practice,* ed. R. Hahn and A. Gaines. Dordrecht: D. Reidel.

Hulka, B.; Kupper, L., and Cassel, J. 1972. Determinants of physician utilization. *Medical Care.* 10:300–309.

Katon, W., and Kleinman, A. 1981. Doctor-patient negotiation and other social strategies in patient care. In *Relevance of social science for medicine,* ed. L. Eisenberg and A. Kleinman. Dordrecht: D. Reidel.

Katon, W.; Kleinman, A.; and Rosen, G. 1982. Depression and somatization. *American Journal of Medicine* 72(1): 127–35; 72(2): 241–47.

Kleinman, A. 1977. Depression, somatization and the new cross-cultural psychiatry. *Social Science and Medicine* 11: 3–10.

———. 1980. *Patients and healers in the context of culture.* Berkeley: University of California Press.

———. 1982. Neurasthenia and depression. *Culture, Medicine, and Psychiatry* 6:117–90.

———. 1983. Cultural meanings and social uses of illness behavior. *Journal of Family Practice* 6:539–45.

———. 1984. Somatization (in Chinese). *Gouwai Yixue, Jingshenbingxue Fence* (Foreign Referential Medical Journal, Psychiatry [Changsha, Hunan, People's Republic of China]) 11(2):65–68.

Kleinman, A., and Katon, W. In press. Somatization and bereavement. In *Background papers: Study of health consequences of stress of bereavement.* Washington, D.C.: Institute of Medicine, National Academy of Sciences.

Labov, W., and Farrshel, D. 1977. *Therapeutic discourse: Psychotherapy as conversation.* New York: Academic Press.

Latour, B., and Woolgar, S. 1979. *Laboratory life: The social construction of a scientific fact.* Beverly Hills: Sage.

Lowy, F. H. 1975. Management of the persistent somatizer. *International Journal of Psychiatry in Medicine* 6:227–39.

Luft, H. S. 1978. *The economic causes and consequences of health problems.* Cambridge, Mass.: Ballinger.

Mayr, E. 1982. *The growth of biological thought.* Cambridge, Mass.: Belknap Press.

Mechanic, D. 1980. The experience and reporting of common physical complaints. *Journal of Health and Social Behavior* 21:146–55.

Mishler, E. 1985. *The discourse of medicine: Dialectics of medical interviews.* New York: Ablex.

Pennebacker, J. W., and Skelton, J. A. 1978. Psychological parameters of physical symptoms. *Personality and Social Psychology Bulletin* 4:524–30.

Plough, A. 1981. Medical technology and the crises of experience: The costs of clinical legitimization. *Social Science and Medicine* 15F:89–101.

Petersdorf, R., and Feinstein, A. 1981. An informal appraisal of the current status of "medical sociology". In *Relevance of social science for medicine,* ed. L. Eisenberg and A. Kleinman. Dordrecht: D. Reidel.

Rothman, D. 1971. *The discovery of the asylum.* Boston: Little, Brown.

Starr, P. 1983. *The social transformation of American medicine.* New York: Basic Books.

Stewart, D. C., and Sullivan, T. J. 1982. Illness behavior and the sick role in chronic disease: The case of multiple sclerosis. *Social Science and Medicine* 16:1392–1404.

Stone, D. 1979a. Diagnosis and the dole: The function of illness in American distributive politics. *Journal of Health Politics, Policy, and Law* 4:510–21.

———. 1979b. Physicians as gatekeepers: Illness certification as a rationing device. *Public Policy* 27:227–54.

Taussig, M. T. 1980. Reification and the consciousness of the patient. *Social Science and Medicine* 14B:3–13.

White, K. L., Williams, T. F.; and Greenberg, B. 1961. The ecology of medical care. *New England Journal of Medicine* 265: 885–92.

WHO. 1973. *International pilot study of schizophrenia.* Vol. 1. Geneva: WHO.

Yelin, E.; Nevitt, M.; and Epstein, W. 1980. Toward an epidemiology of work disability. *Milbank Memorial Fund Quarterly/Health and Society.* 58:386–415.

Zerubavel, E. 1979. *Patterns of time in hospital life.* Chicago: University of Chicago Press.

Zola, I. 1972. The concept of trouble and sources of medical assistance. *Social Science and Medicine* 6:673–79.

———. 1973. Pathways to the doctor: From person to patient. *Social Science and Medicine* 7:677–84.

10 Social Measurement as the Creation of Expert Systems

Aaron V. Cicourel

The history of social science research is in many ways a history of our attempts to create instruments that will make it possible to retrieve information from the mental structures of individuals.[1] We have developed a number of sophisticated strategies with which to elicit information from individuals as a means of inferring either individual differences or group sentiments about a wide variety of capabilities and activities. For example, we have developed mental testing instruments, survey questionnaires, and interviewing strategies in order to assess individuals' attitudes, their understanding of norms, their values, or their intellectual capabilities, and the likelihood that they will succeed in some future endeavor such as academic studies or a new job. Another way of using information from individuals is to obtain the life history, ratings of behavior or check lists, subjective judgments based on interview information, and psychometric test data in order to make predictions about an individual's success after release from prison or a mental institution.

The success of different instruments to elicit and score information on individuals presupposes considerable tacit reliance on the unexplained language use, reasoning, and local comprehension processes of the respondents questioned or tested. But the language, reasoning, and comprehension required has seldom been a topic of research. The frequent assumption made is that the tests and surveys or interview schedules employed are self-contained and self-evident. The use of these instruments has not been accompanied by an explicit effort to study the subjects' or respondents' language, reasoning, and comprehension while being tested, completing a questionnaire, or responding to interview questions that are open-ended. The professional's or researcher's language use, reasoning, and comprehension while constructing, administering, and interpreting test, survey, and interview results have also been taken for granted. Traditional measurement in the social sciences, therefore, has overlooked individuals' mental structures; their information-processing capabilities have been taken for granted.

The past several decades have witnessed an impressive growth in studies of language structure and use and of cognitive processes associated with problem solving or decision making under conditions of uncertainty. These efforts at conceptualizing and studying linguistic, cognitive, and local comprehension processes in actual situations have resulted in considerable clarification of the way information is perceived, represented or reconstructed in memory, and retrieved under different processing and environmental conditions. But there have been few efforts made to reexamine traditional research instruments developed over the past half century in light of these recent developments in information processing. In the pages that follow, I want to examine selective aspects of traditional research methods by making use of information processing ideas as they have been applied to the development of expert systems in medicine. In medicine, the notion of an expert system refers to the formal modeling of the reasoning and decision making of a physician specialist by computer simulation. Additional remarks on what I mean by an expert system will be discussed below.

For at least the past decade, we have witnessed the development of computer-assisted attempts at diagnostic reasoning in medicine that incorporate our understanding of the role of language and cognitive processes in decision making. These recent models of diagnostic reasoning in medicine parallel attempts to model various areas of scientific and everyday, or common-sense, reasoning under laboratory conditions. I assume that the way aspects of diagnostic reasoning are modeled in medicine involves the same decision-making processes required for our understanding of traditional research methods.

I suggest that an understanding of linguistic and cognitive processes in the development of expert systems can clarify the reasoning processes that are often taken for granted in traditional measurement. All social measurement must make explicit the interaction between the formal and the tacit reasoning that is built into our research instruments. Our interpretation of the processes employed by the respondents to understand the instruments and the researcher's reasoning in creating instruments and making inferences from the outcomes that are generated are integral parts of all social measurement. We must come to grips with the following problem: everyday thinking and talk are not self-evident objective processes and products that can be easily subjected to algorithmic, formal modeling. Yet both the researcher and the respondents or subjects make necessary but often tacit use of their everyday knowledge and language. Our efforts at social measurement invariably ignore this issue. I will also explore elements of schematized knowledge and local conditions of interaction and comprehension that are ignored in traditional social science research instruments.

PERCEPTUAL AND SEMANTIC CONTEXT IN EXPERT SYSTEMS

A formal expert system refers to a body of knowledge amenable to a context-free format and mechanical or algorithmic manipulation. Such systems are designed to minimize, if not eliminate or rule out, local conversational and broader institutionalized constraints and to facilitate conditions that can influence decision making in actual settings. For example, interruptions stemming from local talk and telephone calls are not modeled, nor are differences in communication that stem from status differences examined for the way that instructions or elicitation procedures are used.

Formal expert systems share the structural conditions of sentence-based semantic properties to the extent to which they specify explicit but usually restricted semantic domains for the user. Expert systems normally require well-defined bounded domains in order to achieve computational goals. Prior interviews or pretests can be used to anticipate and thus restrict the appropriate vocabulary and problem-solving strategies that can be used. The user, subject, or respondent is provided with a set of options that are permissible and that define a measure on a given set. In the case of computer programs and physician-therapist-patient interviews, the set can be quite extensive and productive in the sense that the user could, on-line, interact with and augment the set of options that can be employed by the system. The goal here is to simulate human learning strategies by providing a program with the capability of creating new schemata based on its interaction with a user or its environment. Psychometric tests and questionnaires, however, cannot leave an interactive trace in the same way that computer programs can, and their restrictive semantic domains are a result of pretesting the items of a questionnaire or of a test to facilitate the use of a mechanical analysis of its outcomes or forced choices.

The psychometric tests and questionnaires could be employed in a computerized format, requiring the researcher or creator to specify more precisely additional aspects of the semantic domains used. Such a task could be something of a problem in a few domains of psychometric tests, but especially in the use of questionnaires seeking opinions, attitudes, and value judgments from respondents. In all expert systems, however, there is a goal of applying algorithms to test or questionnaire items whose content and responses could be perceived and interpreted as self-contained indicators of folk knowledge. Expert systems seek to minimize or eliminate the role of tacit folk knowledge and common-sense reasoning on the part of the researcher in making inferences from a data base. For example, recent work by Clancey (1983) provides us with a sophisticated artificial intelligence program that models a physician's specialized knowledge of infectious diseases. A unique aspect of Clancey's work is the attempt to create an expert system that can reveal the epistemology of the rule-based knowledge employed. To achieve a similar goal, researchers who develop psychometric tests and survey questionnaires would have to clarify for the user both the reasoning employed by the researcher who created each item and the comprehension to be attributed to the respondent. The idea is to capture the researcher's reasoning steps and to clarify the knowledge behind behavior, knowledge that is obscured in the rules used to code outcomes.

The goal of the expert system is to anticipate, in a formal way, the knowledge base and reasoning of the user or subject or respondent. A basic assumption of expert systems research, therefore, is that we are able to identify knowledge domains that can be represented fairly well as context-free computer programs, clinical histories, psychometric tests, or questionnaire items, based on the researcher's use or observation of experts' knowledge under controlled conditions.

An inherent problem in the use of traditional methods of social research, however, is the extent to which they can ever satisfy the ecological validity issue. The ecological validity problem (Cole et al. 1978) refers to how far artificial conditions necessary to guarantee adequate study designs violate circumstances that occur in daily life settings. Or in other words, do our instruments adequately represent the expressed daily life conditions, opinions, values, attitudes, beliefs, and knowledge base of the respondents or subjects we study? Traditional research methods in social science devote considerable effort to the design of studies whose instruments achieve a high level of reliability, but they seldom satisfy ecological validity conditions. The use of expert systems in medicine, however, addresses the ecological validity issue by having users of a program construct diagnoses of actual patients.

SCHEMATIZED KNOWLEDGE AS DECLARATIVE
AND PROCEDURAL DOMAINS

A major thesis of cognitive science research is that our creation, use, and understanding of expert systems presupposes a reliance on personal (Polanyi 1958), common-sense (Cicourel 1964, 1974; Garfinkel 1967; Schutz 1945, 1953), or procedural knowledge (Bobrow & Norman 1975; Rumelhart & Ortony 1977; Rumelhart 1977; Rumelhart & Norman 1978, 1981). Our expertise is also declarative, based on context-free inference rules and general processing strategies.

The idea of declarative and procedural knowledge clarifies the "process" aspects of a representational system from its "data" aspects (Winograd 1975). Declarative systems are said to consist of large numbers of facts and very few special-purpose procedures. Rumelhart and Norman (1981) note that general rules exist for making inferences in declarative systems and that these rules are not dependent on any particular set of facts. The idea of procedural knowledge as a representational system places greater emphasis on processes and the knowledge embedded within these processes. Many special-purpose procedures are involved here, and they contain special knowledge of the kinds of contingencies that are said to be an integral part of the operators that make up the systems. For example, a patient's understanding of particular symptoms and their onset and duration will be embedded in her memory of certain activities (like exercising) and remembering that she stopped at a particular location. Following Winograd (1975), the two types of systems are said to differ vis-à-vis four characteristics: flexibility, learnability, accessibility, and efficiency.

Declarative systems are said to be receptive of new knowledge, without the necessity of new rules of inference yet with the automatic possibility of new inferences. Procedural systems may be said to be "hand crafted by the theorist" (Rumelhart & Norman 1981), and each domain of knowledge is likely to be separate, with little or no transfer from one to the other, thereby making it difficult to add new knowledge. Rumelhart and Norman underscore the importance of context and reasoning ability linked to particular bodies of knowledge in procedural systems. It is this tacit knowledge of how to do something that enables us to produce factual knowledge that is about something. It is relatively easy to comprehend and produce routine linguistic utterances, but difficult to explain the knowledge required for their understanding and production.

A key aspect of declarative knowledge systems is their reliance on inference rules that are known explicitly. The universal format of psychometric tests and questionnaires assumes that respondents can link new knowledge within a task to existing inference rules, or in other words, that new knowledge can be understood without new inference rules. The way the task is framed can mislead a respondent into thinking that special knowledge is needed when actually the example is intended to be analyzed with the same inference rules. Declarative knowledge can be segmented into discrete statements for fairly easy accessibility and identification, while the more context-dependent procedural knowledge is tied to those settings in which it is used. Easily expressed, declarative knowledge is assumed to be stored for easy access.

The use of a standardized format in psychometric tests and sample surveys often means framing problems and questions that are not self-evident to the respondent. Questions may come to mind rather than answers, but the declarative format of standardized instruments does not permit other questions that could clarify the task for the respondent. The way in which a problem or task is framed determines how easy or difficult it is to access declarative and procedural knowledge. The way knowledge is represented externally and internally will either facilitate or inhibit the reasoning needed to access and employ knowledge. Our knowledge about most things we know, therefore, is usually part of a particular, contextualized experience, routine, or activity. We are often unable to discuss this procedural knowledge unless we can be reminded or are able to remind ourselves of the settings in which the information we seek is embedded. Being in a particular situation, therefore, provides us with both environmental and mental cues of the knowledge we seek.

The internal structure of the way knowledge is represented becomes important when we must apply old knowledge to domains that require us to go beyond the way the knowledge was originally intended to be used. This means we compare pieces of knowledge in order to assimilate new knowledge and thus view our knowledge declaratively. Psychometric tests and questionnaires often require a declarative format for what is presumed to be old or existing knowledge, yet the declarative format can force or demand comparisons with contrived or relatively inaccessible procedural knowledge.

Rumelhart and Norman seek a representational system in which all data can be viewed as either data or process. All knowledge may be viewed as knowledge of how to do something or understand something, and the knowledge system may be extended in an analogic way by interrogating it to produce knowledge that is factual or about something. So new schemata can be created by systematic analogical modifications of old ones. Thus our goal in the use of psychometric tests, surveys, and interviews should be the creation of problem-solving tasks or elicitation procedures that create a familiar context, which will enable a respondent to recognize the declarative or procedural knowledge required to complete a task or to elaborate a frame.

Procedural knowledge is tied to experiences and knowledge of how to do or understand something as embedded in particular contexts. The nature of contexts requires empirical study. Knowledge is not static, but changes, is enhanced, or made problematic by the way different participants interact. We need to broaden the way we conceptualize occasions of assumed intersubjectivity and look again at the world we define immediately as normal in a broad sociocultural sense. We need a better understanding of the settings in which participants are anxious to do well on tests, present a good image of themselves in a survey, or convince a parole or psychiatric review board to release them and a better understanding of the emotions, doubts, and fears that accompany physician-patient communication and comprehension. The unfolding interaction becomes a source of new information, of life as usual or some restructuring of what is given and new. We need to learn more about the way the written formats of research instruments and the unfolding interactional contexts of their use frame, constrain, and facilitate the use and modification of the respondent's or user's schemata.

CLINICAL REASONING AND THE LANGUAGE USED TO ESTABLISH A DATA BASE

The clinical-statistical prediction distinction tends to take for granted the subsymbolic and symbolic operations needed to create a data base for both clinical and statistical prediction in medical and psychotherapy settings where clinician and patient must negotiate their perceptual, cognitive, and linguistic activities. These kinds of activities are always presupposed in the production and comprehension of speech and of affectual, paralinguistic, and nonverbal behavior, as well as in planning, problem solving, and decision making in organizational settings and casual encounters.

A physician makes many inferences about medical conditions by interpreting particular lexical items and phrases in the patient's indirect remarks. For example, a cryptic reference to the patient being depressed may be an inference from affect, from negative references to self, and from the patient's general demeanor. The physician may infer factual information on the dosage of a drug by trying to clarify the color of the pill taken. The "facts" seem unequivocal in the written medical history, but the way these elements of a data base are created remains unclear. A patient's rambling and sometimes emotionally confused style of speaking can lead to errors, for example, when dates are not recorded as stated by the patient or when events are transposed because of dates that do not match (Cicourel 1982).

The clinical reasoning of medical and psychotherapeutic personnel can be simulated, but we lack studies of diagnostic reasoning during exchanges or discourse in organized clinical settings. We can specify general methods for understanding and manipulating subsymbolic and symbolic structures and processes and outline heuristics for searching through them, but we cannot take for granted data from clinical and similar settings. Statistical and clinical modes of prediction often take for granted the way clinicians and patients verbalize, comprehend, and represent a problem at hand; in other words, we need to ask how a problem is represented in their talk, memory, or writing. Little attention is paid to patients' knowledge base and their internal representation of problems. We know little about the relation between discourse, internal processing and representation, and behavioral displays in natural settings or the extent to which our expert systems are an adequate representation of these issues.

A patient's knowledge base may be inadequate for understanding a laboratory test. She may not understand why different pap-smear tests within a brief period of time can lead to discrepant outcomes. The physician's explanation that the most recent test was done a little differently and was perhaps the reason for the discrepancy may lead to questions about medical bureaucratic procedures. In one case study (Cicourel 1982), the patient's prior experiences in medical settings as an employee and volunteer contributed to her doubts about the physician's explanations of her problems.

The knowledge-based expertise of the clinician and the processes he or she uses to decide a patient's diagnosis and treatment have become the focus of applied research in artificial intelligence (AI) (Szolovits 1982; Shortliffe 1976; Blois 1980; Duda & Shortliffe 1983). These AI approaches emphasize expert-machine interaction, not the perceptual-cognitive-linguistic processes of the initial and subsequent encounters between a clinician and patient in an organizational context. We need to understand the kinds of referents and comprehension that we arouse in the patient's mind by our questions. By the same token, we need to know the ways in which the physician's or therapist's knowledge base is activated by the kinds of responses the patient supplies.

We know that the organization of questions and responses can facilitate or severely limit the kind of information that a patient might provide a physician or therapist. A narrow or misleading interpretation of the patient's response can lead to a very inadequate clinical history, making it even more difficult for another physician or therapist to understand what the patient may have intended at the time of the original interview. When the physician begins to ask the patient about pain, for example, something of an implicit rating scale is created in order to elicit approximate information about onset, intensity, and duration of the pain. The way in which this informal rating scale is used will constrain the kind of information that the patient can give the physician. Patients must always convert the physician's language into frames that fit their own circumstances, and this means adjusting their responses according to their assessment of their own life experiences and knowledge base in light of past conditions or recent changes. The physician, like many interviewers in survey research, is not always sensitive to this kind of assessment by the patient and may, depending on the patient, assume that the informal rating scale (or set of fixed-choice responses) is context free. But the context is being defined by the extralinguistic conditions of the setting and instructions and by the kinds of questions posed. The questioner must be aware of the effect of words that imply a rating scale to which the respondent must adapt.

Several familiar issues come to mind here. We often inject information into a patient's responses that is not warranted. The language we use is often terse, or we assume that our questions are self-evident and clearly stated. Yet the questions often do not enable the patient to clarify the vagueness of symptoms, beliefs, or past experiences. All too often, ignoring this problem leads to the invention of symptoms or experiences on the spot as the respondents try to satisfy what they think the researcher wants to hear. Our theories have little to say about the fact that respondents often have to deal with a considerable amount of ambiguity in a text or discourse and in their knowledge base. Also, our theories are not oriented to the way information is stored and to its accessibility to the respondent.

Communication requires the creation of mental structures and behavioral contexts that are essential for developing decision frames and accessing tacit or procedural knowledge. When we communicate with a respondent using psychometric tests or a standardized questionnaire, this building of sociocultural contexts is minimal or absent. The building of mental structures and behavioral contexts permits us to activate schemata otherwise closed and also permits a more flexible exchange of information. We can ask for clarification or we can assume that we share enough information that we do not have to state assumed common knowledge each time.

MEEHL'S CLINICAL VERSUS STATISTICAL PREDICTION

Statistical or actuarial methods of prediction, according to Meehl (1954) assign an individual to a class or set of classes by the use of what are felt to be objective facts taken from some account of the person's life history, scores on psychometric tests, ratings of behavior or check lists, and subjective judgments based on interview information. When data from these different sources are combined in some systematic way, we can then classify the individual. The fact of classification enables us to query or enter a previously established table that contains the statistical frequencies of behaviors of different types said to be associated with persons belonging to the class. Statistical prediction therefore includes a kind of algorithmic combination of information that permits classification and a probability measure that is derived from an empirically determined relative frequency. In contrast, clinical prediction, according to Meehl, makes use of interview "impressions" and other information from the subject's history, but it can include the same type of psychometric data used in statistical prediction in order to generate a "psychological hypothesis" about the individual in question. The hypothesis may be produced as part of a psychiatric staff conference and may also be based on "reasonable expectations" about the way "outer events" could unfold. This last procedure defines the clinical or case-study type of prediction for Meehl.

At the time the differences reported by Meehl on statistical and clinical methods were discussed, there was little systematic research on the role of cognitive, linguistic, and pragmatic mechanisms and principles in the use and comprehension of utterances or discourse. Nor was there much concern with using the emerging technology of audio and video recordings as important tools and sources of data. It was little recognized that objective facts derived from a life history, ratings of behavior, check lists, and judgments based on interview information all presume a family of interrelated cognitive, linguistic, pragmatic, and social organizational mechanisms, principles, and processes. Nor was it evident at the time that psychometric tests incorporated unclear assumptions by the tester and the test creator about these mechanisms, principles, and processes. A recent statement by Hunt (1983) covers some of the cognitive issues associated with the use of psychometric tests.

Meehl notes that the distinction between clinical and statistical prediction can be traced to an actuarial format inherent in many if not all clinical judgments. He uses an example in which a clinician accords more weight to a factor than it is given in an actuarial table. The idea is that the clinician "must be using some law or other based upon his previous experience, and this law . . . is actuarial" (Meehl 1954, 24). In defending the clinician, however, Meehl notes that he uses some given facts along with some crudely formulated laws to put together a hypothesis about the status of intervening variables or hypothetical constructs in the patient. The clinician may also use evidence from the Rorschach and Multiphasic profiles, as well as from a patient's slip of the tongue during the interview.

For Meehl, Reichenbach's notion of the "context of discovery" and the notion of justification are not clarified when clinicians and scientific critics discuss clinical judgment. Not all of the hypotheses of the clinician could come about solely by the mechanical use of his data. The context of discovery involves elements not made explicit in the context of justification. Or, in the terms of this paper, many elements of discovery remain procedural and do not get represented in the declarative knowledge base.

In a discussion of clinical intuition, Meehl distinguishes between two types of situations. In the first case, the clinician uses his implicit procedural knowledge to make a diagnosis or prediction or postdictive statement about a patient and cannot be explicit when challenged. Meehl suggests that it would be nice if we could verbalize the basis of our intuitive responses and use "slow-motion photography, the application of group judgments, the graphical and quantitative study of gesture and verbal patterns of patients correctly versus incorrectly identified intuitively, and the like" (1954, 69). In this first case, Meehl notes the difficulty of making explicit what one has said or done as opposed to telling someone how to do something. His remarks sound very much like our comments above on forms of reasoning and schematized knowledge. So it is not that the clinician is unique in making intuitive judgments; he is simply performing in ways that are routine and outside of awareness. Meehl goes on to note that we must investigate individual differences in clinicians' intuitive predictions experimentally in order to gain insight into clinical judgment.

The second case involves the difficulty of clarifying the way a person arrives at a particular hypothesis. The critic is asking for a rule or recipe that cannot be produced, yet hypotheses emerge. So we need to focus on the context of discovery by which experiences from previous interviews combine with what is being heard from the current patient or subject (Meehl 1954, 72). The problem is, notes Meehl, our ignorance about the dynamics of this process and our inability to clarify and formalize the logical steps involved so as to clarify the intuitions (he calls them psychological principles) that are used by the clinician "at the *moment of action* in the clinical interview" (ibid., 82).

The study of discourse processes, textual materials, and their comprehension using a schema-based or related theoretical orientation seems to have been anticipated by Meehl's remarks of some thirty years ago. Cognitive scientists have moved away from the statistical analysis of the psychological principles used by the clinician "at the moment of action in the clinical interview" and instead have tried to simulate, experiment with, and retain in field studies as much of the natural conditions of the behavioral and mental processes as are assumed to be relevant.

INDICATORS AND EXPERT SYSTEMS

Meehl (1954) reviewed different studies that compared the activities of a clinician (usually a psychologist) with those based on a statistical procedure. He found in different tasks, including psychological diagnosis and the prediction of performance of entering college freshmen and recidivism among parolees, that the statistical procedures performed as well or better than human predictors.

The psychologist or physician interacts with a patient who may try to mask symptoms, but we usually assume the patient has contacted a clinician because of wanting to report problems. We also assume that a patient with psychological problems will find it quite difficult to mask them from a skilled clinician during a long initial interview. The key issue, however, is that the actual encounter creates and embodies basic processes and informational objects and referents deemed to be constitutive of a diagnosis.

The tests used for assessing reading comprehension skills in children or adults in a one-on-one context are similar to the clinical case; the reader is likely to display important aspects of normal performance difficulties, aspects probably constitutive of the interaction that takes place. The reading problems are especially likely to be revealed if the tester seeks explanations from the subjects of their understanding of specific items. Tests used for predicting success in college or after parole are less likely to embody the kinds of performance that we would expect to occur on future occasions in natural settings. Future occasions presumably include expected and emergent ecological conditions that are inherent in group and individual actions in organizational settings. Considerable prior information (some of it based on interviews) is needed to construct tests for predicting student success in college and to predict recidivism among parolees. In each case, our indicators rely on procedural and declarative expert knowledge.

In order to understand the advantages and disadvantages of clinical versus statistical prediction, we need to think of the difference between an on-line set of strategies for eliciting and comprehending information and the use of forced-choice responses that have been formally organized into an algorithmic program. We should view statistical predictions as special cases of the use of "expert systems" (e.g., the use of computers to play chess or to simulate diagnostic reasoning in medicine). The central concern here is the way knowledge is to be represented in a declarative format necessary for statistical or computer prediction, as opposed to inherent but tacitly employed procedural or context-dependent knowledge and analogical reasoning that must be part of all clinician-patient interviews and human-machine interaction. Questionnaires and open-ended interviews are variants of these two classes of methods.

A number of diagnostic programs have been created for various types of medical problems (cf. Blois 1984; Clancey 1983; Duda & Shortliffe 1983; Shortliffe 1976; Szolovitz 1982). These programs are said to perform quite well vis-à-vis house staff (interns, residents, and fellows) and consultants or specialists. The programs operate in well-defined domains that have been formalized with the help of medical experts. As Blois notes, the issue is not that a clinician competes with a machine, but that considerable expert judgment has antedated the computer process. The expert judgment relies on prior clinical experiences that are difficult to describe in a declarative format. The declarative knowledge base and procedures of the computer program presuppose that the clinician has negotiated various contingencies in a context where semantic and pragmatic distractions can be common and where processing resources constrain the declarative data base and algorithms that can be employed with the patient. The key issue is the quality of prior judgment and the extent to which the particular data base created corresponds with well-structured medical problems.

In order to understand the use of indicators in statistical prediction or expert systems in clinical diagnosis, we must understand the considerable information processing that must precede the implementation of a statistical procedure or a computer program. The information processing occurs in settings where participants—constrained by their processing capacities and the pragmatic conditions of the interaction—must cooperate, assume common knowledge, and negotiate their understanding of lexical items or phrases or sentences. All of these activities are constitutive of an adequate data base yet are tacit resources rather than topics of inquiry in statistical prediction.

Survey Research and Language Comprehension

A different way of describing the procedural-declarative knowledge problem in social measurement can be found in the passive use of language and the tacit use of personal or procedural knowledge by researcher and respondent in sample surveys.

1. The survey's fixed-choice questions assume that the standardized natural-language sentences are in correspondence with commonly accepted facts, opinions, or beliefs about the world.

2. The standardized natural-language sentences of the questionnaire are presumed to activate only the schematized knowledge in the respondent's memory that corresponds with the researcher's theoretical and substantive intentions.

3. The researcher's scaling, path analysis, or cross-tabulations are formal operations that indirectly model the schematized knowledge and "reasoning" attributed to the respondent's actual responses to questionnaire items.

The survey research model depends on an explicit manipulation of fixed response to natural-language sentences to explain their significance. The analysis of the responses presumes an explicit manipulation of a formal representation that links independent and dependent variables in a principled way. In practice, sophisticated analysis of responses is often based on tacit guesses and ad hoc cross-tabulations of responses. The actual on-line inferences we as ideal readers can make, and those made by respondents from the language used in the survey sentences, do not enter into our justification of the operations carried out formally on the data. The researcher's manipulation of respondents' hypothetical responses is not linked to a theoretical and empirical representation of natural settings in which topics emerge in discourse that are comparable to the questions and responses of a survey.

The analysis of continued and spontaneous discourse, of prepared political speeches, and of the talk between lawyer and client, physician and patient, or therapist and patient has led to the development of complex strategies of cognitive and linguistic investigation. Yet, in the many years we have used survey questionnaires, very little energy has been devoted to an understanding of the language used. Understanding the language of the questionnaire is analogous to comprehending the language of a computer program on natural-language understanding (Winograd 1980): the responses do not reveal the nature of the processing activity by which the respondents are said to reason about the meaning of the questionnaire items. As in the artificial intelligence programs on natural-language understanding, the respondents do not have to use modes of perception or action normally used in the real world. They respond differently than they would if the same or similar questions were posed in natural settings in discussion with others.

The questionnaire items can refer to the economy, arms control, political beliefs, capital punishment, how respondents discipline their children, and so on. Such items presuppose respondents who have some knowledge of the economy, the arms race, a political candidate's qualifications, and the like (LaPiere 1934; Schuman & Johnson 1976; Cicourel 1982). The sentences of the survey are assumed to be free of local contexts of language use. It is the researcher who mediates all connections between the questions, the responses, and the world or worlds they are said to represent. The language of the questionnaire can be said to "simulate" real-world occasions by posing hypothetical issues or policies and by asking the respondent to choose among attitudinal or belief options created by the researcher. A reasoning formalism is created directly by the researcher's formal predictions of likely patterns of responses or indirectly by his manipulating responses after the fact to yield patterns that are then attributed to respondents. The language of the questionnaire simulates a comprehension process and hypothetical action without ever having to observe real-world consequences. The explicit representation of the respondent's internal knowledge base and reasoning is not subjected to conceptual, much less empirical, clarification.

All expert systems employ semantic and syntactic frames to access the respondent's procedural knowledge base despite the necessary declarative format of the instruments used. The declarative format forces the respondent to reorganize procedural knowledge in order to satisfy a format that is not faithful to the context-dependent structure of everyday knowledge. An advantage of current work in medical expert systems is the attempt to capture the user's reasoning steps and to clarify the knowledge behind behavior that is obscured in rule-designed hypothesis testing. We lack a model that can also specify the organizational conditions or constraints that could be expected to prevail when respondents solve problems or express their opinions, attitudes, beliefs, or general knowledge in natural settings.

ASPECTS OF MIND AND EVERYDAY REALITY PRESUPPOSED IN EXPERT SYSTEMS

I have argued that traditional social measurement must incorporate the pragmatic conditions of everyday life in order to satisfy ecological validity conditions in studies of problem solving or decision making and of beliefs, attitudes, opinions, and general knowledge of the world. I have used aspects of expert systems research to suggest modifications in traditional social measurement. Traditional methods of social research also have been characterized as expert systems, but they lack the on-line, adaptive potential of computer simulation models. Below I will outline cognitive and linguistic elements of a folk theory of the mind that are presupposed but often ignored in traditional social measurement and recent developments in expert systems.

Our development and use of expert systems like computer programs that simulate human intelligence and psychometric tests and survey questionnaires that examine cognitive abilities, knowledge resources, and belief systems presuppose cognitive and linguistic elements of the mind. Recent papers by D'Andrade (in press) and Fillmore (1982) discuss elements of a folk model of the mind; both papers reflect recent developments in cognitive science that are integral to our understanding and use of expert systems.

Our use of language presumes various folk models or cognitive schemata of ideas, objects, events, or actions. But when we describe or discuss ideas, objects, events, actions, we are constrained by the number of elements (seven, plus or minus two) human short-term memory can manage or process (D'Andrade 1981; Miller 1956; Wallace 1961). The object, events, or actions that are attended in short-term memory can be complex schemata and thus will include additional knowledge whose access can be facilitated by hierarchical organization leading to many discriminations. Folk knowledge can have a wide range of application, notes D'Andrade, and different models can serve as parts of other models, enabling the members of a culture to take their understanding of their daily environment more or less for granted.

The organization of folk models or common-sense knowledge presumes that aspects of a schema are intersubjective. Intersubjectivity is a necessary assumption on the part of the members of a group or culture, and it refers to knowledge that need not be referenced explicitly, knowledge that is assumed to be shared by participants of a particular setting. Intersubjectivity implies aspects of everyday social reality that are constitutive of social interaction (Cicourel 1964, 1974; Garfinkel 1967; Schutz 1945, 1953) and thus refers to more than the participants' substantive knowledge of a particular setting and each other. What are constitutive and seldom referenced by participants are conditions about the cultural environment such as the "normality" or "strangeness" of the setting; participants assume that they speak the same language and employ similar typifications for ideas and objects in a setting they believe to be the "same" for each. The extent to which all participants experience the setting in similar ways is often a pragmatic accomplishment for the practical purposes of the occasion. Intersubjectivity operates in a practical way when participants use referents that are often anaphoric or deictic. The assumption is that the reciprocity of perspectives of all participants refers to what each knows about the other and that they all share this same perspective, or as D'Andrade (1983) states, "when everybody knows that everybody knows" a schema that is referenced by a glance at some object.

A necessary condition of expert systems is the use of declarative knowledge to elicit responses. The textual presentation of computer programs, psychometric tests, or questionnaire items creates a sense of obvious "facts." The use of an expert system formalizes aspects of folk knowledge while simultaneously using other elements of such knowledge as tacit resources. The resources of procedural knowledge and the local setting are seldom viewed as topics requiring independent conceptual and empirical clarification.

Building on the work of linguistic philosophers like Anscombe (1963), Searle (1969, 1975, 1980), and Vendler (1967, 1972), D'Andrade (in press) describes a series of mental processes and states indicated by English verbals. These include external perceptions, thoughts, feelings, emotions, wishes, desires, intentions, resolution, and will or self-control. Briefly, external perceptions refer to simple (see, hear, smell) and achieved (sight, notice) states and simple processes (look, observe, watch, touch). The central concern of the model is that speech acts, as public events, are especially important markers of internal states and processes (Vendler 1972; D'Andrade, in press). We need to know the extent to which creators and users of expert systems anticipate forced responses of test and questionnaire items and the way that different speech acts can cause different internal states and reactions in respondents, reactions that may or may not be consistent with the intended semantic conceptions employed in the computer program. Current uses of expert systems tend to ignore explicit use of folk models of the mind and rely instead on the researcher's assumed native competence with natural language, beliefs, opinions, and factual information. The issue is not simply one of pretesting instruments but concerns explicit conceptual and empirical tests of the way folk and procedural knowledge can or cannot be accessed, are distorted, or become a source of confusion for individuals and groups using the standardized format of the expert system.

Recent work by Fillmore and Kay (Fillmore 1982) brings us closer to problems of understanding the researcher's use of an expert system to make predictions about a person's capacity to comprehend written materials and to use this comprehension to solve problems. This system can also indicate future academic progress as well as general intelligence and level of achievement. Fillmore and Kay studied children's ability to understand a grade-three test of achievement in two elementary schools. Several questions asked of the students to test comprehension were examined in order to pinpoint the kinds of information that the students would have had to interpret or screen and the specific sentence or sentences that seemed to be central to choosing the correct response.

One goal of the study was the identification of the background knowledge needed by the students and the interpreting and integrating skills required for a reader to comprehend the passages and test questions and provide the answers expected by the test creators. Subjects were interviewed in order to learn if they possessed the knowledge and skills presupposed in the passages and questions making up the test. Fillmore and Kay found that the tests were

seriously flawed and required considerable patience on the part of
the reader because of awkward lexical choices, grammatical structuring, and synonym alterations. Their study examines the ways in
which tests become obstacles to students and the goals of creators
and users of them for practical and research purposes. The reading
tests incorporated cognitive and linguistic difficulties that were not
part of the researcher's model of reading comprehension.

Fillmore and Kay devised a system of annotations to analyze text
materials to say something about the way a passage could be understood. The annotations helped them create a corpus to be used in
selective interview probes and provided the researchers with a
checklist with which to assess the children's performance. After observing the children working with and then retelling the texts, the
researchers used interviews in order to identify the knowledge and
skills they felt were necessary for understanding the texts. In our
terms, the researchers sought to transform the children's procedural knowledge and their ability to communicate some of this
knowledge reflexively in a declarative mode into a more formal
understanding of the knowledge and skills employed by the
children.

Fillmore indicates how an ideal reader might see connections,
create specific expectations, derive inferences, and ask questions
that the annotations are designed to represent. This ideal reader, a
construction of the researcher, is said to employ principles from
compositional semantics, the building of schemata, the detection of
plans and goals, and the making of inferences. The ideal reader
also makes use of tacit and procedural knowledge, for example,
when a text is organized in a way that reminds the reader of things
already known. The construction of an ideal reader enabled Fillmore and Kay to observe differences in the way actual readers
comprehend the text. Their strategy is similar to one devised by
Rumelhart (1977) in which subjects are shown a text one segment
at a time while the researcher seeks a verbal report as to the meaning or significance of each segment.

A central element of the Fillmore and Kay project is the idea
that the reading experience requires the child to create a coherent
picture of the world of the text and of activities congruent with its
language. Several levels of "envisagement" are identified in order
to pinpoint the kinds of inferences the text seems to call for or the
inferences derived from the schemata the child brings to the text in
order to contextualize what is happening within a common framework. The child's personal experiences and imagination are seen as

levels of "envisagement." For our purposes, the most important point is that the reader is able to process or make sense of a given text according to the kinds of linguistic clues that can be found in it and the knowledge it references or that is activated by memorial schemata.

The motion of a folk theory of the mind suggests how we can clarify the way expert systems are created and used, and the way their outcomes can be analyzed. The creator and user of expert systems must clarify the different kinds of schemata the text presupposes for its comprehension and for producing responses that will be appropriate outcomes for analysis. This means (following Fillmore 1982) specifying the relationship between speech acts or textual materials and the grammatical and textual or discourse structure. The expert system should model the kinds of objects, events, or properties in the world of the text, and the kind of knowledge that tells the ideal reader that he or she is dealing with structures of expectations associated with a detective story, a medical interview, a folk tale, a sales transaction, or an obituary.

Concluding Remarks

When we refer to following a rule in the use of expert systems, we always presuppose that our expert will employ a folk model that yields similar if not identical comprehension of instructions, a terminal display, or test and questionnaire items. The primary issue here is the way the language used creates similar or different types of "envisagement" for the expert.

Here we must note the parallel between Goodenough's notion (1957) of culture as what one would have to know in order to behave and be taken as a native and Slobin's discussion (1979) of the behavioral evidence we would need to enable us to say that a person "possesses" or "acts as if he knows" a rule or that the person is "operating according to a particular strategy." Slobin presents evidence for observing behavior according to a rule in the way children use two-word utterances spontaneously. Regularities can be detected immediately. The child also searches for the extension of regularities to new instances, for example, by saying "it breaked" and "two mouses." By the age of three, children show clear signs of correcting their speech as if the production is being checked against some standard or norm. By the time they enter school, they have a good intuitive or procedural grasp of their native language, but they are then taught formal phonological, syntactic, and semantic rules in a declarative mode.

The comments by Goodenough on culture and Slobin on rules of language use imply that the notion of rule-governed behavior is equivocal because of our reliance on unclarified sources of knowledge when we seek to explain the perception and comprehension of subjects and respondents. The kinds of behavior, appearances, and speech acts that enable us to convince others that we are native members of a group or society involve procedural and tacit knowledge that we are not likely to be able to describe to others explicitly. We must anticipate the existence and use of this important knowledge to receive and comprehend the declarative format of a psychometric test or a questionnaire. The knowledge base is notable for its tacit, personal, and collective understanding of language use, appearances, and its negotiated display during social interaction in practical circumstances.

The child's and the adult's ability to monitor their own linguistic realizations and make corrections or adjustments to the processing capabilities of some other person by changing linguistic registers implies that we learn early on how to speak in accordance with rulelike regularities, and we also learn to make appropriate adjustments for others deemed incapable of understanding certain forms of speech and the regularities associated with speech. This latter point would include using a linguistic register or a pidgin when speaking to someone who is viewed as not a native member of one's own group (Gelman & Shatz 1977; Newport 1976; Snow 1972).

We social scientists often design studies that force subjects to behave in a declarative mode even when the task or information we seek presumes tacit knowledge and normally occurs in a procedural mode. Depending on our methodological inclinations, we emphasize one type of study (task oriented) versus another (field oriented), yet we seldom ask the extent to which the use of psychometric tests and questionnaires or reading comprehension tests pose knowledge problems for respondents that cannot be understood by the rather mechanical way we use such expert systems. The expertise of the designer and user of the instrument presumes some understanding of the respondent's knowledge base, yet such conditions are not conceptually clear in the methods employed.

Recent work by Wason and Johnson-Laird (1972) and D'Andrade (1984) has shown the way implicit knowledge is linked to the operations in which we actually use this knowledge (see also Rumelhart & Norman 1981). When subjects are asked to follow a rule in a situation in which their knowledge is embedded in a procedural format that is not easily accessible, rather than in a declarative one where general rules of inference are available, they perform poorly or well according to their relative familiarity with the specific knowledge involved. Thus, unless we are trained or train ourselves to use formal reasoning processes, we cannot perform well on problems requiring general inference rules. But when the problem is framed in a way that resembles everyday problem-solving situations, we "understand" things better because our specific knowledge can be invoked, and we can more easily solve the problem (Rumelhart & Norman 1981). Under these everyday conditions, the knowledge representation system seems to possess the reasoning mechanism we need to solve things.

Exposing subjects to new abstract knowledge or a problem for which they have no schema readily available should proceed by presenting the knowledge or problem in terms that seem familiar, and for which a familiar schema exists, including practical sociocultural conditions that the subjects can understand. People will reason well when they have a framework within which to absorb new knowledge or pursue a problem. Following a rule or understanding when a regularity is appropriate therefore depends on the contexts that can be framed for the subject or respondent and that can be analogically retrieved because of perceived similarities with schemata based on prior experiences. A police officer as an expert tends to rely on everyday experiences in deciding when to arrest, while a lawyer tends to rely on general reasoning processes in deciding on the legality of the arrest. The representation of knowledge is linked to the way we will reason with the knowledge.

The design of expert systems requires an explicit recognition of the way we access the expert's special knowledge by the use of a declarative problem-solving format. Expert problem solving always occurs in an organizational setting that is familiar to the researcher or tester, but this setting is seldom like the everyday situations in which a physician or subject or respondent solves problems. I have called attention to several cognitive, linguistic, and social interaction conditions that tend to be ignored or taken for granted when we seek to measure individual or group problem-solving abilities or when we seek to obtain information about individual or group perceptions and an understanding of their opinions, attitudes, and beliefs about the world.

In conclusion, the practical and formal processes and knowledge we employ as researchers in order to develop and use expert systems are themselves constitutive of the measures we develop and use to understand and predict the expertise of physicians, subjects, and respondents. We must design our expert systems to reflect the ecological validity of problem-solving conditions that are presupposed by general reasoning processes and the use of standardized language and thus model the way everyday reasoning, language, and action enter into all attempts at social measurement or the creation of expert systems.

Note

1. I am grateful to Richard A. Shweder for his helpful comments on an earlier draft of the paper.

References

Anscombe, G. 1963. *Intention.* Ithaca: Cornell University Press.
Blois, M. S. 1980. Clinical judgment and computers. *New England Journal of Medicine* 303:192–97.
———. 1984. *Information and medicine: A hierarchical view of clinical processes.* Berkeley: University of California Press.
Bobrow, D. G., and Norman, D. A. 1975. Some principles of memory schemata. In *Representation and understanding: Studies in cognitive science,* ed. D. G. Bobrow and A. M. Collins. New York: Academic Press.
Cicourel, A. V. 1964. *Method and measurement in sociology.* New York: Free Press.
———. 1974. *Cognitive sociology.* New York: Free Press.
———. 1982. Language and belief in a medical setting. In *Contemporary perceptions of language: Interdisciplinary dimensions,* ed. H. Byrnes. Georgetown University Round Table on Languages and Linguistics 1982. Washington, D.C.: Georgetown University Press.
Clancey, W. J. 1983. The epistemology of a rule-based expert system: A framework for explanation. *Artificial Intelligence* 20: 215–51.
Cole, M.; Hood, L.; and McDermott, R. 1978. Ecological invalidity as an axiom of experimental cognitive psychology. Manuscript.
D'Andrade, R. G. 1981. The cultural part of cognition. *Cognitive Science* 5: 179–95.
———. 1984. Reason versus logic. Manuscript.
———. In press. A folk model of the mind. In *Culture models,* ed. N. Quinn and D. Holland, New York: Cambridge University Press.
Duda, R. O., and Shortliffe, E. H. 1983. Expert systems research. *Science* 220: 261–68.
Elstein, A. S.; Schulman, L. S.; and Sprafka, S. A. 1978. *Medical problem solving: An analysis of clinical reasoning.* Cambridge: Harvard University Press.

Fillmore, C. J. 1982. Ideal readers and real readers. In *Analyzing discourse: Text and talk*, ed. D. Tannen. Georgetown University Round Table on Languages and Linguistics 1981. Washington, D.C.: Georgetown University Press.

Garfinkel, H. 1967. *Studies in ethnomethodology.* Englewood Cliffs, N.J.: Prentice-Hall.

Gelman, R., and Shatz, M. 1977. Appropriate speech adjustments: The operation of conversational constraints in talk to two year olds. In *Interaction, conversation, and the development of language*, ed. M. Lewis and L. A. Rosenblum. New York: Wiley.

Goodenough, W. H. 1957. Cultural anthropology and linguistics. In *Report of the seventh annual round table meeting on linguistics and language study*, ed. P. L. Garvin. Washington, D.C.: Georgetown University Press.

Hunt, E. 1983. On the nature of intelligence. *Science* 219:141–46.

Jackendoff, R. 1975. On belief contexts. *Linguistic Inquiry* 6:53–93.

LaPiere, R. T. 1934. Attitudes vs. actions. *Social Forces* 14:230–37.

Meehl, P. E. 1954. *Clinical versus statistical prediction: A theoretical analysis and a review of the evidence.* Minneapolis: University of Minnesota Press.

Miller, G. A. 1956. The magical number seven, plus or minus two: Some limits on our ability to process information. *Psychological Review* 63:81–97.

Newport, E. L. 1976. Motherese: The speech of mothers to young children. In *Cognitive theory*, vol. 2, ed. N. J. Castellan, D. B. Pisoni, and G. R. Potts. Hillsdale, N.J.: Erlbaum.

Polanyi, M. 1958. *Personal knowledge.* Chicago: University of Chicago Press.

Rumelhart, D. E. 1977. Toward an interactive model of reading. In *Attention and performance* 6, ed. S. Dornic. Hillsdale, N.J.: Erlbaum.

———. 1977. Understanding and summarizing brief stories. In *Basic processes in reading: Perception and comprehension.* ed. D. La Berge and S. J. Samuels. Hillsdale, N.J.: Erlbaum.

Rumelhart, D. E., and Norman, D. A. 1978. Accretion, tuning, and restructuring: Three modes of learning. In *Semantic factors in cognition*, ed. J. W. Cotton and R. Klatzky. Hillsdale, N.J.: Erlbaum.

———. 1981. Analogical processes in learning. In *Cognitive skills and their acquisition*, ed. J. R. Anderson. Hillsdale, N.J.: Erlbaum.

Rumelhart, D. E., and Ortony, A. 1977. The representation of knowledge in memory. In *Schooling and the acquisition of knowledge*, ed. R. C. Anderson, R. J. Spiro, and W. E. Montague. Hillsdale, N.J.: Erlbaum.

Schuman, H., and Johnson, M. P. 1976. Attitudes and behavior. *Annual Review of Sociology* 2:161–207.

Schutz, A. 1945. On multiple realities. *Philosophy and Phenomenological Research* 5:533–75.

———. 1953. Common-sense and scientific interpretations of human action. *Philosophy and Phenomenological Research* 14:1–38.

Searle, J. R. 1969. *Speech acts.* Cambridge: Cambridge University Press.

————. 1975. Indirect speech acts. In *Syntax and semantics*. Vol. 3: *Speech acts*, ed. P. Cole and J. L. Morgan. New York: Academic Press.

————. 1980. The intentionality of intention and action. *Cognitive Science* 4:47–70.

Shortliffe, E. H. 1976. *Computer-based medical consultations: MYCIN*. New York: Elsevier.

Slobin, D. I. 1979. *Psycholinguistics*. Glenview, Ill.: Scott Foresman.

Snow, C. E. 1972. Mother's speech to children learning language. *Child Development* 43:549–65.

Szolovitz, P., ed. 1982. *Artificial intelligence in medicine*. Boulder, Col.: Westview Press.

Vendler, Z. 1967. *Linguistics in philosophy*. Ithaca: Cornell University Press.

————. 1972. *Res cognitans: An essay in rational psychology*. Ithaca: Cornell University Press.

Wallace, A. F. C. 1961. On being just complicated enough. *Proceedings of the National Academy of Sciences* 47: 458–64.

Wason, P., and Johnson-Laird, P. N. 1972. *Psychology of reasoning: Structure and content*. Cambridge: Harvard University Press.

Winograd, T. 1975. Frame representations and the declarative-procedural controversy. In *Representation and understanding: Studies in cognitive science*, ed. D. G. Bobrow and A. M. Collin. New York: Academic Press.

————. 1980. What does it mean to understand language? *Cognitive Science* 4:209–41.

11 The Forms and Functions of Social Knowledge

Donald N. Levine

The quest to identify a kind of knowledge that enjoys a privileged status over common-sense perceptions and understandings of the world has been pursued since the very beginnings of reflection about how we know. The record of responses to that quest provides a capsule summary of major moments in the history of human speculation. The idea of the Good, the authority of Revelation, the clear and distinct truths of geometry, the controlled outcomes of experimental investigation, the self-understanding by humans of human projects, the demystified grasp of real historic forces, the quantification of metric operations, the analysis of unconscious expressions, the enlightenment that follows disciplined meditation— these are some of the well-known historical candidates for that privileged position.

In the last two centuries in the West, and increasingly throughout the world, the single most popular candidate has been known generically as "science." Far and away the most successful rhetoric for establishing superior warrants for a proposition is to claim that it is scientific and that other contenders should be disqualified because they represent only common sense, pseudoscience, or insufficiently scientific science. Yet the success of this candidate has by no means laid to rest the uneasiness that underlay that historic quest. As the last half century of debate in the history and philosophy of science has shown, there has been very little consensus concerning what it is that makes a work of science scientific. From Hempel to Popper to Kuhn to Toulmin to Lakatos to Feyerabend, we have witnessed a succession of inconclusive efforts to establish a diacritical marker for scientificity. At this point, it may perhaps be acknowledged that the very notion of "science" belongs to that category of mental constructs that W. B. Gallie referred to as "essentially contested concepts"—concepts that are so closely linked to

charged substantive debates, normative issues, and historical contexts that their meaning can never be fixed with a single unam-
biguous definition (1964, 157–91).

Yet even without the record of those inconclusive efforts—even
without the massive evidence that underlies Lakatos's claim that
there has been "little agreement concerning a *universal* criterion of
the scientific character of theories" (1978, 124)—one might have
predicted the futility of any such effort. The notion that there is
some single absolute standard of cognitive value belies what has
been a major intellectual achievement of the social sciences during
the last two centuries—the solid awareness that all human expressions are conditioned by their rootedness in the exigencies of
human action. The effort to identify a single diacritical marker for
science, like the quest to find some privileged type of knowledge
more generally, *must* be inconclusive, because of the irreducible variety of values, norms, and motives that organize all kind of action,
contemplative as well as conative or practical.

To acknowledge that fact, however, is not necessarily to assert
that there are no forms of privileged knowledge. Rather it is to
state that sincere adherence to a single criterion of the generically
scientific is to commit oneself to a polemical position that invali-
dates the legitimate claims of other kinds of knowledge. An alternative way to proceed would be to accept the notion of an
irreducible plurality of privileged forms of knowledge.

I

Although the perspective I shall finally use to develop this point of
view is known to sociologists as the theory of action, let me begin by
approaching it from a philosophic perspective. Increased awareness of the plausibility of alternative claims to cognitive privilege
has produced a variety of philosophic efforts to deal with the Babel
of contending intellectual positions in our time. Working on this
problem in the area of literary criticism, Wayne Booth has identified five common responses that appear "when we try to decide
how to listen to the actual clamor of critics' voices today" (1979,
4)—none of which he finds satisfactory. In incorporating his analysis here, I follow Booth's typology but alter his formulations
slightly.

1. The polemicist response—just let everyone get out there and
fight, because what the world needs is more assaults on complacen-
cy and conformity—is unacceptable because it generates destruc-

tive and wasteful exchanges and fosters the vice of misconstruing the ideas of one's intellectual opponents.

2. The semanticist response—just let intellectual antagonists specify the referents of their terms and thus remove ambiguities, and apparent disagreements will disappear—is unacceptable because it assumes that the only real differences among contending intellectual positions are trivial ones, also because it denies that many concepts remain inexorably ambiguous and consequently depreciates those fruitful inquiries that are stimulated by controversies over such ambiguities.

3. The monist response identifies one of the contending positions as valid and portrays all others as wrong, misleading, or unimportant. A more tolerant version of this response would encompass those who view alternative approaches as historically valid but currently outmoded positions or as necessary stages in the evolution of current true belief. This response cannot, however, secure universal assent to such invalidation or depreciation of all other positions.

4. The response of skepticism (or relativism, or nihilism) questions the possibility that any position can arrive at statements possessing truth value. The grounds for such a position are enormously varied; its proponents may appeal to the intractable complexity of observed phenomena, to the incorrigible limitations of observers, or to the hopelessness of arriving at mutual comprehension or intersubjective validation among a plurality of knowers. Such a position is ultimately untenable because it rests both on a logical contradiction (the professed certainty about the impossibility of securing statements beyond doubt) and a practical contradiction (the inhibition of the irrepressible quest for truth).

5. The response of eclecticism acknowledges the validity claims of contending positions or approaches and simply copes with their apparent incompatibility by chopping up the work of others into fragments, salvaging and conjoining whatever of those fragments appear useful. The weakness of this response is its failure to retain the contextual significance of the opposing claims.

In contrast with these responses, Booth espouses a possibility that he terms "methodological pluralism," which holds that "two or more conflicting positions may be entirely acceptable" (1979, 24). Rather than develop de novo the internal texture of such a position, Booth discusses the work of three other critics who in his judgment qualify as exemplary proponents of methodological pluralism.

In philosophy proper, many essential elements of a methodological pluralist position were developed during the last half
century by a scholar who has been Booth's mentor as well as my
own, Richard McKeon. McKeon has grounded the pluralist position historically, by showing ways in which inquiries have been advanced by going through cycles of methodological approaches
(1966a), and systematically, by showing the power of alternative
methods to illuminate commonplace notions like freedom and history (1952). Although a position of methodological pluralism appears implicitly or embryonically in the writings of several social
scientists, I am unaware of efforts comparable to those of Booth
and McKeon in the literature of the social sciences to develop the
rationale and implications of that position. Among the few social
scientists who have sought to articulate such features, I might mention Robert Merton (1976) and Arthur Stinchcombe (1968) in sociology, Henry Briefs (1960) in economics, and Asmarom Legesse
(1973) in anthropology.

My own work over the last three decades has been informed by a
program that seeks to contribute to a framework for a defensible
pluralist position in the social sciences. My dissertation
([1957]1980) articulated the structure and implications of the divergent principles and methods embodied in the work of Georg
Simmel and Talcott Parsons, work that presented two acceptable,
yet largely incommensurable, approaches to the study of society.
My monographs on Ethiopia sought to illustrate, first, the effect of
applying a plurality of observational styles and descriptive
modalities to the study of Amhara tradition and Ethiopia's mod-
ernization and, subsequently, the effect of applying a plurality of
explanatory logics to the question of Ethiopia's historical survival as
an independent nation (1974). In pursuing this line of inquiry over
the years, I have come to emphasize three considerations that perhaps go beyond the analysis provided by Booth and other advocates of methodological pluralism.

II

I would emphasize that it is no longer productive to limit our ad-
vocacy or analysis of pluralism to those rather diffuse entities
denoted by such terms as "intellectual approaches" or "methodological orientations." Insofar as an investigator or intellectual
school sustains a relatively distinctive and consistent orientation, it
necessarily consists of a number of discrete cognitive components.
Although these components exhibit mutual affinities in the work of

a given person or school, they are not necessarily closely linked and in fact usually exhibit the property of independent variability. Failure to realize this has produced those endless confusions that come from calling someone a positivist, a Marxist, an empiricist, a historicist, a Freudian, a Durkheimian, and the like. To say that someone is a Durkheimian, for example—does that mean he follows the master in using aggregate statistics rather than survey data, in analyzing contextual effects rather than individual properties, in talking about anomie rather than alienation, in positing the relativity rather than the universality of moral norms, in searching for functional rather than compositional explanations, or what?

To obviate such confusion, I have found it helpful to distinguish between "approaches," the total concrete orientation of a scholar or a research program, and cognitive "features," the constitutive elements of an approach. Each feature represents a discrete aspect or moment of inquiry. What to identify as a discrete cognitive feature is itself a matter of judgment or controversy, but the following have emerged in my work over the last two decades as unavoidable categories:

1. Categorical frameworks—conceptual forms that identify the units of social phenomena and how they are to be understood in combinations

2. Empirical procedures—operations forms that enable one to make observations

3. Descriptive modalities—conceptual forms that specify the types of observation one should make

4. Explanatory logics—conceptual forms that specify how sets of observations are to be construed in relationships of independent to dependent variables

5. Epistemic methods—conceptual forms that organize the strategic pattern of any inquiry or research program

6. Interpretations—conceptual forms that specify how to relate observations of phenomena to notions of what is real

7. Epistemic products—rhetorical forms by which one organizes and makes public the results of inquiry

Some of the variance among divergent approaches reflects differences in the weighting of various features. Thus survey research highlights the feature of empirical procedures, "rational choice" research gives primacy to categorical frameworks, while ethnomethodology stresses the feature of what is here called "interpretations." More complex approaches, like Marxian, Freudian, or Weberian social science, pay serious attention to a number of features—one reason why their proponents so often engage in controversy over what is truly the essence of their respective approach.

Every cognitive feature, moreover, can be realized in a variety of ways, which I call "forms." Thus the feature of explanation can take a genetic, a structural, a compositional, or a functional form. Most of the variation and controversy in the social sciences stems from divergences among forms. Just as one finds the "empiricist" and the "theorist" each denouncing what the other does as not "really science" because of their investment in different features or aspects of the cognitive process, so one finds proponents of different forms of the same feature depreciating one another's work in similar wise. It follows from the pluralist position I am advocating, however, that knowledge gained through any form can be valid and indeed can constitute a privileged kind of knowledge when it is pursued on the basis of special training and experience. The name I would give to this type of knowledge is "disciplined."

In addition to transforming a general pluralist appreciation of different approaches into one that appreciates different features and forms, I would stress that the question of the relationship that obtains among divergent forms is genuinely an open question. At this point, at least, I can find no grounds for arguing a priori that the relationship between any two divergent forms is necessarily of a single kind when applied to any problem whatsoever. That relationship can and does take a number of possible forms. It can be the case that divergent forms are *mutually irrelevant,* as when they define and address themselves to wholly different problems. It can be that they *cross-cut* one another, as when they generate different definitions of a similar problem. It can be that they are *competitive,* as when they address a similar problem but lead to different solutions. They can be related in a *collaborative* mode, as when they address different parts of the same problem. Or, when they address different aspects of the same problem, we can view their relationship as *complementary.* Finally, we can see their relationship as lodged in some *architectonic* synthesis when they appear to be performing different tasks that are integrated or integrable in some hierarchical or sequential structure.

III

The third consideration I would stress in articulating a pluralist position is one that brings the array of cognitive forms back into a context of human action. Although the analysis of forms by itself can bring clarity of understanding and enhance the possibilities of mutual comprehension, it remains sterile if not finally tied to some sense of the significance of forms in relation to human purposes. This is so in two senses. To understand the forms as historical products, we must examine the evolutionary context in which they were created and utilized. This not only makes them more fully intelligible but also enables us to ask whether or not the forms we have inherited still serve those matrical purposes, other purposes that have subsequently replaced them, or no good purpose at all. Moreover, the connection to currently defensible purposes provides a central criterion for assessing each cognitive form and indeed for deciding what order of claim to the production of privileged knowledge it may now be said to possess.

The complete pluralist program, then, must include an effort to inventory the array of defensible human purposes no less than to conduct an inventory of cognitive forms. As in the latter case, any schematic inventory must limit itself to a small number of rather broad categories, categories that involve a somewhat arbitrary element of judgment and cannot be specified absolutely. In thinking about the array of purposes that disciplined forms of social knowledge have been thought to serve at some point or other, I have found it convenient to order them by recourse to the well-established categories of the "general theory of action" formulated in the last generation by Talcott Parsons and many of his colleagues. The central tenets of the Parsonian theory include the assumptions (1) that all action is organized toward the attainment of ends; (2) that action is structured in four levels of boundary-maintaining systems, the levels of the behavioral system, the personality system, the social system, and the cultural system; and (3) that each of these systems in turn is organized toward the fulfillment of the four basic systemic functions of marshalling adaptive resources, coordinating energies to attain goals, integrating the elements of the system, and providing support for maintaining the value patterns of the system.

On the basis of the foregoing considerations, then, I have prepared the following paradigm of the forms and functions of social knowledge.[1]

AN ACTION-THEORETIC PARADIGM FOR ASSESSING THE FORMS AND FUNCTIONS OF SOCIAL KNOWLEDGE

I. A framework for inquiry into and assessment of alternative types of social scientific work

A. Inquiry re: The forms of social science (How does one
learn about disciplinary resources?)
1. What are the properties of each feature? To what kinds
of issues is it relevant?
2. What are the properties of each form? What is it good
for? What is it bad for?
3. How does it relate to other forms? To what extent is it
independently variable? What elective
affinities/incompatibilities does it have with forms of
other features?
B. Inquiry re: The relationships among different forms
1. Mutually irrelevant (wholly different problem)
2. Cross-cutting (different definitions of the problem)
3. Competitive (similar problem, different solutions)
4. Collaborative (same problem, different parts)
5. Complementary (same problem, different aspects)
6. Architectonic (different tasks, hierarchically or
sequentially integrated)
C. Inquiry re: The functions of social science (How does one
produce nonalienated social knowledge?)
1. What are the defensible objectives of social scientific
inquiry? How are they defended?
2. What are the most appropriate features and forms for
each function?
D. The critical assessment of features and forms (How does
one identify excellent, decent, wasteful, alienated, or
harmful social science?)
1. Criteria of validity
a) accuracy
b) logical consistency
c) clarity
d) completeness or scope
2. Criteria of significance
a) heuristic value
b) appropriateness to content of inquiry
c) appropriateness to purpose of inquiry
d) quality of relevant purposes and values
3. Criteria of quality of execution
a) extent to which forms are properly or
elegantly realized
b) extent to which forms remain linked to
defensible purposes

II. Toward a critical inventory of the forms of disciplined social
    knowledge
  A. Categorical frameworks (How does one conceptualize the
     units and organization of social phenomena?)
     1. Choices and markets (A. Smith, G. Becker)
     2. Controls and hierarchies (Marx, Dahrendorf)
     3. Affects and connections (Simmel, Bales)
     4. Beliefs and consensus (Durkheim, Benedict)
     5. Needs and mechanisms (Spencer, Parsons)
     6. Themes and patterns (Kroeber, Lévi-Strauss)
     7. Intentions and conjoint actions (Toennies, Weber)

  B. Empirical procedures (How does one make observations?)
     1. Unobtrusive-noninduced (direct observation, content
        analysis)
     2. Unobtrusive-induced (questionnaires, concealed
        experiments)
     3. Intrusive-noninduced (participant observation)
     4. Intrusive-induced (depth interviews, lab experiment)

  C. Descriptive modalities (What does one observe?)
     1. Externals (behavior, artifacts)/internals (thoughts,
        sentiments)
     2. Simple properties/rich detail
     3. Dominant trends/contradictory tendencies
     4. Parts/elements
     5. Microscopic/mesoscopic/macroscopic
     6. Behavioral system/personality/social system/culture
     7. Types of social facts
        a) global
        b) analytic
        c) interactional
        d) institutional
     8. First-person/second-person/third-person accounts

  D. Explanatory logics (How does one relate sets of
     observations construed as independent/dependent
     variables?)
     1. Genetic (explaining y as a consequence of some
        antecedent process or event)
     2. Compositional (explaining y as a result of the properties
        of its constitutive elements)
     3. Structural (explaining y as a consequence of its position
        in a set of ordered relationships)

        4. Functional (explaining *y* with reference to the needs of
           x that it fulfills)
   E. Epistemic methods (Where does one start, toward what
     does one move, and how does one proceed?)
        1. Logistic—by construction and decomposition
        2. Dialectic—by assimilation and exemplification
        3. Problematic—by resolution and question
        4. Operational—by discrimination and postulation
   F. Interpretations (How does one relate observations of
     phenomena to notions of what is real?)
        1. Ontological: reality is transcendent, appearances are
           imperfect manifestations thereof (Plato, Hegel)
        2. Entitative: reality is underlying nature, appearances are
           secondary derivatives thereof (Marx, Freud, Lévi-
           Strauss)
        3. Essentialist: reality is phenomena, properties and causes
           that are natural functions or acquired conditionings
           (Durkheim, Malinowski)
        4. Existentialist: reality is phenomenal, socially
           constructed (Schütz)
   G. Epistemic products (How does one organize and present
     findings?)
        1. Case studies
        2. Narratives
        3. Graphs, tables
        4. Propositions
        5. Ideal types
        6. Models
        7. Axiomatized systems
        8. Discursive syntheses
III. Toward a critical inventory of the functions of disciplined
   social knowledge
   A. Cultural functions
        1. Grounding a world view (Marx)
        2. Grounding normative criteria (Durkheim)
        3. Providing aesthetic symbolism (Nisbet)
        4. Providing empirical understanding
           a) of universals and variants
           b) of self-experience and others
   B. Social systemic functions
        1. Technical knowledge (Spencer, Coleman)
        2. Counsel to rulers/insurgents (Machiavelli, Lenin)

      3. Shared beliefs/enhanced communication (Comte, Dewey)

      4. Clarifying collective values and enhancing their transmission (Lasswell, Skinner)

   C. Personality functions

      1. Increasing consciousness about self and self's situation (Berger)

      2. Increasing clarity about one's values (Weber)

   D. Behavioral system functions

      1. Enhanced cognitive competence

IV

What, now, is the potential usefulness of a paradigm of this sort? First, it enables us to analyze more efficiently the structure of a given approach by constraining us to identify and locate the forms of its central defining features. Second, it may facilitate constructive communication among proponents of different approaches, and provide a less polemical way for them to talk about their differences. Above all, it provides a more coherent way for critics to assess the value of different kinds of social knowledge—to indicate what kinds of social knowledge may legitimately claim privileged states and why.

Section I.D of the paradigm schematizes three sets of appropriate criteria. There is no mechanical way to indicate the relative weighting of these criteria. That is a matter of value judgment that will vary with the background and purposes of each critic. What this part of the paradigm can do is constrain critics to be aware of a broader range of legitimate criteria than they would be likely to acknowledge otherwise and prod them to be more articulate in defending the criteria they choose to stress.

One set of criteria concerns the validity of cognitive efforts. These are the criteria familiar to scientists, who, however, are not always aware that the criteria are seriously competitive among themselves. Disciplined work that ranks high according to all of these criteria has a very special claim to privilege with respect to its truth value. Yet validity has never been the exclusive general criterion for assigning special merit to scientific work. Not only may one criterion of validity be sacrificed for another—as when accuracy is sacrificed for logical consistency, or scope is sacrificed for accuracy—but other kinds of criteria may or should be invoked as well. What may be called the criteria of significance also became prominent. These include (1) the extent to which a given finding, idea, or research program opens up new areas of discovery or new ways of looking at some part of the world; (2) the consideration of how appropriate a given cognitive form is to the type of phenomena being studied; (3) the consideration of how appropriate a given cognitive form is to the purpose of the inquiry; and (4) the quality of the purpose served and the values embodied in or promoted by the research program.

Finally, there are criteria that have to do with what may be called the quality of execution of a program. Two chief criteria of this sort stand in chronic tension with one another. On the one hand, there is the consideration of how well a given form is realized in practice. To what extent is its integrity respected? What is the level of technical ability with which it is employed? How elegantly is its script performed? On the other hand, there is the consideration of how closely the execution of form remains linked to defensible purposes. It is often the case that the integrity of a form is sacrificed on behalf of a given purpose; it is perhaps even more often that the integrity of purpose is sacrificed to the intrinsic requirements of the form. Yet no final claim to privileged knowledge can be made without addressing these two concerns.

These remarks have been abstract and schematic. I hope they have been sufficiently clear and suggestive to elicit some support for their central thrust: that the time is ripe for articulating a self-conscious pluralist program in the social sciences in which the point will be, not to scrap the demarcationist project, but to sophisticate it.

Note

1. The typology presented under II.C.7 is based on Lazarsfeld and Menzel (1961). Typology II.D may be viewed as a transmutation of Aristotle's four causes. Typologies II.E and F are adapted from McKeon (1966b).

References

Booth, W. C. 1979. *Critical understanding: The power and limits of pluralism.* Chicago: University of Chicago Press.

Briefs, H. W. 1960. *Three views of method in economics.* Georgetown Economic Studies. Washington, D.C.: Georgetown University Press.

Gallie, W. B. 1964. *Philosophy and the historical understanding.* London: Chatto and Windus.

Lakatos, I. 1978. *The methodology of scientific research programs.* Cambridge: Cambridge University Press.

Lazarsfeld, P. F., and Menzel, H. 1961. On the relation between individual and collective properties. In *Complex organizations,* ed. A. Etzioni. New York: Holt, Rinehart and Winston.

Legesse, A. 1973. *Gada: Three approaches to the study of African society.* New York: Free Press.

Levine, D. N. 1965. *Wax and gold: Tradition and innovation in Ethiopian culture.* Chicago: University of Chicago Press.

———. 1974. *Greater Ethiopia: The evolution of a multiethnic society.* Chicago: University of Chicago Press.

———. 1980. *Simmel and Parsons: Two approaches to the study of society.* New York: Arno Press.

McKeon, R. 1952. *Freedom and history.* New York: Noonday Press.

———. 1966a. Philosophy and the development of scientific methods. *Journal of the History of Ideas* 27:3–22

———. 1966b. Philosophic semantics and philosophic inquiry. Manuscript.

Merton, R. K. 1976. Structural analysis in sociology. In *Sociological ambivalence and other essays.* New York: Free Press.

Stinchcombe, A. L. 1968. *Constructing social theories.* New York: Harcourt, Brace and World.

12 Nonlinear Behavior

Frank M. Richter

The social sciences are by no means unique among the sciences in worrying about scientific virtue. Geology twenty years ago was very conscious of comparisons between the "soft" earth sciences and "hard" sciences such as physics and chemistry; indeed the shadow of these harder sciences would have led many to argue, as Kelvin had a hundred years before, that geology could not claim to be truly scientific until mathematics and the laws of physics and chemistry were brought to bear on geological problems. An interesting episode involves Kelvin's attempt to illuminate, for geologists to follow, the virtuous path by using physical law to once and for all settle the question of the age of the earth. Perhaps it was fortunate that his physics was incomplete (radioactive heat production in the earth had not yet been discovered nor had the importance of convective heat transfer been recognized), leading him to underestimate the true age by more than two orders of magnitude. Fortunate, because the general argument became less than persuasive, leaving room for a variety of other approaches that in some cases gave rise to very important advances in the understanding of the earth.

Kelvin's eventual comeuppance does not of itself invalidate the general argument of a single standard for scientific achievement. The single standard breaks down once one can point to different traditions leading to important new developments. In the earth sciences, plate tectonics is the best example of this, being a scientific revolution that has none of the attributes of canonical physical science law. Plate tectonics is a representation: The earth's surface is composed of a small number of rigid spherical caps (plates) in relative motion, with deformation confined to narrow zones at their boundaries. It is only approximately true, not equally applicable everywhere, and not capable of being modified so as to account for those regions where it fails. It contains no reference to the laws of motion even though it describes motions. Yet it is scientific and revolutionary in that it provides a whole new framework for discussing, and in some cases resolving, problems involving large-scale geological processes. By its success it legitimizes (for the time being at least) the whole of the earth sciences, dispelling the shadows of the harder sciences.

This is a particular example of what might well be a general theme: comparisons between scientific fields for purposes of value judgments are more a symptom than a cure for a transient sense of unease. Furthermore, such comparisons typically involve broad generalizations about fields and their success, with little or any reference to the distinct measures of success that are applied to the different fields. Once one recognizes that measures of success, in the absence of an absolute standard, are socially negotiated quantities, a special disadvantage of the social sciences becomes clear. The scientific fields that can most easily claim to be successful are those in which the measures of success are internalized, sometimes even self-fulfilling. Astronomy defines the measures of success and succeeds. The social sciences, in contrast, are often faced with measures of success beyond their control. In many cases, the larger society defines the relevant problems for the social sciences and has strong prejudices as to what constitutes an acceptable answer. This externalized valuation system seems to be a source of much of the present unease in the social sciences.

Externalized measures of success might be degraded as being less than profound, yet they do serve a very powerful legitimizing or devaluing role. Physics and chemistry derive large measures of esteem, even self-esteem, from their success as contributors to technological innovation. Geology draws credit from its relation to mineral exploration. One can also point to cases where external criteria serve to make topics disreputable. Again in geology, earthquake prediction comes to mind. The external demand is clear and simple: predict the time, location, and magnitude of large earthquakes. The frustration of not yet being able to satisfy this specific demand devalues what progress has been made in understanding particular aspects of the earthquake source. "Don't bother me with details, the fact of the matter is that you still can't predict earthquakes" may be unfair, but it is an effective indictment. Early optimism and false claims only add to the sense of inadequate science.

The problem with social science is, then, not so much that it studies man, but that all men judge its success. The reaction of the

social sciences to external demands and externalized measures of
success is made difficult in part by the natural tendency of intellectual communities to be disputatious, overemphasizing differences
at the expense of those aspects of a field for which convergence
and consensus do exist. This continuous argument at the frontiers
of our knowledge hides the ground successfully conquered and to
the outsider gives the impression of chaos and fragmentation. In
many cases, it is the role of the applied science enterprises to suggest that out of such chaos eventually comes progress. But even in
terms of applied science, the social sciences seem at a disadvantage
compared to the physical sciences because strategies developed in
the social sciences often seek some statistical enhancement of a desirable outcome—thus they don't succeed or fail in the same binary
sense that a trip to the moon and back succeeds or fails.

The process of negotiating and renegotiating measures for
seeing oneself and for being seen as successful is an essential part
of the well-being of a scientific field. An interesting example of
renegotiation is Robert R. Wilson's testimony to Congress as to the
worth of the Fermilab accelerator: "It has nothing to do directly
with defending our country except to make it worth defending." In
terms of the social sciences, Fiske (chap. 3, this volume) might be
seen as arguing for restricting their subject matter to those aspects
that have the highest likelihood of meeting the present (scientistic)
success standard while Campbell (chap. 5, this volume) seems much
more interested in renegotiating.

Restricting the subject matter so as to conform to some specific
success ethic seems the worst of all paths, given the nature of many
of the issues the social sciences seek to understand. Let me use the
"central equation" mentioned by Converse (chap. 2, this volume) to
make my point. In this "machine view" of behavior we have

$$B = f(p,s)$$

where behavior B is some as yet unspecified function of person p
and situation s. The function represents the totality of interactions
between the person and himself and the person and situation leading to behavior. By sufficiently restricting what we mean by behavior, person, and situation, a series of correlations could no doubt be
found, including one between acceleration (behavior), mass (an attribute of person), and an external force (a component of situation
space). It would read

$$a = (1/m)F$$

more familiar in the standard form $F = ma$. This early success of the central equation would be somewhat misleading as to the future potentialities of success. It was obtained by a very fortuitous set of restrictions, for example, ignoring such other attributes of person as color, size, composition, in fact everything else imaginable except for mass. An even more misleading aspect of $F = ma$ is that it is linear, in the sense that it can be extended to cases of more than one force acting by simply adding the behavior caused by each of the forces taken one at a time. This is crucial to the generalizability of the law. The "central equation" on the other hand is demonstrably nonlinear in that if

$$B_1 = f(p,s_1)$$

and

$$B_2 = f(p,s_2),$$

it is not necessarily true that $B_1 + B_2 = f(p,s_1 + s_2)$. In many cases, one can imagine that the behavior resulting from combining two elements of situation space will be quite different from the behavior each element would elicit if it were acting alone. In other words, the effect in terms of behavior space of any single element of situation space depends on what else is contained in situation space. This nonadditivity of the results from simpler situations when dealing with a more complex situation is a well-known obstacle in predicting the response of systems governed by nonlinear dynamics. Systems of this kind are characterized by instabilities such that very small changes in the parameters (attributes of person or situation) can cause drastic changes in the outcome (behavior). Another common feature is a multiplicity of possible solutions for the same point in parameter space. Social scientists might do well to note the difficulties that other fields have, and the diverse strategies they have to adopt, once they leave those realms governed by linear dynamics.

In order to illustrate the complexity and richness of behavior governed by nonlinear dynamics, let me construct a simple hypothetical model relating fear, aggressiveness, and guilt in a person confronted with an accusation of a serious infraction, malpractice, for example. The external situation (the accusation) enters the problem only as an initial impulse to the subsequent behavior as a function of time. The different degrees of aggressiveness, fear, and guilt are measured by variables z, y, and x defined as follows:

z measures aggressiveness on a scale of positive values starting from zero

y measures the level of fear and can be either positive (high
fear) or negative (low fear)

x measures the person's perception of his own guilt (positive
values) or innocence (negative values) of the infraction he is
accused of

The rules relating these variables are assumed to be as follows:

Rule 1: $dz/dt = -bz + xy$

Rule 2: $dy/dt = -y + (r - z)x$

Rule 3: $dx/dt = -\sigma x + \sigma y$

Here b, r, and σ are constants to be specified, and the left-hand side
of each rule represents the rate of change with time of the variable
involved. These rules, which are in fact the Lorenz equations, are
mildly nonlinear in that they contain terms involving products of
variables, such as xy in rule 1.

The rules when stated in words contain the following effects:

Rule 1: Aggressiveness tends to decay away with a time constant b if left to itself. Aggressiveness can be increased or
decreased depending on the correlation of fear and guilt.
Aggressiveness tends to increase when both fear and guilt
are high ($y > 0$, $x > 0$) or when both are low ($y < 0$, $x < 0$).
These effects might be plausible in that high fear and guilt
lead to a loss of control while low fear and guilt lead to aggressiveness out of a sense of outrage with the accusation.
When fear is high and guilt is low ($y > 0$, $x < 0$) or fear is low
while guilt is high ($y < 0$, $x > 0$), aggressiveness decreases.
These effects might result from fear causing the person to
become cautious in the first combination and, in the latter
case from a sense of resignation.

Rule 2: Fear tends to decay when left to itself, owing to the
$-y$ term. It will increase (decrease) due to guilt (innocence)
when the level of aggressiveness z is less than r. If z is greater
than r, the effect of guilt on fear reverses. Again these effects are plausible if we associate increasing irrationality with
increasing aggressiveness.

Rule 3: The sense of guilt decays toward zero with time constant σ if left to itself. If the level of fear is sufficiently high (*y* > *x*), then the sense of guilt will tend to increase. This might result from emphasizing one's possible guilt as one becomes increasingly frightened of the consequences.

If these rules seem somewhat contrived, it is in part because I want to keep a structure that is governed by the Lorenz equations, equations that are having a profound impact in many areas of the physical and natural sciences for reasons that will become clear once we begin to inspect the solutions.

Figure 1 illustrates the everchanging behavior that follows the accusation when *b* = 8/3, σ = 10, and *r* = 30, shown as trajectories in the guilt (x) and aggressiveness (z) plane. Fear is also continuously changing and thus the trajectories in fact never intersect, or for that matter never repeat, when seen properly in three dimen

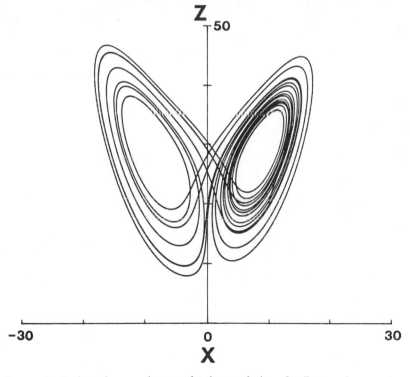

FIGURE 1. Trajectories mapping out the time evolution of guilt (*x*) and aggression (*z*) when *b* =8/3, σ = *10*, and *r* = 30 in the Lorenz equations. Fear (*y*), also continuously changing, is not represented in this projection.

sions. Having started out in the $x > 0$ quadrant, the person oscillates in aggressiveness while in that quadrant but then jumps into
the low guilt quadrant ($x < 0$), oscillates there for a while, then
jumps again, and so on. Despite the deterministic nature of the
system (we know the rules), one cannot predict what quadrant the
person will be in some sufficiently long time later. For some periods of time, guilt is positively correlated with aggressiveness, but
then suddenly the correlation reverses. This type of behavior,
called chaos in the evolving jargon associated with these equations,
is better seen in figure 2, which shows x (sense of guilt) as an unpredictable function of time. It is this unpredictability despite the simple governing rules that has drawn so much attention.

To complicate matters further, consider what happens when r is
changed from 30 to 20. The rules are still the same, only the level at
which aggressiveness can reduce fear has been lowered. Figure 3
gives the resulting behavior for two different starting points. Behavior now converges onto one of two stable points in the x,z plane,
with a similar stabilization of the level of fear. A slight change in the
specifications has made the outcome completely predictable, if
somewhat complicated by the fact that the eventual stable behavior

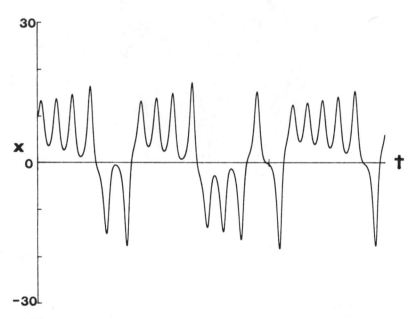

FIGURE 2. Guilt (x) as a function of time for the case shown in fig. 1.

does depend on the person's "state of mind" at the time the accusation is made.

The Lorenz equations used above (Lorenz 1963) have attracted an enormous amount of attention and serious study over the past twenty years (Sparrow 1982) because of the striking contrast between their simplicity (mildly nonlinear, constant coefficients, no external forcing) and the richness and complexity of their solutions and because of the implication that complicated, natural nonlinear systems might be usefully modeled in terms of equally simple equations. On the other hand, there is the troublesome point that systems may remain unpredictable on some time scales despite a full knowledge of the deterministic laws governing their evolution. More generally, the excitement and wonder at the richness of this simple nonlinear system is a reflection and a commentary on how new and how limited the present understanding of systems gov-

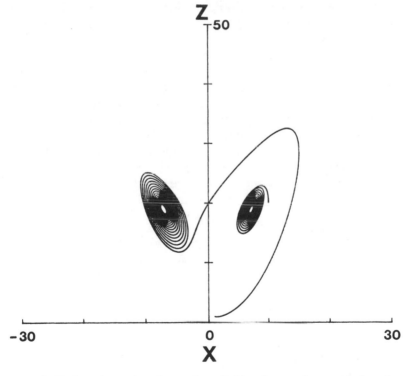

FIGURE 3. Trajectories projected onto the guilt (x) and aggressiveness (z) plane for two different starting points; $b = 8/3$, $\sigma = 10$, $r = 20$.

FRANK M. RICHTER

erned by nonlinear dynamics really is. And it is with such systems that many of the topics of the social sciences must contend.

To the extent that the social sciences are studying nonlinear systems, several conclusions can be drawn. Complexity need not be a reflection of some deficiency in the modes of discourse or analysis but may well be an inherent property of the systems being studied. That generalizations about behavior "don't travel well," are very context dependent, or may even be contradictory when derived from different sets of observations taken at different times, is exactly what one might expect for behavior such as that shown in figure 1. It is not at all surprising that clinical or laboratory studies, by restricting some of the interacting variables or the coupling between variables, may elicit behavior that seems quite unrelated to what is realized once the restrictions are removed. Differences in behavior such as that shown in figures 1 and 3 can easily result from very minor restrictions being added to the system. Since figures 1 and 3 do have a common underlying dynamics, laboratory studies should be aimed at understanding particular elements of this dynamics, instead of seeking universally valid statements about behavior itself.

Once complexity is seen as the natural outgrowth of the dynamics governing behavior, it loses its negative connotation regarding scientific legitimacy and becomes instead a strong argument for renegotiated standards of success that accept that simple and urgent questions need not have simple answers. The best and possibly only guide to the potentialities for future knowledge is, then, what has already been achieved, and these achievements should be valued all the more as the true complexity of the background from which they have emerged comes more clearly into focus.

References

Lorenz, E. N. 1963. Deterministic non-periodic flows. *Journal of Atmospheric Science* 20:131–41.

Sparrow, C. 1982. *The Lorenz equations: Bifurcations, chaos, and strange attractors.* Applied Mathematical Series, 41. New York: Springer & Verlag.

13 Heuristics and the Study of Human Behavior

William C. Wimsatt

Frank Richter (chap. 12, this volume) has argued that many social scientists misunderstand the paradigm that the physical sciences provide; predictability and simple lawlike behavior are frequently as elusive (or nearly so) in the natural sciences as they are in the social sciences.[1] As the recent explosion of interest in chaotic behavior in various scientific disciplines suggests, the phenomenon of detailed unpredictability is quite common (and for quite simple nonlinear systems) throughout all of the natural sciences and, I would argue, in the biological and social sciences as well (e.g., Wimsatt 1980a). To the extent that the misleadingly named "covering law" model applies in the natural sciences, it is only because we can more frequently get away with our simple idealizations there, more simply isolate our systems (in the human sciences, most importantly from our own unintended interventions), more readily treat their relevant properties as context independent, and through it all, focus on questions and parameter ranges that yield simple equilibrium behavior. I don't want to suggest that there are no qualitative differences between the physical, biological, and social sciences—I think that Roy D'Andrade's picture is fine as a first approximation (see chap. 1, this volume)—but I do believe that many of the things touted as differences in kind are merely differences in degree.

Does this mean that we are doomed to unpredictability everywhere? Chaotic behavior does not imply total unpredictability, but only that initial uncertainties will increase in time if we demand a deterministic account of the behavior of a system. At other levels of description, chaotic behavior is quite regular in its properties (see Feigenbaum 1980 or Hofstadter 1981). The lack of total predictability raises no new epistemological problems that we did not already have with theories of decision making under uncertainty

293

(Luce & Raiffa 1957; Kaufmann 1974). Indeed, one natural response to deterministic complexity that exceeds our capabilities of analysis is to treat the behavior as "random" (Wimsatt 1980a). Chaotic systems, for the purposes of prediction, are simply pseudo-random number generators in which, because they are real systems, rather than computer algorithms, we don't know the "seed" or initial conditions (or often the algorithm) exactly.

I wish to turn to another matter that receives little attention in this book and that seems to me to be an important new direction in the social sciences. This is the question of what we do when the complexity of the systems we are studying exceeds our powers of analysis. This too is an old problem in social science methodology, but it does not indicate a cause for despair, since exactly the same thing has happened frequently in the natural and biological sciences. Roughly, the therapy is the same in both cases: introduce idealizations, approximations, or other devices that, perhaps artificially, reduce the complexity of the problem. Here, however, we needn't be looking only to the natural sciences for guidance, for the best developed theory of such devices has arisen in psychology and the social sciences. I have in mind the work of Simon, Lenat, Tversky and Kahneman, and others on problem-solving heuristics. (While it might be argued that this is a part of cognitive psychology or artificial intelligence, it is worth noting that Simon's interest in heuristics springs from his "satisficing" theory of decision making, which in turn was motivated jointly by his interest in decision making, in administrative organizations [1957] and his dissatisfaction with rational decision theory [1955,1981].)

It is important to note that to regard a system as using heuristics is to regard it as a kind of engineering system. This is implicit in Simon's characterization of the scope of "the sciences of the artificial" (1981)—artificial things are products of design processes or, more generally, of selection processes. In this, I am also following Campbell, who has argued the same point from a somewhat different perspective (see, for example, Campbell 1974). A similar view has been advocated by Dennett (1979) in his characterization of the "design stance" as a perspective for analyzing functionally organized systems. To the extent that heuristics are important in the analysis of our reasoning processes and action or behavior, the boundary between D'Andrade's second and third perspectives (or Dennett's analogous ones) is at least blurred; I think it becomes a matter of degree. I will return to this after I say something more about the nature of heuristics.

HEURISTICS

"Heuristic" has become one of the most widely used terms in artificial intelligence and cognitive psychology and, as with other such terms, shows wide variance in its use. To my knowledge, it was introduced in its present context by Herbert Simon, who borrowed it from the mathematician, George Polya, who used it to describe "rules of thumb" used in solving mathematical problems. For a recent rich and constructive discussion of the nature of heuristics in artificial intelligence work, see Lenat 1982. As I understand them, heuristic procedures, or heuristics, have four important properties that between them explain a number of characteristics of their use:

1. By comparison with truth-preserving algorithms or with other procedures for which they might be substituted, heuristics make no guarantees (or if they are substituted for another procedure, weaker guarantees) that they will produce a solution or the correct solution to a problem. A truth-preserving algorithm correctly applied to true premises must produce a correct conclusion. But one may correctly apply a heuristic to correct input information without getting a correct output.

2. By comparison with the procedures for which they may be substituted, heuristics are very "cost-effective" in terms of demands on memory, computation, or other resources in limited supply (this of course is why they are used).

3. The errors produced by using a heuristic are not random but systematically biased. By this, I mean two things. First, the heuristic will tend to break down in certain classes of cases and not in others, but not at random. Indeed, with an understanding of how the heuristic works, it should be possible to predict the conditions under which it will fail. Second, where it is meaningful to speak of a direction of error, heuristics will tend to cause errors in a certain direction, which is again a function of the heuristic and of the kinds of problems to which it is applied.

4. The application of a heuristic to a problem yields a transformation of the problem into a nonequivalent but intuitively related problem. Most important this means that answers to the transformed problem may not be answers to the original problem. (This property of heuristics was pointed out to me by Robert McCauley, see McCauley, in press).

Traditional philosophy of science is a philosophy of deductive structures and algorithms for computationally omnipotent computers—LaPlacean demons for which computation has a negligible cost. Theories are assumed to have an axiomatic structure, and they are assumed to be closed under entailment; that is, anything that follows from a set of axioms is a part of that theory. Thus, for example, discussions of reductionism are full of talk of in-principle analyzability or in-principle deducibility, where the force of the in-principle claim is something like "If we knew a total description of the system at the lower level and all of the lower-level laws, a sufficiently complex computer could generate the analysis of all of the upper-level terms and laws and predict any upper-level phenomenon." Of course, we don't have such a complete lower-level description of higher-level systems in any science, we are not even sure that we have all of the relevant lower-level laws, and we have not yet succeeded in producing any such apocalyptic derivations of the total behavior of any higher-level systems—but these are supposed to be merely "technical" difficulties.

I have criticized this unattainable picture of reductive explanation elsewhere (Wimsatt 1976a, 1976b), and I have suggested an alternative account that dovetails naturally with the "heuristic" picture. But the original picture persists widely in philosophical analyses and in "rationalistic" theories in the social sciences, particularly in decision theory, linguistics, and other areas where algorithmic models are found. Its persistence is aided by regarding such theories as "normative"—as specifying what is the optimal behavior, usually under impossibly idealized circumstances (when we have no computational limitations and make no errors in our calculations). The search for larger computers, which can calculate faster, and for various technical improvements to increase reliability (such as doing computations in parallel and cross-checking regularly) shows that our best equipment falls short of this ideal. The gap is far larger if we note that all of our models of phenomena involve simplifications and approximations done to increase analytical tractability, so that the problems we are solving are already less complex than the real world they are designed to mimic.

We are not LaPlacean demons, and any image of science that tells us how to behave as if we were still fails to give useful guidance for real scientists in the real world. In fact it may suggest viewpoints and methods that are less than optimal for the dinky and error-prone equipment we possess. A more realistic model of the scientist as problem-solver and decision-maker includes the existence of such limitations and is capable of providing real guidance and better fits with actual practice in all of the sciences. In this model, the scientist must consider the size of computations, the cost of data collection, and must regard both processes as "noisy" or error-prone. A central feature of it is the use of "cost-effective" heuristic procedures for collecting data, simplifying problems, and generating solutions.

Although a growing number of philosophers and cognitive psychologists have become interested in heuristics, the two groups have focused on different properties of heuristics. Philosophers for the most part have focused on their computational efficiency (property 2 above) and argued the heuristics play an important role in scientific inference and discovery. Note that essentially all "inductive" and discovery procedures in science are heuristic principles, failing as algorithms in part because they do not represent logically valid argument forms. Indeed, psychologists have focused on this fact and gloried in the "irrationality" of our everyday heuristics, by which they mean that we will in the appropriate circumstances draw erroneous conclusions using them (see, e.g., Tversky & Kahneman 1974; Nisbett & Ross 1980; Shweder 1977).

Both of these properties need to be examined together. It is not irrational to use a procedure that may under some circumstances lead you into error if you take pains to avoid those circumstances and if using it saves you a great deal of effort. All instruments in the natural, biological, and social sciences are designed for use in certain contexts and can produce biased or worthless results if they are used in contexts that may fail to meet the conditions for which they were designed. A fair amount of effort in these sciences is devoted to determining the conditions under which instruments can be used without bias or to "calibrating" them to determine their biases so that they can be corrected for. This is one of the major activities of statistical methodologists—either constructing new instruments or calibrating or criticizing the use of existing ones.

Campbell's notion of a "vicarious selector" (1974) is employed widely by him to explain and characterize a hierarchy of selection processes in perception, learning, and cultural evolution. It follows from his characterization of vicarious selectors that they are heuristic procedures (see Wimsatt 1981a, 155). I believe that Campbell's conception of a hierarchy of selection processes acting to produce structures' "fit," whether physical or ideational, with their relevant environments is the most productive form for functionalist theories in the social sciences. It lacks their panfunctionalist tenor and also has a much closer connection with evolutionary ideas in the biological sciences, which have recently begun to move toward productive models for the microevolution of culture (see Boyd & Richardson 1985).

Biological adaptations (and in Campbell's scheme, social and psychological ones as well) all meet the defining characteristics of heuristic procedures. First, it is a commonplace among evolutionary biologists that adaptations, even when functioning properly, do not guarantee survival and production of offspring. Second, they are nevertheless cost-effective ways of contributing to this end. Third, any adaptation has systematically specifiable conditions under which its employment will actually decrease the fitness of the organism. These conditions are, of course, seldom found in the "normal" environments of the organism, or the adaptation would be maladaptive and selected against. Fourth, these adaptations serve to transform a complex computational problem about the environment into a simpler problem, the answer to which is usually a reliable guide to the answer to the complex problem. Thus shorter day length is a good predictor of oncoming winter and is used by a variety of plants and animals to initiate appropriate seasonal changes in morphology and behavior—even though heavy cloud cover or artificial conditions in the laboratory can "fool" this adaptation. Similarly, rapid decreases in general illumination in the frog's visual field are taken to indicate the approach of a predator. Though the frog may be fooled frequently by this adaptation (e.g., cows are not predators but may be frequent parts of the frog's environment), the cost of being wrong is sufficiently great that this is a "cost-effective" solution.

The third property, that the errors produced in using a heuristic are systematic, is widely exploited in the analysis of organic adaptations. It is a truism of functional inference that studying how a system breaks down (and the conditions under which it does) is a powerful tool for determining how it functions normally and the conditions under which it was designed to function. This fact can also be used systematically in the study of our reasoning processes. First, from an analysis of the heuristic, we can determine the conditions under which (and how) it will break down, thus "calibrating" the heuristic. This, as already pointed out, is the task of the methodologist, but it should be applied to our heuristic reasoning processes no less than to the study of our machines or to organic adaptations. But a more interesting insight, first employed by Tversky and Kahneman (1974), is that the widespread occurrence of systematic errors is to be recognized as the "footprint" of a heuristic procedure or procedures. Different heuristics leave characteristically different footprints, so an analysis of the biases can lead to plausible inferences about the character of the reasoning processes that produced them. Usually, we need some knowledge of these reasoning processes in order to pare down the field of appropriate candidates, but this can be done. For example, I conducted a study of the systematic biases in mathematical models of group selection, a heated controversy in evolutionary biology, and was able to trace the origin of these biases to heuristics for problem simplification characteristic of reductionistic problem-solving strategies. I will discuss this in the next section since reductionistic problem-solving methods are widely used and just as widely criticized in the social sciences (more details of this specific case can be found in Wimsatt 1980b, 1981a).

REDUCTIONIST RESEARCH STRATEGIES AND THEIR BIASES

If reductionistic problem-solving heuristics have a generic bias, it is to ignore, oversimplify, or otherwise underestimate the importance of the context of the system under study. A number of writers (including several in this volume) have complained about the frequency with which properties of the systems they study are assumed to be independent of context, when in fact they are disguised relational properties. Context dependence is a frequent problem of translation for linguists. I have argued that context dependence of biological fitness components at a lower level is a necessary (but not sufficient) condition of the existence of higher-level units of selection (Wimsatt 1980b, 1981b). If reductionistic problem-solving heuristics lead to illegitimate assumptions of context independence, there is a prima facie case for believing that biases of reductionistic problem-solving strategies are extremely pervasive in the social sciences.

How these biases arise can be easily seen from a general characterization of the problem-solving context of a reductionistic problem-solver. First, assume that a scientist starts by choosing, designating, or constructing a system for analysis. This immediately partitions his world of study into that system and its environent (see Star 1983a for relevant simplification processes here; Griesemer's concept [1983] of the "conceptual map" as fixing the environment in which problem solving takes place is relevant at this stage of analysis.) Second, we must make Simon's "assumption of bounded rationality" that any real-world system is too complex to study in all of its complexity, so we must make simplifications—through selection of properties or objects for study, simplified assumptions about relationships between these properties or objects, assumptions about what variables must be controlled or randomized, and the like. Third, I will assume a very general characterization of what it is to be a reductionist; that is, a reductionist is interested in understanding the character, properties, and behavior of the studied system in terms of the properties of its parts and their interrelations and interactions. (This is a sufficiently inclusive description that it probably captures any analytic methods in general, even those of many who would not call themselves reductionists. It should in any case be acceptable to any reductionist.) This means that the reductionist is primarily interested in the entities and relations internal to the system of study. But this fact, together with the assumption of bounded rationality, has an interesting consequence. While simplifications will in general have to be made everywhere, the focus of the reductionist will lead him to order his list of "economic" priorities so as to simplify first and more severely in his description, observation, control, modeling, and analysis of the environment than in the system he is studying.

Any reductionist who began with the assumption that his system was totally homogeneous in structure and constant through time would have nothing to study: there would be no parts or relations between them. But commonly found in simple models of systems (and even in not-so-simple ones) is the assumption that the system is isolated (in effect, that it has no environment) or that its environment is constant in space and time. This asymmetry in simplifications is indicative of the kinds of biases induced by using reductionistic problem-solving strategies.

Below I outline reductionistic problem-solving strategies. Each one is used in some circumstance because its adoption transforms the initial problem into one that is easier to analyze and to solve. Each of them can be seen as an application of the general schema for making simplifications to a specific scientific activity, whether conceptualizing the system for study and analysis, building or modifying models of its behavior, observing its behavior, designing controlled experiments (or looking for natural data sets that meet desired control conditions), or testing the models. This partial list should suggest a variety of relevant cases in various disciplines. I have somewhat arbitrarily divided the heuristics into heuristics of conceptualization, model building and theory construction, and observation and experimental design, though these activities are seldom as separable as this division might suggest.

Heuristics of Conceptualization

1. *Descriptive localization.* Describe a relational property as if it were monadic or a lower-order relational property. Note that if a property is a function of system properties and environment properties, keeping the environment constant will make the property look as if it is a function only of system properties. Thus, for example, fitness is a relational property between organism and environment. Keeping the environment constant makes it look as if fitness can be treated as a monadic property of organisms. Many context dependencies are hidden in this fashion.

2. *Meaning reductionism.* Assume that new redescriptions of a property at a lower level or an account of that property in terms of the intrasystemic mechanisms that produce it can result in meaning changes (through redefinition) of scientific terms, whereas higher-level redescriptions (or an account of the property in terms of intersystemic mechanisms) cannot. Result: Since philosophers regard themselves as concerned with meaning relations, they are inclined to a reductionistic bias. Note that this is not a bias when it is applied to properties that are "correctly" regarded as monadic at the level of analysis in question, that is, that are context independent for wide ranges of conditions like those normally studied. But if the property in question is a disguised relational property or a functional property (both of which impose conditions on properties or entities outside of the system under study), this assumption can lead to serious mistakes.

Heuristics of Model Building and Theory Construction

3. *Modeling localization.* Look for an intrasystemic mechanism rather than an intersystemic one to explain a systematic property, or if both are available, regard the former as "more fundamental." As derivative corollaries, structural properties are regarded as more important than functional ones, and mechanisms as more important than context (see, e.g., discussions of the assumed stability of personality traits in Shweder 1979a, 1979b, 1980a).

4. *Context simplification.* In reductionistic model building, simplify the description of the environment before simplifying the description of the system. This strategy often legislates higher-level systems out of existence or leaves no way of describing inter-

systemic phenomena appropriately. This is, in effect, a redescription of the account given above of the origin of reductionistic biases against the importance of context but even at this general level of description has been exceedingly important in some areas. This is perhaps the most striking bias in mathematical models of group selection (see Wimsatt 1980b).

5. *Generalization.* When setting out to improve a simple model of the behavior of a system in its environment, focus on generalizing or elaborating the internal structure of the system at the cost of ignoring generalizations or elaborations of external structure. Because a number of simplifications will have been made both internal and external to the system, there will always be room for improving its internal description and analysis. In effect, this strategy involves the following working maxim: If a model fails to work or predict adequately, it must be because of oversimplifications in the description of internal structure, not because of oversimplified descriptions of external structure (see Star 1983a, 1983b for a sociological perspective on this).

Heuristics of Observation and Experimental Design

6. *Observation.* The reductionist will tend not to model environmental variables and will thus fail to record data necessary to detect interactional or larger-scale patterns. Note that this can apply on a temporal as well as on a spatial scale. Thus one who studies patients without having taken appropriate case histories may be committing this error, as well as one who does not record appropriate contextual variables of the experiment.

7. *Control.* The reductionist in experimental design will construct experimental arrangements so as to keep environmental variables constant (or will often merely assume that they are constant!). He then tends to miss dependencies of system variables on them. This heuristic is particularly interesting, since it follows straightforwardly from an application of Mill's canon—"Vary the factors one at a time, keeping all others constant"—to the context of reductionistic problem solving. If the reductionist is interested in determining causal relations among intrasystemic variables, he will try to vary the intrasystemic variables one at a time, keeping all of the other intra- and extrasystemic variables constant. As he stud-

ies different intrasystemic variables, he will be keeping the other intrasystemic variables constant in different combinations and will thus tease out the various intrasystemic causal relations. But the extrasystemic variables will also be kept constant in each of these experiments, so he will never have done an experiment appropriately designed to determine effects of any extrasystemic variables on system properties. One can imagine a reductionist replying to the claim of the causal importance of some extrasystemic variable "But we have been studying these systems for years, and no one has ever reported any effect of that variable!" But of course not—it has always been kept constant! This is another instance of the old maxim that there are no "universal" control setups. What one must control is a function of what relationships one is studying.

8. *Testing.* Make sure that a theory works out locally (or in the laboratory) rather than testing it in appropriate natural environments or doing appropriate robustness analyses to suggest what are important environmental variables and what are relevant ranges of these parameters for study. (This is such a frequent criticism of experimental studies that I won't even attempt to illustrate or document it. I am sure that you can provide your own favorite examples.)

An Example of Reductionistic Biases: Models of Group Selection

I have studied in detail the use of these heuristics in model building in population biology. It may help to illustrate how they operate if I provide a partial description of one case of their operation in the development of models of group selection in evolutionary biology. In recent evolutionary biology, group selection has been the subject of widespread attack and general suspicion. Most of the major theorists have argued against its efficacy. A number of mathematical models attempting to assess the relative efficacy of individual and group selection have been constructed, and virtually all of them seem to support this scepticism: it appears that group selection could be significant only rarely and under very special conditions on the relevant parameter values.

Wade undertook an experimental test of the relative efficacy of individual and group selection—acting in concert or opposition— in laboratory populations of the flour beetle, Tribolium. This work produced surprising results. Group selection was a significant force in these experiments, capable of overwhelming individual selection in the opposite direction for a wide range of parameter values. The conflict between his findings and the then known mathematical models of the process led him to a closer analysis of these models (Wade 1978).

The models surveyed made a variety of simplifying assumptions. Although most of them were different, Wade found that five of the assumptions were widely held in common. (Of the twelve models surveyed, each made at least three of them, and five of the models made all five assumptions.) Crucial for present purposes, all of the assumptions were biologically unrealistic and incorrect, and each independently had a strong negative effect on the possibility or efficacy of group selection. Furthermore, these assumptions were made by friends and foes of group selection alike, so one could not argue they were making those assumptions that would buttress their favorite conclusions. Why, then, did they all make assumptions strongly inimical to group selection? Such a coincidence cries out for explanation: We have found a systematic bias suggesting the use of problem-solving heuristics.

These assumptions are analyzed more fully elsewhere (Wade 1978; Wimsatt 1980b), and I will discuss only one of them here. It was first introduced by Richard Levins, an advocate of group selection, and is known as the "migrant pool" assumption. This is the assumption that all of the migrants from any groups (the "offspring" of these groups) go into a common pool from which new groups are drawn at random. It won ready acceptance for two reasons. First of all, it provided substantial analytic simplifications (the need to keep track only of gene frequencies in a single migrant population, rather than recording the independent gene frequencies in a single migrant population, rather than recording the independent gene frequencies of the migrants from each parent group). Second, it was equivalent to a time-honored simplifying assumption of population genetics, "panmixia," the assumption that all members of a population have an equal probability of mating with any one member.

Unfortunately, when the process of reproduction is examined at the group level (rather than the individual level at which most theorists conceptualize the problem), this assumption is seen to be equivalent to the assumption of a particularly strong form of "blending inheritance," which (as R. A Fisher pointed out in 1931 at the individual level) results in a rapid loss of variance, leaving evolution with little variation to act upon. The striking thing is that while all population geneticists know that "blending inheritance" is a thing to avoid (it is avoided at the individual level by the processes of Mendelian segregation), they were unable to recognize that they had made assumptions equivalent to introducing it at the group level in their models of group selection. To put the point in another way, to assume panmixia is the same as assuming that with respect to probability of mating, there are no groups! It is thus not surprising that reductionists should have found little effect of group selection in their models.

A particularly crucial factor in explaining the inability to see the consequences of this assumption is what I have called "perceptual focus" (Wimsatt 1980b, 248–49). If groups are thought of as merely "collections of individuals," as they are by most of these people—a hypothesis that has since been confirmed by interviews with some of the protagonists—then the description of processes is referred to the individual level, and one cannot see that assumptions that appear benign at that level may be dangerous oversimplifications when viewed at a higher level. This phenomenon appears to explain, not only the ready acceptance of the "migrant pool" assumption, but also some of the other assumptions Wade discusses. It also suggests a technique for correcting the systematic biases of the reductionistic problem solving strategies that I will discuss further on.

Heuristics Can Hide Their Tracks

One of the remarkable things about the case just discussed is that the biases in these models had not been discovered—in spite of the fact that a variety of models of the processes of group selection had been investigated. One would hope that this "sampling from a space of possible models" (Levins 1968) would be an unbiased sampling and would turn up models with different conclusions if the conclusions were artifacts of the simplifying assumptions that were made (see Wimsatt 1981a). But in this case, it clearly was a biased sample. The question is, Why?

The answer resides in the fact that all of the modelers were using a variety of reductionistic modeling strategies and assumptions. While they approached their models in somewhat different ways, this commonality of generic approach constrained the results. Each of the heuristics in the list of reductionistic modeling strategies independently biases the models against the inclusion or proper consideration of environmental variables. If one then cross-checks these models as a way of validating the results, one will get an apparent robustness of the conclusions, but a spurious one, a case of pseudorobustness. It is tempting to suggest that much of the appearance of success (I do not want to deny that there have been real successes as well) of reductionistic methodologies comes from this phenomenon—that different reductionistic methods hide their mutual inadequacies by covering each others' tracks.

Another important means through which methodologies (regarded as related bundles of heuristics and practices) can "hide their tracks" (and this applies not just to reductionistic methodologies) is through the fourth property of heuristics—that use of a heuristic causes a redefinition or transformation of the problem to which it is applied. If a transformation yields an analytically tractable, and therefore successful, problem, there will be a tendency to act as if the new problem (to which there is now a solution) captures the core issues of the old problem and thus to argue that the old problem is "really" solved by the solution to the new problem. With one step further, the new problem may be taken as defining the proper formulation of the original, and thus it has replaced the old in a manner rendered largely invisible since it is now regarded as a "clarification of the old problem" that preserves the spirit of the research tradition while removing "confusions" that had earlier prevented solution of the problem. This is a "hidden revolution," a more modest paradigm shift masquerading as none at all. The philosopher Ludwig Wittgenstein (1960) has argued that this kind of phenomenon characterizes rule-following behavior and the use of concepts in general. We assimilate new kinds of application of a rule to its original domain of interpretation and thus have the anomalous phenomenon that before it is applied to the new situation, it looks as if we have a real choice as to whether to apply the rule or not, but after the fact, it appears as if we had no other choice!

This kind of invisible paradigm shift has many of the properties Kuhn (1970) ascribes to paradigm shifts in general, except for those connected with the explicit recognition of a revolutionary change. It is still true that the new paradigm carries with it valuational judgments and defines explanatory standards; but instead of arguing that this represents a rejection of the old paradigm, the reductionist will argue that this is the proper interpretation of the old problems and theory, that this was "contained in the old view all along." When this kind of paradigm shift is accompanied by the acceptance of a new formal model, it will result in a bias of over-simplification—often accompanied by the reification of the abstract system to define a kind of (Weberian?) ideal type, which is talked about as if it existed in the real world. Thus thermodynamicists talk about "ideal gases" or "van der Waal's gases," denoting gases whose behavior fits the ideal-gas law and van der Waal's equation of state respectively. Biologists, similarly, talk about "Mendelian genes," "Mendelizing traits," "Lotka-Volterra communities," and "panmictic populations"—in each case indicating a supposed conformity of a real-world system with the abstract conditions of the model.

While one may decry this kind of reification, the tendency to do it indicates a real and often ignored function of theoretical models. Although we sometimes set out to test our models, far more often we use them as patterns to organize phenomena and to classify results as fitting or not fitting the model. Using the model as a pattern-matching template in this way enormously simplifies the task of finding order in the data, but it also introduces a kind of inertia (or as Tversky and Kahneman would say, an "anchoring" bias), which opposes change in the system. When the results don't fit, we do not throw away the model but instead redescribe the system: the population is *not* panmictic, the gene is *not* Mendelian, the community *not* Lotka-Volterra. The only problem with this activity is that if such pattern matching is mistaken for genuine testing, it can lead advocates of the model to believe that the model has been confirmed, and critics to accuse the advocate of ad hoc–ery and of converting the model into a "meaningless schema" or "covert tautology." The difference between this kind of activity and a real test of the model is that in pattern matching, there often is no attempt to determine the values of the parameters of the model independently. Values are chosen so that the model fits the data, producing a kind of sophisticated curve fitting, rather than a legitimate test of the model. (See Tribe's excellent discussion [1972] of the misuse of the assumptions of rational decision theory in attempts to make real-world decisions.)

A parallel kind of thing can happen when the paradigm is an experimental system rather than a theoretical model. If an experimental system is highly successful, it can become a normative paradigm for how a class of studies should be pursued. "Drosophila genetics" and "Tribolium ecology" mark off, not only model organisms, but sets of procedures for studying them and preferred questions for consideration that were extended as paradigms for studying other organisms in other situations because they represented ideal conceptions of how to study genetics and ecology respectively. When these conceptions are attacked, they elicit spirited defenses of the general methodological approach (see, e.g., Mertz & MacCauley 1980). The bias introduced here is one of overgeneralization—whether of the limited model or of the experimental protocol and design or of the questions asked.

Both of these kinds of promotion of a theoretical or experimental model to a paradigm can reinforce the biases of the other problem-solving techniques by hiding the need to reconceptualize the system or the formulation of the problem of analyzing it. They can defer for a long time the noticing or analyzing of questions that were far more obvious at the start of this line of investigation. This phenomenon—the increasing entrenchment of a theoretical or experimental paradigm—in part serves to explain why disciples of an approach are often far less flexible and far less methodologically conscious than the originators of that approach. I have attempted to model and to explore the consequences of this kind of entrenchment in a variety of contexts, in biological evolution and development, cognitive development, and in models of scientific and cultural change (see Glassman & Wimsatt 1984; Wimsatt 1985a, 1985b).

Two Strategies for Correcting Reductionistic Biases

I know of two general strategies for correcting for the artifacts and biases of problem-solving heuristics. The first is truly general but is subject to specific problems when applied to reductionistic problem solving. The second can be regarded as a specific application of the general approach to reductionistic problem solving, with an eye to addressing the special problems of a reductionistic approach.

The general approach is what Campbell has called "triangulation," which Campbell and Fiske have incorporated in the now classic "multitrait-multimethod" matrix (1959). I have discussed the variety of functions and applications of this method, which I call "robustness analysis," in general review of the topic (Wimsatt 1981a). By using a variety of different models, approaches, means of detection, or of derivation and comparing the results, we can hope to detect and correct for the biases, special assumptions, and artifacts of any one approach.

But we have already seen that this approach does not guarantee success. It too is a heuristic procedure. The models of group selection display an ingenious variety of assumptions and approaches, but they all share biasing assumptions in common, assumptions whose biasing effects were not apparent before Wade's review (1978). How can we prevent our array of models and approaches from being a biased sample? To this question, there is no general answer, but there is an answer derived from the character of the biases in this specific case. Recall that the effect of each reductionistic bias is to ignore or to underestimate the effects of variables in the environment. But is this attached unalterably to the variables in question? No—it occurs merely because of where they are located. This bias would be removed for anything that could be brought within the system, and this can be accomplished merely by changing the boundaries of the system being investigated. Thus the strategy for eliminating biases in the description and analysis of groups as collections of individuals is to build models in which the groups are treated as individuals in a larger system in which they are parts and in which we focus on modeling intergroup relations. (This strategy is deliberately exploited in Wimsatt 1981b in the development of models of group inheritance.) The biases of the reductionistic heuristics will still apply, but because the system boundaries have changed, they will have different effects. The comparison of intragroup with intergroup models is the right comparison for testing the robustness or artifactuality of lower-level reductionistic assumptions. A comparable strategy should be equally appropriate for analogous problems in the social sciences.

Similarly, going down a level is the right medicine for testing more holistic models, which may ignore microlevel details. Geneticists regularly (and rightly) complain when higher-level optimization models predict optimal states that may not be genetically possible or that may take some time to attain so that the "equilibrium state" cannot be assumed (see, e.g., the last chapter of Oster & Wilson 1979 for a detailed critique of optimization modeling in population biology). I have called this approach "multilevel reductionistic analysis" (Wimsatt 1980b), though it is misleading to regard it as reductionistic when the move is from a lower to a higher level. It is reductionistic only in that the approach uses reductionistic problem-solving techniques at any given level. It is not reductionistic in the suggestion that one should go to a higher level of analysis to correct for the biases induced at a lower level.

THE IMPORTANCE OF HEURISTICS IN THE STUDY OF HUMAN BEHAVIOR

I have argued that the study of our heuristics, of the nature of our real reasoning processes, their "cost-effective" advantages, and their systematic biases should be a major topic on the agenda for the human sciences. Let me summarize the reasons why I think this is important. It is important first of all because these heuristics of reasoning are part of our equipment, and as with any equipment, they must be calibrated and used as tools for evaluating hypotheses and experimental and observational studies. This has already been done, for example, in the original investigation of Tversky and Kahneman (1974), as well as their more recent work (Kahneman, Slovic & Tversky 1983; see also Mynatt, Doherty & Tweney 1977; Tweney, Doherty & Mynatt 1981; Shweder 1977, 1979a, 1979b, 1980; and Wimsatt 1980b).

Second, as part of our equipment, these heuristics are part of our subject matter, one of our objects of study. This is true of us, not only as individual problem solvers, but also as social beings. I should at this point confess that I have fallen prey to my own reductionistic biases with my limited focus on the processes of individuals. We should focus also on the heuristics of group processes and upon the biases of groups on the social processes of science. There are, for example, group identification processes that suppress intragroup disagreement, processes of competition that exacerbate disagreements between groups and restrict flow of information and recruits between them, disciplinary and subject-matter biases that lead us to overestimate the importance of and to overextend the subject matter and theories that we know well and to take insufficient account of those we do not. I have formulated these as processes in the sociology of science, but they obviously apply more broadly to other spheres of human action. We need to understand these biases, both for their own sake and also to learn how to correct for their effects.

The new movements in sociology of science (e.g., Latour & Woolgar 1979) are making useful progress in this direction, but from a determinedly "externalist" perspective. Campbell and I agree strongly that a more appropriate approach would be to try to integrate internalist and externalist perspectives. Two recent studies that have taken important and productive steps in this direction are those of Star (1983a, 1983b) and Griesemer (1983). Star focuses on the development of the localizationist perspective in neurophysiology from 1870 through 1906 and has important new analyses of the individual and social processes for handling anomalies and other processes used for legitimizing data and methodological approaches (Star & Gerson, 1983a, 1983b). Griesemer focuses on the recent macroevolution controversy in evolutionary biology and develops tools for analyzing "conceptual maps" (a scientist's models of the relationships between subject areas in his domain and the resultant structure of the problem to be solved) and for tracking the changes in these maps in the conceptual life history of individual scientists or in the diffusion of ideas and research problems from one research group to another.

Third, we need to take stock of and to incorporate an understanding of our reasoning heuristics and their biases into our accounts of human action. These act as constraints on our decision processes, and can lead to a variety of unintended suboptimal consequences, as is documented in the theory and case studies of Janis and Mann (1977). On the positive side, things of which we cannot take account are things we can afford to ignore in an explanatory theory of human behavior. It is a truism that it is not the way the world is but how we conceive of and conceptualize it that determines our actions. If we do conceive it in various oversimplified ways, this can lead us into various sorts of error, but if these ways are indeed simpler than the way the world is, our explanatory tasks should be correspondingly simpler as well. We must be careful to correct for these biases in studying human action, but at the same time we must expect to find them in our accounts of it.

For these reasons, I do not see D'Andrade's third world of meanings and intentions as being quite so different from the engineering and functional systems studied in the biological sciences as he supposes. If I am right in believing that meanings, intentions, plans, strategies, decisions, beliefs, and the like are basically engineered structures, then we should expect them to have the same mix of strengths and weaknesses as any of our artifacts and to be best studied with tools that have at least a family resemblance to the conceptual tools of the other engineering disciplines. Less predictable they may be, but complex machines have always been less predictable than simpler machines—and our cognitive and social worlds are nothing if not complex.

If this sounds like facile reductionism, it is not: if our cognitive structures share design principles with evolutionary and engineering artifacts, this does not (by itself) make them biological or hardware entities. It rather reflects principles of optimal or "satisficing" design common to all three areas. I fully expect that elucidation of some of our social and cognitive heuristics—as studied by social scientists—will provide insights that will be useful in these other disciplines, just as work in them has provided (for better or worse) metaphors and paradigms for social scientists. Before the rise of Darwinism, genetics, and molecular biology gave biology distinctive well-established theories, biologists borrowed freely from psychology and theories of society, and they are now doing so again. Thus evolutionary biologists have recently adopted the theory of games and claim that much more is to be mined for application to biological problems from economics and learning theory (Maynard-Smith 1983), and at least two computer scientists argue that large parallel-processing computers should be developed with an architecture modeled on the structure of the scientific research community (Kornfeld & Hewitt 1981). I suspect that much more is soon to follow.

Note

1. I would like to thank Donald Fiske, Jim Griesemer, and Leigh Star for very useful comments on an earlier draft of this paper. This work was supported by the Systems Development Foundation, Grant no. 6357.

References

Boyd, R., and Richerson, P. 1985. *Cultural evolution*. Chicago: University of Chicago Press.
Campbell, D. T. 1974. Evolutionary epistemology, In *The philosophy of Karl Popper*, vol. 1, ed. P. A. Schilpp. LaSalle, Ill.: Open Court.
Campbell, D. T., and Fiske, D. W. 1959. Convergent and discriminant validation by the multitrait-multimethod matrix. *Psychological Bulletin* 56:81–105.
Dennett, D. C. 1979. *Brainstorms*. Cambridge: Bradford Books–MIT Press.
Feigenbaum, M. 1980. Universal behavior in nonlinear systems. *Los Alamos Science* 1:4–27.
Fisher, R. A. 1931. *The genetical theory of natural selection*. Oxford: Cambridge University Press.
Glassman, R., and Wimsatt, W. C. 1984. Evolutionary advantages and limitations of early developmental plasticity. In *The behavioral biology of early brain damage*. Vol. 1: *Research orientations and clinical observations*, ed. C. R. Almli and S. Finger. New York: Academic Press.
Griesemer, J. L. 1983. Communication and scientific change: The role of conceptual maps in the macro-evolution controversy. Ph.D. diss., University of Chicago.
Hofstadter, D. 1981. Metamagical themas: Strange attractors. *Scientific American*, November, 22–43.
Janis, I. L., and Mann, L. 1977. *Decision making*. New York: Macmillan.
Kahneman, D.; Slovic, P.; and Tversky, A. 1983. *Decision under uncertainty: Heuristics and biases*. London: Cambridge University Press.

Kaufmann, A. 1974. *The science of decision making*. New York: McGraw-Hill.

Kornfeld, W., and Hewitt, C. 1981. The scientific community metaphor. *IEEE Transactions on Systems, Man, and Cybernetics*, SMC-11: 24–33.

Kuhn, T. S. 1970. *The structure of scientific revolutions*. 2d ed. Chicago: University of Chicago Press.

Latour, B., and Woolgar, S. 1979. *Laboratory life: The social construction of scientific facts*. Beverly Hills: Sage.

Lenat, D. B. 1982. The nature of heuristics. *Artificial Intelligence* 19: 189–249.

Levins, R. 1968. *Evolution in changing environments*. Princeton: Princeton University Press.

Luce, R. D., and Raiffa, H. 1957. *Games and decisions*. New York: Wiley.

McCauley, R. M. In press. Competence, heuristics, and scientific discovery. *British Journal for the philosophy of Science*.

Maynard-Smith, J. 1983. *Evolution and the theory of games*. London: Cambridge University Press.

Mertz, D. B., and MacCauley, D. 1980. The domain of laboratory ecology. *Synthese* 43:95–110. Reprinted 1982 in *Conceptual Issues in Ecology* ed. E. Saarinen. Dordrecht: D. Reidel.

Mynatt, C.; Doherty, M.; and Tweney, R. 1977. Confirmation bias in a simulated research environment. *Quarterly Journal of Experimental Psychology* 29: 85–95.

Nisbett, R., and Ross, L. 1980. *Human inference: Strategies and shortcomings of social judgment*. Englewood Cliffs, N.J.: Prentice-Hall.

Oster, G., and Wilson, E. O. 1979. *Caste and ecology in the social insects*. Princeton: Princeton University Press.

Shweder, R. A. 1977. Likeness and likelihood in everyday thought: Magical thinking in judgments about personality. *Current Anthropology* 18:637–48.

———. 1979a. Rethinking culture and personality theory, part 1. *Ethos* 7:255–78.

———. 1979b. Rethinking culture and personality theory, part 2. *Ethos* 7:279–311.

———. 1980a. Rethinking culture and personality theory, part 3. *Ethos* 8:60–94.

———, ed. 1980b. *Fallible judgment in behavioral research*. New Directions for Methodology of Social and Behavioral Science, no. 4, San Francisco: Jossey-Bass.

Simon, H. A. 1955. A behavioral model of rational choice. *Quarterly Journal of Economics* 69:99–118.

———. 1957. *Administrative behavior*. 2d ed. New York: Macmillan.

———. 1981. *The sciences of the artificial*. Cambridge: MIT Press.

Star, S. L. 1983a; Scientific theories as going concerns: The development of the localizationist perspective in neurophysiology, 1870–1906. Ph.D. diss., University of California, Berkeley.

————. 1983b. Simplification in scientific work: An example from neuro-science research. *Social Studies of Science* 13:208–226.

Star, S. L., and Gerson, E. 1983a. Management of anomalies in scientific research. Part 1: Varieties of anomaly. Manuscript.

————. 1983b. Management of anomalies in scientific research. Part 2: Properties of artifacts. Manuscript.

Tribe, L. 1972. Policy science: Analysis or ideology? *Philosophy and Public Affairs.* 2:66–110.

Tversky, A., and Kahneman, D. 1974. Judgment under uncertainty: heuristics and biases. *Science* 185:1124–31.

Tweney, R.; Doherty, M.; and Mynatt, C. 1981. *On scientific thinking.* New York: Columbia University Press.

Wade, M. J. 1978. A critical review of the models of group selection. *Quarterly Review of Biology* 53:101–14.

Wimsatt, W. C. 1976a. Reductionism, levels of organization, and the mind-body problem. In *Consciousness and the Brain,* ed. G. G. Globus et al. New York: Plenum.

————. 1976b. Reductive explanation: A functional account. In *Proceedings of the meeting of the Philosophy of Science Association, 1974.* ed. C. A. Hooker et al. Dordrecht: D. Reidel.

————. 1980a. Randomness and perceived-randomness in evolutionary biology. *Synthese* 43:287–329. Reprinted 1982 in *Conceptual issues in ecology,* ed. Esa Saarinen. Dordrecht: D. Reidel.

————. 1980b. Reductionistic research strategies and their biases in the units of selection controversy. In *Scientific discovery.* Vol. 2: *Case studies,* ed. T. Nickles. Dordrecht: D. Reidel.

————. 1981a. Robustness, reliability, and overdetermination. In *Scientific inquiry and the social sciences,* ed. M. Brewer and B. Collins. San Francisco: Jossey-Bass.

————. 1981b. Units of selection and the structure of the multilevel genome. In *PSA-1980,* vol. 2, ed. P. D. Asquith and R. N. Giere. East Lansing, Mich.: Philosophy of Science Association.

————. 1984. Generative entrenchment, developmental constraints, and the innate-acquired distinction. Paper given at the conference "Integrating Scientific Disciplines," Georgia State University, May 1984.

————. 1985. Von Baer's law, generative entrenchment, and scientific change. Manuscript.

Wittgenstein, L. 1960. *Remarks on the foundations of mathematics.* London: Blackwell.

14 What Social Scientists Don't Understand

P. E. Meehl

In the papers prepared for the conference on which this book is based and in the discussion, there were some matters almost universally agreed upon but repeated unnecessarily. Then there were some things that should have been agreed upon but were not. Finally, there were matters that were not agreed upon that needed more intensive examination—matters playing a central role in the philosophy of the social sciences and in the present intellectual gloominess that seems to prevail in all of the disciplines represented.

THINGS GENERALLY AGREED ON FROM THE BEGINNING

It was agreed that logical positivism and strict operationism won't wash. Logical positivism, in anything like the sense of Vienna in the late twenties turned out not to be logically defensible, or even rigorously formulatable, by its adherents. It is epistemologically unsound from a variety of viewpoints (including ordinary-language analysis), it is not an accurate picture of the structure of advanced sciences such as physics, and it is grossly inadequate as a reconstruction of empirical history of science. So it is dead. All old surviving logical positivists agree, including my friend and teacher Feigl, who invented the phrase "logical positivism" and was the first to introduce the approach in the United States in 1931. The last remaining defender of anything like logical positivism was Gustav Bergmann, who ceased to do so by the late 1940s.

Why, then, the continued attack on logical positivism and its American behaviorist near-synonym "operationalism"? My answer to this is unsettling but, I think, correct. Our conference on social science came about partly because of widespread dissatisfaction about the state of the art, and we have always been more introspective methodologically than the physicists and biologists, who en-

315

gage in this kind of thing only under revolutionary circumstances. My perhaps cynical diagnosis is that one reason the conference members spent needless time repeating that logical positivism and simplistic operationalism are incorrect views of scientific knowledge is that this relieves scientific guilt feelings or inferiority feelings about our disciplines. It's as if somebody said, "Well, maybe clinical psychology isn't up to the standards of historical geology or medical genetics, let alone theoretical physics; but we needn't be so fussy about our concepts and empirical support for them because logical positivism, which was so stringent on that score, is a nefarious doctrine and we are no longer bound by it."

I see a connection here with the concern about the social sciences as "science" and what it takes to be really scientific. I have never had much interest in this labeling question. I don't see how anybody familiar with various disciplines in the life sciences, and even some of the "inorganic" sciences, could see it as a clear-cut or interesting question. Skinner points out in *The Behavior of Organisms* (1938, 41, 419) that the curves obtained from a single organism in the operant conditioning chamber ("Skinner box") are smoother and more reproducible than many of the curves obtained by medical students in their introductory physiology lab course. The verbal report of a sophomore, experiencing for the first time a negative afterimage, is reproducible enough so that you can afford to bet $10,000 at 100-to-1 odds that a subject pretested for having normal color vision and not insane will report that what he sees after presentation of a red circle and being asked to fixate a distant gray wall is a large, faded blue-green circle. Avoiding the mass media identification of the word "science" with test tubes, and instead attending to reproducibility, degree of quantification, and conceptual neatness (while allowing open concepts), my own discipline of psychology has subareas that are highly scientific, such as some branches of visual perception, cognitive processes, behavior genetics, and animal learning. Others are of intermediate "scientificalness," like trait theory, differential psychology, and psychophysiology of emotion. Still others, like projective techniques and psychoanalytic dream interpretation (which I practice), do not deserve to be called scientific at all. Some branches of historical geology, especially the paleontology involved in evolutionary theory, are much overrated as to their scientific status, being in a primitive degree of quantification, with highly speculative components. That doesn't mean we call geology or paleontology unscientific. Some branches of organic medicine are in a primitive state, while others are almost in as advanced a scientific state as chemistry or physics. It seems to me pointless to argue about these matters and mentally unhealthy for a social scientist to get involved in the semantic hassle as to whether he is engaged in science or not. It would be desirable to strike that question (perhaps even the very term "science") from the methodological vocabulary of conferences like ours. In addition to being hygienic, this would conduce to greater intellectual honesty because it would force us, instead of warding off semantic attacks by administrators or skeptical intellectual laymen with an antiscience bias, simply to ask the question "To what extent does this discipline contain knowledge that brings some sort of credentials with it?" Whether there is any kind of credentialed knowledge that is not, in some carefully specified sense, "scientific" knowledge is an interesting philosophical query, but one we need not answer for our purposes.

In psychology, at least, there is a tendency to conflate "experimental" with "quantitative" and then in turn to mix up "statistical" with "mathematical" as if they were the same thing, which they are not. Social science has many more statistical methods and findings than it does mathematical models, except in economics, where the connection between the mathematical models and the empirical statistics is regrettably tenuous. One can proceed experimentally without being quantitative; one can be quantitative in the sense of statistical counts without having a mathematical model for the causal structure underlying the processes; one could be highly quantitative, both in the sense of statistics of observations and in the sense of the postulated causal model being formalized in differential equations, and not be capable of experimenting at all, as in astronomy. Even worse is the conflation of the word "empirical" to mean "experimental and quantitative," a tendentious mistake that begins by failing to look up the word in Webster (for more detailed discussion of this, see Meehl 1983).

Another thing that seemed universally agreed upon is that a classical Newtonian model of science is incorrect. In my college days, nobody thought that Hull (1943) or Skinner (1938) or Thurstone (1935) was "the Newton of psychology," or that there was even ever going to be such a person. There are at least three broad classes of scientific theories, and all three kinds are to be found in all three major divisions of science (physical, biological, or social). First, there are *functional-dynamic theories,* Newton's, the theory of heat, Skinner's laws of learning, or the mathematical principles of population genetics being examples. Many of these, and certainly the impressive ones, are expressed in mathematical form and look like the Newtonian business, but not always. Functional-dynamic theories relate states to states or events to events and are most like Aristotle's concept of efficient causes. We say that when one variable changes, certain other variables change in such and such ways; their ideal form is the partial differential equation. Functional-dynamic theories do not, however, have to be completely general in the way that classical mechanics or thermodynamics purport to be. If, for instance, Hull's 1943 book had held up, we would have been overjoyed, even if those equations for habit strength held only for mammals and not for fishes or invertebrates. No one would have been disappointed by such departures from generality. What was disappointing is that the basic qualitative aspects (e.g., even the necessity for reinforcement) did not hold up—the latent learning experiments falsified it. It was by no means clear that the function form (simple positive growth function) was correct.

What scientists hoped (and believed?) was that the qualitative listing of intervening variables in Hull's famous set was general over at least mammalian species and that these variables would all be growth or decay functions of input like number of reinforcements, or extinction trials, deprivation time, and so on. What turns out from the research, especially that of the Skinnerians, is that no such mathematical construct as habit strength can be justified, even within a single species, the white rat, and in the controlled conditions of the laboratory on which the theory was based. So the distressing thing about Hull's heroic effort was not that it doesn't work for earthworms or that sometimes it's hard to estimate the growth constant or that for some species the reinforcers are strange. The disappointing thing about Hullian theory was that it didn't even hold up in the Skinner box or in the maze for the white rat, given hunger as a drive and food as a reinforcer. That is, on the very species, drives, rewards, and historical variables that were its origin, the theory did not do an adequate job, even as first-level description, let alone as causal analysis.

Second, there are theories that are *structural-compositional*. Their main idea is to explain what something is composed of, or what kind of parts it has and how they are put together. I think it is unfortunate to speak, as some did at the meeting or in papers, about reductionism as an evil force, to be exorcised by incantation. Some of the most impressive achievements in other sciences have been highly reductionist, and there are disciplines in which the reductionist aim could be almost described as the main scientific program (e.g., biochemical genetics). The main thing Crick and Watson made possible with the DNA business (in itself, mainly a big piece of reduction) was an entire research program, a proliferating enterprise of Kuhnian "normal science," in which the whole point is to reduce. What biochemical geneticists are mainly engaged in, other than the technology of manipulation, is precisely the reduction of something called a "gene," previously understood solely in terms of the mathematics of linkage and population genetics plus approximate location on a chromosome, to a specified sequence of codons. Whether or not the phenomena of a domain can be successfully reduced to those of another is an empirical question.

I suspect part of the problem here is our fear, connected with trade union considerations or vested interests, that if somebody, somewhere, somehow, someday were to reduce one's favorite concepts to lower-order ones, one's enterprise would have been shown feckless, which is of course absurd. Even when an almost complete job of reduction has been carried out in a highly corroborated theory in the physical sciences, nobody in his right mind proposes to liquidate discourse carried out for certain purposes at a higher level. We know what goes on about heating a building in terms of kinetic theory, but when a heating engineer talks with an architect or economist, he does not formulate the subject matter in terms of kinetic energy of molecules. I have always thought it foolish for some of my colleagues in sociology to get upset at the possibility that some psychologist might claim that all social symbolic interactions must ultimately be "based upon psychology," that is, reduced to individual organismic principles of learning (Skinnerian or otherwise). I think this kind of worry is partly what seduced such a smart and methodologically aware scholar as Durkheim into making some elementary bloopers in statistical inference in his classic book *Suicide*.

People who have thought through the "pyramid of sciences" problem are free of the worry—witness Skinner. As a good solid materialist and biological psychologist, Skinner entertained not the faintest doubt that every one of his learning principles involved structural changes in CNS. When pressed in conversation, he could argue, "When the laws of behavior are sufficiently worked out in mathematical detail (in the next generation following me), and when the anatomy, especially the microanatomy, and the physiology of the brain are very thoroughly understood, there will be no problem of prematurely forcing a speculative translation be-

cause it will be perfectly apparent how the brain/behavior dictionary will read." Similarly, Freud, who through his entire life always
assumed that basically everything happening was in the brain and
attempted an ambitious project along those lines, was perfectly
clear in his arguments as to why brain language was not useful at
this stage of our knowledge of psychopathology. The appropriate
language in which to discuss the mental machinery is mental.

Third, some theories are *evolutionary* (historical or developmental), for example, Darwin's theory, Wegener's theory of continental
drift, Freud's early theory of the life-historical origins of the obses-
sional versus the hysterical neurosis, historians' theories as to the
fall of Rome.

THINGS THAT SHOULD HAVE BEEN AGREED UPON

The question as to whether, how much, and what kind of quantification is useful is again an empirical one not to be decided from
the philosophical armchair, nor on the basis of either a scientistic
obsession with mathematics or worship of physics on the one side
or a humanist antiscientist bias on the other. The question is
whether or not the use of a certain theoretical formalism, or the use
of a certain kind of statistical procedure in data reduction, does or
does not help matters. It is necessary to think clearly about words
and to realize that many of the words—I would say most words—
both in ordinary language and in scholarly discourse that purport
to explain anything are quantity words intrinsically. Not always, but
almost always. That Freud doesn't express libidinal cathexis in *lib*
units doesn't detract one whit from the fact that part of his explanatory system involves making comparisons between quantities of it.
When a social scientist speaks of something—anything, a tribal
custom or suicide tendencies or unconscious memories or a white
rat's lever-pressing disposition—he typically uses words like "always," "frequently," "typically," "rarely," "never," "oddly," "weakly," "under special conditions," "mostly." Every single one of these
words is a claim of the degree to which some force or entity exists
or influences; every single one indicates a frequency or probability
with which something happens or the magnitude of a disposition
(propensity). It is foolish for social scientists to try to get away from
this simple fact about the descriptive language of their disciplines.
The question is, What are the circumstances under which it pays
off at a given state of knowledge to re-express these quantity words
of ordinary English in explicitly numerical form? How strong is the
claim that can be made for the resulting metric—that is, does it

have certain nice properties such as a ratio scale or interval scale? Does it demand them?

There should have been more agreement on the legitimacy of open concepts. The writings of Waismann (1945), Pap (1953, 1958, chap. 11), and Carnap (1936, 1937) should have taken care of that question. The famous "testability and meaning" paper, whatever Carnap's main intentions at the time, was at least partly a logician's explication and justification for the use of open concepts in science, and Carnap subsequently became much less operational than he was in that paper. I had thought that a sufficiently satisfactory exposition of it for many social science disciplines was provided by Cronbach and myself thirty years ago (1955).

As Pap and others have clearly shown, considerable openness of concepts exists even in the most advanced sciences, and a great deal in the primitive early stages of any science; they abound in the life sciences. There isn't any good reason for saying that social scientists may not employ them once you have seen that the problems are methodological. My own view is that the proper way to deal with open concepts in psychology, including partially defined constructs like the heritable component of g, lies in the application of an appropriate stochastic mathematics. We don't get rid of open concepts by pseudooperational definitions, nor ought we to rejoice (like an obscurantist) in their persisting openness. What we ought to do is to tighten the stochastic nomological net increasing the strands, improving the instrumentation, and thereby reducing the stochastic feature. There is no reason to require that the end state of such process be to liquidate probability notions from the object language, which is fortunate, because there is no hope of doing so.

There is still a little bit of confusion between probability as an epistemic concept, referring to the degree of evidentiary support or corroboration for some fact or theory, and probability as a metrical concept of the object language, built into the theory itself and considered likely to remain (regardless of the future state of evidence) because it is part of the theoretical substance. This second meaning of "probability" is not epistemological but has either a purely formal frequency interpretation or, as I would prefer, a Popperian propensity interpretation.

Should anyone still worry about the legitimacy of a contextual or implicit definition of an inferred causal entity based on covariation of observations? I had thought that was settled thirty or forty years ago, when philosophers of science (partly the positivists themselves and certainly their critics and amenders) recognized that only a

proper subset of theoretical terms is directly "coordinated" to observational functors and predicates. The rest of them, the majority,
acquire their meaning via a complicated mixture of at least three
components: (a) their formal role in the theoretical network, a contextual partial interpretation similar to the implicit definitions of
point and line in geometry; (b) the fact that the net as a whole is
tied to minimally theoretical or pure observational terms, called
"upward seepage"; and (c) informal explications in an associated
text that uses models, analogies, even occasional mentalistic metaphors to contribute to meaning.

As to realism, I have never met any scientist who, when doing
science, held to a phenomenalist or idealist view; and I cannot force
myself to take a nonrealist view seriously even when I work at it. So
I begin with the presupposition that the external world is really
there, there is a difference between the world and my view of it,
and the business of science is to get my view in harmony with the
way the world really is to the extent that is possible. There is no
reason for us to have a phobia about the word "truth." The idea
that you shouldn't ask whether a scientific statement is true, separate from the anthropologist's or the Hogo Bogos' belief in it, because you can't be absolutely certain, is a dumb argument, refuted
by Carnap in his famous replies to Kaufmann (Carnap 1946a,
1946b, 1948; see also Carnap 1949). Nor does it denigrate any
culture's (or subculture's) values or forms of life to say that its deni-
zens are mistaken as to certain causal facts. The point is not to
conflate our admiration for the Hogo Bogo form of life or Faustian
man's techniques in the moon shot with a factual question.

Regarding the imputation of motives or intentions on the basis
of fallible behavior indicators, I believe it correct to say that the
basic ideas involved were, for psychology, handled pretty well by
Tolman (1932). In fact, Tolman relied heavily, although with a
greater emphasis on the preeminence of the "docility" criterion,
upon a powerful analysis by McDougall (1923) sixty years before
our conference (cf. Murray 1938, 54–76). So I found it a little discouraging that social scientists were reinventing McDougall's wheel
after six decades. If the McDougall or Tolman kind of analysis
(spontaneity, persistence with variation, cessation on goal reaching,
anticipatory preparation for goal situation, improved performance
contingent on getting results [= docility]) strikes some as too mentalistic (an objection I myself would have trouble understanding, let
alone accepting), one could turn instead to Skinner (1938), whose
discussion of why we introduce state variables like drive and emo-

tion after doing our preliminary analysis of behavior in terms of reinforcement and extinction is highly sophisticated and adequate to most—I do not say all—scientific purposes. Or for that matter, one may consult Freud's 1916 paper on the unconscious, where his discussion of how the rationale of imputing unconscious motives to oneself is at bottom no different from that of attributing motives, conscious or unconscious, to other people.

I am not such an optimist as to suppose that there are no technical problems involved here. One could say that a souped-up generalization of the Campbell-Fiske multitrait-multimethod matrix is the answer, with plenty of room for time factors and cross-lag correlations included in the statistical tool kit. But my main point here is that the subject was discussed at the conference as if nobody had ever thought of it before. Furthermore, there was confusion between the problem of vagueness of meaning (if you like, "partial interpretation" or "open concept" definition) where a motive is imputed and the probabilistic character of the inference to it from fallible behavioral indicators. A motive is itself an open concept, and it is partly because of that openness—that is, the stochastic character of the strands in the nomological net and even the qualitative incompleteness of the net itself—that there is epistemic doubt, in some cases very great.

Of course, it is silly to think that the fact that you can have warranted doubt about an empirical statement somehow makes it illegitimate, and even sillier to think that there should be differences in degree of doubtfulness under such circumstances. I don't think that Tolman or McDougall or Skinner or Freud needed to be philosophically sophisticated or to use any technical philosophy-of-science jargon in expounding this, but it is perhaps a help in this day and age to have some of that available. So here we have another example of where a rather unphilosophical, tough-scientist approach will enable you to make progress, as will a highly sophisticated and technically competent philosophy-of-science approach.

Nobody today holds a strict deductive model, including Hempel, who propounded it. However, nobody has succeeded in presenting a useful meaning of scientific explanation that is totally unlike the Hempel model. All explanations that people are willing to take seriously look somewhat like that model, given the allowance of statistical laws together with suitable *ceteris paribus* clauses. Until somebody shows us what an explanation is that differs radically from a modified deductive model, I am not going to be impressed with the admittedly valid criticism of Hempel. This is made easy for me—and, I gather, difficult for some people—because I take it as perfectly appropriate to overlap "causes" with "reasons," and I totally reject the ordinary-language claim that this cannot be done. Abstract reasons in Plato's heaven are not causes. But the hearing of reasons, stating of reasons, believing in reasons, tokening of sentences that mean reasons are events in the world and partake in the causal order. I would maintain with Tolman that the difference between a lawyer making a complicated argument to the Supreme Court in order to protect the taxpayer and a rat turning right in order to get food at the end in the goal box has not been shown to be other than a difference of very great and impressive degree, that is, not of kind. The imputation of motive to a person performing an instrumental act does not differ in any essential qualitative way from the implication of an unconscious motive, as in psychoanalysis, or a nonworded motive to the white rat. It's a matter of vagueness and a matter of degree of evidentiary support.

TESTING A WEAK THEORY

It seemed to me that our preoccupation with the demise of positivism and our worries (or self-reassurances) about obtaining some sort of "scientific ideal" in the social sciences led us to spend considerable time on the wrong things rather than on the really important topics. The latter are mostly variations on the same theme, namely, how weak theories can be strongly tested. I agree with Sir Karl Popper that talking about the meanings of words, or more sophisticatedly, about the nature of scientific concepts, is almost always a waste of time.

The important thing to clarify is the structure of the theoretical network and the resulting empirical tests. When do reductionist strategies work? How does one tell whether they are working, preferably early on, before a lot of time is wasted on them prematurely? Is it possible to concoct fairly strong tests of weak theories, and how should this be done? When is quantification worthwhile and when is it premature, or even fake? Can there be a general strategy for sequencing research studies of interaction effects of high order with an eye to generalizability? How should we relate the power function in statistical significance testing to the desire for strong falsifiability, since we know that the null hypothesis in social science is always false? Is meta-analysis a satisfactory solution of the crude pro/con count of studies found in a typical *Psychological Bulletin* review article? Is Lakatos's distinction between progressive and degenerating research programs, despite recent criticisms of it, a worthwhile distinction that could be helpful to the social scientist? How should the *ceteris paribus* clause be used in early stages of theory building? In saving what might be a good theory from premature death by quick falsification, when we use what we hope is "legitimate ad hoc–ery," can any useful rules of thumb be stated about degrees and kinds of ad hoc–ery, such as Lakatos's three kinds? Are any generalizations possible from the history of science about the fruitfulness or wickedness of ad hoc–ery of various sorts at different stages in the testing of a theory?

Obviously each of these topics deserves a separate paper longer than the present one. So I confine myself to a more intensive discussion of only one, the biggest one, as I see it. I shall propound a controversial thesis, deliberately stated in strong language.

> Thesis: Owing to the abusive reliance upon significance testing—rather than point or interval estimation, curve shape, or ordination—in the social sciences, the usual article summarizing the state of the evidence on a theory (such as appears in the *Psychological Bulletin*) is nearly useless.

The distribution of obtained significant and nonsignificant results is an arbitrary and complex artifact of eight methodological factors largely unrelated to a theory's verisimilitude, namely, (a) experimental design, (b) inherent construct validity of measures, (c) reliability of measures, (d) properties of the statistical power functions, (e) presence and size of higher-order interactions, (f) verisimilitude of auxiliary theories relied on in deriving empirical predictions, (g) differential submission rate of manuscripts reporting significant versus nonsignificant findings, and (h) editorial bias as to the same. The net result of these influences on the pro/con count is that usually such a heap of studies is well nigh uninterpretable.

Colleagues think I exaggerate in putting it this way. That's because they can't stand to face the scary implications of the thesis taken literally, which is how I mean it. Even though it is stated in all good elementary statistics texts, including the excellent and most widely used one by Hays (1973, 415–17), it still does not seem generally recognized that the null hypothesis in the life sciences is almost always false—if taken literally—in designs that involve any sort of self-selection or correlations found in the organisms as they come, that is, where perfect randomization of treatments by the experimenter does not exhaust the manipulations. Hence even "experimental" (rather than statistical or file data) research will exhibit this if interaction effects involving attributes of the persons are studied. Consequently, whether or not the null hypothesis is rejected is simply and solely a function of statistical power.

Now this is a mathematical point; it does not hinge upon your preferences in philosophy of science or your belief in this or that kind of theory or instrument. Whether investigator Jones, in testing theory T with a predicted observational relationship, succeeds in refuting H_o depends upon the eight factors listed above. Expanding a bit on these, the region of the independent variable hyperspace in which the levels of a factor are chosen is something Fisher didn't have to worry much about in agronomy, for obvious reasons; but most psychologists have not paid enough attention to Brunswik on representative design.

There will usually be wide variation over studies in the intrinsic qualitative construct validity of the measures (both of input and output variables). The reliability of the measures will typically vary widely from values as low as .4 to as high as .95, and hence highly variable upper bounds are set on the net construct validity after attenuation by unreliability. As a result, the ordering of two measures as to their net attenuated construct validity may be quite different from the ordering as to their intrinsic qualitative construct validity because of marked differences in reliability.

While sample size exerts the biggest impact upon a statistical power for a given degree of real difference, N will be only partly a function of rational considerations stemming from the research problems but heavily a function of historical and geographical accidents, chronological age and status of the investigator, whether a study is a Ph.D. dissertation or part of a five-year project. Now the frightening (and hence repressed) point is that when we scramble these different factors and get a net power function for refuting H_o, the relationship between the probability of successfully refuting it and the verisimilitude of the substantive theory can hardly be large. I know of no realistic way of saying how small it could be, but any such relation would necessarily be markedly attenuated because of these other factors, none of which is of small magnitude in its impact.

This effect would be there even if the size of a difference in standard score form were itself a monotone function of the verisimilitude of the theory, which nobody claims it is. Most psychological theories in the "soft areas" of psychology do not even attempt to say how large an effect ought to be if perfectly measured, or even whether the theory implies that the main effect of a theoretical variable should be bigger than that from other compatible theories that contribute to determining what happens in the domain. For example, I might think that failure would have a different kind of effect on upper- and lower-class teenagers but that there would also be an interaction with IQ and also with the kind of task in which they failed (which already gives me some bad interaction problems). But even if I thought I had a powerful theory, I would not be likely to say that the self-concept from social class is therefore the biggest factor influencing a child's response to failure or success. And I certainly would not be in a position to say anything metric about these values. Even if the hapless reviewer is more sophisticated than most of them seem to be, when he looks at this pattern of "$p < .05$," and "$p < .01$," and "$n.s.$," he is not in a position to judge the extent to which the obtaining or nonobtaining of a statistically significant effect is artifactual with respect to the testing of the theoretical substance. So it seems to me that the first step is to get that message across to psychologists who write and read such literature surveys. So far as I can make out, not one in twenty scholars in may field is appreciably aware of the problem.

I believe there's a scandalous underestimation of the net impact of a number of factors on what the usual crude pro/con tally of significant and nonsignificant results probes. What my colleague Lykken calls the "ambient noise," or "crud factor," is of unknown average value, but it can hardly be supposed to be less than, say, in correlation terms, Pearson $r = .25$ in the soft areas of psychology. "Everything is correlated with everything," and .25 is probably not a bad average value. Randomly chosen individual differences variates do not tend to correlate zero. Of course in real life, the experimenter is usually correlating variates that belong, at least commonsensically, to some restricted domain. We don't usually do studies correlating social dominance with spool-packing ability or eye color. So a more realistic guesstimate of the crud factor, the expected correlation between a randomly chosen pair of variates belonging to a substantive domain, would be higher than that, maybe as high as .30.

Suppose an experimenter divides a group of subjects at the median on an input variable and includes all of these in the study as "high" and "low." If the input variable is normally distributed, then the difference in mean value between subjects in the high and the low group is around 1.6 sigma. If the crud factor is .30 in a broadly demarcated behavior domain, it would yield about a .5 sigma deviation expected difference on the dependent variable. If $N_1 = N_2 = 32$, we have a statistical power of around .50. So aside from the

verisimilitude of the theory—it might in the extreme case have absolutely no truth in it—the research has about an even chance of
getting a statistically significant result at $\alpha = .05$. Now of course the
trend could be in either direction, so we might say there is about
a .25 probability of getting a statistically significant result "in the
right direction," that is, in the direction "predicted from theory,"
even though the theory has nothing to do with obtaining the effect.
A random matching of theories with trend direction is, of course,
set too low at $p = 1/2$, since the crud factor in most research areas is
heavily concentrated in positive correlations and in some domains
(e.g., ability, psychopathology) may yield a positive manifold.

When one surveys a body of research literature under these circumstances, a pro/con outcome tally of, say, 16:4 is far less favor-
able to the theory than it appears. There is an editorial bias in favor
of significant results, partly due to Fisher's true but misleading dic-
tum that H_o cannot be proved, partly to power function problems,
and perhaps to some feeling that they are more interesting or more
informative. This editorial bias multiplies by an author's bias in
submitting papers. Suppose the editorial bias favoring significant
outcome (after excluding papers unacceptable for gross errors in
design) were 2:1, and the author submission bias the same. This
yields a pro/con bias of 4:1 in what studies finally appear in the
literature. So an impressive box score of 16:4 (new theories' box
scores rarely look better than that in *Bulletin* reviews) has arisen
from a latent true pro/con outcome ratio about 1:1; that is, in reality about half of the experiments performed support the theory.

Now assume the investigators (having taken to heart the strictures of Cohen [1977]) have designed their experiments so as to
achieve a power equal to .75, a bit lower than he recommends.
Then the likelihood ratio L_t/L_o of the theory against the crud factor
is about an even 1:1. The true split pro/con (reported + unre-
ported outcomes) being also even, the posterior probability of the
theory on all evidence to date would be the same as the prior. Taking the prior on theories in soft psychology to be, say, $P \leq .10$
(their long-term survival rate is surely no better than that), the Bayesian posterior will then read $P(T/e) \leq .10$. This pessimistic but realistic computation is very different from the usual reviewer
summary that a theory with 16:4 success/failure rate is doing
rather well, is "quite promising," or "deserves further research"; in
reality the posterior odds are 9 to 1 against the theory.

Now I don't mean to say that we all ought to be literally comput-
ing Bayes's theorem and numerical probabilities in this way (al-

though some statisticians would say "Why not?"). Nor do I argue that at this point research on a 16:4 "hits" theory should be stopped. I only emphasize that the apparent 16:4 box score favoring the theory does not really favor it at all.

At this stage, another disturbing element appears. Suppose one accepts the philosophers' maxim "Do not make a mockery of honest ad hoc–ery," and the Lakatosian notion that we forbid the *modus tollens* arrow to be directed at the theory's "hard core" instead of at its protective belt. That's all very well, but the examples that Lakatos and others adduce are from astronomy, physics, and. chemistry, in which the hard core of the theory is clung to (despite a few prima facie falsifiers) because the theory has a lot "in the bank" already. We recognize the unwisdom of premature discarding because of anomalies that are apparent falsifiers. Such a policy does well in sciences where it's possible for a theory to get a lot in the bank early on, as with Kepler, Newton, Mendeleev, or Morgan. But in psychology, what is taken as having a lot in the bank is usually one of these 16:4 tallies.

The point is that understanding the logic and statistics of the situation—the asymmetry between corroboration (which is weak) and falsification (which is strong), the properties of the power function, and the fact that H_o is always false if taken as a literal value—shows us that we get an illusion of having a lot in the bank empirically for theories that are extremely weak and that have as yet passed only feeble tests. So that "honest ad hoc–ery" is here being performed on a theory that we have very little reason to believe has appreciable verisimilitude on the basis of its early track record of 16:4 "successful" outcomes. This mess arises partly from the inherent difficulty of testing weak theories, but also from slavish adherence to significance testing as the research method.

For the reader who is wondering whether he follows the preceding reasoning, I can provide a short, simple litmus test. An objection occurs to what I have just said: "But surely there is some author and editor bias in submitting articles in the biological and physical sciences, and they're doing pretty well; so why are you making it out to be so terrible in psychology and sociology?" If that strikes you as a tough question, then you haven't fully got the point yet. The point is this: A selective bias in manuscript submission and editorial acceptance exerts its malignant effect via the widespread abuse of null hypothesis refutation, treated as if it were a powerful method of testing weak theories. Social scientists have a tendency to think that this bias in what subset of performed investigations reaches the published research literature is a sort of minor blemish on our research methods, perhaps suggesting mild social pressure (advice to editors) to change these habits and some slight modification of the way we think about the published corpus. That is a gross understatement of the case I am making here. The asymmetry between falsification and so-called confirmation in inductive logic is insufficiently appreciated by investigators and scholars. Combined with the relative feebleness of the hurdle that a theory has to pass if all we require is that "the girls be different from the boys," this asymmetry has the result that even a rather small bias in article submission, in addition to another small to moderate bias in acceptance, means that the tally of pro/con empirical outcomes on a particular theory should undergo some correction down toward the pro/con midline. Even if the bias were equally present in physics or astronomy, it would not have the catastrophic consequence it does for the social sciences because physicists and astronomers do not normally test theories by refuting the null hypothesis. In the rare instances when a significance test is used in physics, chemistry, or genetics, it is used in precisely the reverse of the way we use it in psychology and sociology, as I pointed out seventeen years ago (Meehl 1967). When the equivalent of a significance test is employed in physics, astronomy, chemistry, and most of genetics, it is employed to falsify the substantive theory by showing that the empirical results lie outside the range of instrumental and sampling error. Physicists, of course, were using the old "probable error" this way before R. A. Fisher was born. And it is worth noting that the invention of chi-square by Karl Pearson at the turn of the century was intended to be used in this way, namely, to measure "frequency discordance." That is, the question was whether the observed frequencies in a table of frequency distribution departed from that specified by the substantive theory. But when we have only a directional expectation, such as is generated by the weak theories of soft psychology and sociology, such a point prediction is not made. What we do is refute the null hypothesis and then take its contrary as being strongly corroborative of the theory, whereas in reality, it is only weakly corroborative. That means that significance tests are used in the opposite way in the physical sciences from the way they are used in the social sciences, except in those rare cases where the social sciences generate a sufficiently powerful model to make numerical point predictions or narrow interval predictions.

In physics it wouldn't matter much if a few investigators failed to send in their negative result papers. Given ten investigations of a theory prediction that such and such point values within such and such narrow tolerances should be found in the laboratory, and eight of those come out right, it would be an astounding coincidence if the theory had no verisimilitude. It is extremely difficult to explain eight of them coming out correctly, assuming low verisimilitude, whereas it is not nearly as difficult to explain that two of the ten depart significantly outside the tolerance. That is a totally different state of affairs from the case of refuting H_o in a weak psychological theory, where the crud factor is available to explain all sorts of tendencies, and a box score of eight to two, even if wrongly taken at face value, does not speak strongly for the theory substance.

The physicist, chemist, or astronomer can put good money in the theory bank by a rather small run of successes because of the fact that they all involve point predictions or narrow interval predictions. And this money in the epistemic bank is what warrants physical scientists engaging in honest ad hoc–ery, lest a good theory with high verisimilitude be prematurely slain. The point is that a box score of 16:4 in psychology, given the bias in what appears in the journals, puts very little money in the bank, so that when combined with the low prior ratio on almost any theory in these fields, it means a posterior in Bayes' formula that is unimpressive.

I don't know the facts about selective reporting in the physical sciences, but it is obvious that a discipline in which a "negative result" means a significant deviation from a theoretically predicted point value constitutes very much stronger information than the failure to refute H_o in the social sciences. For that reason, I would be surprised if the reluctance of authors to submit insignificant results, or the leaning of editors in favor of accepting significant results, were anywhere near as strong in physics as in psychology and sociology. Because of the problems of the statistical power function, even a falsification in psychology doesn't count as heavily as a measurement of a velocity falling outside the experimental error counts against a theory in physics.

One hesitates to paint such a bleak picture without having a clever and convincing "cure" up his sleeve, but, alas, I am unable to provide one. I do, however, have some constructive suggestions. An absolute precondition for improving matters with regard to the testing of theories and the early elimination of theoretical turkeys is "negative," to wit, to see that a bad problem exists. There is a widespread, massive intellectual inertia in my profession with respect to null hypothesis refutation as a tactic, witness the fact that the ma-

jority of psychologists in the soft areas continue to proceed un-
apologetically in this way, despite numerous articles (going back
almost a quarter of a century in highly visible journals) that have
raised the problem from a variety of standpoints and a whole book
dealing with the significance test controversy at a high level of philosophical and statistical sophistication that appeared almost a decade and a half ago (Morrison & Henkel 1970).

The first thing we must do is to increase the general awareness
of the younger generation of teachers and researchers that, given
the nature of our subject matter and the ubiquitous crud factor, the
corroboration of weak theories by a moderately successful run of
refutations of H_o is a feeble research strategy. The widespread
adoption of that strategy accounts in part for the long history of
failed psychological and sociological doctrines, each of which gave
the illusion of great promise in its early phase. People just don't
want to face the unpleasant fact that the base rate of long-term
survival of theories in the social sciences is very small, so that the
combination of this with the peculiarities of the significance test do
not objectively yield the degree of corroboration of substantive theories that is generally supposed they do.

SUBSTANCE AND SIGNIFICANCE

For scholars to get the full point, it is not sufficient that they understand about the crud factor and about the statistical power function
in relation to the crud factor. It is crucial also to understand the
difference between a substantive theory and a statistical hypothesis
that is indirectly related to it. It is salutary to reflect upon the reason why null hypothesis testing was fairly successful in the area of
its first application (agronomy), namely, the very small (negligible
except to a professional philosopher) logical distance or difference
in meaning between the counter–null hypothesis and the substantive theory. I find that few psychologists and sociologists are clear
about that, which I think reflects the manner in which undergraduate (and even some graduate) teaching of statistics is conducted. In
such instruction, no professor should introduce students to the
idea of doing a significance test without first distinguishing between substantive theory and statistical hypothesis, and then going
on to point out that in agriculture, where Fisher made his great
contributions, there is essentially no difference between the statement "The fertilized plots yielded more bushels of corn" and the
statement "Fertilizing causes more corn to grow." When we refute
H_o statistically (directionality being taken for granted in agron-

omy), we corroborate its alternative, the counter–null hypothesis, which is the first statement. The confidence with which H_o is refuted is in essence identical with the confidence we are entitled to have in our substantive causal statement.

In contrast, when refuting the null hypothesis as a means of corroborating a complex structural (compositional), functional, or developmental theory of neurosis, or perception or social dominance or whatever, this quasi-identity between the content of what we prove by refuting H_o and what we want to prove substantively does not exist. This is partly because of the nature of the subject matter, since psychological theories usually involve hypothetical constructs while the agronomy theory is essentially a first-level observational inductive statement, and partly because of the ubiquitous and non-negligible crud factor, which could be understood by a Bayesian as a sizeable box of viable competitive theories that go in the denominator of Bayes's formula. There is a surreptitious tendency to mentally subtract the significance level from one, so that the complement $(1 - \alpha)$ gets vaguely "attached" to our confidence in the theory. Nobody explicitly does this. But the presence of those double and triple asterisks in a table of t-tests or F-tests (Meehl 1978) produces a misleading degree of subjective confidence by an unconscious assimilation of this complement value $(1 - \alpha)$ to the probability of the substantive theory. People commit, without being aware of it, the fallacy of thinking "If the theory weren't true, then there is only a probability of .05 of this big a difference arising," when of course we are not entitled to say anything even vaguely approaching this.

If there were adequate appreciation of the relative feebleness of null hypothesis refutation as a theory tester, as well as of its malignant combination with manuscript submission and editorial acceptance policies to give a biased box score in the published literature, what then might be done constructively? I trust my comments will not be misconstrued to mean that I disagree with the desirability of adequate statistical power as proposed forcefully by Cohen (1977), an important methodological thesis still not properly recognized by social scientists. It should be more widely emphasized that in order to set up a meaningful test of a substantive scientific theory, one needs, if employing significance testing at all, an adequate value of the power function. If more people met this requirement in conducting their research, then editors would not be presented with a dilemma of "keeping something out of the literature that should be known" while realizing that failure to refute the null hypothesis does not speak strongly against a particular substantive theory in the investigation because the power was too low. The APA Board of Publications should address itself to this question and adopt a strong policy.

I think it is scandalous that editors still accept manuscripts in which the author presents tables of significance tests without giving measures of overlap or such basic descriptive statistics as might enable the reader to do rough computations, from means and standard deviations presented, as to what the overlap is. In my view, it is inexcusable to present quantitative data in such a form that the reader is unable even to ask how many standard deviation units the experimental group was above the controls. Such data reporting is as incomplete as it would be not to mention which group intelligence test was used or how many degrees of freedom or where the sample was obtained. This is a gross defect in reporting scientific findings. Editors ought to arbitrarily reject such papers, so that members of the profession would come to take it for granted that measures of overlap and effect size must be presented. I don't wish to be dogmatic about what form should be used, although my own view is that both a metrical and a counting form should normally be employed and, if possible, the proportion of variance accounted for by the experimental factor.

It goes without saying that any statement of hits and misses by a cutting score should be accompanied by sufficient base-rate information and information about distribution shapes, so that the reader with clinical interest can make a meaningful assessment of how much has been achieved (Meehl & Rosen 1955). One of the best ways to reduce the illusion of scientific power that comes from writing "$p < .001***$" would be an accompanying table indicating—as would be very often the case with a test advocated for clinical purposes—that by using Fisbee's Projective Tennis Ball Test you can do 5 percent better at diagnosing schizophrenia in your clinic than you could by flipping pennies or guessing the base rate.

Ideally, of course, one would like to have stronger substantive theories, that is, theories that are capable of generating point predictions or relatively narrow interval predictions so that the significance test would have a meaning comparable to what it has in chemistry and physics or genetics. That is, we inquire whether our data depart significantly from the point value or the narrow interval that the theory demands. In such cases, the theory takes a high risk of falsification and consequently, if it succeeds in passing the hurdles, receives substantial corroboration. It should be realized that moderately strong theories can sometimes generate predictions of patterns, of decreasing values of rank orders, of function shapes (e.g., that something will be "more or less ogival," even though not exactly the integral of Gaussian function), and so forth.

I sometimes think that we social scientists suffer from a strange mixture of optimism and pessimism in this respect. On the one hand, we have been brainwashed by Fisherian statistics into thinking that refutation of H_o is a powerful way of testing substantive theories. On the other hand, when urged to generate point or narrow-range predictions, we take it for granted that in the soft areas of psychology, it will be totally beyond our powers. Maybe the latter is the case, but I'm not convinced that it is. When one talks to applied mathematicians working in new fields like catastrophe theory, for instance, one hears that rather weak semiqualitative statements can sometimes be put together in ways that lead to rather specific quantitative predictions with a modicum of mathematical ingenuity. For example, one does not have to know the microstructure of a system in a way that points to predicting actual numerical values in order to be able to say that with increases in x, y must increase in a decelerated fashion up to the place that a third variable z equals 0, after which the derivative of y with respect to x increases.

There's an educational problem in psychology in this respect because we have a chicken and egg situation. Psychologists in the soft areas do not learn much of any mathematics (I don't count memorizing how to do an F-test as "mathematics"), and it is hard for the faculty to insist that they do so (especially if the faculty themselves don't know much math) because the student understandably wants to know what good it will do him since they don't *use* very much mathematics, but only t-tests, in his subdiscipline. But of course if nobody working in a given discipline knows any mathematics, they will never be able to find out whether it's possible to generate stronger semiquantitative predictions from relatively weak substantive theories.

It is interesting to ask whether research methods courses should explain the problem of higher-order interactions as a source of poor generalizability. There is nothing sinful about working with minitheories confined to a narrow domain. But a minitheory whose domain is narrowly restricted by, say, demographic variables is likely to be a rather poor minitheory. One suspects it would be possible, based on a careful literature survey, to write down a list of a dozen demographic factors and another dozen major methods factors that turn out to be the most nefarious in preventing strong generalizability of findings. It seems that there ought to be a research strategy that would take account of such expectable higher-order interactions, so that when a substantive theory of some process, say, social dominance or visual-perceptual learning or whatever, is proposed, there would be a recommended sequence for research studies aiming to test it, based upon our prior knowledge of the demographic and methods factors that seem to be most commonly a source of failures to replicate.

There is a problem here about the degree of densification in the nuisance parameter space that philosophers of science and statisticians should work on. It arises partly from the neglect of Brunswik's emphasis upon sampling situations as well as organisms. The "levels" of an experimental factor are not usually very problematic in agriculture, and reasonable levels are sometimes easy to select in fields like education. In domains where reasonable levels cannot be chosen on purely economic or ethical grounds, the problem of the distribution of patterns of experimental factors in a study of interactions becomes more difficult and complicated.

Finally, despite the absence of a rigorous definition of verisimilitude by the philosophers of science, I remain persuaded that some such concept is crucial in thinking about theory evaluation. Even a strong falsification (in which the auxiliary hypotheses are hardly in reasonable doubt) should be regularly viewed in fields like psychology and sociology as speaking strongly against the theory in its present form, rather than proving the theory to be deserving of instant execution and all further investigation of it abandoned forthwith. My emphasis upon falsification and the feebleness of H_o refutation as a corroborator on the positive side does not mean that I disagree with the important qualifications and amendments of the original Popperian position by such critics as Lakatos.

I think some epistemological problems in social sciences cannot profitably be discussed unless the discussants are quite thoroughly familiar with concepts in philosophy of science. I note a tendency in some quarters to think that you can do philosophy of science quite casually. That is a grave mistake. My position is definitely not that all or most social scientists should know technical philosophy of science. What offends me is that from a state of philosophical ignorance, they advance methodological arguments that are inherently philosophical. My point is that if you are going to make use of what are in their very nature philosophical or epistemological arguments to defend or criticize a substantive or methodological scientific position (such as a certain research strategy or a preference for certain kinds of measuring instruments or a certain class of theories having properties in common), if you are going to employ philosophy of science for this purpose, you ought to know something about it.

If social scientists are going to proceed satisfactorily to some set of near-consensus conclusions on an accurate description of the state of affairs in a specified domain and what we should start doing instead, matters of philosophy of science and basic epistemology must either not come up because the nature of the topics being discussed does not inherently move to them or come up but be "settled" easily because the scientists already agree on at least an implicit philosophy of science, no matter how wrong-headed it may be. If the subject matter does force confrontation of philosophy of science and epistemology issues but the social scientists do not agree about those issues, they must possess technical competence—almost as much as the philosopher himself—before they can consider them fruitfully.

References

Carnap, R. 1936. Testability and meaning, part 1. *Philosophy of Science* 3: 420–71.

———. 1937. Testability and meaning, part 2. *Philosophy of Science* 4: 2–40.

———. 1946a. Remarks on induction and truth. *Philosophy and Phenomenological Research* 6: 590–602.

———. 1946b. Rejoinder to Mr. Kaufmann's reply. *Philosophy and Phenomenological Research* 6: 609–11.

———. 1948. Reply to Felix Kaufmann. *Philosophy and Phenomenological Research* 9: 300–304.

———. 1949. Truth and confirmation. In *Readings in philosophical analysis,* ed. H. Feigl and W. Sellers. New York: Appleton-Century-Crofts.

Cohen, J. 1977. *Statistical power analysis for the behavioral sciences.* 2d ed. New York: Academic Press.

Cronbach, L. J., and Meehl, P. E. 1955. Construct validity in psychological tests. *Psychological Bulletin* 52: 281–302.

Hays, W. L. 1973. *Statistics for the social sciences.* 2d ed. New York: Holt, Rinehart and Winston.

Hull, C. L. 1943. *Principles of behavior.* New York: Appleton-Century.

McDougall, W. 1923. *Outline of psychology.* New York: Scribner's.

Meehl, P. E. 1967. Theory-testing in psychology and physics: A methodological paradox. *Philosophy of Science* 34: 103–115.

————. 1978. Theoretical risks and tabular asterisks: Sir Karl, Sir Ronald, and the slow progress of soft psychology. *Journal of Consulting and Clinical Psychology* 46: 806–34.

————. 1983. Subjectivity in psychoanalytic inference: The nagging persistence of Wilhelm Fliess's Achensee question. In *Testing Scientific Theories*, ed. J. Earman. Minnesota Studies in the Philosophy of Science, vol. 10. Minneapolis: University of Minnesota Press.

Meehl, P. E., and Rosen, A. 1955. Antecedent probability and the efficiency of psychometric signs, patterns, or cutting scores. *Psychological Bulletin* 52: 194–216.

Morrison, D. E., and Henkel, R., eds. 1970. *The significance test controversy.* Chicago: Aldine.

Murray, H. A. 1938. *Explorations in personality.* New York: Oxford University Press.

Pap, A. 1958. *Semantics and necessary truth.* New Haven: Yale University Press.

————. 1953. Reduction-sentences and open concepts. *Methodos* 5: 3–30.

Skinner, B. F. 1938. *The behavior of organisms.* New York: Appleton-Century.

Thurstone, L. L. 1935. *The vectors of mind.* Chicago: University of Chicago Press.

Tolman, E. C. 1932. *Purposive behavior in animals and men.* New York: Century.

Waismann, F. 1945. Verifiability. *Proceedings of the Aristotelian Society, Supplement* 19: 119–50.

15 Philosophy of Science and the Potentials for Knowledge in the Social Sciences

Alexander Rosenberg

A great deal of the preconference material, and much of the deliberation of the conference, was taken up with matters in the philosophy of science (for examples, see chaps. 6 and 8, this volume). In the discussions, I maintained that this focus was misplaced and that we should have broached more distinctively social scientific problems and solutions. In this paper, I attempt to sketch the role that philosophy can be expected to play in determining the potentials for knowledge in social science. This sketch will at least explain, if it does not justify, my view that at this stage philosophy has little to contribute and my appeal that such discussions stay clear of philosophy.

Our aim was to assess the potentials for knowledge in social science. It is natural to suppose that this is a question to which philosophy is directly relevant, since one traditional task of philosophy has been to provide theories of what knowledge is, of its sources and justification. This is the province of epistemology and its subdivision, the philosophy of science. The definitions and theories of knowledge elaborated in these subjects are often advanced as implicit or explicit prescriptions for how to proceed in the acquisition of knowledge. Such alternative theories, and there have been many, compete with each other to the extent each claims to be exhaustive and exclusive as an account of knowledge. However, exponents of each theory have often been satisfied with a more limited writ. Each of the different kinds of knowledge satisfying a different definition may be acceptable for a limited range or kind of objects of knowledge, though none is universal in its applicability. Thus some writers have distinguished religious knowledge, ethical knowledge, natural knowledge, common-sense knowledge, linguistic knowledge; and they have claimed that differences among the objects of each of these sorts of knowledge make for differences in the nature, scope, and justification of our knowledge of God, values, natural phenomena, persons, language, and so on. Accordingly, all the different kinds of knowledge (and theories of them) will be compatible, because none competes with another when their ranges of application are properly circumscribed.[1] Such epistemological relativism has all the virtues of tolerance, and all of its vices.

If we adopt such an attitude, the serious question becomes which of the indefinitely many kinds of knowledge thus defined is a fruitful one to attempt to acquire. In other words, which definition of knowledge shall we adopt for purposes of social science? The widespread dissatisfaction evinced at the conference with the account of knowledge of the logical empiricists and their followers reflects the view that their definition of knowledge is not a fruitful one for the human disciplines. Employing it has not seemed to enable us to acquire much knowledge about human behavior. There are two alternative morals to draw from this failure. One is to deny that the logical empiricist account is a useful or fruitful definition of the sort of knowledge we seek in social science (Gergen 1982, chap. 2). The second is to admit that since this is the kind of knowledge we seek, and we are not likely to succeed in providing any, there is not much potential for knowledge in social science.[2]

The first of these two alternative is of course vastly to be preferred. And that is why much effort, at the conference and elsewhere, has been expended by social scientists to show that this definition of knowledge is unsuitable either for the study of human phenomena or, more generally, for the study of any phenomena whatever, natural or human (cf. Manicas & Secord 1983). It is to establish one or the other of these two conclusions that so many social scientists who are dissatisfied with progress in their own disciplines engage in philosophy and why they treat Kuhn's *Structure of Scientific Revolutions* (1970) as a work of signal importance. They hope to undermine the claims of one definition of knowledge for their domain of objects and to generate a new one that does justice to their disciplines by sanctioning their results as "knowledge." This, I venture to say, is why so many social scientists turn to philosophy when faced with the question of limning the potential for knowledge in the social sciences. If we settle for the received view of what knowledge is, the potential looks pretty slim. So the first task is to provide a new definition of knowledge.

Accordingly, we find among social scientists some considerable controversy about which characterizations of knowledge will provide the most fruitful prescriptions for its accumulation. But if this controversy is pursued purely at the level and with the tools of philosophy, it is no more likely to be solved than Hume's two-hundred-fifty-year-old problem of induction, or Plato's two-millennia-old problem of the ontological status of numbers. A purely epistemological exploration of the strengths and weaknesses of alternative theories of knowledge will neither come to any philosophical consensus, nor will it advance social science in the slightest.

Given a range of alternative accounts of knowledge, the only way to decide which will really be fruitful for social science, which will make the potentials for knowledge considerable, is by actually employing them in the work of social scientists. This is what makes the work of Kleinman so arresting, no matter what one's disagreements with him over matters of philosophy. His employment of a controversial conception of knowledge, with determinable results, is reported and discussed in Kleinman 1980 (see also Eisenberg & Kleinman 1981).

It is the agreed upon successes in solving the problems facing the social scientist that must in the end determine the choice between differing philosophical conceptions, for the relation of philosophy to the social sciences is one ultimately of dependence and not priority. Like all very general and abstract theory, philosophical claims are decided after the less theoretical facts are "in," when consensus on lower-level findings has been attained and now begins to need explanation. The reason is that philosophy is nothing more or less than extremely general and abstract theory, on a cognitive par with theory in the rest of science, natural and social. For too long, social and natural scientists have viewed philosophy either as empty speculation or as a necessary a priori preliminary, an essential foundation, which must be firmly and finally fixed in order to establish the rules and prescriptions whereby the rest of science can proceed. Both of these conceptions are profoundly mistaken.

If the history of the twentieth-century philosophy of science has shown anything, it is that there is no demarcation principle between philosophy and science proper. This is something that both antipositivists and postpositivists have agreed on. What it means is that there is no difference in kind between methodological rules, metaphysical theses, epistemological analyses, and substantive science. Claims that come under each of these headings are all on a par with respect to "cognitive significance," evidence, coherence, and explanatory power.

For a long time, some of these types of claims, especially the avowedly metaphysical and epistemological ones, were viewed as empirically meaningless, as pseudosolutions to pseudoproblems. At the same time, methodological principles were treated as conventions, definitions that scientists could take or leave. By contrast with such "analytic" statements—true in virtue of the meanings of the terms they contain—real scientific claims were held to be "synthetic," to have empirical content; their truth or falsity was a function of their factual content, and they differ from these other sorts of claims in being open to direct or indirect observational confirmation and disconfirmation.

However, the distinctions these categorizations were based on turn out to be without justification, or at any rate without the sort of justification that will meet the logical positivist's high standard. (The locus classicus of this now widely accepted conclusion is Quine 1953.) We cannot distinguish the metaphysically meaningless from the empirically significant because no adequate principle of empirical meaningfulness or cognitive significance can be formulated. There is no formal way to legitimate the physicist's quark while delegitimating Hegel's *Weltgeist*. We cannot separate analytic statements, true in virtue of form alone, from synthetic ones, true or false in virtue of the facts, because we cannot identify the form of a statement independently from its content. And the assessment of methodological conventions has been shown to be indistinguishable from that of empirical hypotheses. The succession of methodologies from essentialism to inductivism to hypotheticodeductivism tracks the succession of dominant research programs from Aristotle's through Newton's to contemporary microphysics.

This means that we cannot draw lines between philosophy and science. Rather, there is a continuum along which both lie. It is a continuum from reports of the most minute, factual, ideographic detail, up through generalizations, across theory, along toward whole research programs, and all the way up to rank philosophical speculation. Questions in the philosophy of science are clearly on the research program–rank speculation end of the continuum. How are such questions to be decided? When do they need to be faced? The answers to these two questions are the same as the answers to questions about how and when other highly theoretical issues are to be decided.

The function of theoretical claims is that of explaining and systematizing lower-level findings and generalizations. Their relations to the lowest level factual claims of a discipline are always highly indirect and mediated by a vast network of auxiliary hypotheses.

For example, quantum theory explains and systematizes the high school experiments of reagent chemistry only via its connection to atomic theory and the periodic table of the elements. And because the connection to findings is indirect and mediated, a given high-level theory is in itself consistent with a larger number of mutually incompatible possible findings at the most concrete levels of findings and reports. Equally, any particular finding is compatible with an indefinitely large number of broad theories that might ultimately explain it and link it to other findings. This is what makes theory construction so undisciplined and creative an undertaking. But it is nonetheless an essential one, at the right time and place. A set of findings, no matter how large, never points unambiguously to a single theory, and a small set of them does not even pick out a manageable range of possible theories. Therefore no theory can sensibly be assessed until a great deal of data is in. This means that theories can only be assessed relatively late in the scientific process. For only then will there be enough data and enough auxiliary information to narrow the field to a small number of theories.

Two examples of this relation between very general theory and fairly restricted findings are provided by physical geometry and linguistic translation. The local, terrestrial findings of surveyors and mapmakers about spatial relations are compatible with an indefinite number of alternative global geometries, both Euclidean and non-Euclidean. They do not point to a unique geometry or even to a very small set of geometries as the correct axiomatization of the spatial relations uncovered by terrestrial investigation. The twenty-five-hundred-year-old conviction that they did pick out a unique geometry, Euclid's, turned out to be quite false. And yet it would have been hopelessly premature to suggest that this axiomatization was mistaken until new astronomical data, and several important auxiliary hypotheses, saw the light of day. Moreover, this new data undid, not only the physicist's conviction that space was Euclidean, but also the philosopher's theory that Euclidean geometry was a body of a priori necessary propositions.

The relation of a theory of the semantics and syntax of a language to a body of translation equivalences between that language and another presents a similar example, nearer home for the social scientist. Any finite body of biconditionals equating expressions in one language to those of another is consistent with any of an indefinitely large number of different and incompatible dictionaries and grammars for the two languages. Similarly, the two quite incompatible translation schemes can systematize the same finite set of translation equivalences. These equivalences are produced initially with no theory about the structure of the language being translated, and hypotheses about this structure are premature until a considerable body of accepted equivalents is built up. In fact, an articulated theory about the semantics and syntax of the language to be interpreted is quite superfluous for many purposes in any case.

So, data never point to a unique theory and are always compatible with mutually inconsistent theories. In many cases, a great deal of data is needed before the class of potentially explanatory theories is even narrowed to an interesting one. Accordingly, many theoretical disputes may be very premature, and some entirely irrelevant to the uses we put the nontheoretical findings to.

Substitute "philosophies of science" for "theories" in the above passage and the role of such philosophies becomes as clear as that of theories. The stage at which, and the grounds on which, philosophies of science are to be assessed are no different from those on which theories are to be assessed. Deciding on which philosophy of science is right is not a necessary preliminary to doing science. It is a late product of success in other, less theoretical parts of the scientific enterprise. This is what makes debates about the philosophy of science fruitless at this point in the career of the social sciences. We are not yet at a late enough stage in the development of these disciplines to make theoretical discussion very profitable, let alone philosophical treatment illuminating. We are not even at the stage of determining which general, nonphilosophical theory of human behavior is to be preferred, let alone which philosophy of science best accommodates and explains such a theory.

The decision on which is the correct philosophy is no more preliminary to successful social science than is the decision on which is the correct theory of human behavior. Like theories, philosophies do have an important motivating role in the development of a research program. No one can undertake the collection of findings unguided by theory and by at least implicit methodological prescriptions. Whether or not such theoretical and methodological motivation is or ought be explicit, its necessity for organizing research cannot be denied. The same must be said for alternative philosophies of science. They too motivate and direct research, and to the extent research requires theory to guide it, philosophy has the same kind of role that theory has in determining the direction of scientific work.

In denying that philosophical issues need be decided before we can get on to doing science, I do not mean to deny that social scientists can or should take sides on these issues. Only, they should not expect to settle them. Having taken sides, the social scientist must turn away from philosophy, and from theoretical dispute. He must turn to piling up the sort of findings that will in the long run settle these disputes, or that will at any rate narrow the field among alternative social theories or philosophies of science. Moreover, since findings are consistent with diverse and incompatible philosophies of science, we should expect social scientists differently motivated nevertheless to find broad agreement about many, indeed most, of the urgent matters on the current agenda of the social sciences. Given our present state of factual knowledge, differences in philosophy are just much too abstract to make a difference for our understanding of mental illness, or the sociology of crime, aggregate voting behavior, or international relations.

So in plotting the near-term potential for knowledge in social science, philosophical differences should really not intrude at all. Social scientists motivated by different conceptions of knowledge should pretty well agree on the immediate agenda for the acquisition of knowledge; they should agree about what we need to know, and also about what we already know, without recourse to philsophy. Immediate agreement on an epistemology is not needed to address the question of social science's potential to produce knowledge, and it is superfluous at this stage to any estimate of the potential itself, as well as to the kind of knowledge we seek, for estimates of our potential to provide any sort of knowledge in social science can only be framed in the light of actual successes and failures to advance knowledge. On the identification of these successes and failures, there is a prospect of far broader consensus than the vast philosophical differences among scientists would lead us to believe.

Notes

1. This approach to reconciliation among competing routes to knowledge is illustrated and advocated in Donald Levine's contribution to this volume (chap. 11).

2. This is the conclusion of Rosenberg (1983). This pessimism born of the acceptance of empiricist strictures on science is also reflected in Converse (chap. 2, this volume) and in Meehl (1978).

References

Eisenberg, L., and Kleinman, A., eds., 1981. *The relevance of social science for medicine.* Dordrecht: D. Reidel.

Gergen, K. J. 1982. *Toward transformation in social knowledge.* New York: Springer-Verlag.

Kleinman, A. 1980. *Patients and healers in the context of culture: An exploration of the borderline between anthropology, medicine, and psychiatry.* Berkeley: University of California Press.

Kuhn, T. S. 1970. *The structure of scientific revolutions.* 2d ed. Chicago: University of Chicago Press.

Manicas, P. T., and Secord, P. F. 1983. Implications for psychology of the new philosophy of science. *American Psychologist* 38: 399–413.

Meehl, P. E. 1978. Theoretical risks and tabular asterisks: Sir Karl, Sir Ronald, and the slow progress of soft psychology. *Journal of Consulting and Clinical Psychology* 46: 806–34.

Quine, W. V. 1953. Two dogmas of empiricism. In *From a logical point of view.* Cambridge: Harvard University Press.

Rosenberg, A. 1983. Human science and biological science. In *Scientific explanation and understanding,* ed. N. Rescher. Lanham, Md.: University Press of America.

16 Similarity and Collaboration within the Sciences

Philip S. Holzman

SIMILARITY

I should like to select only one aspect of Aaron Cicourel's paper for discussion, although there are many issues that could be addressed in this rich presentation of a method. The issue that I shall focus on concerns the attitude social science adopts toward its own status as a science.

Dr. Cicourel has told us about his study of expert systems. He is concerned with those factors in a medical setting that make a difference in patient care. He asks what it is that helps a physician come to a particular diagnostic conclusion ("Aha! this is rheumatoid arthritis or amyotrophic lateral sclerosis") or to a particular modification of treatment. Dr. Cicourel has detailed for us the many variables that must be considered by the expert in reaching these conclusions, and he has shown how context is an extremely critical variable. The procedures he describes relate to the establishing of a causal analysis of decision making by the expert physician or by the medical team. In this effort, Dr. Cicourel, I believe, has taken an implicit stance supporting the idea that the social sciences are composed of disciplines that deal with causes, in contrast to those who insist that the social sciences deal only with reasons. Therefore the canons of procedure do not differ from those of the natural sciences.

I agree with Dr. Cicourel's implicit stance, and I wish to make that stance explicit by underscoring what I think is a potentially malignant position adopted by some social scientists: namely, that the social sciences are in a domain separated from the natural sciences and that the social sciences do not deal with causes but are concerned with "reasons" and with context to a far greater degree than are the natural sciences.

Dr. Cicourel's work illustrates that the physician and the medical expert system are constantly dealing with relevant causes—not necessary or sufficient causes, but surely relevant ones. For example, cigarette smoking is neither a necessary nor a sufficient cause for developing cancer, but it is a relevant cause. And, I submit, in social sciences as in medicine, we deal mostly with relevant causes. In this respect, I find it hard to understand the essentially apologetic attitude on the part of social scientists with respect to their own discipline that because there is a paucity of discoveries of necessary and sufficient causes, the discipline is essentially in a separate domain together with those hermeneutic disciplines like literary criticism and textual interpretation. The stance of these scholars has been essentially to agree with the logical positivists' position and thereby to acquiesce to the argument that such disciplines as sociology and anthropology are, not sciences, but disciplines concerned with meaning, reasons, and context.

But all phenomena—not only those studied by the social scientists, but the natural sciences as well—are context dependent. The idea that physics deals with phenomena that are not context oriented is a myth. Elasticity, electromagnetic hysteresis, and Coulomb's law illustrate the overwhelming influence of context. The philosopher of physics Adolf Grunbaum has called attention to the fact that if one wants to measure the effect of a particular charged particle, one must consider its velocity, which is finite, and its past history, which goes back throughout its entire existence in all past time. Yet, for the solution of certain problems, aspects of that context do not make a measurable difference. Sometimes it is important to know the context and sometimes it is not. Now, with respect to Dr. Cicourel's work, we need to know when it does make such a difference to diagnosis and treatment if a doctor does not understand a particular patient's folk language. When does ethnicity make a difference in the evaluation of psychotic symptoms? When does socioeconomic status not make a difference with respect to behavior or group phenomena? When can such contextual issues be ignored?

It is not sufficient for the social scientists to tell the scientific public and each other that context and history are important and that social scientists deal with meanings and not causes. Surely, almost anything we do has a meaning, but sometimes the meaning is irrelevant for the purposes of establishing lawfulness of certain variable occurrences. To assume that the social sciences are composed of disciplines that are concerned only with meaning is to retreat to and accept the position foisted upon us by the logical positivists. I question that position for two reasons. First, it accepts the separate domains of the natural sciences and social sciences, a separation that Popper has shown to be erroneous, since all science is conjectural. Second, it places the social sciences within the class of hermeneutic disciplines, those concerned with interpreting texts, and this classification, I submit, is misplaced on at least three counts:

1. If one interprets a passage from Shakespeare or a passage in one of Saint Paul's letters, the text that will be interpreted is the same one that had been interpreted 300 years ago or 1,000 years ago. No matter what violence the interpretation does to the text, no matter how wrong the interpretation is, the text does not change. But in social science, or in therapeutics—for example, psychotherapy—the text does indeed change in response to the interpretation. Unlike the Pauline letters or the Shakespearean text, the patient changes in some way and the text is no longer the same after the interpretation.

2. As every therapist will attest, when an interpretation of the meaning of the patient's behavior is offered to the patient, the patient will resist that interpretation. But Saint Paul's letters have never resisted interpretation. Therefore one is obliged to state the regularities that describe both the resistance to the interpretation and those that describe the changes that take place as a result of the interpretation. Once this process is entered upon, we are no longer within the discipline of hermeneutics. We are within the realm of nomothetic science.

3. Within a discipline concerned with meanings, meanings have relevance and existence only with respect to the awareness of another person. Lawful regularities of behavior exist on levels other than the interpretative. To restrict social science to the level of meanings only would rule out a whole set of regularities that call for social science investigation with respect to lawful regularities. These include nonconscious, or even unconscious, phenomena, the behavior of groups, the sociology of decision making, the problem of testimony, to name only a few.

I submit that the position that social science deals only with reasons and not with causes muddies the scientific waters. Surely many reasons are causes, although some reasons are not causes, as for example, incorrect reasons or rationalizations. It is a type of verbal thaumaturgy to formulate method in terms of reasons and thereby to believe that we have excluded ourselves from the search for causal regularities.

Dr. Cicourel's paper underscores for us the critical issue that social science must be concerned with issues of nomothetic science. Too often in this conference I have heard it stated almost as an axiom that social science is concerned only with the idiographic, the unique event, the irreproducible, and the historical context that is never repeatable. This focus prevents the social science disciplines from going forward to the formulating of lawful regularities that are the hallmark of nomothetic science, and therefore to the stating of critical and important issues for study. I should like to see a conference convened with social scientists who will ask what questions in social sciences cry out to be asked. What should social scientists be investigating? Such a focus would probably not tarry long over the philosophical foundations of the discipline. Yet the idiographic approach is important only as a phase in the developing of knowledge. It is the phase in which hunches are developed and creative clues are sifted. But to remain at that level restricts the social sciences to descriptions of events, to essays about the human condition that elude scientific adjudication.

I thank Dr. Cicourel for presenting to us his work because I think it illustrates how, in trying to understand the way expert systems develop, social science is challenged to go beyond the single case, the stage of meaning, the hermeneutic, and to move toward a discipline that is nomothetic.

COLLABORATION

I shall address the question of why it is that social science research has not contributed very much to the field of mental health and mental illness. I suppose I should document the contention that social science has contributed very little to the mental health field, but I will ask you to take that assertion on faith and use as the evidence the fact that we are having a lot of trouble supporting social science research with tax money, and that cases for such support are difficult to make. A second bit of evidence is that several years ago, the Foundations Fund for Research in Psychiatry ran a conference on the interaction of environmental and genetic factors in the schizophrenias. The focus of that conference was on what the social sciences had contributed. Recall that much of the research in mental illness prior to the mid-1950s was heavily oriented to social science. At that conference we were all disappointed, for there were pitifully few solid findings and data. Compare this to the relatively large number of significant advances within the biological aspects of mental illness and health, particularly relating to psychoses. Many of those advances in the biological aspects of mental diseases have come about because of a happy liaison between several branches of medical science, biological science, and the practitioners, that is, those who were "on the line" treating patients. Take just one example. A French surgeon, Laborit, was searching for a compound that would calm his presurgical patients without sedating them, in order to facilitate their undergoing anesthesia. He worked with a pharmaceutical company that eventually modified the molecule of an antihistamine drug, phenergan, and produced a compound that worked for the surgeon. Laborit believed that this new compound, chlorpromazine, calmed his anxious presurgical patients so effectively that he recommended the drug to his psychiatric colleagues for use with their difficult psychotic patients. It indeed seemed to calm those patients as well. Although psychiatrists had long been used to seeing new treatments introduced with fanfare and enthusiasm only to be shown ineffective soon after the initial enthusiasm waned, this drug was different. It seemed to work, not only as a calming agent, but as an unmistakable ameliorator of the psychotic condition. This observation resulted in efforts to understand why it was effective and how it worked. A new ferment within the field of psychopathology began, with members of disparate disciplines collaborating on these problems: neuroanatomy, neuropharmacology, biochemistry, psychology, psychiatry, sociology, epidemiology. Representatives from all of these disciplines began and continue a fruitful collaboration that has been producing knowledge in a productively cumulative manner. True, there have been many false leads, wrong hypotheses, errors of judgment, but there has been an unmistakable advance in knowledge and in therapeutics in the setting of easy communication between basic and applied research.

With few exceptions, we do not have such activity in the social sciences. Some of the exceptions center about the mental health field, for example, John Clausen's laboratory at the National Institute of Mental Health, which flourished in the fifties, and the epidemiological work in New Haven, St. Louis, and a few other cities. This work contrasts with much insular work within the social sciences that has the cast of triviality. The isolation of many social sciences from other branches of science shuts off the accretion of knowledge. The overconcern of the social sciences with problems of methodology and the underrepresentation of issues of substance, as well as an insistence in many quarters on a retreat from nomothetic science, should come to an end.

But how? I believe the University of Chicago could well oversee a renaissance of social science such that the discipline can realize its potential for generating major contributions to mental health, the understanding of mental illness, and the general improvement of life. The University of Chicago committee system can promise much in this respect. Consider a committee with medical, legal, anthropological, sociological, psychological membership. Such a group could direct efforts to discovering the important issues that need study. I am not suggesting that biology alone can or even should do this. I am suggesting that social sciences alone cannot. The critical ingredient in the scientific success story of biological psychiatry is the breakdown of the insularity of psychiatry, that is, the collaboration by several disciplines. I am making a case for institutional support of such collaboration between the social sciences and the biological sciences, and the University of Chicago is in a strategic position to pioneer such a movement.

17 Two Extremes on the Social Science Commitment Continuum

Barbara Frankel

Two important issues in the preceding chapters need further examination. First, I want to discuss some implications of the great variety of epistemic and methodological commitments among social scientists; and second, I want to raise yet again the problem of reductionism, which poses the paradoxical threat that in pursuing physicalist rigor, social scientists may end by studying nonsocial phenomena.

The outlook appears most dim to those strongly committed to traditional norms of unified science, and least so to those willing to consider that "science" may not be unifiable. Converse's notion of "textures" suggests the latter, as does D'Andrade's paper, with its two kinds of social science cutting across usual disciplinary boundaries (see chaps. 1 and 2, this volume). Decades ago, in fact, Poincaré (1952) suggested the possibility that different methods might be appropriate to different sciences (though he had nothing kind to say regarding the social sciences, to be sure). My first comments stem from those opposing outlooks and the questions raised by the existence of varied—indeed contrasting—epistemic commitments and methodological loyalties within the social sciences.

In these reflections, I shall focus primarily upon Fiske's "Specificity of Method and Knowledge in Social Science" (chap. 3). His discussion serves as my platform because it seems to exemplify one extreme of what I shall call the "commitment continuum" in the social sciences—what I think of as the unity-of-science end. People occupying this position are committed to what one might call methodological unitarianism: They take it as given that all inquiries calling themselves scientific must employ the classical scientific method—a method, one should note, first devised to facilitate rigorous study of nonhuman aspects of nature.

This understanding of science prescribes a hypothetico-deductive logic of investigation, quantifies results, states its conclusions in propositional form, and demands that these propositions be falsifiable in principle. Its project is the discovery of causes, and its unit of study is ideally typified by the atom. Although there is a marked problem as to the way in which such atoms (i.e., minimal units) ought to be conceptualized at the levels of organization that social scientists investigate, the general strategy is to reduce sociocultural phenomena in order to study them, with the aim of attaining that well-known trio of traditional scientific goals: prediction, explanation, and (where possible) control of the behavior of discrete variables.

Clearly, Fiske's essay is a cry of pain echoing from this end of the commitment continuum—a cry we should heed respectfully, coming as it does from one who has labored long and hard to honor his commitment to the unity of science. In "Specificity of Method," however, we are presented with something of a paradox, for Fiske is both disappointed with the fruits of the sort of scientism I have just described and firm in his belief that the road to salvation lies in the application of more of the same—that is, in still more rigorously reductionistic natural science methods.

As I read his argument, he sees at least four fundamental sources of problems that, taken together, add up to the curse of "method specificity"—the chief reason for our failure to link bodies of knowledge together so that social science can progress. First of all, people are involved in data production, and the judgments produced by people employed as "measuring instruments" tend to vary. Second, social science researchers rely upon words, and the connotations—or even the denotations—of words vary among both researchers (be they judges, coders, or observers) and those they study (be they subjects, respondents, or informants), all of whom are incurably idiosyncratic language users. Third, the research styles, even the norms, of researchers (including their demands for precision and what Meehl calls "big effects") also vary, leading to noncomparability of studies. And finally, time itself is the enemy of progress in the social sciences. Since time usually passes between protocol events and their recording, data are subject to both memory lapses and retrospective distortions, making them generally unreliable.

An unfriendly critic might be sorely tempted to caricature "Specificity of Method" as a statement lamenting the confusion and noise introduced into social science by the humanness of human beings. What a beautiful social science we could have, after all, if only observers were all identical, unbiased, infallible measuring instruments, if only researchers and subjects didn't have to communicate through the fuzzy medium of words from natural language, if only our standards of success were uniform, and if only we were not time-bound animals. I am not, however, an unfriendly critic. In a way, in fact, I sympathize with Fiske's persistent and loyal adherence to his faith in methodological unitarianism, that is, to the work of making the social sciences scientific as physics is scientific, despite all obstacles. My aim, therefore, is not to caricature his position but, rather, to examine it and perhaps even suggest some cure for his malaise.

Certainly Fiske's stance is a minority position in this volume; only Campbell and Holzman, among the social scientists, appear still to be in sympathy with any version of neopositivist social science. But Fiske does not assume a priori, as Holzman does, that atomistic-causal, nomothetic social science is both what we should be doing and what we unproblematically can be doing. Nor does he sidestep such problems, as Campbell seems to, by focusing upon the way social science communities might be organized so that approximations to truth will inevitably improve. His concern is, rather, with the way designs for research might be organized so as to deal with the failure of conventional methods to yield cumulative improvement in our knowledge of "common, basic processes of behavior." Fiske's unhappiness at this failure—and the intuition that such basic processes surely must exist—lead him to advocate ever more microscopic methods of investigation.

Such an approach might be characterized as an atomistic foundationalism, that is, the attempt through reduction to arrive at certainty. It seems to me that this quest for indubitable truth, and the concomitant failure to accept our human plight as knowers, is one underlying cause of Fiske's malaise. If I am right, he is doomed to continued disappointment, not only because certain knowledge is impossible, but because the very strategy of reductionism is rooted in two serious misconceptions that I will discuss in more detail below.

Like many anthropologists, I occupy a position somewhere close to the opposite end of the commitment continuum. Since mine lies opposite to that position I have called the unity-of-science pole, it seems logical to call this position the pluralism-of-science end of the commitment continuum. And, having charged Fiske with methodological unitarianism, perhaps my own position should be dubbed methodological polytheism—a fitting faith, surely, for an anthropologist. Though less well established than the opposite extreme, the outlines of this position are becoming clearer as disillusionment among social scientists trained in the older tradition becomes more widespread. Gergen and Cronbach, I think, fit this description, showing marked signs of what could be miscalled "humanistic" leanings (a term so often used to refer to a species of softheadedness that I have consciously avoided it here). Such leanings entail, in the first place, at least a partial rejection of the narrow view of science characterizing the unity-of-science position.

From this standpoint, any systematic effort to learn about nature may qualify as science, and a plurality of methods for unlocking her secrets is acceptable. Pluralists assume that research methods appropriate to the study of nonliving, living, and specifically human aspects of the natural world may well be fundamentally unlike one another. In particular, they assume that because humans are self-conscious beings whose behavior is not independent of their notions of the way humans are supposed to behave, the social sciences may normally require different methods than any of the natural sciences. At this end of the continuum, the logic of investigation is as likely to be inductive as deductive (despite the so-called scandal of induction),[1] and results may not be quantifiable, nor even fully replicable. Conclusions are not always stated as propositions—and if they are, these may not be strictly falsifiable (partly because some classes of observations fail to be reproducible, in the very nature of the case).

The project of scientific pluralism is to understand, to render intelligible and preserve whole and intact (i.e., without reduction to qualitatively different atoms) the phenomena of interest. This may involve describing patterns rather than discovering causes; thus the language used may be one in which signification matters more than statistical significance, and unique events matter more than the repetitive ones that permit one to speak of quantifiable variables. The effort at this end of the continuum is less likely to be aimed at reducing the world to its atoms than at reconstituting it by giving it a "thick description" (Geertz 1973) leading to a plausible and coherent interpretation. The scientific pluralist does not exclude an atomistic-causal approach to knowledge, even in the study of social life, but sees it as only one kind of possible endeavor deserving the name of science. Since no method can be presumed to yield knowledge that is indubitable, complete, or foundational, only the ingenuity and persuasiveness of the scientist place limits upon our research strategies.

There are discomforts, however, in the catholicity that obtains at this end of the continuum. These derive from the absence of clear canons for deciding upon methods appropriate to particular subject matters, and the consequent difficulties that attend efforts to justify knowledge within one's scientific community (even by the dilute standard of "having good reasons to believe"). I do not think the discomforts of pluralism are insurmountable, however. Needed are regulative principles that are based—like those of all science—on the sort of consensus that both Kuhn's notion of the "exemplar" and Campbell's image of a disputatious community quarreling about the truth commend to our attention. The vagueness of this recommendation is intentional, for I don't pretend to have a pluralist substitute for the self-assurance of the methodological unitarian at the other end of my continuum. The comforting certainty of a one-possibility world, however, has always carried with it the costs of a limited vision, whether it is a world of aborigines or of scientists.

Now to comment on a second issue raised by my reading of Fiske's paper—the problem of reductionism in the social sciences. I have earlier alluded to two serious misconceptions that underlie reductionism as a research strategy, and now I shall specify them. First, reductionism in the form most common in social science directs our attention to a unit of study that is intrinsically nonsocial; that is, it still seeks to discover what causes the observed behavior of physically discrete biological individuals rather than seeking to understand the interactions in which social persons participate. Second, it ignores, because it cannot accommodate, questions of context.

I should confess, at this point, that my personal version of scientific pluralism is less akin to polytheism within the tribe of social scientists than it is to cultural relativism among the several disciplines. Thus it acknowledges that different tribes need different gods and rituals (i.e., different explanatory goals and methods) because the levels of organization of natural phenomena these disciplines investigate are not alike; but it also advocates ethnocentrism to the extent that it wants to differentiate the goals and methods of physics from those of biology, and the goals and methods of biology from those of psychology or sociology. A certain tolerance of dissent within disciplines is surely healthy, but the uncritical adoption of faiths imported from more "successful" sciences probably isn't. Indeed, it smacks of the inferiority complex often suffered by indigenous peoples when colonized by more "successful" (read better-armed or more arrogant) invaders.

I will not recapitulate here the arguments for emergentism (of a materialist, nonmystical, nontranscendental sort), for these have been eloquently stated on many occasions (see Campbell 1974). A simple aphorism sums them up: All the laws of physics, chemistry, or biology—taken together or separately—cannot explain or predict the existence (much less the motivations) of physicists, chemists, or biologists. Admittedly these laws control, in the sense of constraining, the forms terrestrial scientists—not to mention their hard-won knowledge—can take, but not even the latest evolutionary biology can tell us how any species could possibly have evolved such ornate social arrangements as to produce the assemblage of colleagues who attended this conference.

In posing the danger of confusing biological individuals with social persons, it seems to me that Fiske's scientism leads to an inability to deal conceptually with contexts and meanings, as opposed to objects or forces. The social sciences must cope uniquely with the former, though they must also take the latter into account. Indeed, our feelings of frustration in the social sciences might stem from the need to include in our calculations all the laws lower down in nature's hierarchy; that is, such theories of social behavior as we may one day devise cannot contradict physics or biology (at least if we are materialists, rather than transcendentalists). Given this constraint, it is perhaps no wonder that we have discovered so few nontrivial laws of social phenomena.

If we agree that the social sciences must define minimal units without reduction, it would seem that we are long overdue for a rethinking of categories. How can we assure that the units of social science investigation will be genuinely "social"—as cells and organisms are genuinely biological, and as subatomic particles and galaxies are genuinely physical? One alternative to Fiske's implicit assumption that the way to go is toward ever-finer levels of analysis within the same conceptual framework employed in the past is hinted at by Bateson (1972, 1979). The premises of his analysis are cybernetic: what is central for human thinking, acting, and choosing are not forces and objects, but information and messages that define social contexts and order human behavior within those contexts.

In this connection, I like the image used when Bateson asks us to consider the "self" of a blind man navigating by means of a stick. "Where," we are asked, "does the blind man's self begin? At the tip of the stick? At the handle of the stick? Or at some point halfway up the stick? These questions are nonsense, because the stick is a pathway along which differences are transmitted under transformation, so that to draw a line *across* the pathway is to cut off a part of the systemic circuit which determines the blind man's locomotion. . . . The total self-corrective unit which processes information, or, as I say 'thinks' and 'acts' and 'decides,' is a *system* whose boundaries do not at all coincide with the boundaries either of the body or of what is popularly called the 'self' or 'consciousness'" (Bateson 1972, 318–19).

What intrigues me about Bateson's manner of phrasing the question "What is the self?" is that selves—or what I would call "persons' arc not conceived as coterminous with biological organisms, or what most of us would call "individuals." They are, rather, links in systems of communication. The human communicative systems we usually call culture and society are foremost among these, but certainly Bateson would also include things like tools (the blind man's stick) that enable humans to interact with their physical environment and to receive information from it. Such a view allows the social scientist to avoid being distracted by the physical boundary of the human skin, and to think in terms of minimal units that have a meaningful social character.

If, for example, one's research problem involved "role behavior," the social unit might be defined as including the incumbents of complementary pairs of roles, neither of which can really be said to exist in the absence of the other. Thus there is no mother unless there is a child, no husband unless there is a wife, no teacher unless there is a student.[2] "Persons" or "selves" as studied by social scientists might then be thought of as the sum of an individual's achieved and ascribed social roles, as nodes in a network of communication, or as the sum of all character traits attributed to particular "personalities" by some set of customary vis à vis. (Some comfort may come to Fiske from this way of looking at things, since personality thereby becomes something chiefly in the eye of the beholder. Because each social actor perceives any "personality" only from the perspective of a particular sort of relationship, it should no longer surprise us that different observers fail, on the whole, to corroborate one another's descriptions). The specific ways in which researchers might choose to define their units of study would then become functions of their substantive interests and research questions, so long as the social character of these units was maintained.

What I have said is not really new, having been broached fifty or more years ago by G. H. Mead (1934) and others. All human social action is interaction—with others, ourselves, our natural and created physical world—within culturally defined contexts that largely determine, not only action, but its meaning. As social scientists, we take as our subject matter the level of organization that we call the social. Given this, we must take seriously the notion of social persons as entities created by and existing only within systems of interaction, and as bounded, not by the skins of biological individuals, but by contextual boundaries that may be (as things stand thus far) of indefinite extent. If we do so, I predict that the effects upon our research methods will not be inconsequential.

But to speak of context is a peculiarly difficult matter. It is, after all, a slippery concept, for there is no telling a priori where a context begins or ends. Humans live within a set of Chinese boxes, as it were, a social universe composed of contexts of ever-widening extent, from the dyad to the world-system, and from microseconds to millennia. It follows that an indefinite number of bounded contextual units are potentially definable between the poles of the time-space continuum. One problem implied by any contextual approach, then, is to specify for scientific purposes what sort of context we are looking at, so that the universe of discourse is defined in a way making it amenable to critical appraisal by peers.

What is being suggested here, not for the first time—but perhaps at a time when the sagging self-confidence of social scientists makes change look more attractive than it once did—is reconsideration of the conceptual system whereby research on human social and cultural life has traditionally been conducted. Like other sciences in the course of their development (including physics), we may have reached the point of asking whether the common-sense categories we have traditionally employed are adequate. Though one does not lightly discard common sense, its underlying assumptions need to be periodically examined to see whether they obstruct understanding rather than aid it. Two examples of dubious common-sense assumptions and the errors they generate have already been mentioned here: basing a strategy of reduction upon the assumption of identity between biological individuals and social persons, and basing inquiry upon the assumption that forces and objects have the same causal relevance for social as for physical phenomena. There are surely more.

Reformulation of the categories through which we come to understand nature, and ourselves as part of nature, is the kind of operation Gregory Bateson called Learning III (1972, 279–308). It is an enterprise that inevitably makes the world look different. Never is it easy, for it requires doing a lot more of what this conference has, I think, begun to show evidence of doing—breaking out of old ways of thinking and bringing the light of critical examination to bear upon the most basic premises and dearly held beliefs of all our disciplines. I do not know whether such a proposal will diminish Fiske's despair; certainly I hope it doesn't increase it. Clearly what these comments have offered is not a program, but merely a few insights that we might wish to keep in mind in case any of us feel moved to relocate our positions on the commitment continuum.

Notes

1. I note with some amused satisfaction the recent discovery that there is a parallel "scandal of deduction," which, logician Susan Haak asserts, results from the necessity of presupposing deduction in order to justify it (cf. Barnes & Bloor 1982, 41–42.)

2. Hsu (1965) has long believed the dyad to be the basic social building block. His thesis is that each culture derives its uniqueness from social emphasis upon a characteristic pair—Chinese culture being focused upon the father son pair, ours upon husband-wife, and so on.

References

Barnes, B., and Bloor, D. 1982. Relativism, rationalism and the sociology of knowledge. In *Rationality and relativism*, ed. Martin Hollis and Steven Lukes. Cambridge: MIT Press.

Bateson, G. 1972. *Steps to an ecology of mind.* New York: Ballantine.

———. 1979. *Mind and nature.* New York: Dutton.

Campbell, D. T. 1974. "Downward causation" in hierarchically organized biological systems. In *Studies in philosophy of biology*, ed. F. J. Ayala and T. Dobzhansky. Berkeley: University of California Press.

Geertz, C. 1973. Thick description: Toward an interpretive theory of cultures. In *The interpretation of cultures.* New York: Basic Books.

Hsu, F. L. K. 1965. The effect of dominant kin relationships on kin and non-kin behavior. *American Anthropologist* 67:638–61.

Mead, G. H. 1934. *Mind, self, and society.* Chicago: University of Chicago Press.

Poincaré, H. 1952. *Science and method.* New York: Dover.

18 Pluralisms and Subjectivities

Donald W. Fiske and Richard A. Shweder

"Potentialities for Knowledge in Social Science" was the title of the conference in the invitation to the participants. In planning the composition and the conduct of the conference, the organizers decided they they should not impose an a priori structure. Although a list of background readings (see Bibliography) was circulated in advance and some guidelines for possible papers were suggested, the authors of invited papers were under minimal constraints: they were asked to reflect on the state and nature of social science knowledge. At the conference itself, most of the discussions started with a given paper and then moved in whatever directions the participants saw as relevant. As the conference proceeded, no attempt was made to achieve consensus. It is likely that general agreement would have been obtained on very few issues, and majority votes seemed hardly worth seeking.

As a consequence, it would be foolish—even presumptuous—of us to formulate conclusions for conferees who were selected to form a diverse group, having in common perhaps only a concern for examining the current and future states of social science. Hence, in this closing chapter, we can more profitably consider just what the book is: What does this set of chapters present? What do they indicate about social science?

The contents of this book are intentionally heterogeneous. Its purpose will have been met if it generates thought and controversy as did the papers when discussed at the conference. Yet, as an outside reader has noted, the book has a fundamental unity: the chapters advocate deliberate reexamination of what we have been doing in social science, not just more of the same; they urge greater flexibility in research strategies and procedures; they recommend more deliberation in drawing conclusions and more caution in proposing generalizations.

362

Certain topics were examined by several authors and recurred in the conference discussions. One was the comparison of social science to natural science (physical and biological). Given that their contents, their objects of study, are manifestly different, should scientific investigation and thinking be much the same across all science? Campbell argues that the requirements for being scientific are identical in all science, and Fiske urges social scientists to see how far they can go toward achieving knowledge of social science phenomena by eliminating the confounding aspects of their current methods. On the other side, D'Andrade differentiates the three world views central to the physical, natural, and semiotic sciences and shows that each must investigate in its own way. Cronbach and Secord, each by his own route, develop arguments for the inadequacy of the hard science norms in social inquiry. Underlying this issue is the question "Just what is science? What is distinctive about it?" Every scientist gives a somewhat different answer to that question. While some of the contributors leave their answers implicit, Richter holds that success in a science is a matter for social negotiation and renegotiation.

Linked to that topic is the issue of universal laws or generalizations. D'Andrade argues that the notion of covering law has not worked well as a norm for all science. Joining him, Secord holds that science is not composed of universal laws based on regularities. Converse asks whether the stereotype of "the universal laws of true science" may be misleading. The issue needs a clearer formulation. In social science as in all science, regularities have been observed or empirically demonstrated. No one would deny that any statement of a regularity is insufficient without accompanying statements about the circumstances, the conditions under which the regularity occurs. But scientists seek more general principles that account for diverse sets of regularities. Yet when people consider a theoretical proposition, they seem to feel that it should have no limits, no restrictions. Are there any laws in any science that hold at all times, in all places, under all conditions? Even when a mathematical equation is central to a theory, the terms of that equation must be translated into specific concepts. The explanatory value of a quantified law varies with its application. All too often, attention is focused on what the law accounts for, putting aside the obvious fact that it was intended to explain, not everything, but only certain regularities among particular things or events as observed under specified boundary conditions.

Holzman argues that all phenomena in all sciences are context dependent. Certainly in social science, a fruitful generalization or theoretical proposition should be taken as applying to some particular events and not to the behavior of all people at all times. Although some biological generalizations may apply to all living people at all times, the content to be understood by social science clearly differs with the context. As Converse suggests, behavior does vary with the setting, and our task is to determine how. But social scientists are, according to Secord, unable to specify pertinent conditions. It is notorious that psychologists have been unable to arrive at a standard taxonomy of situations—in part because such a classification must be set up for each major class of behaviors being investigated. Distinctions critical for understanding one aspect of behavior may be irrelevant for another. Experimental researchers avoid the problem by establishing a constant set of conditions within which aspects are systematically varied to determine their effects. Experimenters are most successful when studying processes that seem to be the same inside and outside the laboratory.

Another topic receiving repeated attention in papers and discussions was the matter of meaning, the area of hermeneutics. Among the sciences, only social science is concerned with the meanings that people assign to persons, things, words, and other actions. D'Andrade identifies a set of semiotic sciences. Shweder distinguishes the positivist and the hermeneutic poles in order to locate a distinctive science of subjectivity between them. Even Campbell wants to include hermeneutic interpretation within his unified approach. Gergen goes beyond the question of the meanings held by our subjects to focus on multifaceted richness in our language about actions and in our understanding of everyday experience. All of the conferees seemed interested in the matter of meanings, although some were silent about the kind of discipline appropriate for studying them.

PLURALISMS

A major characteristic of the chapters and the discussion was the putting aside of traditional disciplinary or departmental categories (like anthropology, psychology, and sociology) in favor of alternative ways of structuring the field of social science. Each of the traditional disciplines is of course pluralistic: anthropology has physical, cultural, linguistic, and archeological subfields; among specializations in psychology are biological, cognitive, and developmental approaches; sociology has many subareas including demography, stratification, and intergroup relations. The conferees, however, developed different, often cross-disciplinary categorizations of the phenomena of social science, of the things to be understood (cf. topic II.A in the paradigm presented in Levine's chapter).

These chapters present a plurality of viewpoints. Each chapter offers a distinctive way of looking at the content of social science and has an emphasis shared only to some degree with that of any other contributor. This results in part from each writer's selecting a particular approach to the phenomena of social science, an approach that focuses on one body of content or that categorizes the material of social science in a given way. Each approach, each categorization, is based on a conceptualization; each involves its own abstractions from the raw material. Each position has been derived by the contributor from a conceptual reference point (see chap. 7), that point being determined by a small hierarchy of primary values to which the contributor adheres. Primary values are preemptive and constrain the development and formulation of each viewpoint. Since scientists, like everybody else, rarely modify their basic value systems, it can safely be predicted that the pluralism expressed in this volume will endure for years to come.

DIVERSE PLURALISMS

In addition to the pluralism of the volume as a whole, most of the authors present a pluralistic viewpoint, some structuring their chapters in such terms and others giving their categorizations a less central position. Among the more comprehensive schemas, D'Andrade contrasts three world views, each concentrating on its own set of things to be understood: the physical sciences, the natural sciences, and the semiotic sciences. Others, such as Secord, stress the distinction between the physical and the social sciences. Meehl refers to the classic pyramid of the sciences. Converse emphasizes the distinctive textures of the various sciences, and suggests that separate textures exist even within each established discipline. Even broader than any of these is Rosenberg's list of kinds of knowledge: religious, ethical, natural, common-sense, and linguistic. In contrast to these positions, two of the authors argue against such comparisons. Richter says that the standard for scientific achievement is relative, and hence it is unprofitable to make value judgments comparing scientific fields. In Campbell's view, the requirements for being scientific are the same for the physical and the social sciences; within each "disputatious community of truth seekers" busy constructing scientific knowledge, belief change is brought about by using established procedures for persuading one's colleagues. The implicit pluralism of individual views is to be overcome by generating consensus within the community.

Other contributors examine pluralisms within social science. The most systematic and differentiated is Levine's paradigm for social knowledge; his complex classification is based on several facets of disciplined social inquiry. He presents a strong case for "an irreducible plurality of privileged forms of knowledge." After contrasting two polar positions, the positivistic and the hermeneutic, Shweder advocates a science of subjectivity founded on a broadened concept of rationality. Frankel presents a continuum of degrees of commitment to traditional scientific method, as contrasted to a belief in methodological pluralism, and locates several conference participants on it. In Fiske's view, the products of scientific activity in the social sciences are multiple and discrete bodies of knowledge, each generated by the application of a specific method to a given protocol. Cronbach asserts the need for a pluralism of conceptualizations and explanations, bringing to bear multiple perspectives from different disciplines. He notes that while social science has produced knowledge at two levels (descriptive and historical reports, and concepts), achievement at two higher levels (generalized propositions and systematic explanations) is more problematic. The aspirations of Gergen take a different direction. Emphasizing the relative independence, even autonomy, of the language of person description and explanation from the activity it is intended to describe, he stresses the importance of new conceptualizations, of generative theories that give us new perspectives on the world of daily life. The distinctions made in other papers are pluralistic in somewhat different senses. Basic differentiations in Cicourel's chapter are between declarative and procedural knowledge and between the clinical and actuarial approaches to prediction. Secord notes that persons and social structures are stratified at different levels: physical, biological, psychological, and sociological.

More generally, the range of viewpoints taken by the contributors reflect the conventional levels of analysis emphasized by various social scientists. These levels differ in the size and temporal duration of the units to be studied, as discussed by Fiske. In an inventory of the forms of disciplined social knowledge, one of Levine's categories is "Descriptive Modalities (What does one observe?)." Among the range of his classifications are "microscopic, mesoscopic, macroscopic" levels. Thus Shweder writes about a culture or a society as a thing to be understood. The analysis of Cicourel's expert systems involves understanding how a group functions. Other authors look at a class or type of individual: Kleinman discusses people who are ill. At the level of the individual, Secord examines capacities and incapacities. Still smaller and more ephemeral is the action with which Gergen is concerned. At the bottom are the behavioral processes considered by Fiske.

Note that for most of the contributors, the pluralism offered is orderly. Rather than being isolated categories, the separate components are arranged along a continuum of some sort, for example, the levels in reductionism as discussed by Wimsatt. Even more striking is the relative absence of evaluative judgments. The typical stance is that many types of investigation should be encouraged, each enterprise doing its own thing in an appropriate manner. While there is active promotion of one strategy or another as being particularly promising and needed, there is little contentiousness, little depreciation of alternative approaches.

In sum, coming from diverse backgrounds, the contributors perceive social science—its activities and its products—in many ways. The majority of these writers approve such pluralisms; a minority are distressed by them or merely accept this diversity as unavoidable. Most of the authors are cautiously optimistic, with only an occasional voice expressing concern about the quantity of systematic knowledge that has been generated to date.

SUBJECTIVITIES

The pluralisms of the contributors are related to various subjectivities, different degrees of emphasis on subjectivity, diverse views about how subjective experience is to be used or avoided in social science, and opposed positions on the extent to which science is compatible with subjectivity. Above and beyond the personal subjectivity of each scientist, what are the roles of subjectivity in the work of social scientists? Indeed, what is subjectivity?

Of little relevance to the present discussion is one definition of "subjectivity," that it is the subjective quality of a person's writing. Although all scientific writing has this quality, it is most evident and most pertinent in the voluminous literature of speculation and theorizing in social science, especially by writers who have not engaged in systematic empirical research. Another meaning is commonly called "bias": according to *Webster's* "The quality of an investigator that affects the results of observational investigation." Most social scientists agree that such subjectivity is to be minimized in scientific activity. Subjectivity can also mean "the testing of truth solely by standards which can be applied only by the individual subject making a judgment . . . instead of by some objective criterion accessible to others . . . or even by some traditional external authority frankly recognized as such." This form of subjectivity is the opposite of the scientific community's agreement on facts as presented in Campbell's paper.

The subjective, in the sense of arising within a mind or in the sense of being seen from one perspective rather than another, pervades science in obvious ways. In the context of discovery, an idea comes to a scientist's mind, is examined and developed, modified, or rejected. Each scientist's choice of what is to be observed is always a personal decision. In science, most of the basic observations involve a subjective or personal experience in the observer and are affected by the conceptualizations of the investigator (so-called facts are theory-laden). And once the observations have been analyzed and integrated, the results are open to interpretation, a process that is subjective to a considerable degree.

Also pertinent is the sense of subjective that refers to what is to be understood, to the phenomena being investigated. Some events are located by social scientists within an individual person; others occur externally, so they are at least potentially accessible to direct observation by others. A feeling is an internal event; a grimace or a smile is external. The identification of an event as internal does not mean that it is unique or idiosyncratic: a clap of thunder generates highly similar sensory-perceptual events in the individuals who hear it.

There is little controversy about the possibility of studying internal events indirectly. In addition to the use of psychophysiological procedures (as in the study of dreaming), the latency of response can be an effective indicator, as cognitive psychology has shown for many years, starting with the comparative times for simple and complex reactions. More controversial is the use of verbal reports from the person in whom the event occurred. Ericsson and Simon (1984) have made a convincing analysis of the conditions under which such reports can be used as dependable scientific data.

In contrast, sharp controversy exists about the degree of subjectivity that is acceptable in efforts to understand social science phenomena, even external events. Within this volume, the views of Gergen and Fiske are divergent. Although Fiske agrees with Gergen that our language about action must be considered as independent and autonomous from action itself, he disagrees with the goal advocated by Gergen. Gergen seeks an enriched understanding stemming from diverse interpretations that enable us to view from new perspectives. He calls for generative theories making proposals that clash with our common-sense ways of seeing the world. While granting the enriched experience that such theories provide, Fiske persists in believing that social science can achieve cumulative, systematic knowledge about behavior by using methods that minimize or eliminate the forms of subjectivity or individualistic experience that intrude into most observation and thinking in social science today. He urges a concerted attack on subjectivity as bias in our methods of observation and the "testing of truth . . . by some objective criterion accessible to others."

Subjectivity of content, of that which is to be understood, and subjectivity in approaches to understanding come together in the primary values of the contributors. One group takes internal events, internal attributions of meaning and the resultant evaluative judgments, to be of central importance, and certainly more important than external behavior per se. Those who give primacy to such internal experience are willing to use subjective methods and ordinary language where necessary in observing and interpreting these materials. Some of the authors, such as Gergen, might argue that traditional scientific method is useless in such work, that positivism and neopositivism simply ignore these vital areas in social science. Others, like D'Andrade, Campbell, Secord, and Kleinman, might accept Shweder's position that a rigorous science of subjectivity is possible. Whatever the author's position, the issue of subjectivity is pervasive in these papers, either implicitly or explicitly (as in several elements of Levine's categorical frameworks for social phenomena).

Another group of the authors, not only take objectivity of investigation in the context of justification or confirmation as their primary value, but also believe that such investigation is more feasible with external events. For those authors, manifest behaviors are the objects of study, since there must be intersubjective consensus on observations and since public techniques must be used for processing data to arrive at replicable findings. They are pessimistic about the possibility of achieving systematic, "scientific" knowledge about internal events, especially those that do not represent processes common to most people. Holzman, Rosenberg, and Fiske seem to exemplify that position, and Converse appears to be close to it. Some of the contributors might object to being placed squarely in any of these groupings.

It is obvious that social science is not a single integrated discipline; rather it is a collectivity of endeavors sometimes working cooperatively, sometimes borrowing from each other, and only occasionally collaborating in joint enterprises. It is a range of disciplines and methodologies, above and beyond the somewhat anachronistic categories in university catalogs. It includes biological investigations and humanistic efforts. It studies highly heterogenous phenomena—the same thing or event often being studied from disparate perspectives by epistemological approaches with various kinds and roles of subjectivities.

Some thirty years ago, there was an optimism that seems rather naive to us today. The prevailing view was that social science was developing so rapidly that it was only a matter of time before hard work would generate an integrated, systematic body of science of both individual and collective behavior (see White, *The State of the Social Sciences* [1956]). Today social scientists are more cautious about what the accomplishments of the social sciences will be two or three decades hence. While the optimism has not completely vanished, it is more sober. Among social sciences, the level of optimism varies widely. As the Introduction and the other papers in this volume suggest, and as the quarter-century follow-up of the White book (Kruskal 1982) and many other volumes bring out, the quest for cumulative, integrated knowledge within social science is less easy than anticipated.

In sum, this volume presents the multiple products of a collective effort by six psychologists, three sociologists, three anthropologists, two psychiatrists, two philosophers, and a geophysicist to work through basic controversies about the nature and forms of social science knowledge, bringing out how those controversies are both fruitful and relevant to the practice of social research.

References

Ericsson, K. A., and Simon, H. A. 1984. *Protocol analysis: Verbal reports as data.* Cambridge: MIT Press.

Kruskal, W. H., ed. 1982. *The social sciences: Their nature and uses.* Chicago: University of Chicago Press.

White, L. D., ed. 1956. *The state of the social sciences.* Chicago: University of Chicago Press.

Bibliography

Adams, R. McC.; Smelser, N. J.; and Treiman, D. J., eds. 1982a. *Behavioral and social science research: A national resource.* Part 1. Washington, D.C.: National Academy Press.

————. 1982b. *Behavioral and social science research: A national resource.* Part 2. Washington, D.C.: National Academy Press.

Allport, D. A. 1975. The state of cognitive psychology. *Quarterly Journal of Experimental Psychology* 27: 141–52.

Arensberg, C. M. 1972. Culture as behavior: Structure and emergence. In *Annual review of anthropology,* vol. 1, ed. B. J. Siegel. Palo Alto: Annual Reviews.

Armistead, N., ed. 1974. *Reconstructing social psychology.* Baltimore: Penguin.

Behavioral and Social Sciences Survey Committee. 1969. *The behavioral and social sciences: Outlook and needs.* Englewood Cliffs, N.J.: Prentice-Hall.

Bernstein, R. J. 1976. *The restructuring of social and political theory.* New York: Harcourt Brace Jovanovich.

Bhaskar, R. 1978. On the possibility of social scientific knowledge and the limits of naturalism. *Journal for the Theory of Social Behaviour* 8: 1–28.

————. 1982. Emergence, explanation, and emancipation. In *Explaining human behavior: Consciousness, human action, and social structure,* ed. P. F. Secord. Beverly Hills: Sage.

Birtchnell, J. 1974. Is there a scientifically acceptable alternative to the epidemiological study of familial factors in mental illness? *Social Science and Medicine* 8: 335–50.

Blau, P. M., ed. 1975. *Approaches to the study of social structure.* New York: Free Press.

Booth, W. C. 1979. *Critical understanding: The powers and limits of pluralism.* Chicago: University of Chicago Press.

Boulding, K. E. 1980. Science: Our common heritage. *Science* 207: 831–36.

Brewer, M. B., and Collins, B. E., eds. 1981. *Scientific inquiry and the social sciences: A volume in honor of Donald T. Campbell.* San Francisco: Jossey-Bass.

371

Campbell, D. T. 1972. Herskovits, cultural relativism, and metascience. Introduction to *Cultural relativism: Perspectives in cultural pluralism* by M. J. Herskovits. Ed. F. Herskovits. New York: Random House.

Cicourel, A. V. 1964. *Method and measurement in sociology*. New York: Free Press.

Cole, S.; Cole, J.; and Dietrich, L. 1978. Measuring the cognitive state of scientific disciplines. In *Toward a metric of science: The advent of science indicators*, ed. Y. Elkana et al. New York: Wiley.

Collins, R. 1975. *Conflict sociology*. New York: Academic Press.

Connerton, P., ed. 1976. *Critical sociology: Selected readings*. New York: Penguin.

Cook, T. D., and Campbell, D. T. 1979. *Quasi-experimentation: Design and analysis issues for field settings*. Chicago: Rand McNally.

Cronbach, L. J. 1975. Beyond the two disciplines of scientific psychology. *American Psychologist* 30: 116–27.

————. 1982a. *Designing evaluations of educational and social programs*. San Francisco: Jossey-Bass.

————. 1982b. Prudent aspirations for social inquiry. In *The social sciences: Their nature and uses*, ed. W. H. Kruskal. Chicago: University of Chicago Press.

Devereux, G. 1967. *From anxiety to method in the behavioral sciences*. The Hague: Mouton.

Easton, D. 1962. Introduction: The current meaning of "behavioralism" in political science. In *The limits of behavioralism in political science*, ed. J. C. Charlesworth. Philadelphia: American academy of political and social science.

————. 1969. The new revolution of political science. *American Political Science Review* 63: 1051–61.

Eisenberg, L., and Kleinman, A., eds. 1981. *The relevance of social science for medicine*. Dordrecht: D. Reidel.

Elkana, Y.; Lederberg, J.; Merton, R. K.; Thackray, A.; and Zuckerman, H., eds. 1978. *Toward a metric of science: The advent of science indicators*. New York: Wiley.

Elms, A. C. 1975. The crisis of confidence in social psychology. *American Psychologist* 30: 967–76.

Feyerabend, P. 1975. *Against method: Outline of an anarchistic theory of knowledge*. Atlantic Highlands, N.J.: Humanities Press.

Fiske, D. W. 1978. *Strategies for personality research: The observation versus interpretation of behavior*. San Francisco: Jossey-Bass.

————. 1979. Two worlds of psychological phenomena. *American Psychologist* 34: 733–39.

Friedrichs, R. W. 1970. *A sociology of sociology*. New York: Free Press.

Geertz, C. 1973. *The interpretation of cultures*. New York: Basic Books.

————. 1980. Blurred genres: The refiguration of social thought. *American Scholar* 49: 165–79.

Gergen, K. J. 1973. Social psychology as history. *Journal of Personality and Social Psychology* 26: 309–20.

———. 1976. Social psychology, science, and history. *Personality and Social Psychology Bulletin* 2: 373–83.

———. 1980. The emerging crisis in life-span development theory. In *Life-span development and behavior,* vol. 3 ed. P. B. Baltes and O. G. Brim, Jr. New York: Academic Press.

———. 1982. *Toward transformation in social knowledge.* New York: Springer-Verlag.

Giddens, A. 1976. *New rules of sociological method: A positive critique of interpretive sociologies.* New York: Basic Books.

Glass, G. V. 1972. The wisdom of scientific inquiry on education. *Journal of Research in Science Teaching* 9: 3–18.

Gouldner, A. W. 1970. *The coming crisis of Western sociology.* New York: Basic Books.

Harré, R. 1974. Blueprint for a new science. In *Reconstructing social psychology,* ed. N. Armistead. Baltimore: Penguin.

Harré, R., and Secord, P. F. 1972. *The explanation of social behavior,* chaps. 1–3. Oxford: Blackwell.

Harris, M. 1964. *The nature of cultural things.* New York: Random House.

Hempel, C. G. 1965. *Aspects of scientific explanation and other essays in the philosophy of science.* New York: Free Press.

Hesse, M. 1972. In defense of objectivity. *Proceedings of the British Academy* 58: 275–92.

Hicks, J. 1976. "Revolutions" in economics. In *Method and appraisal in economics,* ed. S. J. Latsis. Cambridge: Cambridge University Press.

Homans, G. C. 1967. *The nature of social science.* New York: Harcourt, Brace and World.

Hutchison, T. W. 1977. *Knowledge and ignorance in economics.* Chicago: University of Chicago Press.

Hymes, D., ed. 1972. *Reinventing anthropology.* New York: Pantheon.

Kaufmann, F. 1944. *Methodology of the social sciences.* New York: Oxford University Press.

Keat, R. 1981. *The politics of social theory.* Chicago: University of Chicago Press.

Kelman, H. C. 1968. *A time to speak: On human values and social research.* San Francisco: Jossey-Bass.

Kleinman, A. 1980. *Patients and healers in the context of culture: An exploration of the borderline between anthropology, medicine, and psychiatry.* Berkeley: University of California Press.

Koch, S. 1974. Psychology as science. In *Philosophy of psychology,* ed. S. C. Brown. London: Macmillan.

———. 1981. The nature and limits of psychological knowledge: Lessons of a century qua "science." *American Psychologist* 36: 257–69.

Kruskal, W. H., ed. 1982. *The social sciences: Their nature and uses.* Chicago: University of Chicago Press.

Lachenmeyer, C. W. 1971. *The language of sociology.* New York: Columbia University Press.

———. 1973. *The essence of social research: A Copernican revolution.* New York: Free Press.

Latsis, S. J., ed. 1976. *Method and appraisal in economics.* Cambridge: Cambridge University Press.

Leach, E. R. 1961. *Rethinking anthropology.* London: Athlone Press.

Lindblom, C. E., and Cohen, D. K. 1979. *Usable knowledge: Social science and social problem solving.* New Haven: Yale University Press.

McCoy, C. A., and Playford, J., eds. 1967. *Apolitical politics: A critique of behavioralism.* New York: Crowell.

McGuire, W. J. 1969. Theory-oriented research in natural settings: The best of both worlds for social psychology. In *Interdisciplinary relationships in the social sciences,* ed. M. Sherif and C. Sherif. Chicago: Aldine.

———. 1973. The yin and yang of progress in social psychology: Seven koan. *Journal of Personality and Social Psychology* 26: 446–56.

MacIntyre, A. 1981. *After virtue: A study in moral theory.* Notre Dame: University of Notre Dame Press.

Mackenzie, B. D. 1977. *Behaviourism and the limits of scientific method.* Atlantic Highlands, N.J.: Humanities Press.

Manicas, P. T., and Secord, P. F. 1983. Implications for psychology of the new philosophy of science. *American Psychologist* 38: 399–413.

Meehl, P. E. 1978. Theoretical risks and tabular asterisks: Sir Karl, Sir Ronald, and the slow progress of soft psychology. *Journal of Consulting and Clinical Psychology* 46: 806–34.

———. 1983. Subjectivity in psychoanalytic inference: The nagging persistence of Wilhelm Fliess's Achensee question. In *Testing scientific theories,* ed. J. Earman. Minnesota Studies in the Philosophy of Science, vol. 10. Minneapolis: University of Minnesota Press.

Mischel, W. 1968. *Personality and assessment.* New York: Wiley.

Morganthau, H. J. 1965. *Scientific man versus power politics.* Chicago: University of Chicago Press.

Moscovici, S. 1972. Society and theory in social psychology. In *The context of social psychology: A critical assessment,* ed. J. Israel and H. Tajfel. New York: Academic Press.

Mussen, P. 1977. Choices, regrets, and lousy models (with reference to prosocial development). Presidential address to Division 7, presented at meeting of American Psychological Association, August 1977.

Myrdal, G. 1973. How scientific are the social sciences? *Bulletin of the Atomic Scientists* 28: 31–37.

Nagel, E. 1961. *The structure of science: Problems in the logic of scientific explanation.* New York: Harcourt, Brace and World.

———. 1971. Theory and observation. In *Observation and theory in science,* ed. E. Nagel, S. Bromberger, and A. Grünbaum. Baltimore: Johns Hopkins University Press.

Neisser, U. 1976. *Cognition and reality: Principles and implications of cognitive psychology.* San Francisco: Freeman.

Newell, A. 1973. You can't play twenty questions with nature and win: Projective comments on the papers of this symposium. In *Visual information processing,* ed. W. G. Chase. New York: Academic Press.

Pepitone, A. 1976. Toward a normative and comparative bicultural social psychology. *Journal of Personality and Social Psychology* 34: 641–53.

Personality and Social Psychology Bulletin. 1976. 2: 371–465. Papers discussing Gergen's "Social psychology as history."

Phillips, D. L. 1973. *Abandoning method: Sociological studies in methodology.* San Francisco: Jossey-Bass.

Popper, K. R. 1957. *The poverty of historicism,* 130–43. New York: Basic Books.

Prewitt, K. 1981. Usefulness of the social sciences. *Science* 211: 659.

———. 1982. Assessing the significance of social science research. In *The five-year outlook on science and technology 1981.* Vol. 2: *Source materials.* Washington, D.C.: National Science Foundation.

Putnam, H. 1973. Reductionism and the nature of psychology. *Cognition* 2: 131–46.

———. 1978. Lecture 6. In *Meaning and the moral sciences.* London: Routledge and Kegan Paul.

Rabinow, P., and Sullivan, W. M., eds. 1979. *Interpretive social science: A reader.* Berkeley: University of California Press.

Reason, P., and Rowan, J., eds. 1981. *Human inquiry: A sourcebook of new paradigm research.* New York: Wiley.

Ring, K. 1967. Experimental social psychology: Some sober questions about some frivolous values. *Journal of Experimental Social Psychology* 3: 113–23.

Roberts, M. J. 1974. On the nature and condition of social science. *Daedalus* 103: 47–64.

Rosenberg, A. 1980. *Sociobiology and the preemption of social science.* Baltimore: Johns Hopkins University Press.

———. 1983a. Human science and biological science: Defects and opportunities. In *Scientific explanation and understanding,* ed. N. Rescher. Lanham, Md.: University Press of America.

———. 1983b. If economics isn't science, what is it? *Philosophical Forum* 14: 296–314.

Sampson, E. E. 1977. Psychology and the American ideal. *Journal of Personality and Social Psychology* 35: 767–83.

———. 1981. Cognitive psychology as ideology. *American Psychologist* 36: 730–43.

Sarbin, T. R. 1976. Contextualism: A world view of modern psychology. *Nebraska Symposium on Motivation* 24: 1–41.

Schlenker, B. R. 1974. Social psychology and science. *Journal of Personality and Social Psychology* 29: 1–15.

Scriven, M. 1956. A possible distinction between traditional scientific disciplines and the study of human behavior. In *The foundations of science and the concepts of psychology and psychoanalysis*, Minnesota Studies in the Philosophy of Science, vol. 1, ed. H. Feigl and M. Scriven. Minneapolis: University of Minnesota Press.

———. 1969. Psychology without a paradigm. In *Clinical-cognitive psychology: Models and integrations*, ed. L. Breger. Englewood Cliffs, N.J.: Prentice-Hall.

Sechrest, L. 1976. Personality. *Annual Review of Psychology* 27: 1–27.

Secord, P. F., ed. 1982. *Explaining social behavior: Consciousness, human action, and social structure.* Beverly Hills: Sage.

Selby, H. A. 1970. Continuities and prospects in anthropological studies. In *Current directions in anthropology: A special issue*, ed. A. Fisher. Washington, D.C.: Bulletin of the American Anthropological Association.

Shackle, G. L. S. 1972. *Epistemics and economics: A critique of economic doctrines.* Cambridge: Cambridge University Press.

Shils, E. 1977. Social science as public opinion. *Minerva* 15: 273–85.

Shweder, R. A. 1979a. Rethinking culture and personality theory. Part 1: A critical examination of two classical hypotheses. *Ethos: Journal of the Society for Psychological Anthropology* 7: 255–78.

———. 1979b. Rethinking culture and personality theory. Part 2: A critical examination of two more classical postulates. *Ethos: Journal of the Society for Psychological Anthropology* 7: 279–311.

———. 1980. Rethinking culture and personality theory. Part 3: From genesis and typology to hermeneutics and dynamics. *Ethos: Journal of the Society for Psychological Anthropology* 8: 60–94.

Simon, H. A. 1976. From substantive to procedural rationality. In *Method and appraisal in economics*, ed. S. J. Latsis. Cambridge: Cambridge University Press.

———. 1980. How to win at Twenty Questions with nature. In *Perception and production of fluent speech*, ed. R. A. Cole. Hillsdale, N.J.: Erlbaum.

Smedslund, J. [1972]1973. *Becoming a psychologist: Theoretical foundations for a humanistic psychology.* New York: Halsted.

Smelser, N. J. 1968. *Essays in sociological explanation: Theoretical statement on sociology as a social science and its application to processes of social change.* Englewood Cliffs, N.J.: Prentice-Hall.

Smith, M. B. 1973. Criticism of a social science. *Science* 180: 610–12.

———. 1974. *Humanizing social psychology.* San Francisco: Jossey-Bass.

Somerville, J. 1941. Umbrellaology; or, methodology in social science. *Philosophy of Science* 8: 557–66.

Stabler, E. P., Jr. 1982. Review of *Sociobiology and the preemption of social science*, by A. Rosenberg. *Philosophy of Science* 49: 648–51.

Stent, G. S. 1975. Limits to the scientific understanding of man. *Science* 187: 1052–57.

Stinchcombe, A. L. 1968. *Constructing social theories.* New York: Harcourt Brace Jovanovich.

Surkin, M. 1970. Sense and non-sense in politics. In *An end to political science: The caucus papers,* ed. M. Surkin and A. Wolfe. New York: Basic Books.

Surkin, M., and Wolfe, A., eds. 1970. *An end to political science: The caucus papers.* New York: Basic Books.

Taylor, C. 1964. *The explanation of behaviour.* London: Routledge and Kegan Paul.

———. 1971. Interpretation and the sciences of man. *Review of Metaphysics* 25: 4–51.

Thorngate, W. 1976. Possible limits on a science of social behavior. In *Social psychology in transition,* ed. L. Strickland, F. Aboud, and K. Gergen. New York: Plenum.

Toulmin, S. 1969. Concepts and the explanation of human behavior. In *Human action: Conceptual and empirical issues,* ed. T. Mischel. New York: Academic Press.

Triandis, H. 1975. Social psychology and cultural analysis. *Journal for the Theory of Social Behaviour* 5: 81–106.

Tulving, E. 1979. Memory research: What kind of progress? In *Perspectives on memory research,* ed. L.-G. Nilsson, Hillsdale, N.J.: Erlbaum.

von Wright, G. H. 1971. *Explanation and understanding.* Ithaca: Cornell University Press.

Ward, B. 1972. *What's wrong with economics?* New York: Basic Books.

Wilson, P. 1980. Limits to the growth of knowledge: The case of the social and behavioral sciences. In *The role of libraries in the growth of knowledge,* ed. D. R. Swanson. Chicago: University of Chicago Press.

Zeisel, H. 1981. Social science rubrics? A review of *Usable knowledge,* by C. E. Lindblom and D. K. Cohen. *American Bar Foundation Research Journal* 1: 273–81.

Ziman, J. 1978. Social knowledge. In *Reliable knowledge: An exploration of the grounds for belief in science.* Cambridge: Cambridge University Press.

Author Index

Ackerknecht, E., 223
Adams, R., 3
Agar, M., 25
Albert, S., 216
Alexander, L., 231
Almond, G., 104
Argyris, C., 153
Aristotle, 172–73, 282, 318, 342
Aserinsky, E., 72
Atkinson, M., 140
Austin, J., 152
Averill, J., 142
Ayers, M., 205

Bales, R., 69, 279
Barker, R., 4
Barnes, B., 112, 116–17, 132, 138, 177, 361
Baron, R., 211
Bartok, B., 104
Bastian, A., 123
Bateson, G., 358–59, 361
Bateson, W., 116
Bayes, T., 178, 328, 331
Bechtoldt, H., 131
Becker, G., 279
Beethoven, L., 104
Benedict, R., 279
Bennett, J., 128
Berger, P., 142, 215, 281
Bergin, A., 77
Bergmann, G., 131, 315
Berkowitz, L., 207
Berlin, B., 4, 178
Bhaskar, R., 73, 197–98, 200, 206, 208, 212–13, 215
Blalock, H., 198
Bloch, S., 78
Bloor, D., 112, 361
Blumhagen, D., 231

Bohr, N., 175
Bond, G., 78
Booth, W., 272–74
Bosk, C., 232, 234
Bourne, E., 149
Boyd, R., 298
Bradburn, N., 66
Brady, I., 128
Bramel, D., 100
Bransford, J., 210
Brewer, M., 98
Brickman, P., 47
Briefs, H., 274
Broca, P., 223
Brown, G., 238
Brownell, W., 91–92, 95, 102
Brunswik, E., 326, 336
Bultmann, R., 110

Campbell, D., 9–10, 35, 62, 71, 73, 94, 96, 103, 108, 111–12, 115, 119–20, 122, 124–25, 127, 130–31, 150, 286, 294, 297, 308, 323, 355, 357–58, 363–65, 368–69
Carnap, R., 137, 321–22
Cartwright, D., 77
Cartwright, N., 174
Casson, R., 192
Cavell, S., 179
Chalip, L., 80
Child, I., 171
Chomsky, N., 144
Chrisman, N., 226, 230, 234
Christoph, P., 78
Cicourel, A., 10–13, 23, 25, 32, 64, 140, 347, 366–67
Clausen, J., 3, 351
Clausner, J., 126
Clements, F., 223
Cofer, C., 98

Cohen, J., 328, 333
Cohen, P., 95–96, 101, 328
Cole, M., 30
Coleman, J., 95–96, 280
Collingwood, R., 146
Collins, B., 98
Collins, H., 112, 114–15, 122
Comte, A., 59, 281
Converse, P., 5, 7–9, 22, 42, 56, 59,
    136, 286, 345, 353, 364–65, 369
Cook, T., 35, 71, 94, 96, 103, 125
Coulter, J., 140
Crano, W., 73
Crick, F., 319
Cronbach, L., 5, 8–9, 27–28, 42–43,
    59, 74, 80, 83, 85, 92, 101–3, 105,
    124, 131, 136, 214, 321, 356, 363,
    366
Csikszentmihalyi, M., 73
Cummings, W., 235
Cummins, R., 203–5, 216

Dahrendorf, R., 279
Dalton, J., 86–87
D'Andrade, R., 7, 9–10, 19, 23, 34, 38,
    69, 130, 149, 178, 183, 185, 293–94,
    311, 353, 363–65, 369
Darwin, C., 91, 100, 163, 320
de Man, P., 145
Demers, R., 230
Dennett, D., 294
Derrida, J., 145
Descartes, R., 7, 104
Dewey, J., 281
Dickson, W., 100, 102, 105
Dilthey, W., 98, 146
Dixon, R., 4
Docherty, J., 78
Doherty, M., 310
Dollard, J., 163
Donnerstein, E., 207
Duhem, P., 113, 116, 125–26
Dumas, M., 87
Duncan, S., 69, 73
Durkheim, E., 168, 175, 215, 279–80,
    319

Edelson, M., 5, 178
Edwards, A., 102
Einstein, A., 172
Eisenberg, L., 341
Ekman, P., 4
Eliot, T., 7, 47
Epstein, W., 231
Ericsen, C., 73

Ericsson, K., 68, 368
Estes, W., 99
Estroff, S., 233

Fanshel, D., 233
Feigenbaum, M., 293
Feigl, H., 315
Feinstein, A., 224
Feldstein, S., 69–70
Fennell, R., 63, 100
Ferber, A., 69
Feyerabend, P., 114, 120, 177, 271
Feynman, R., 21
Fidler, I., 200–201
Figlio, K., 231
Firth, R., 128, 227
Fisher, R., 102, 120, 305, 326, 328, 330,
    332
Fiske, A., 80
Fiske, B., 80
Fiske, D., 1, 8–9, 16, 31, 61–63, 66, 69,
    71, 73, 77, 86, 131, 191, 212, 286,
    308, 312, 323, 354–55, 357–59,
    361–63, 366–69
Follette, W., 235
Fortes, M., 175
Foucault, M., 233
Fox, R., 234
Frankel, B., 16, 353
Frazer, J., 123
Frederick, V., 171
Freeman, D., 128
Freidson, E., 233
Freud, S., 39, 157, 163, 169, 214, 280,
    320, 323
Friend, R., 100
Fuller, S., 138

Gadamer, H., 144, 148, 184
Gaines, A., 232
Gallie, W., 163, 271
Garfield, S., 77
Garfinkel, H., 25, 140
Garner, W., 73
Gay, J., 30
Geertz, C., 5–6, 26, 85, 95, 104, 191,
    356
Genco, S., 104
Gendlin, E., 80
Gergen, K., 5, 9–10, 15, 27, 30–32, 44,
    59, 85, 95, 105, 123, 136, 143, 147,
    149, 157, 173–74, 340, 356, 364,
    366–69
Gergen, M., 143
Gibson, J., 210–11

Giddens, A., 215–16
Gieryn, T., 115, 119, 132
Gilligan, C., 154
Glass, G., 70
Glassman, R., 308
Glick, J., 30
Glymour, C., 86, 105, 214
Goffman, E., 157
Goodfield, J., 83, 96
Goodman, N., 173–75, 191
Goodnow, J., 23
Gouldner, A., 153
Gray, H., 43
Greenberg, B., 230
Greenberg, J., 4
Gregor, T., 182
Grice, P., 179
Griesemer, J., 299, 310, 312
Grunbaum, A., 348
Guy-Lussac, J., 87

Haak, S., 361
Habermas, J., 109, 119, 148
Hahn, R., 225, 232, 234, 241
Hake, H., 73
Haldane, J., 190
Hanson, N., 141–42, 178
Harlow, H., 84
Harré, R., 129, 143, 146, 197, 200, 202, 205, 211
Harris, T., 238
Hartman, G., 145
Harwood, A., 232
Hatano, G., 88
Hayek, F., 99
Hays, W., 325
Heelas, P., 149
Hegel, G., 280
Helman, C., 231
Hempel, C., 7, 19–20, 26, 28, 39, 271, 323
Henkel, R., 332
Herskovits, M., 111
Hesse, H., 83
Hesse, M., 97, 104, 173, 177–78
Hewitt, C., 312
Hirsch, E., 148, 184–85
Hoffer, T., 95
Hofstadter, D., 293
Hollis, M., 111, 145
Holmes, L., 128
Holzman, P., 15–16, 78, 347, 355, 363, 369
Horton, R., 170, 172, 174–75
Hsu, F., 361

Hubble, E., 96
Hulka, B., 230
Hull, C., 63, 317–18
Hull, D., 119
Hume, D., 141, 202, 341

Jaffe, J., 69
James, T., 96
Janis, I., 311
Jones, M., 63, 100
Jung, C., 157, 163

Kagan, J., 191
Kahneman, D., 169, 171, 178, 294, 297–98, 307, 310
Kant, I., 83, 104, 141
Kasschau, R., 98
Katon, W., 224, 226, 232, 242
Katz, D., 58
Kaufmann, A., 294
Kaufmann, F., 322
Kay, P., 4, 178
Kelley, H., 146
Kelvin, K., 284
Kendon, A., 69
Kepler, J., 214, 329
Kessing, R., 192
Kessler, S., 140, 216
Kilgore, S., 95
Kipling, R., 183
Kirk, J., 25
Kirshner, J., 191
Kirtner, W., 77
Klein, L., 90
Kleinman, A., 11–12, 16, 191, 222, 224–26, 229–32, 234, 237, 241–42, 341, 367, 369
Kleitman, N., 72
Knorr-Cetina, K., 25, 112, 118
Kohlberg, L., 182, 186–88, 190
Kohut, H., 163
Kornfeld, W., 312
Krauss, E., 66
Kroeber, A., 279
Kruskal, W., 59, 85, 99, 370
Kuhn, T., 69, 110, 121, 126–27, 141–42, 151, 163, 172–73, 177, 271, 306, 340, 357

Laborit, 351
Labov, W., 233
Lacan, G., 144
Lakatos, I., 96, 177, 271–72, 324–25, 329, 336
Lakoff, G., 23

Lalljee, M., 143
Larson, R., 73
Lasswell, H., 281
Latour, B., 25, 112, 118, 132, 143, 225, 232, 310
Laudan, L., 132
Laundauer, T., 30
Laurendeau, M., 182
Lazarsfeld, P., 282
Leary, D., 145
Le Corbusier, 104
Legesse, A., 274
Lenat, D., 294–95
Lenin, V., 280
Lentz, R., 78
Lévi-Strauss, C., 33, 144, 279–80
Levin, H., 96
Levin, S., 78
Levine, D., 13, 58, 64, 271, 274, 345, 366, 369
LeVine, R., 182, 189
Levins, R., 304–5
Levy, D., 78
Lewin, K., 211
Lewin, R., 46
Lewis, O., 128
Lindblom, C., 95–96
Lipton, R., 78
Livingston, E., 25
Lock, A., 149
Locke, J., 141
Loos, C., 164, 167–68, 172
Lorenz, E., 288–89, 291
Lowy, F., 235
Luborsky, L., 78
Luce, R., 294
Luckmann, T., 142, 215
Luft, H., 233
Lunn, A., 190
Lutz, C., 149
Lykken, D., 327
Lynch, M., 25

McAndrew, C., 140
McArthur, L., 211
McCarthy, T., 119
MacCauley, D., 308
McCauley, R., 295
McClintock, M., 73, 77
MacCorquodale, K., 131
McDougall, W., 322–23
Machiavelli, N., 280
McKenna, W., 140
MacKenzie, D., 116–17, 132
McKeon, R., 274, 282

Mackie, J., 92
Madden, E., 197, 200, 202, 205
Malinowski, B., 25, 280
Manicas, P., 38, 87, 197, 208, 215, 340
Mann, L., 311
Mannheim, K., 112
Marshall, J., 30
Marx, K., 163, 279–80
Matson, F., 175
Mauss, M., 175
May, W., 178, 185
Maynard-Smith, J., 312
Mayr, E., 46, 225
Mead, G., 360
Mechanic, D., 231
Meehl, P., 3, 14–15, 28, 78, 85, 90, 96, 105, 131, 315, 317, 321, 330, 333–34, 345, 354, 365
Mendeleev, D., 329
Menzel, H., 282
Merton, R., 85, 97, 119, 132, 274
Mertz, D., 308
Milgram, S., 207
Mill, J., 120, 141, 178, 302
Mill, J. S., 141
Miller, G., 179–80
Miller, J., 164, 186, 188–90
Miller, M., 25
Miller, N., 163
Miller, T., 70
Mintz, J., 78
Miron, M., 178, 185
Mischel, W., 38
Mishler, E., 232
Mook, D., 95
Morgan, T., 117, 329
Morrison, D., 332
Moser, H., 91, 95
Moyer, D., 126
Much, N., 186–87
Mummendey, A., 143
Murdock, G., 168, 170–71
Murray, H., 86, 97–98, 322
Mynatt, C., 310

Nagel, E., 4–5, 20
Nagel, T., 168, 176
Neurath, O., 137
Nevitt, M., 231
Newcomb, T., 44, 58
Newell, A., 61
Newton, I., 43–44, 47, 172–73, 317, 329, 342
Nietzsche, F., 141
Nisbet, R., 280

Nisbett, R., 169, 297
Nucci, L., 187

O'Flaherty, W., 183
Osawa, K., 88
Osgood, C., 178, 185
Ossorio, P., 149
Oster, G., 309
Overton, W., 146

Pap, A., 321
Parsons, T., 24, 274, 277, 279
Paul, G., 78
Pavlov, I., 111
Peake, P., 38
Pearson, K., 116–17, 330
Penick, S., 78
Pennebaker, J., 231
Pepper, S., 67, 145, 175
Petersdorf, R., 224
Phillips, D., 105
Piaget, J., 163
Pierce, R., 56
Pinard, A., 182
Piranesi, G., 104
Planck, M., 96
Plato, 280, 324, 341
Plough, A., 231, 234
Poincaré, H., 353
Polanyi, M., 131
Polya, G., 295
Popper, K., 71, 85, 271, 324, 349
Piaget, R., 77
Provine, W., 116–17
Prytulak, L., 67
Putnam, H., 86, 90, 97, 105, 173–74

Quine, W., 113, 116, 125–26, 139, 151, 342
Quinn, N., 23

Radcliffe-Brown, A., 25
Raiffa, H., 294
Ravetz, J., 127
Reese, H., 146
Richardson, P., 298
Richter, F., 13–14, 191, 284, 293, 363
Rickert, H., 146
Ricoeur, P., 144, 148, 176, 184
Rivers, W., 223
Rodgers, J., 200
Roethlisberger, F., 100, 102, 105
Rogers, C., 163
Roll-Hansen, N., 117, 132
Rorer, L., 86

Rorty, R., 178
Rosen, A., 334
Rosen, G., 224, 226, 232, 242
Rosenberg, A., 3, 5, 15, 31, 36, 211, 339, 345, 365, 369
Ross, L., 169, 297
Rothman, D., 233, 235
Russell, B., 137

Sabini, J., 142
Sackheim, H., 78
Sahlins, M., 178
Sampson, E., 145
Sarbin, T., 146
Saussure, F., 144
Schachter, S., 142
Scheff, T., 140
Scheffler, I., 197
Scheibe, K., 146
Schleiermacher, F., 109
Schlick, M., 137
Schneider, D., 31, 168–69, 171
Schopenhauer, A., 141
Schultz, T., 99
Schutz, A., 142, 280
Secord, P., 11, 38, 64, 146, 197, 207, 211, 214, 340, 363, 365–67, 369
Segall, M., 111
Shaffer, P., 97–98
Shapin, S., 112
Sharp, D., 30
Shaw, R., 210
Shimony, A., 126
Shotter, J., 145
Shweder, R., 1, 9–11, 16, 38, 69, 149, 158, 163–64, 169, 171, 181–82, 186–90, 297, 301, 310, 362, 364–67, 369
Silver, M., 142
Simmel, G., 274, 279
Simon, H., 68, 88, 294–95, 299, 368
Sivananda, S., 181
Sivin, N., 127
Skelton, J., 231
Skinner, B., 31, 157, 163, 281, 316–17, 319, 322–23
Slovic, P., 171, 178, 310
Smedslund, J., 149
Smelser, N., 3
Smetana, J., 187
Smith, A., 163, 279
Smith, H., 175
Smith, M., 70
Sonnenfeld, J., 100
Sparrow, C., 291

Spence, D., 176
Spence, K., 63
Spencer, H., 279–80
Spencer, W., 123
Spengler, O., 123
Sperry, R., 72
Spinoza, B., 141
Spiro, M., 169, 171–72
Stanley, J., 35, 124–25
Star, S. L., 299, 302, 310, 312
Starr, P., 233
Stegmuller, W., 121
Sternberg, R., 66, 77
Stevenson, I., 181–82
Stewart, D., 231
Stinchcome, A., 274
Stolzenberg, G., 156
Stone, D., 231, 233
Sudman, S., 66
Sullivan, D., 231
Sullivan, H., 163

Taussig, M., 228
Taylor, C., 147
Teggart, F., 123
Thibaut, J., 146
Thorngate, W., 90
Thurstone, L., 317
Toennies, F., 279
Tolman, E., 63, 99–100, 322–24
Torres, A., 59
Toulmin, S., 83, 87, 96–98, 104–5, 271
Toynbee, A., 123
Treiman, D., 3
Trevor-Roper, H., 164–66
Tribe, L., 307
Turiel, E., 186–87
Turner, C., 66
Turner, V., 33
Tversky, A., 169, 171, 178, 294, 297–98, 307, 310
Tweney, R., 310
Tyler, S., 192

Vessell, E., 63

Vico, G., 98
Virchow, R., 223
von Neumann, J., 84
von Wright, G., 20

Wade, M., 303–5, 309
Waismann, F., 321
Wallace, A., 182–83
Watson, J. B., 111
Watson, J. D., 319
Webb, N., 103
Weber, M., 24, 39, 146, 215, 279, 281
Wegener, A., 320
Weinberg, S., 29
Weiss, C., 84, 95
Welkowitz, J., 70
Westermarck, E., 123
White, G., 4, 149
White, K., 230
White, L., 370
Whiting, J., 171
Whorf, B., 185–86
Widiger, T., 86
Wigner, E., 74
Williams, T., 230
Wilson, E., 309
Wilson, R., 286
Wilson, S., 171
Wimsatt, W., 14, 293–94, 296–97, 299, 302, 304–5, 308–10, 367
Winch, P., 146
Winograd, T., 184
Wish, M., 23
Wittgenstein, L., 139, 306
Woolgar, S., 25, 112, 118, 143, 225, 232, 310
Wothke, W., 80

Yalom, I., 78
Yelin, E., 231, 233

Zajonc, R., 55, 213
Zerubavel, E., 234
Zola, I., 230
Zuckerman, H., 118

Subject Index

Abstraction, level of, 64–65, 69
Accounts of behavior, 211–12
Action, 10, 31, 37, 177; human, 276; as interaction, 360; science of, 152
Actualism, 205
Adaptation, biological, 298
Ad hoc-ery, 307, 325, 329
Aggregation: of data, 99; level of, 49
Aggression, 139, 287–91
Algorithms, 295
Alienation, 64
Analogies, 322
Analysis, levels of, 49, 64–65, 218, 366
Animism, 175
Anthropology, 20, 25; medical, 230–31
Argument structures, 189
Artifacts, 305, 311
Artificial intelligence, 12, 254, 295
Atomic theory, 86
Attitude, 207

Bayes' theorem, 328, 331, 333
Behavior: chaotic, 293; complexity of, 209, 287; consistency in, 38; equation for, 45, 286–87; nonlinear, 13, 284
Behavioral indicators, 322–23
Behavioral medicine, 227
Belief change, 112–15, 119
Bias: anchoring, 307; editorial, 325, 328; reductionistic, 301, 308–9; in sample, 305; submission, 325, 328; systematic, 295, 299
Biochemistry, 351
Biological sciences, 8, 11
Biology, 45–48, 51
Biomedicine, 240
Boundary conditions, 7, 28, 91
Brain language, 320

Capacities, 87–88, 213–14; in laboratory, 210
Categories, common-sense, 360
Causal law, 177, 203
Causal powers, 199–203, 205, 217
Cause, Humean conception of, 199
Causes, 324, 347–48; necessary and sufficient, 348; reasons as, 212; relevant, 348
Ceteris paribus clauses, 123, 207, 323
Chemistry, 45, 47
Cognitive features, 275–76
Cognitive science, 12
Commitment: continuum, 353; epistemic, 353; in social sciences, 353–61
Communication, 255
Communities of scholars, 98; disputatious, 9, 119, 123–24
Complexity, 13, 48–49, 294; of persons, 199
Composition laws, 203
Concepts, 88–89; open, 321, 323
Conceptual maps, 310
Conceptual reference points, 164, 174, 181, 188–91, 365
Conditions: antecedent, 19; external, 34; internal, 34
Confirmation, 113
Constructionism, 150
Constructivism, 10
Constructs: cultural, 169; mental, 168, 174
Construct validation, 85
Construct validity, 325
Context, 301, 347–48, 360; dependence, 15, 299, 301, 348, 363–64; of discovery, 256–57; independence, 293, 299, 301; of justification, 256

Contextualism, 10, 142, 150
Contextual variables, 302
Control, 76, 302
Convergence, 6, 8, 61
Correspondence theory, 10, 139
Covering law, 7, 363
Covering law model, 28–29, 39, 363; of
    explanation, 14, 19–20; in natural
    sciences, 21–22, 293; in semiotic sci-
    ences, 26
"Crud factor," 327–28, 332
Cultural rationales, 189
Culture, 177

Data, process of producing, 65–68, 76
Decision making, 247
Decision theory, rational, 294, 307
Deconstructionism, 10, 143, 151
Definition: contextual, 321; implicit,
    321
Degrees of freedom, 124
Dependability, 75
Description: autonomy of, 149; as neu-
    tral, 153; perspective-free, 176
Devil, 164–67
Diagnosis: clinical, 258–59; computer,
    258
Diagnostic and Statistical Manual, 238
Diagnostic procedures, 11
Dichotomies, standard, 177
Disease, 230, 255
Disposition, 320
Dissonance theory, 123
Dream, 182–83

Ecology, referential, 121–24
Economics, 90, 317
Effect size, 92
Emergentism, 358
Empiricism, 110
Epidemiology, 351
Epistemological relativism, 9
Epistemology, 110, 339, 341, 345
Errors, systematic, 298
Essentialism, 342
Ethnography, 128
Ethnomethodology, 24, 140
Experiment, 55, 121, 207, 317; as
    closed world, 208; conditions in,
    209
Experimental design, 302
Experimental method, 34–35
Expert systems, 12, 246; development
    of, 247; and folk knowledge, 249,
    262–63, 265; formal, 248; indica-

tors in, 257–59; knowledge used in,
    250, 267; in medicine, 247, 261,
    347–48
Explanation, 19–20, 28, 88, 177, 198;
    psychological, 203; scientific, 22; in
    the social sciences, 197
Extrapolation, 94–95

Falsification, 113
Focus, perceptual, 305
Folk knowledge, 249, 262
Folk model, 23, 265; of mind, 261, 263,
    265
Foundationalism, 108
Foundations Fund for Research in Psy-
    chiatry, 350
Functional analysis, 205

Generality, 52, 186
Generalization, 29, 90, 94; boundaries
    of, 28, 91; context-dependent, 13–
    14; cross-national, 56; of findings,
    93, 336; law-like, 21–23, 26; lim-
    ited, 27; in model building, 302; in
    natural sciences, 21, 25; in physical
    sciences, 20; in semiotic sciences,
    25–26, in social sciences, 4, 42,
    49, 53, 85; universal, 4–5, 19, 178,
    363
General law, 7, 19, 21–22, 26–27, 30,
    39
Generative mechanisms, 11
Generative theory, 157
Geology, 8, 15, 47
Geometry, 343
Group selection, 299; models of, 303

Hawthorne research, 9, 84, 100–101
Hermeneutic: approach, 350; disci-
    plines, 348–49; method, 33
Hermeneuticists, 176–78, 184
Hermeneutics, 16, 364; deconstruc-
    tionist, 10; scientific, 10; in social
    sciences, 108–11
Heuristic, errors from, 298
Heuristic procedure, 295, 298
Heuristics, 293, 311; calibrated, 310;
    characteristics of, 295, 297, 306; of
    conceptualization, 300–301; of ex-
    perimental design, 302; of group
    processes, 310; irrationality of, 297;
    of model building, 300–301; of ob-
    servation, 302; problem-solving, 14,
    294, 299, 304; of theory construc-
    tion, 300–301

Historical circumstance, 8, 44–45, 51, 53
Historical knowledge, 89
Historicism, 108
Historicity, 136
Humanities, 177
Hypotheses: rival, 125; statistical, 332
Hypothesis testing, 101
Hypotheticodeductivism, 342

Idealism, 14
Idealist, 177
Ideological region, 164, 171, 181; rationality of, 166
Ideology, 6, 164, 170
Idiographic approach, 350
Illness, 230–31; behavioral view of, 236; theories of, 170–71
Induction, 341
Inductivism, 342
Information processing, 247
Inquiry, object of, 74
Instantiation laws, 203–4
Institution as machine, 24–25
Intentionality, 175
Intentional state, 36–37
Intentions, 31, 148, 176–77, 322
Interactions: higher-order, 325, 335–36; interpersonal, 69
Interpretation, 32–33, 97; indeterminacy of, 148; of text, 349
Intersubjectivity, 31, 262
Interview, 34, 246, 252, 254
Intrasystemic mechanism, 301
Investigator, individuality of, 67
Irrational processes, 171, 180

Knowledge: bodies of, 61–62, 67–72; conceptions of, 345; declarative, 12, 250–51, 256, 258–59, 262, 266; definition of, 340; disciplined, 276; implicit, 266; kinds of, 339–40, 365; objects of, 339; privileged, 272; procedural, 12, 250–52, 259–62, 266; representation of, 267; schematized, 248; specificity of, 8; tacit, 213, 250; theories of, 339; useful, 6, 17. See also Social knowledge
Knowledge base, 249, 253

Laboratory, 113
Language, 22–23, 265–66; of action, 151; everyday, 248; intentional, 147; natural, 178, 184, 259; and observation, 137–38; ordinary, 211–

12; of person description, 148; rules of, 179; of social description, 136
LaPlacean demons, 296
Law. See Causal law; Covering law; General law; Generalization; Natural law; Scientific laws; Universal law
Laws, in economics, 90
Liabilities, 198, 213–14
Logic, 178–80
Logical empiricism, 340
Logical positivism, 15, 131, 315, 342, 348–49

Malpractice, 166
Materialist, 177, 319
Mathematical models, 14
Mathematics, 317
Meaning: conception of, 178, 183; connotative, 185; contextual dependency of, 138–40; object-like, 185; of propositions, 138; in semiotic sciences, 20, 22–24; study of, 15, 31–37, 39; subjective, 185; of theoretical terms, 322; vagueness of, 323; of words, 66–67, 139, 186
Meanings, in social science, 348–49
Measurement: fundamental unit of, 65; social, 261
Mechanism, 21, 175, 301
Medicine, 11–12, 170, 348; in social science, 222; social science views of, 228
Mental health, 11, 16, 155–56, 158, 350–51
Mental illness, 3, 155, 239, 345
Meta-analysis, 70, 324
Metaphor, 30, 145, 181, 189, 322; physical, 175; root, 163, 191
Metaphysics, 341
Method, 61; specificity of, 62, 66, 71, 354. See also Procedure, measuring
Methodology, 4, 16, 306, 341–42
Method variance, 8, 165
Mill's canon, 120, 178, 302
Minitheories, 335
Model, 181, 322; deductive, 323; as template, 307
Modus tollens, 329
Monism, 16
Monists, 174
Moral development, 186–87
Moral obligations, 188
Moral understandings, 186

Motives: imputation of, 322; uncon-
scious, 323–24
Multiple worlds, 174
Multitrait-multimethod model, 71, 131,
308, 323
Myth, 6

National Academy of Sciences, 3
National Institute of Mental Health, 3,
239
Natural law, 164, 170
Natural sciences, 7, 9, 177, 347. *See also*
World view, natural sciences
Nature, 177; "personified," 175
Neopositivism, 16
Neuroanatomy, 351
Neuropharmacology, 351
Nihilism, 9
Nihilists, 174
Nomic attributions, 203–4
Nomic correlations, 203
Nomological net, 323
Nomothetic science, 350
Null hypothesis, 325, 329–31, 333

Objective, 168, 175, 177, 184
Objectivism, 184
Objectivity, 10, 16, 164–65, 170, 172,
177–78, 182, 186, 191, 369; claim
to, 137; transcendent, 176
Objects, subject-dependent, 175, 178,
186, 191
Observer, specificity of, 77
Operant conditioning, 316
Operationalism, 174, 315
Operationism, 316
Order, imposed, 22–23
Oversimplification, bias of, 307

Paradigm, 5–6, 163, 306, 308, 366; ac-
tion-theoretic, 277–81; shift, 306
Performative utterances, 152
Personality, 37–38; research on, 86
Perspectives, 163, 262, 310
Phenomenology, 85; social, 142
Philosophy, as theory, 341
Philosophy of science, 15, 336, 339,
341–42, 344; of social science, 197
Physical sciences, 7–9, 108–9, 126. *See
also* World view, physical sciences
Physics, 46–48; Newtonian, 199
Pluralism, 362; methodological, 13,
273–74; scientific, 16, 355–57; in
social science, 1, 9, 97, 164, 274; of
viewpoints, 364–67

Pluralists, 174
Point of view, native, 10
Political behavior, 55–56
Positivism, 10–11, 15, 108, 176–79,
184
Postpositivism, 9, 16–17, 110
Power, statistical, 326, 333
Pragmatic implications, 179
Prediction, 19–20, 28, 177; clinical,
252, 255–58; interval, 331, 334;
point, 331, 334; statistical, 252,
255–59
Probabilistic information, 92
Probability, 320–21
Problems, social, 77
Problem solving, reductionistic, 300,
305, 309
Procedure, measuring, 61–63, 67–68
Processes, 247, 294, 297; behavioral,
73, 76, 257; design, 294; discourse,
257; nonrational, 180; personality,
38; rational, 180
Propensity, 320
Property: functional, 301; object-like,
186; relational, 301; structural, 301
Protocol, behavioral, 61, 63, 72
Pseudorobustness, 306
Psychiatry, 351
Psychology, 20, 30, 351; cognitive, 295;
scientific, 316
Psychotherapy, 39, 77–78, 218, 235;
research in, 64
Purposes, human, 277

Quantification, 317, 320
Questionnaires, 246, 248–49, 251,
259–61

Randomization, 54
Rationalism, 117, 141
Rationality, 10, 166, 178, 182–83;
bounded, 299; divergent, 10–11,
163, 180–82, 186–91
Reading comprehension, 263–65
Realism, 90, 322; internal, 174
Realist, 11
Reality: correspondence with, 185; ex-
ternal, 169; physical, 169; psychic,
169, 171; representation of, 172;
theory-independent, 173; thought,
169
Reason, 164, 168
Reasoning, clinical, 253; diagnostic,
247, 256–57
Reasons, 324, 347–49

Reductionism, 14, 16, 296, 300, 318, 357
Reductionistic analysis, 309
Reductionistic biases, 301, 308–9
Regularities, 15–16, 28–29, 74–75; in behavior, 11, 198; limits for, 363; observed, 8; in universal laws, 199
Reincarnation, 181
Relativism, 14, 112, 357; epistemological, 9, 108, 117; ontological, 110; radical, 9–10
Reliability, 296
Religion, 6, 10, 164
Religious concepts, 171–72
Replicability, 75, 121
Replication, 122, 130
Representative design, 326
Representativeness, 75
Reproducibility, 75, 93–94, 316
Research: applied, 84; exploratory, 102; and understanding, 158
Robustness analysis, 303, 308

Satisficing, 294, 311
Science, 7, 10, 52, 164; conceptual foundations of, 14; criteria for progress, 1–3; definition of, 271; idealization of, 175; models of, 44, 47; Newtonian model, 317; normal, 319; preparadigmatic, 163; realist view, 210; single standard for, 284; standard view, 197–98; as subject-dependent, 178; unity of, 15–16, 355; value-free, 177
Sciences, comparative success of, 285; hard, 46–47, 50, 82; psychological, 8; pyramid of, 319
Scientific communities: critical mass for, 127; insulation of, 126. See also Communities of scholars
Scientific laws, 11
Scientific method, 9, 120, 353
Scientism, 108, 354
Semantic domains, 248
Semantics, 23
Semiotic sciences. See World view, semiotic sciences
Significance, cognitive, 341–42
Significance testing, 15, 329–30, 334
Signification, 356
Situations, 54–56, 99; taxonomy of, 364
Social change, 154
Social construction, 118; of reality, 140; scientific knowledge as, 115

Social knowledge: forms and functions of, 277–81; levels of, 88, 271; value of, 281
Social psychology, 30, 37–38, 45, 48; crisis in, 44
Social science, 6, 42–44, 108, 127–28; applied, 217–19; complexity in, 8, 48; crisis in, 1–3; criteria for, 281–82; cumulation of knowledge in, 136; expectations for, 43–44; and hermeneutics, 109; as a humanity, 176; interdisciplinary, 98; isolation of, 351; knowledge in, 1, 4; laws in, 4; in medicine, 12, 222–41; and natural science, 176–77, 347, 363, 365; optimism about, 370; philosophy of, 315; pluralism in, 274; policy for, 32–35; potential knowledge in, 339–40; progress in, 1, 8, 104, 157, 199; as science, 316; state of, 43, 362; texture of, 46–50; thought, 173; uneasiness in, 1–2, 4–5
Social structures, 214–17, 219
Social thought, 175
Social utility, 3
Sociology, 20, 351; medical, 232
Sociology of science, 109, 112–16, 121–22; relativist, 112
Somatization, 231–32
Soul, reincarnating, 181
State variables, 322
Statistics, 317
Structuralism, 143
Subjective, 168, 173, 175, 177, 184; experience, 7, 12; phenomena, 368; states, 186
Subjectivism, 184
Subjectivity, 177, 184, 186, 362, 367–69; object-like, 178, 191; and objectivity, 10, 16, 164, 172, 186, 191; science of, 7, 11, 176–79, 183, 192; in social science, 6; study of, 5
Supernatural belief, 164
Superstition, 10, 164, 168; anthropologists and, 168–70
Survey, 246, 252, 259–61
Systematic distortion hypothesis, 38
Systems, 11; closed, 198; cultural meaning, 24; declarative, 250; nonlinear, 13, 292–93; open, 198, 208. See also Expert systems

Test, psychometric, 246, 248–49, 251–52
Testability and meaning, 321

Testing of theory, 303
Textures of sciences, 8, 45–47, 54, 365
Theories: alternative, 345; auxiliary,
    325; developmental, 320; diversity
    of, 5–6; evolutionary, 320; func-
    tional-dynamic, 317; historical, 320;
    inconsistent, 344; normative, 296;
    structural-compositional, 318; test-
    able, 62; weak, 324, 329–30, 332,
    335
Theory: and findings, 342–43; of
    human behavior, 344; ontology of,
    172–73; substantive, 332, 334; value
    bias of, 154; verisimilitude of, 325–
    26
Thick description, 5, 356
Thought: religious, 170, 172; scientific,
    170
Translation equivalences, 343
Triangulation, 308
Truth, 322

Understanding, 177
Universal law, 52, 363; deduction from,

    11; limits for, 4, 51; science as, 198–
    99; in social psychology, 44
Universals. *See* Generalization,
    universal
University of Chicago, 351–52
Unpredictability, 14, 293

Validity, 112, 118; ecological, 13, 249,
    268
Value, 176
Values, primary, 365, 369
Variables: extrasystemic, 303; intra-
    systemic, 303
Verifiability, 137
Verstehen, 98

Witches, 170, 172
Witch hunts, 164–66, 169
Words, meanings of, 66–67, 139, 186
World Health Organization, 239
World view, 7, 9, 20, 363, 365; natural
    sciences, 21–22, 24–26, 29; physical
    sciences, 21, 29; semiotic sciences,
    22, 25–26, 29, 311